Business History around the World

This book offers the first in-depth international survey of current research and debates in business history. Over the past two decades, enormous advances have been made in writing the history of business enterprise and business systems. Historians are documenting and analyzing the evolution of a wide range of important companies and systems, their patterns of innovation, production, and distribution, their financial affairs, their political activities, and their social impact. This volume is a reference work that will be of immense value to historians, economists, management researchers, and others concerned to access the latest insights on the evolution of business throughout the world.

Each essay is written by a prominent authority who provides an up-to-date assessment of the state and significance of research in his or her area. Part I debates the identity and parameters of the discipline, followed in Part II by wide-ranging surveys of the business history literature in the United States, Europe, Latin America, Japan, and the Chinese-speaking world. Part III examines international comparative research on multinationals, family business, and government relations.

Franco Amatori is Professor of Economic History at Bocconi University in Milan, Italy. He has written extensively on Italian business history. He edited, with Alfred Chandler and Takashi Hikino, *Big Business and the Wealth of Nations* (Cambridge, 1997).

Geoffrey Jones is Professor of Business Administration at Harvard Business School. He is the author or editor of more than twenty books in the field of business history and is the coeditor of the quarterly journal *Business History*.

COMPARATIVE PERSPECTIVES IN BUSINESS HISTORY

At the dawn of the twenty-first century the world economy is in the midst of the most profound transformation since the industrial revolution. Firms, communications systems, and markets for products, services, labor, and currencies are all breaking out of national boundaries. Business enterprises today must negotiate a global environment in order to innovate and to compete in ways that will protect or enhance their market shares. At the same time, they are finding it essential to understand the different perspectives growing out of local, regional, and national experiences with business and economic development. This has become a crucial competitive advantage to companies and a vital skill for those who study them. *Comparative Perspectives in Business History* explores these developments in a series of volumes that draw upon the best work of scholars from a variety of nations writing on the history of enterprise, public and private. The series encourages the use of new styles of analysis and seeks to enhance understanding of modern enterprise and its social and political relations, leaders, cultures, economic strategies, accomplishments, and failures.

Series Editors

Franco Amatori, *Bocconi University*
Louis Galambos, *The Johns Hopkins University*

Managing Editor

Mary Butler Davies

Sponsors

Associazione per gli Studi Storici sull'Impresa (ASSI), Milan
Istituto di Storia Economica, Bocconi University, Milan
The Institute for Applied Economics and Study of Business Enterprise,
The Johns Hopkins University

Other Titles in the Series

Pier Angelo Toninelli, *The Rise and Fall of the State-Owned Enterprise in the Western World* (ISBN 0 521 78081 0)

Business History around the World

Edited by

FRANCO AMATORI

Bocconi University

GEOFFREY JONES

Harvard Business School

CAMBRIDGE
UNIVERSITY PRESS

PUBLISHED BY THE PRESS SYNDICATE OF THE UNIVERSITY OF CAMBRIDGE
The Pitt Building, Trumpington Street, Cambridge, United Kingdom

CAMBRIDGE UNIVERSITY PRESS
The Edinburgh Building, Cambridge CB2 2RU, UK
40 West 20th Street, New York, NY 10011-4211, USA
477 Williamstown Road, Port Melbourne, VIC 3207, Australia
Ruiz de Alarcón 13, 28014 Madrid, Spain
Dock House, The Waterfront, Cape Town 8001, South Africa

http://www.cambridge.org

First published 2003

Printed in the United Kingdom at the University Press, Cambridge

Typeface ITC Garamond Book 10.25/13 pt.   *System* LATEX 2_ε [TB]

A catalog record for this book is available from the British Library.

Library of Congress Cataloging in Publication Data
Business history around the world / edited by
Franco Amatori, Geoffrey Jones.
p.   cm. - (Comparative perspectives in business history)
Includes bibliographical references and index.
ISBN 0-521-82107-X
1. Economic history - 1990-   2. Business - History.   3. Industrial organization - Cross-cultural studies.
I. Amatori, Franco.   II. Jones, Geoffrey.   III. Series.
HC59.15 .B88   2003
338.09′0511-dc21   2002031343

ISBN 0 521 82107 X hardback

Contents

Contents   ix

Acknowledgments

This book is the outcome of a long and demanding process. We could not have completed it without the active support of many friends and colleagues. We want to thank all the authors for their patience in responding vigorously to the reports of their referees and in some cases substantially rewriting the original papers presented at the Milan conference. Persons working at a number of institutions that sponsored the series were particularly helpful. At Bocconi, Marzio Romani, Director of the Economic History Institute, has been very supportive – as always when business history is involved. Andrea Colli put at our disposal his outstanding organizational capacity. Nicola Crepax, secretary of ASSI (the Italian Association of Business Historians) at the time the project was being undertaken, was wonderfully helpful. On the ASSI side, we benefited greatly from the many comments by Pier Angelo Toninelli, secretary of the scientific committee of the association. Equally useful were the observations of Giuseppe Berta, Duccio Bigazzi, Renato Giannetti, Giovanni Federico, Anna Grandori, Luigi Orsenigo, Vera Zamagni, Takashi Hikino, and Patrick Fridenson, all of whom served as discussants at the Milan colloquium (October 1998) when the project started. At Johns Hopkins University we would like to thank Chairperson Gabrielle Spiegel of the History Department, the Deans of Arts and Sciences, the Institute for Applied Economics and the Study of Business Enterprise, and in particular,

Elizabeth Kafig, for the support they gave to this international undertaking. At the Centre for International Business History at the University of
Reading, Margaret Gallagher was as efficient as usual in making administrative arrangements. Cambridge University Press did an excellent job
in providing us with first-rate referees whose observations contributed
considerably to the improvement of the final product. At Cambridge the
helpful and friendly support of Frank Smith and Barbara Chin was greatly
appreciated. The final outcome of this long process depended to a great
extent upon the dedication and editorial skills of Mary Butler Davies and
Lou Galambos. As always, the editors and the authors remain ultimately
responsible for the text.

Franco Amatori and Geoffrey Jones

Milan and Boston

Contributors

Franco Amatori is Professor of Economic History, Bocconi University, Italy.

María Inés Barbero is Professor of Economic History, Universidad de Buenos Aires, and Professor of Economic History, Universidad de General Sarmiento, Argentina.

Giorgio Bigatti is Lecturer of Economic History, Bocconi University, Italy.

Albert Carreras is Professor of Economic History and Institutions, Department of Economics and Business, Universitat Pompeu Fabra, Spain.

Youssef Cassis is Professor of Economic History, University Pierre Mendès France, Grenoble, France, and Visiting Research Fellow, Business History Unit, London School of Economics, UK.

Alfred D. Chandler, Jr., is the Isidor Strauss Professor of Business History, Emeritus, Harvard Business School, USA.

Andrea Colli is Assistant Professor of Economic History, Bocconi University, Italy.

Margarita Dritsas is Professor of Economic and Social History, Department of European Studies, Hellenic Open University, Greece.

Louis Galambos is Professor of History and Co-Director, the Institute for Applied Economics and the Study of Business Enterprise, Johns Hopkins University, USA.

William J. Hausman is Chancellor Professor of Economics, Economics Department, College of William and Mary, USA.

Geoffrey Jones is Professor of Business Administration, Harvard Business School, USA.

Matthias Kipping is Associate Professor, Department of Economics and Business, Universitat Pompeu Fabra, Spain.

Akira Kudô is Professor, Institute of Social Science, University of Tokyo, Japan.

Chi-Kong Lai is Director, Asian Business History Centre and Senior Lecturer in Modern Chinese History, University of Queensland, Australia.

William Lazonick is University Professor, University of Massachusetts Lowell, USA, and Distinguished Research Professor, INSEAD (the European Institute of Business Administration), France.

Håkan Lindgren is Professor of Economic History, Department of Economics, Stockholm School of Economics, Sweden.

Mary B. Rose is Senior Lecturer in Business History, The Management School, Lancaster University, UK.

Harm G. Schröter is Professor, Department of History, University of Bergen, and Professor, Department of Economics, Norwegian School of Economics and Business Administration, Norway.

Keetie E. Sluyterman is Senior Researcher, Institute for History and Culture, Utrecht University, the Netherlands, and Visiting Fellow, Centre for International Business History, Reading University, UK.

Xavier Tafunell is Professor of Economic History, Department of Economics and Business, Universitat Pompeu Fabra, Spain.

Eugenio Torres is Professor of Economics, Department of Applied Economy, Universidad Complutense of Madrid, Spain.

Jonathan Zeitlin is Professor of History, Sociology, and Industrial Relations, University of Wisconsin-Madison, USA.

Business History around the World

1

Introduction

FRANCO AMATORI AND GEOFFREY JONES

Business history in the broadest sense includes everything about our business past, from the history of individual firms to that of entire business systems. While its boundaries and scope remain the subject of intense debate, business history research has yielded rich insights into the nature and origins of innovation and the wealth of nations. We have, as a result of this research, come to understand the role of business in momentous and sometimes horrendous historical events. Books and articles by business historians have had a profound impact upon the concerns of scholars working in management, history, and a broad range of social sciences. An important goal of this book is to make the enormous empirical wealth generated by business historians available to nonspecialists.

With that in mind, the book is organized in three parts. Part I consists of essays that seek to define the identity and borders of the discipline. It reviews some of the most important theoretical positions, including the so-called alternative approach, and the relationships of the field to economic theory. The contributors come from very different methodological backgrounds, and there is little consensus among them. They are engaged in ongoing debates.

Part II turns to the literature on national and regional cases. It begins with the historic core of modern capitalism in northwestern Europe and the United States. The subsequent essays consider the European countries of the Mediterranean – Italy, Spain, and Greece. Finally Japan, Chinese-speaking cultures, and Latin America are discussed. The geographical coverage is not comprehensive; the distinctive experiences of major Asian economies such as those of India and Korea, the Middle East, Turkey, and North and Sub-Saharan Africa are not addressed. Nor are the substantial literatures on the business history of Australia, New Zealand, and Canada. The initial hopes of the editors to include essays on the eastern European transition economies were dashed.

Nevertheless this volume provides the widest geographical coverage of the state of business history yet published. It shows clearly that there is no single model for successful or unsuccessful capitalism, and that interpretations of the business past have changed dramatically over time. British business history, for example, was long conditioned by a search for the causes of Britain's relative economic decline since the late nineteenth century, an issue that, as Geoffrey Jones and Keetie Sluyterman in this volume show, has been greatly redefined by recent research. Conversely, Japanese business history was long driven by a search for the reasons behind Japanese post–World War II economic growth. Akira Kudô shows that the field is currently undergoing a major revision following the acute problems of the Japanese economy since the 1990s.

The book concludes with Part III on comparative business history. Although the doyen of business history, Alfred D. Chandler Jr. – whose latest work graces the end of this volume – has been an active proponent of international comparisons in the study of business history, and although Japanese scholars have worked to promote comparative research, the significant comparative business history literature remains rather limited. The reasons are not difficult to discern; the meaningful comparison of the history of firms and business systems among countries requires a thorough understanding of the political, economic, social, and institutional contexts. This information is in most cases published largely in national languages, adding greatly to the tasks of investigators in a subject where research is already labor-intensive. The three essays here consider three subject areas – multinationals, family business, and the relationship between business and government – where comparative work has made some headway. There are many other themes of central concern to business historians – marketing, innovation, human resource management, gender, and ethnicity among them – which the editors were constrained from covering, not only because of lack of space, but because comparative perspectives remain limited. Fortunately, many of the national and regional surveys in Part II refer directly to these issues.

We believe the essays in this volume demonstrate the remarkable scope and vitality of business history. Business history emerged as a discrete subdiscipline at the Harvard Business School in the United States in the interwar years, though in Europe several historians were also by that time interested in explaining the history of industries and firms, usually employing a broader framework than that seen in the United States. During the 1950s, major scholarly histories based on confidential corporate archives and written by academics – such as R. W. and M. E. Hidy's study of Standard Oil, *Pioneering in Big Business* (New York, 1955), and Charles Wilson's *The History of Unilever*, Volumes 1 and 2 (London, 1954) – began to appear in both the United States and Europe. Such works continued to coexist – as they still do – with thousands of more "popular" histories of firms.

Over time the subject established its own credentials and is now represented by an impressive array of books, journals, newsletters, research centers, associations, specialized libraries, and conferences. Much of the credit for the maturing of business history as an academic discipline lies with the U.S. scholar Alfred D. Chandler. Chandler remains the business historian whose work is most widely read beyond the discipline of business history itself – by historians, management scholars, and institutional economists. They regard him as one of the founding fathers of strategic management and identify him as a major formative influence. However, Chandler's work matured within the context of a highly talented generation of American business historians that included Allan Nevins and Ralph Hidy and a younger generation including Louis Galambos and Mira Wilkins.

Chandler's work – the latest example of which appears at the end of this volume – has been distinguished by a sharp focus on the enterprise. He succeeded in taking business history beyond the lurches of ideological disputes by fostering dialogue with scholars in related fields, including economists, management specialists, and lawyers. Chandler's work remains central to business history, most notably through his generalizations about the relationship between strategy and structure, the distinction between core and peripheral sectors, and the role of big business and management in innovation. His generalizations remain controversial and disputed, but they still provide the most central framework for discussion in this immensely rich field of study.

Chandler has never claimed to cover all aspects of business history. At the end of *Scale and Scope* (Cambridge, 1990), his breathtaking comparative work on big business, after more than 600 pages of detailed analysis, he writes, "indeed this book has only begun to map the history of the institution before World War II. Much more work needs to be done at every level. . . ." But Chandler, like Karl Marx, claimed he was studying the most significant elements of the past, and he has not shirked the responsibility for making bold statements. As a result, he has sometimes been treated as a straw man who claimed that the development of any national industrial system must necessarily pass through a similar set of stages in the rise of large managerial corporations. Considered in this way, it is clear that Chandlerism could not satisfy even the most orthodox of his followers. For instance, those who write about Mediterranean Europe cannot avoid the role of state intervention, which, for Chandler, has been of secondary importance. At the same time, they have been forced to consider the enormous importance of small enterprise to national business systems. Similarly, scholars on overseas Chinese business need to make family firms rather than large managerial enterprises central units of analysis. Even in the United States, scholars have made it clear that there is a diverse and vibrant world beyond large firms, a world that requires our attention.

This volume includes contributions from several of the leading U.S.-based critics of Chandler's approach, as well as those who consider his interpretation of national cases outside the United States to be only partial. William Lazonick, an economist by training, emphasizes the need to consider companies in their broad social setting and not just through their entrepreneurial and managerial aspects. At the same time, he says we should think about the organizational capabilities of firms but also examine the process of their formation. He emphasizes "social conditions of innovative enterprise," a new perspective, building in part on the writings of both Chandler and the economist Edith Penrose. Insofar as there is a methodological spectrum between theory and empiricism in business history, this essay is an extreme example of a theoretical approach to the subject. Many scholars whose primary allegiance lies with history would dispute Lazonick's assertion that "business history needs a theory of innovative enterprise" and might be critical of an essay that talks very little about actual firms. Certainly there is an enormous methodological gap between Lazonick and Chandler. While Chandler has sought to generalize from rich empirical research, Lazonick's work provides a theory in search of evidence.

The "alternative approach" that characterizes Jonathan Zeitlin's essay is an alternative to Chandler, whose architecture Zeitlin deconstructs in favor of a vision that does not distinguish between subject and context, between opposed ways of production, and between epochs. In contrast to Chandler's emphasis on the critical role of large, professionally managed firms engaged in mass production, Zeitlin stresses the diversity of production systems that have always been present. He also stresses "the rediscovery of flexible production as a pervasive feature of industrial history prior to its contemporary resurgence since the 1970s." Zeitlin's methodological approach is drawn from history and the social sciences and differs profoundly from those of Lazonick. However Zeitlin's approach, like that of Lazonick, is heavily theoretical, and it is noteworthy that he refers to "industrial history" rather than "business history."

The essay by Louis Galambos offers a different post-Chandlerian approach. The author describes those who have challenged the stronghold of business history, the history of the industrial company. Why should we not consider the social or ecological impact of enterprise, ethnicity in business, or enterprise and gender? Influenced by approaches popular in university history departments, a new generation of business historians in the United States is heading in new directions. U.S. scholarship, which in the past was heavily biased toward the study of big business and organizational systems, is recently gravitating toward gender and culture. This has contributed – as Galambos notes – to a proliferation of approaches to the subject, in contrast to the Chandlerian orthodoxy that prevailed in the United States two decades earlier.

In some ways, business history stands at a crossroads at the beginning of the twenty-first century. The choices are whether to seek to embed the subject more firmly within the multiple concerns of history, or whether to position it as part of the discipline of management, seeking to establish valid generalizations about the role and performance of firms, entrepreneurs, and business systems. Postmodernists, who tend to view such conceptualizations as self-serving constructions, have little regard for the archival evidence that has been so important in traditional business history. Conversely, scholars who stress that the future of business history lies with its ever-closer integration into management studies would stress its potential for enriching and extending our current understanding of business behavior and performance by providing empirical evidence on our business past. Although these tensions are real and growing, as William Hausman notes in his essay, "debate over what constitutes the essence of business history is not new."

The surveys in Part II are indicative of some of the continuing national differences in business history research, often reflecting the national academic context in which they developed. Almost certainly a process of convergence is now underway, most strikingly in Europe, where the formation of the European Business History Association in the 1990s has led to enormous growth in interaction and networking between European scholars, who formerly often knew more about what was happening in the United States than in their neighboring countries. However considerable differences of emphasis remain. In Scandinavia, Håkan Lindgren notes, business history remains firmly rooted in economic history and centrally concerned with the study of the firm – in other words, wholly different from recent trends in the United States. In Greece and Spain, too, the links of business history with economic history have been strong, though the subdiscipline has developed a noticeably quantitative dimension in the latter country. In Britain, France, and Italy, business history has shown far more vitality than economic history and to a large extent has superseded it, and business historians have increasingly worked in the context of management and business studies. Meanwhile, in Japan, the large number of business historians largely work and teach within faculties of management and commerce, and for many years there has been a sharp distinction between business and economic history. As Akira Kudo stresses, Japanese business historians have a long tradition of international comparative research, and Japanese scholars have an almost unique interest in studying the business histories of other countries. Much of this research is not translated from Japanese and represents almost an "alternative" business history literature.

The chapters about the various nations also reveal some striking differences in the forces stimulating research in business history. In Germany, Harm Schröter shows that public concern about the country's Nazi past has stimulated a new interest in business. In Italy, companies were important in stimulating research into business history, in part to improve their image. In some countries, such as the Netherlands, the lack of academic institutionalization has made business historians dependent on commissions from companies as their main source of employment. In others, such as Britain and Japan, commissioned corporate histories are primarily undertaken by scholars who hold established university positions in business history.

Over the past twenty years, business history has become of greater interest to a wider range of emerging economies, and in this volume Chi-Kong Lai and María Inés Barbero review the cases of Chinese-speaking and Latin American cultures, respectively. Both show growing literatures with distinct biases. In Latin America, research has been heavily focused on entrepreneurs rather than firms. In China, too, there have been only a limited number of firm-specific studies. One of the major challenges facing business historians in many emerging countries is that there is virtually no tradition of private companies devoting resources to preserving corporate archives and even less of a tradition of allowing access to them by outsiders. Fortunately, the widespread activities of Western multinationals in many Asian, African, and Latin American countries provide a partial solution to this problem, as their archives can often provide substantial information not only on their specific affiliates, but also on the general business environment in their host economies. The essay in this volume on multinationals by Geoffrey Jones reviews some of the literature on foreign companies in emerging countries.

Business history lies in a peculiar position between the micro and macro explanations of economic growth and performance. In the best examples, its goal is that of beginning with a micro institution for the purpose of outlining the path of growth of a national economic model. In this way, business historians have traced the emergence of an American corporate economy, the cooperative capitalism of Germany, and the privileged role of government in France and the southern European countries. It is the way in which micro and macro intertwine that often makes the Chandlerian unit of analysis – the firm – appear inadequate. The essays in this volume demonstrate the value of including in the historical analysis not only the internal organization and strategies of firms, but also the national culture in which they operate, along with their legal and political environment.

As this volume indicates, business history is today an academic subdiscipline of remarkable potential and diversity. Its diversity is reflected in the fact that its academic practitioners are to be found contributing in many different contexts, and this is reflected in its eclectic methodology and still-developing research agendas. What is evident is the potential for business history research. In the world of academia, the attention of economists and management scholars has shifted from representative firms to unique firms. They are seeking to identify the differences between individual firms or key actors as a means of explaining technological innovation and the achievement of competitive advantage. Business history still has great potential to reach a wider audience, that is, people who almost never read academic books but have a great interest in – and perhaps even a right to know – something about the history of the firms that employ them and the branded goods and services they use in everyday life. We believe the essays in this volume demonstrate the remarkable scope and vitality of business history.

PART I

General Issues, Open Questions, Controversies

2

Identity and the Boundaries
of Business History

An Essay on Consensus and Creativity

LOUIS GALAMBOS

For most of its early history, business history evolved as an isolated American subdiscipline, separated by a wide gulf from the strong intellectual currents reshaping the larger discipline of history in the United States.[1] It was not the only subdiscipline that was isolated in this way during the period between 1930 and 1960. As Charles Neu has pointed out, diplomatic history had a somewhat similar phase of insular historiographical development that did not end in the United States until the

I would like to thank Julie Kimmel, Gabrielle Spiegel, and Jane Eliot Sewell for their suggestions. The usual disclaimers apply.

[1] I have written on aspects of the historiography of business history before. I have tried not to repeat myself in this essay, but I have probably failed; those who would like to check should consult the following: "U.S. Business History and Recent Developments in Historical Social Science in the United States" in *Proceedings of the Conference on Business History, October 1994, the Netherlands*, eds. Mila Davids, Ferry de Goey, and Dirk de Wit (Rotterdam, 1995), 112-20; "What Makes Us Think We Can Put Business Back into American History?" *Business and Economic History*, 2d series, no. 20 (1992): 1-11; "What Have CEOs Been Doing?" *Journal of Economic History* 48, no. 2 (1988): 243-58; "Technology, Political Economy, and Professionalization: Central Themes of the Organizational Synthesis," *Business History Review* 57, no. 4 (1983): 471-93; "The Emerging Organizational Synthesis in Modern American History," *Business History Review* 44, no. 3 (1970): 279-90; *American Business History* (Washington, D.C., 1967).

volatile 1960s.[2] But the isolation of business history was particularly extreme. Its origins in a business school setting made it suspect to many
historians, as did the ideology of its founder and the first generation of
his followers. N. S. B. Gras left no doubt as to where he stood on the contributions business had made to American society (they were positive)
or the damage the New Deal had done to a once vibrant U.S. political
economy (it was negative).[3] At a time when most American historians
were moderate reformers aligned with the U.S. brand of modern liberalism, this style of conservatism was scorned if it was noticed at all. For
the most part, it was just ignored.

In 1939, Gras published the first general synthesis in the subdiscipline,
Business and Capitalism, which he modestly subtitled *An Introduction
to Business History*. The book was, in fact, more than an introduction,
because the author synthesized much of what was known at that time
about the evolution of business policy and business management. At
the heart of his synthesis was a simple set of stages or eras: Pre-Business
Capitalism, Petty Capitalism, Mercantile Capitalism, Industrial Capitalism,
Financial Capitalism, and National Capitalism. The description within
these chronological categories, especially the early ones, was frequently
excellent, but what was lacking was an analytical engine to explain why
the system moved from one stage to another. This weakness was particularly evident in Gras's interpretation of the transition from Financial
to National Capitalism, a compromise system, he said, that left capital
in private hands while putting "government at the top." Thus, a history
written in terms of business policy and management reached a political
climax grounded in "dissatisfaction with such industrial capitalists as lin-
gered on but primarily with the system of financial capitalism. . . ."[4] As
this statement suggests, the author generally had trouble dealing with

---

[2] Charles Neu, "The Changing Intellectual Structure of American Foreign Policy," in
Twentieth-Century American Foreign Policy, eds. John Braeman, Robert H. Brenner, and
David Brody (Columbus, 1971), 1-57.

[3] N. S. B. Gras, *Business and Capitalism: An Introduction to Business History* (New York,
1947; originally published in 1939), 323-581. Gras concluded (356), "In the long run, the
New Deal would corrupt democracy and necessitate its abolition. It is the tammanyization of
the people on a national basis. It tends to oust opponents as enemies and it seeks scapegoats
for the misdeeds of others. In Germany and Italy the Jews have been the scapegoats and in
America financial capitalists." Gras also said (355), "The New Deal tends to ever-increasing
taxation and costs and therefore to inflation. It tends towards public financial bankruptcy
on a private business basis (and therefore ultimately to communistic capitalism). It tends
toward war. . . ."

[4] Ibid., 337. See also N. S. B. Gras and Henrietta M. Larson, *Casebook in American Business
History* (New York, 1939).

twentieth-century developments, in part because so little research had been done on the modern corporation and the administrative state. These weaknesses notwithstanding, there was little chance that scholars outside of business history were at that time going to pay much heed to a study that placed the New Deal in the same historical category as German and Italian fascism.[5]

Intellectual isolation would not have been so damaging to business history if there had been a great deal of intellectual ferment within the subdiscipline. But alas, there was very little. Gras's immediate followers were determined to fill out in an objective, systematic, inductive way the structure provided by the founder. They would fill in the blank spaces, adding details to the stage analysis.[6] They achieved their objective: business history began to generate information at an impressive rate, and the early practitioners devoted increasing attention to twentieth-century developments in the United States. The subdiscipline developed a strong identity and clear boundaries, across which there were very few intellectual exchanges.[7]

The subdiscipline's isolation was particularly painful to some of its practitioners because they knew they should have been closely aligned with and making important contributions to economic history. After all, Gras had been an economic historian before he launched the enterprise of business history.[8] Most business historians belonged to the Economic History Association, whose longtime secretary-treasurer, Herman Krooss, knew that the history of business was an intrinsic part of economic history.[9] But during the post–World War II years, a new

---

[5] Even as distinguished an historian as Richard Hofstadter found it impossible in 1948 to distance himself from Franklin D. Roosevelt and the New Deal. He thus was unable to impose on Roosevelt the same demands he did on the other presidents in *The American Political Tradition and the Men Who Made It* (New York, 1948).

[6] To a considerable extent, the second generation of business historians ignored the problems of synthesis and was satisfied with developing correctives to the "progressive" analysis of businesspersons as robber barons. The post–World War II generation of U.S. political historians, the so-called revisionists (with the prominent exception of Daniel Boorstin), occupied themselves along similar lines, developing correctives to progressive (that is, U.S.-style liberal) history rather than a new paradigm.

[7] See the items cited in Ralph W. Hidy, "Business History: Present Status and Future Needs," *Business History Review* 44, no. 4 (1970): 483-97.

[8] See, for instance, N. S. B. Gras, *Industrial Evolution* (Cambridge, Mass., 1930).

[9] In his textbook *American Economic Development* (New York, 1957), 271-2, Krooss said, "The epic hero of American economic history should be the business entrepreneur, not the statesman, the military leader, or the intellectual." It was difficult, he said, to generalize about business history, but he guided his readers to Gras and Larson, *Casebook in American*

cadre of economists were revolutionizing economic history in the United States, and these cliometricians were, if anything, even more contemptuous of business history than were the nation's political historians. Neoclassical economics was their common paradigm, and in that body of theory the historical and internal dimensions of business were, by definition, eliminated from consideration.[10]

This was not the case at Harvard University's Research Center in Entrepreneurial History, and the Research Center sparked a substantial amount of intellectual exchange within business history and between it and other disciplines. The Research Center failed to achieve its goal of creating a new, Schumpeterian subdiscipline. It failed to establish a viable, dynamic alternative to static or comparative static equilibrium analysis within economics. But the intellectual reverberations from the Research Center would continue to be felt in business history to the present day.[11] It was at the Research Center that Tom Cochran worked out his sociological approach to comparative business history and began to build a socially oriented synthesis that encompassed small as well as large enterprise and the political context, sans Grasian vituperation. It was at the Research Center that Alfred D. Chandler, Jr., began to blend Schumpeterian dynamics with Weberian social categories (by way of Talcott Parsons) and point business history toward the study of large enterprise.

As a result of the work of these two scholars, business history became a substantially less isolated and significantly more productive discipline in the 1960s and 1970s. We can afford to pause for a moment and ask why the Research Center was so productive. The people were talented, but there is usually an oversupply of intelligence in all corners of academic life. The Harvard Business School did not lack talent in those same years, but it did not produce the intellectual breakthroughs that came out of the Research Center. What distinguished the Research Center, I believe, was a collection of talented people who were working within a

---

Business History, which, he said, was "indispensable." Krooss was, however, much kinder to the New Deal (see 480–521) than Gras had been.

[10] Robert William Fogel and Stanley L. Engerman, eds., The Reinterpretation of American Economic History (New York, 1971), provide a convenient guide from a time before that academic cycle peaked.

[11] I have depended heavily upon Steven A. Sass, "Entrepreneurial Historians and History: An Essay in Organized Intellect" (Ph.D. diss., Johns Hopkins University, 1977) for my comments on the Research Center. But also see Explorations in Enterprise, ed. Hugh G. J. Aitken (Cambridge, Mass., 1965), especially 3–19, an essay on "Entrepreneurial Research: The History of an Intellectual Innovation" by the editor.

well-defined paradigm in a setting that encouraged debate and experimentation. The central paradigm was a dynamic theory of capitalist
evolution that had a clearly specified drive wheel, the entrepreneurial
function à la Schumpeter. Schumpeterian theory was, in the style of
Marx and Weber, an all-embracing theory with important political and
social components.

While the Research Center's major paradigm was all-embracing, it was
relatively abstract, lacking (again, in the Marxian and Weberian traditions)
historical specificity and depth. That left each of the participants in the
program plenty of intellectual room in which to develop a distinctive
approach to "entrepreneurial history." Thus, the paradigm facilitated intellectual exchanges without requiring the kind of consensus that stifles
creativity. Nor did the Research Center's leaders try to impose a single
language, theory, or set of categories on the participants.[12]

Indeed, business history could not have had more stark alternatives
than the ones formulated by Cochran and Chandler. Cochran's was the
broader of the two; he would go on to study everything from the rise
of the administrative state to child-rearing habits, from the U.S. beer
industry to Latin American business practices.[13] Chandler's approach
was to pick out the business institution he thought was most important
to the evolution of modern capitalism and to pursue that subject, the
large corporation, with bulldog determination for the rest of a career
that is still unfolding.

While employing Weberian categories and even absorbing some
elements of the kind of equilibrium analysis Parsons was promoting,
Chandler created his own unique synthesis.[14] Business bureaucracy in
the form of professional management became in his vision a major source
of innovation and was, in fact, one of the innovations that enabled capitalism to generate new income and wealth. Like Schumpeter, he made
innovation the motor of change, but unlike Schumpeter, Chandler was

---

[12] It would have been difficult to impose a single line of analysis or synthesis on this group
of scholars (which included, among others, Douglass North), but the Research Center, to
its credit, did not try.

[13] David B. Sicilia, "Cochran's Legacy: A Cultural Path Not Taken," *Business and Economic
History* 24, no. 1 (1995): 27–39.

[14] Others have provided analyses and narrative accounts of the development of Chandler's
scholarship. See, for instance, Thomas K. McCraw, "Introduction: The Intellectual Odyssey
of Alfred D. Chandler, Jr.," in *The Essential Alfred Chandler: Essays Toward a Historical
Theory of Big Business*, ed. Thomas K. McCraw (Boston, 1988), 1–21; Richard R. John,
"Elaborations, Revisions, Dissents: Alfred D. Chandler, Jr.'s *The Visible Hand* after Twenty
Years," *Business History Review* 71, no. 2 (1997): 151–200.

not skeptical about the ability of large, bureaucratized firms to remain entrepreneurial.[15]

Chandler altered the identity of business history without, however, completely abandoning Gras's values. Both were positivists who wrote a teleological style of history in which business was the prime mover. Both were skeptical about the modern administrative state, although Chandler was considerably more constrained in his judgments than Gras. More important were their differences. Unlike Gras, Chandler understood that the subdiscipline would thrive only if it acquired a new blend of induction and deduction, that is, a more sophisticated theoretical framework. His combination of sociological theory with a refurbished dynamic economic theory became the central paradigm that dominated work in the field for three decades.

The driver that provides Chander's theory with its dynamic element is the business firm and, in particular, the large corporation that responds creatively to changes in its technological and market environments. Those creative responses generate the innovations that enable companies to provide their customers with the goods and services they need (including entirely new commodities and services) more efficiently than other forms of enterprise. Unlike Schumpeter, Chandler did not venture into political history, but he left no doubt as to his evaluation of the respective roles of government and the large corporation in promoting economic growth.

Chandler's synthesis attracted other scholars to aspects of business behavior that they had heretofore ignored and encouraged them to study business in new ways. The Chandlerian paradigm was grounded in a powerful if implicit ideology that seemed likely to provoke substantial controversy within the subdiscipline and across its boundaries. At first, however, the new synthesis promoted consensus.

AN EMERGING AND DANGEROUS CONSENSUS

Initially, Chandler's work attracted very little attention outside of business history, and within the subdiscipline it produced more consensus than controversy. In business history, on the pages of the leading journal in the field, and in the few graduate programs offering instruction in this subdiscipline, Chandler's ideas became omnipresent. Students tended to

---

[15] Joseph A. Schumpeter, *Capitalism, Socialism, and Democracy* (New York, 1947), especially 134, 207, 219.

focus on large corporations and, even more narrowly, on their strategies and structures. In some cases, their instructors warned them that if they did not mention Chandler in the first paragraph or two of their manuscript, it might well not be published in the *Business History Review*. By the late 1980s, this word had apparently gotten around rather far; in the autumn issue of the *Business History Review* in 1989, all of the articles cited Chandler's work.[16] Chandler's academic gravitational field was so strong that the external aspects of business began to receive less and less attention as scholars young and old followed the master into the inner workings of the large corporation.

While this was happening, Chandler was doing much to promote the study of business history in the United States and abroad. He trained a cadre of young business historians and assisted in various ways a number of more advanced scholars. He helped historians from Great Britain, France, Italy, Japan, and Germany at a time when the study of business history was just coming of age in several of these countries. Personally and intellectually, he was the leader of a field of study that he had remolded along the lines of his paradigm. Most of his students worked on subjects that fit comfortably within that paradigm. While not all of the affiliated scholars did, most of their work was at least on the edge of the Chandler synthesis.

One of those attracted to Chandler's ideas was a radical economist, William Lazonick, whose prior interests had been primarily in comparative economic history. Attracted by a Chandleresque style of business history, Lazonick's career took a sharp turn. For one thing, he began to publish – at an astonishing rate – a series of articles and books that elaborated on Chandler's ideas and defended them from what he perceived as a threat from the transactions-costs analysts in economics, in particular Oliver E. Williamson. Actually, Williamson thought he was supportive of and supported by Chandler's history in the form it had acquired in *The Visible Hand* (Cambridge, 1977). But Lazonick thought otherwise and vigorously defended one of the crucial boundaries of business history from the intrusion of neoclassical, equilibrium theory.[17]

This phase of Lazonick's work in business history is important because it tells us much about what was happening to the subdiscipline

---

[16] Between 1985 and 1989, the number of citations of Chandler's work in the *Business History Review* were 5, 14, 14, 14, and 34; the figure in 1989 was high in spite of the fact that one special issue on real estate included no references to Chandler's publications.

[17] William Lazonick, *Business Organization and the Myth of the Market Economy* (New York, 1991).

as consensus reigned. Despite his solid grounding in economics and in
Marxist analysis, Lazonick did not directly challenge any of Chandler's
central interpretations or evaluations. Neither did Richard Tedlow,
Richard Vietor, or Tom McCraw, three of Chandler's distinguished
colleagues at the Harvard Business School.

Richard Tedlow wrote an excellent book on marketing that could have
provided a creative new twist to the study of modern U.S. business. But
instead, the author ignored some of the most interesting aspects of his
own evidence and left it sitting, rather uncomfortably, in the Chandler
context.[18] I am not singling out this book because it is a bad example
of business history. To the contrary, I use the book in both my graduate seminar and upper-level undergraduate courses because it is a good
book. But it is also a book that tells us something about the intellectual
environment at the Harvard Business School during those years. Unlike
the Research Center for Entrepreneurial Studies, the Harvard Business
School was and still is a powerfully consensus-oriented institution. It
encouraged elaboration, not dissent, in much the same way that most
modern bureaucracies do. This was important, because it meant that in
this vital center for business studies, the subdiscipline was sliding toward the situation that had stultified its intellectual development in the
Gras era.

CONVERGENCE WITH OTHER DISCIPLINES
AND CREATIVE CONTROVERSY

Fortunately, business history had become by this time a much broader
and more vibrant enterprise than it was in the Gras years, thanks in
large part to Chandler. The Lazonick–Williamson debate is instructive
in this regard. When Gras was writing, economists were contemptuous
of business history. Many still are today. But clearly, Oliver Williamson
was not. While, à la Lazonick, Williamson may have misread Chandler,
he did read him and thank him profusely for the evidence he provided
to support some of the important theoretical additions Williamson was
making to the neoclassical theory of the firm.

Those particular emendations necessitate some comment, because
Williamson and others were moving economics closer to history and
closer to the point where they might find it necessary to develop a

[18] Richard Tedlow, *New and Improved: The Story of Mass Marketing in America*
(New York, 1990).

dynamic rather than a static theory of the firm and of its role in the economy.[19] A dynamic theory in the manner of Schumpeter had the potential to spark another burst of creative interaction between economics and history, something along the lines of what had happened at the Research Center in Entrepreneurial History. Williamson introduced or elaborated a number of concepts that should now be familiar to most business historians. They include bounded rationality, opportunism in principal–agent relationships, embedded knowledge, and an analysis of hierarchy, in addition to transactions costs.[20] As a result, time and historical particularity, two essential aspects of history, were creeping down this theoretical path into the economics of the firm and corroding the frictionless mechanism of mathematical analysis.

These developments spawned a collaborative effort under the auspices of the National Bureau of Economic Research (NBER) to bring economics and business history even closer together. Peter Temin, Daniel M. G. Raff, and Naomi R. Lamoreaux have led this ongoing program to build collaboration on the intellectual platform of a modified neoclassical paradigm. Of special interest in this regard is the volume that Lamoreaux and Raff edited on *Coordination and Information: Historical Perspectives on the Organization of Enterprise*.[21] As the editors explained, the convergence of transactions-cost analysis and Chandlerian history of the large firm created a new opportunity for "collaboration between business history and economic theory." By making problematic the means of coordination within the firm, the role of information flows in business activity, and the decision-making processes and boundaries of the enterprise, they looked forward to a post-Chandlerian style of analysis that would be informed by "game-theoretic methods." For help in uncovering "the complexities that need to be addressed in the analysis of economic coordination under conditions of imperfect information," they turned to scholars in history, economics, finance, and business management.[22]

---

[19] So too was Paul David, who was developing the idea of path dependency as a means of theorizing about specific historical patterns of innovation.

[20] Oliver E. Williamson, *Markets and Hierarchies: Analysis and Antitrust Implications* (New York, 1975); and the same author's "Hierarchies, Markets and Power in the Economy: An Economic Perspective," *Industrial and Corporate Change* 4, no. 1 (1995): 21–49. I do not mean to understate Williamson's debt to Coase; that relationship is well established. See Ronald H. Coase, "The Nature of the Firm," *Economica* 4 (1937): 386–405.

[21] The NBER project began with *Inside the Business Enterprise: Historical Perspectives on the Use of Information*, ed. Peter Temin (Chicago, 1991); I have discussed that volume in the paper I delivered in the Netherlands. See footnote 1.

[22] Lamoreaux and Raff, *Coordination and Information* (Chicago, 1995), 3–8.

Each of the resulting historical essays provided a narrative. Several were guided, in varying degrees, by one or more concepts drawn from the theory. Thus, Raff found a business system in which the pattern of innovation displayed an "economic rationality at its core" but was "well leavened with culture, meanings, and the heavy hand of history." Similarly, Daniel Nelson found that the efforts (1890–1940) of industrial engineers to reshape coordination within U.S. firms left a "mixed legacy." W. Bernard Carlson returned to the history of General Electric and discovered that the emergence of a powerful oligopolistic competitor could be understood only in terms of conflict resolution within an organization that included several important "mind sets" and related interest groups. David Mowery looked again at research and development in the United States and learned (contra Chandler) that transactions costs could be shaped dramatically by the political environment in which firms operated. The other essays developed similar "complexities," some of which were linked to information imperfections, principal–agent relationships, and suboptimal regulatory regimes.[23]

What does not emerge from the book is an alternative paradigm of business history built on game-theoretic methods. None of the essays dealt specifically with secular patterns of development for the entire business system or even that part of it that has occupied most of the attention of Chandler and his followers. For the present, then, the NBER project has yielded and seems likely to continue to produce a series of excellent analyses – many of them economics-informed; all of them

---

[23] Ibid., 27–8, 48, 57–61, 147–76. One of the major challenges to the editors was, of course, to guide historians who felt uncomfortable with the concepts and language of economics to use theory in reworking material they had already researched and published. Thus, Daniel Nelson wrote an excellent essay on "Industrial Engineering and the Industrial Enterprise, 1890–1940," 35–48, but did not, so far as I can tell, directly employ economic theory. W. Bernard Carlson, "The Coordination of Business Organization and Technological Innovation within the Firm: A Case Study of the Thomson–Houston Electric Company in the 1880s," 55–94, turned to an historian of technology, Reese Jenkins, for his guiding concept. Tony Freyer, "Legal Restraints on Economic Coordination: Antitrust in Great Britain and America, 1880–1920," 183–202, added a new twist to his conclusion but no new economic concepts to his methodology. On the other hand, David C. Mowery ("The Boundaries of the U.S. Firm in R&D," 147–76), Kenneth A. Snowden ("The Evolution of Interregional Mortgage Lending Channels, 1870–1940: The Life Insurance–Mortgage Company Connection," 209–47), and Charles W. Calomiris ("The Costs of Rejecting Universal Banking: American Finance in the German Mirror, 1870–1914," 257–315) all used economic analysis to good effect in their studies. All three had done so before, and all three were trained in economics. It may also be important that all three were analyzing the external aspects of businesses – either the boundaries of firms or the relationships between them.

historically researched – of past business behavior, without a dynamic synthesis that would be an alternative to the Chandlerian context.

Richard Nelson, Sidney G. Winter, and others have long been convinced, however, that such a new paradigm could be constructed in a manner consistent with certain methodological aspects but not with most of the central ideas of "orthodox neoclassical economic theory." Working from a different starting point, they jumped with both feet into the realm of dynamic economic analysis.[24] Evolutionary economics represented a more dramatic break with static or comparative static economics than Williamson's work or the NBER project. As the evolutionary perspective currently stands, it is not entirely clear whether evolution is a metaphor or is actually the driving force of the analysis, but in either case, this group of economists has also added time and historical particularity to their theory. Indeed, they have added much more.[25] Like Williamson, they and their colleagues in the evolutionary school have begun to reach out toward history, looking in one case at the historical development of "national innovation systems," in another at the "sources of industrial leadership" in seven important industries, and at the early development of biotechnology.[26]

The last study, Maureen McKelvey's book on *Evolutionary Innovations: The Business of Biotechnology* (Oxford 1996), provides an excellent indication of how close this branch of economics has moved to business history, how fruitful the interaction can be, and how much of a gap still remains between these subdisciplines. McKelvey's comparative historical case study of genetic engineering in the United States and Sweden is explicitly situated in evolutionary economics. The author's meticulous historical treatment of two firms and their innovations is an outstanding addition to business history and to the history of technology in a modern science-based industry. McKelvey also succeeds in illustrating some important features of the evolutionary model. But she is unable to close the gap between the economic abstractions of the model and her time-, place-, person-, and institution-particular data. Her book indicates that much remains to be done before convergence on this front will be

---

[24] Richard R. Nelson and Sidney G. Winter, *An Evolutionary Theory of Economic Change* (Cambridge, Mass., 1982).

[25] See, for instance, the discussion of "Organizational Capabilities and Behavior," ibid., chap. 5, 96–136.

[26] Richard R. Nelson, ed., *National Innovation Systems: A Comparative Analysis* (New York, 1993); David C. Mowery and Richard R. Nelson, eds., *Sources of Industrial Leadership: Studies of Seven Industries* (Cambridge, 1999).

complete but that intellectual transactions across the remaining gap will continue to be fruitful.

Insofar as the work in evolutionary economics generates productive controversies, they are analytical and empirical in nature. The same can be said for the controversies developing along the boundary between business history and the history of technology. An energetic and productive subset of the historians of technology has in recent years stimulated considerable analytical debate about business history. The works of Thomas Hughes, David Hounshell, John Smith, Bernard Carlson, Leonard Reich, Steve Usselman, and others – to mention only a few – have brought into question the focus of Chandler and some of his closest followers on the internal aspects of business development. The studies in the history of technology suggest that public policy, cultural values, and scientific and engineering institutions deserve a place beside strategy and structure as factors shaping corporate evolution.[27]

A somewhat different style of controversy, ideological as well as analytical, has arisen along the boundaries between business history, sociology, and political science. In addition to challenging industrial organization theory, Chandler's paradigm was a threat to those social scientists who were committed to any one of the numerous varieties of neo-Marxist interpretation of modern society. The prescient Charles Perrow saw this challenge very early and launched what has become an extended dialogue with Chandlerian history. Others followed, especially after the collapse of communism and the decline of the left seemed to put capitalism in the driver's seat throughout the world. The threat from a conservative historical synthesis now seemed important enough to prompt a number of leading scholars to offer alternative explanations of the rise of big business and of its impact on social classes, political systems, and the developed and developing economies. In addition to the indefatigable Perrow, William G. Roy, Neil Fligstein, and Mark Granovetter have mounted counterattacks that have, I believe, enlivened business history and broadened its scope.[28] While they have yet to develop a paradigm

---

[27] See the insightful discussion in David A. Hounshell, "Hughesian History of Technology and Chandlerian Business History: Parallels, Departures, and Critics," *History and Technology* 12 (1995): 205–24.

[28] For a sympathetic but critical account of Perrow's substantial body of work, see Christiane Diehl-Taylor, "Charles Perrow and Business History: A Neo-Weberian Approach to Business Bureaucratization," *Business and Economic History* 26, no. 1 (1997): 138–58; William G. Roy, *Socializing Capital: The Rise of the Large Industrial Corporation in America* (Princeton, 1997); Neil Fligstein, *The Transformation of Corporate Control*

that is likely to attract many business historians who do not already share their ideological concerns, they have certainly helped to collapse the consensus that for a time threatened the health of the subdiscipline.[29] Their work also promises to meld with the new postmodern studies discussed subsequently.

Controversy has erupted within as well as along the boundaries of business history, and in the 1990s it became the norm. As the subdiscipline matured in a number of European and Asian countries, its scholars developed national perspectives that no longer could be comfortably accommodated in the Chandlerian historical framework. The work of Leslie Hannah is a case in point, as are some of the studies published and edited by Geoffrey Jones.[30] Active business history associations and publications now existed in a number of countries, and a single paradigm could no longer encase their diverse conclusions. What was emerging was a perspective in which the American model of modern large-scale enterprise could no longer be assumed to be the end toward which business history was marching in the twentieth century. This conclusion seemed all the more reasonable given the problems many U.S. companies were experiencing in meeting foreign competition during the years following the 1965-75 transitional decade.[31]

One of the markers for the new era in business history was the emergence of the journal *Industrial and Corporate Change* (*ICC*). Initially a joint product of Italian and U.S. scholars, *ICC* created a new and exciting intellectual space situated between the microeconomics of the firm, managerial studies, and business history. I have found in recent years that *ICC* is the journal I read first and most completely (unless, of course, I have an article in one of the three U.S. journals, the *Business History Review,*

(Cambridge, Mass., 1990); Mark Granovetter, "Coase Revisited: Business Groups in the Modern Economy," *Industrial and Corporate Change* 4, no. 1 (1995): 93-130.

[29] The same can be said for the work of Martin J. Sklar; see *The Corporate Reconstruction of American Capitalism, 1890-1916: The Market, the Law and Politics* (Cambridge, 1988).

[30] See Leslie Hannah, "The American Miracle, 1875-1950, and After: A View in the European Mirror," *Business and Economic History* 24, no. 2 (1995): 197-220. The comments by Alfred D. Chandler, Takashi Hikino, Mary O'Sullivan, Wilfried Feldenkirchen, and Patrick Fridenson and the reply by Leslie Hannah, 221-62, are also instructive in this regard. Geoffrey Jones, "Global Perspectives and British Paradoxes," *Business History Review* 71, no. 2 (1997): 291-8.

[31] The British association had, of course, been active since the 1950s. For a recent review of Italian historiography see Francesca Carnevali, "A Review of Italian Business History from 1991 to 1997," *Business History* 40, no. 2 (1998): 80-94. See also the selections by Louis Galambos (an introduction), Geoffrey Jones (Britain), Etsuo Abe (Japan), and Franco Amatori (Italy) in *Business History Review* 71, no. 2 (1997): 287-318.

Enterprise & Society (formerly *Business and Economic History*), or
Essays in Economic and Business History).

Within business history, consensus was supplanted by vigorous elements of controversy, and that was true even with those scholars who
were most closely aligned to the Chandlerian paradigm. We can return to
the work of William Lazonick, who added to his elaboration and defense
of Chandler some distinctly non-Chandlerian themes. One involved his
return to the study of labor – an interest of his earlier radical years –
and his recognition that U.S. corporations suffered because they did not
encourage innovation from the shop floor, as did Japanese companies.
Chandler's brand of top-down business history had little to say about the
shop floor, but Lazonick found there one of the primary reasons that
America's hierarchical organizations had fallen on such difficult times in
the 1960s, 1970s, and 1980s.[32] Economies of scale and scope did not
enable U.S. firms to hold their market shares when they failed to achieve
innovation from the bottom up as well as the top down. Lately, Lazonick and Mary O'Sullivan have probed corporate governance in search of
other aspects of U.S. companies in need of reform.[33]

I would place my own work on government and lately on innovation in the same category. While building on Chandler, I looked beyond
the firm to its political context, power relations, and links to the profes-
sions. While giving considerable emphasis to structure, scale, and scope,
I looked outside the firm for important sources of innovation and made
that process far more contingent than Chandler had. Recently, my work
has emphasized the networks of public, private, and nonprofit institutions that sustain innovation in those science-based, high-tech companies
that have leaders capable of responding effectively to the frequent transformations that characterize these networks and industries.[34] Those firms
that have lacked this kind of leadership have been pushed aside by more
innovative organizations. First movers or not, they have lost market share
to more creative institutions.

Other scholars who were less inclined to build on Chandler have also
generated new perspectives. Philip Scranton and Jonathan Zeitlin have
led a growing chorus proclaiming the role of the small and medium-
sized firm in promoting business development in the late nineteenth and

---

[32] William Lazonick, *Competitive Advantage on the Shop Floor* (Cambridge, Mass., 1990).
[33] William Lazonick and Mary O'Sullivan, "Organization, Finance and International Competition," *Industrial and Corporate Change* 5, no. 1 (1996): 1–49.
[34] Louis Galambos with Jane Eliot Sewell, *Networks of Innovation: Vaccine Development
at Merck, Sharp & Dohme, and Mulford, 1895–1995* (New York, 1995).

twentieth centuries.[35] The work by Scranton, Zeitlin, et al.; the British studies of family firms; and analyses of recent business developments in northern Italy suggest that we are going to learn a great deal in the coming years about the different settings that conduce to innovation and about large-firm/small-firm relationships in successful economies.

Zeitlin's essay in this book ("Productive Alternatives: Flexibility, Governance, and Strategic Choice in Industrial History") provides an excellent guide to the development of this line of analysis in the years since the early 1980s. Often labeled the "historical alternatives" school, these scholars have altered the historiographical landscape of business history in ways prefigured by the work of Thomas Cochran. Unlike Cochran, however, Zeitlin et al. have developed a paradigm that is grounded in economics, not sociology, and that is itself extremely flexible. It can be used as an alternative to or an addition to the Chandlerian synthesis. It has been used as an "ideal type," but in Zeitlin's most recent characterization, this model is employed primarily as an antidote to technological determinism and a means of getting at the many successful national and regional variations that modern capitalism has produced.

Although it seems unlikely in 2003 that the "virtual corporation" or the mini-firm will supplant the large public corporation in most sectors of the global economy, the boundaries and internal structures of the dominant companies have remained in flux for several decades. Patterns of innovation have shifted in a number of science-based industries. Economists, scholars in management studies, and historians of business and technology have all analyzed these changes, without as yet establishing a new, commanding synthesis of modern business history.[36] All that seems

---

[35] Philip Scranton, *Endless Novelty: Specialty Production and American Industrialization, 1865–1925* (Princeton, 1997), focuses on batch production. Charles Sabel and Jonathan Zeitlin, eds., *World of Possibilities: Flexibility and Mass Production in Western Industrialization* (Cambridge, 1997), provide an historical context for the alternative to large-scale production. *The Second Industrial Divide: The Possibilities for Prosperity*, by Michael Piore and Charles Sabel (New York, 1984), was written while the U.S. business system was suffering from intense global competition and experiencing a formidable organizational transition; by the mid-1990s, when the United States had recovered its leadership role in the world economy, the Piore–Sabel prescription would begin to look dated. I have discussed the transition in "The U.S. Corporate Economy in the Twentieth Century" in *The Twentieth Century*, eds. Stanley Engerman and Robert Gallman, vol. 3 of *The Cambridge Economic History of the United States* (Cambridge, 2000), 927–67.

[36] Some of the most interesting small firm/large firm developments in recent years have involved the biotechnology industry. See, in addition to McKelvey, *Evolutionary Innovations*, Luigi Orsenigo, *The Emergence of Biotechnology: Institutions and Markets in Industrial Innovation* (New York, 1989); Gary P. Pisano, *The Development Factory:*

certain is that lively debate will continue and that historiographical as well as business innovation will continue to be central concerns of the subdiscipline.

While all of this was happening, the historical profession in the United States and, to a lesser extent, abroad was steadily moving away from the subject matter and central concerns of business history. In the United States, histories that focus on class, gender, and race have in recent years dominated the national professional organizations and their agendas, journals, and programs. The profession's normative ideology has drifted to the left and away from market-related phenomena at about the same pace as the world has drifted to the right and toward the market.

POSTMODERNISMS AND DIVERGENCE

These changes in the history profession, which I will lump into a category called "postmodernisms," have influenced all of the subdisciplines, including business history. I use the plural form, "postmodernisms," because the new approaches take several forms. Sometimes postmodernism is an ideological position grounded in a post-Marxist or neo-Marxist radical opposition to multinational capitalism of the sort that developed in the post–World War II period.[37] Sometimes postmodernism is an approach to literary criticism that defines what one can and cannot say on the basis of a particular written source. Whether used in literary criticism or history, this variety of postmodernism propounds a brand of relativism that is used to break down traditional structures of interpretation and open a field to new, sometimes highly idiosyncratic concepts. Pressed far enough, these approaches to knowledge can be considered a philosophy, a new approach to what can and cannot be known. Finally, postmodernism is frequently used to characterize the culture of modern society. Used in this way, it is a structure, a synthesis much like the Chandlerian paradigm but with a much broader purview. Everything, except some remnants of modern society, is seen as possessing a postmodern character. These three forms of postmodernism are

---

Unlocking the Potential of Process Innovation (Boston, 1997); and Henry G. Grabowski and John M. Vernon, "Innovation and Structural Change in Pharmaceuticals and Biotechnology," *Industrial and Corporate Change* 3, no. 2 (1994): 435–49.

[37] I have discussed postmodernism at greater length in "Myth and Reality in the Study of America's Consumer Culture," in *The Modern Worlds of Business and Industry: Cultures, Technology, Labor*, ed. Karen Merrill (Turnhout, Belgium, 1998), 183–203.

linked by the central assumption that reality is socially constructed and contingent.[38]

The development in recent years of women's studies gave a great boost to cultural history, and both helped foster certain brands of postmodern analysis. Their impact can be seen in business history, especially but not exclusively among a younger group of scholars. Recently, the Center for the History of Business, Technology, and Society at the Hagley Museum and Library in Wilmington, Delaware, has become a leading promoter of this style of business history through its publications, seminars, and conferences. Published under the rubric "The Future of Business History," one of their recent conference proceedings provided a full sample of postmodern thought. As the volume's editors, Philip Scranton and Roger Horowitz, noted, they wanted to explore "the points of intersection between business history and studies of culture, gender, ideology, race, work, the environment, and of course, technology. . . ." At these intersections, they said, "scholars (few of whom described themselves as business historians) were accomplishing intriguing and innovative research on the activities of businesses."[39]

The resulting essays covered a broad range of subjects and employed a number of different conceptual frameworks and ideologies. The various authors brought to the surface "blatant and forthright attempts to harness gendered values"; "anxieties" among antebellum Southerners; a rush by the corporation of the 1930s "to occupy" the turf between the company and society; the potential for a new history that would demonstrate business contributions to "species extinction" and "ecosystem degradation"; "managerial noncompliance" with safety regulations; a "neo-Fordist 'discourse of enterprise'"; an antebellum Philadelphia plagued by "racial tensions" that constrained the social progress of even a successful African American businessman; an economic history best "seen as a series of political struggles over the legitimate nature of social order"; a Machiavellian Air Force successfully constructing "the military industrial complex"; and a new post-1970 business order in which some of the

---

[38] I am indebted to Gabrielle Spiegel for this observation. Of course, one does not have to be a postmodernist to believe history is contingent. My own work on innovation stresses contingency and the construction and reconstruction of intellectual contexts associated with particular forms of science, technology, and organizational theory and practice.

[39] Scranton and Horowitz, "The Future of Business History," *Business and Economic History* 26, no. 1 (1997): 1–4.

most successful sectors – biotech and information technology – "have been organized and governed without large, hierarchical organization structures."[40]

Stitched together, these essays provide a glimpse of what a postmodern business history might resemble. While the volume contained several essays that were distinctly modern – those by Naomi Lamoreaux, Daniel Raff, Peter Temin, Sally Clarke, JoAnne Yates, and Robert E. Weems, Jr. – most of the contributors were oriented more to David Harvey than to Alfred Chandler, more to Jackson Lears than to Joseph Schumpeter.[41] Their foundation was thus the ideological brand of postmodernism, either in a structuralist or a poststructuralist form.

The postmodern movement in professional thought is, of course, not confined to the United States or to any one center. Its intellectual origins were in Europe, and indeed, most of business history's associations, conventions, and publications have been touched by postmodern influences. There is every reason to believe that these influences will become stronger, not weaker, in the years ahead and that they will produce a new style of business history, if not an overarching paradigm. It seems possible that postmodern business history will elide with the neo-Marxist critiques of modern capitalism and develop something resembling the old "robber baron" synthesis. But in this case, the critique of capitalism will be more sophisticated than it was in the 1930s and 1940s, when the robber baron interpretation was most popular.

Postmodern business history will no longer be built on the assumption that has facilitated intellectual exchanges between business history, economics, economic history, and economic sociology – the assumption that, all other things being equal, the institutions and systems that make available the most goods and services are best for society.[42] The brand of postmodernism that describes all developed societies as imbued with a single culture of consumption has already developed an alternative to

[40] Ibid., 25, 43, 96, 136, 154, 195, 227, 230, 264, 278, respectively.
[41] David Harvey, *The Condition of Postmodernity: An Enquiry into the Origins of Cultural Change* (Oxford, 1989); Richard Fox and T. J. Jackson Lears, eds., *The Culture of Consumption* (New York, 1983).
[42] Two exceptions to this rule are Sally Clarke and Kenneth Lipartito, both of whom are functioning as intellectual "brokers," maintaining links with the paradigms that give a positive twist to consumption while exploring new, postmodern approaches to business history. See, for instance, Sally Clarke, "Consumer Negotiations," *Business and Economic History* 26, no. 1 (1997): 101–22; Kenneth Lipartito, "Culture and the Practice of Business History," *Business and Economic History* 24, no. 2 (1995): 1–41.

that assumption. The culture of consumption turns the central idea that more is better on its head. More goods and services become, in fact, a destructive element that leaves populations wandering through malls and staring at TV advertisements in search of a salvation that can never be achieved.[43]

This intensely ideological brand of business history will, for the most part, simply bypass Chandler and concentrate on its critique of global capitalism. Today, this line of interpretation is already being applied to studies of post-Soviet societies and their economic problems. Gender analysis is fostering critiques of what has been for much of its history a male-dominated business system. Poststructuralists are presenting new stories, new narratives of business behavior, most of which offer negative perspectives on the class, racial, and gender aspects of business.

WELL?

There will, in short, be turmoil in business history in the years to come. There are at least five constellations of scholarly work that offer alternatives to an unreconstructed Chandlerian synthesis. One is a reconstructed form of Chandler's paradigm. Another is the modified neoclassical approach associated with the NBER project. A third is work linked to evolutionary economics, and a fourth draws upon the central concepts of the flexible alternatives school. A fifth is the postmodern constellation, in both its structuralist and poststructuralist varieties. Clearly, there will continue to be a large number of intellectual transactions across the boundaries of the subdiscipline, and, indeed, these boundaries are likely to be threatened and the subdiscipline's identity seriously challenged. As the centrifugal forces grow stronger, there will be an increasing possibility that business history as presently constituted, or at least its subject matter, will be completely absorbed by another discipline or subdiscipline.

Consensus has been vanquished. There will be no end to the controversy, competition, bitterness, and exasperation. At least I hope there is not an end to it, because it is, I am certain, the life of any academic trade and the best sign that business history is today more interesting than it has been at any time since the founding of the subdiscipline in the 1930s.

---

[43] Fox and Lears, *The Culture of Consumption*. See Galambos, "Myth and Reality."

KEY WORKS

Chandler, Alfred D., Jr. *The Visible Hand: The Managerial Revolution in American Business.* Cambridge, Mass., 1997.

Scale and Scope: The Dynamics of Industrial Capitalism. Cambridge, Mass., 1990.

Galambos, Louis. "The U.S. Corporate Economy in the Twentieth Century." In *The Twentieth Century*, edited by Stanley Engerman and Robert Gallman, 927–67. Vol. 3 of *The Cambridge Economic History of the United States.* Cambridge, 2000.

Galambos, Louis with Jane Eliot Sewell. *Networks of Innovation: Vaccine Development at Merck, Sharp & Dohme, and Mulford, 1895-1995.* Cambridge, 1995.

John, Richard R. "Elaborations, Revisions, Dissents: Alfred D. Chandler, Jr.'s *The Visible Hand* after Twenty Years." *Business History Review* 71, no. 2 (1997): 151–200.

Lamoreaux, Naomi and Daniel Raff, eds. *Coordination and Information: Historical Perspectives on the Organization of Enterprise.* Chicago, 1995.

Lazonick, William. *Business Organization and the Myth of the Market Economy.* New York, 1991.

Competitive Advantage on the Shop Floor. Cambridge, 1990.

McCraw, Thomas K. "Introduction: The Intellectual Odyssey of Alfred D. Chandler, Jr." In *The Essential Alfred Chandler: Essays Toward a Historical Theory of Big Business,* edited by Thomas K. McCraw, 1–21. Boston, 1988.

McKelvey, Maureen. *Evolutionary Innovations: The Business of Biotechnology.* Oxford, 1996.

Sabel, Charles F. and Jonathan Zeitlin. *World of Possibilities: Flexibility and Mass Production in Western Industrialization.* Cambridge, 1997.

Sicilia, David B. "Cochran's Legacy: A Cultural Path Not Taken." *Business and Economic History* 24, no. 1 (1995): 27–39.

Tedlow, Richard. *New and Improved: The Story of Mass Marketing in America.* New York, 1990.

Williamson, Oliver E. *Markets and Hierarchies: Analysis and Antitrust Implications.* New York, 1975.

3

Understanding Innovative Enterprise

Toward the Integration of Economic Theory and Business History

WILLIAM LAZONICK

What determines the growth of an economy? How does a society share among its members the costs of generating economic growth and the benefits that are derived from it? These fundamental questions of growth and distribution are as old as the discipline of economics. But modern economics has not been very successful in providing cogent answers. The main problem is that the conventional theory of the market economy lacks a theory of economic development.

This intellectual deficiency is neither inevitable nor accidental. During the nineteenth century, the elaboration of a theory of economic development was the central project of what came to be called "classical" economics. But during the twentieth century, the economics discipline displayed an ever-growing commitment to the individualistic ideology and ahistorical methodology of "neoclassical" economics. Given these ideological and methodological orientations, adherents to the neoclassical

The original version of this essay was prepared for the conference "Business History around the World at the End of the Twentieth Century," Milan, October 15–17, 1998. A revised version was presented at the Business History Workshop, Saïd Business School, University of Oxford, March 19, 1999. The substantial elaboration, amendment, and refinement of the arguments in this essay have been made under a grant from the Targeted Socio-Economic Research Programme of the European Commission, DGXII, Contract No. SOE1-CT-98-1114. I am grateful to Louis Galambos and Mary O'Sullivan for comments on various drafts.

perspective neglected to build a theory of economic development that can comprehend the historical experiences of economic growth and income distribution in the world's most advanced national economies.[1]

Indeed, the neoclassical research agenda by its very definition – the study of *the allocation of scarce resources among competing uses* – places the process of economic development beyond its analytical scope. Using this definition, conventional economic analysis assumes that, in the determination of economic performance, technological and market conditions can be taken as exogenous. The neoclassical economist takes the "scarcity" of resources – technology – and the "competing" uses to which they can be allocated – markets – as given constraints in the resource allocation process. Economic actors are assumed to operate subject to these exogenously determined constraints as they seek to optimize their objectives.

In contrast, a theory of economic development takes as given neither the quantity nor the quality of productive resources available, nor the uses to which these resources can be applied. Economic development occurs through the transformation of prevailing technological and market conditions so that higher-quality, lower-cost goods and services become available to enhance the standards of living of the society's population. The neoclassical economist considers as optimal those outcomes that reflect responses to *given* technological and market conditions. Yet it is precisely such optimal outcomes that must be changed for the wealth of nations to grow.

A theory of economic development indicates how transformations of technologies and markets occur and how these transformations affect the creation and distribution of income and wealth. The quest for such a theory raises a number of key questions for empirical analysis, with methodological implications for how this research is to be performed:

- What technological and market conditions stand in the way of economic development at any point in time? The very notion that conditions that constrained economic activity at a point in time can be transformed to generate economic development means that the study of the economy requires a *historical analysis of the process of change*.[2]

---

[1] I have elaborated on this argument in William Lazonick, *Business Organization and the Myth of the Market Economy* (New York, 1991).

[2] Such was the great analytical insight of Joseph A. Schumpeter. For a discussion of Schumpeter's ideas on historical analysis, see Lazonick, *Business Organization*, 122–30,

- Are such historical transformations the work of entrepreneurial individuals, innovative enterprises, nonprofit institutions, or developmental states? The answer to this question determines the social units of analysis that are the foci of our research and ultimately permits us to determine *how different social units interact in the process of economic development.*

I call the analytical approach that seeks to integrate theory and history in this way the "historical-transformation methodology" – an approach that stands in sharp contrast to the constrained-optimization methodology that conventional economists use to analyze the economy. In this essay, I offer a perspective on the interaction of different social units in the historical-transformation process. In particular, I focus on the role of *innovative enterprise*, as distinct from entrepreneurial individuals, nonprofit organizations, and developmental states, in this historical-transformation process. I argue that the innovative enterprise is a *social organization* that is central to the processes of change that results in economic development and that, as a social organization, its investment strategy, organizational structure, and productive capabilities reflect to some extent the institutional environment in which it operates.[3]

How then do we analyze innovative enterprise? Innovation entails the transformation of productive inputs into salable outputs to generate products and services that are higher in quality – more desirable to users – and lower in cost – more affordable to users – than the previously attainable quality/cost of those goods and services at prevailing factor prices. "Innovative enterprise" refers to the business organization, both within a firm as a distinct unit of strategic control and across an allied network of firms, that undertakes this transformation process. I shall argue that, whether within a firm or across a network of firms, innovation must be analyzed as a collective process requiring the *organizational integration* of the activities of large numbers of people who participate in a specialized division of labor.

and id., "The Integration of Theory and History: Methodology and Ideology in Schumpeter's Economics," in *Evolutionary and Neo-Schumpeterian Approaches to Economics*, ed. Lars Magnusson (Norwell, Mass., 1994), 245–63.

[3] This insight, which is by no means readily apparent to someone trained in modern economic theory and analysis, derives from the work of business historians, the current state of the art of which is summarized in the contributions to this volume. See also *Big Business and the Wealth of Nations*, ed. Alfred D. Chandler, Jr., Franco Amatori, and Takashi Hikino (New York, 1997).

The particular types of specialized activities that the innovative enterprise integrates into a collective process depend on the particular transformations of prevailing technological and market conditions that current competitive conditions require. The intellectual challenge is to develop a theory of the social processes that transform *industrial* (technological, market, and competitive) conditions to yield innovative outcomes. The prime purpose of this essay is to articulate a theoretical perspective on those processes.

In the following section, drawing on research carried out by Mary O'Sullivan and me over the past several years, I outline what I call "the social conditions of innovative enterprise," or the "SCIE," perspective.[4] Then I go on to consider how Edith Penrose's theory of the growth of the firm and Alfred Chandler's strategy-structure approach relate to the SCIE perspective. I conclude by briefly considering the relation of the SCIE perspective to two recent attempts by economists to bring economic theory and business history into closer relation to one another.

THE SCIE PERSPECTIVE

How does an innovative enterprise transform technological and market conditions to generate higher-quality, lower-cost products? To undertake the research that can begin to answer this fundamental question requires a theoretical perspective on the processes of historical transformation in which business organization is central. Given that business enterprises are social structures that are embedded in broader (typically national) institutional environments, the theory models the relations among *industrial conditions*, *organizational conditions*, and *institutional conditions* in the process of historical transformation. I thus provide a theoretical perspective on the social conditions of innovative enterprise. The fundamental assumptions, relations, and principles of the SCIE perspective are themselves derived from prior comparative-historical research.[5] Central to this perspective is the specification of

[4] See our elaboration of this perspective in William Lazonick and Mary O'Sullivan, "Perspectives on Corporate Governance, Innovation, and Economic Performance," report to the European Commission, Targeted Socio-Economic Research Programme, under contract number SOE1-CT98-1114 (http://www.insead.edu/cgep).

[5] William Lazonick and Mary O'Sullivan, "Organization, Finance and International Competition," *Industrial and Corporate Change* 5, no. 1 (1996): 1–49; id., "Finance and Industrial Development, Parts I and 2," *Financial History Review* 4, nos. 1 and 2 (1997): 7–39, 113–34; id., "Big Business and Skill Formation in the Wealthiest Nations: The Organizational

the key characteristics of the industrial, organizational, and institutional conditions that can promote or constrain the innovation process. The key characteristics are

- industrial conditions: *technological, market*, and *competitive*
- organizational conditions: *cognitive, behavioral*, and *strategic*
- institutional conditions: *employment, financial*, and *regulatory*

To understand how these different social conditions influence the innovation process, I also specify the key characteristics of that process. Drawing on the theoretical and empirical literature on innovation and relating it to resource allocation in the economy as a whole, Mary O'Sullivan has argued that the innovation process can be characterized as *cumulative, collective*, and *uncertain*.[6] The innovation process is cumulative because the possibilities for transforming technological and market conditions today and tomorrow depend on the development of those conditions in the past. Hence, an innovative enterprise engages in cumulative learning. The innovation process is collective because the transformation of technological and market conditions requires the integration of large numbers of people with specialized knowledge and skills so that they interact to develop and utilize productive resources. Hence, an innovative enterprise engages in collective learning. The innovation process is uncertain because the cumulative and collective processes that can transform technological and market conditions to generate higher-quality, lower-cost products are unknown at the time when resources are committed to these processes. Hence, an innovative enterprise must be strategic in how it engages in cumulative and collective learning.

Revolution in the Twentieth Century," in *Big Business and the Wealth of Nations*, ed. Chandler, Amatori, and Hikino, 497–521; William Lazonick, "Organizational Learning and International Competition," in *Globalization, Growth, and Governance*, eds. J. Michie and J. G. Smith (Oxford, 1998), 204–38. For the development of the analysis of strategic control as a critical condition of innovative enterprise and the role of financial, employment, and regulatory institutions in setting social conditions through which strategic control affects the allocation of corporate resources and returns, see Mary O'Sullivan, *Contests for Corporate Control: Corporate Governance and Economic Performance in the United States and Germany* (Oxford, 2000).

[6] See Mary O'Sullivan, "The Innovative Enterprise and Corporate Governance," *Cambridge Journal of Economics* 24, no. 4 (2000): 393–416, which analyzes the implications of the characterization of the innovation process as cumulative, collective, and uncertain for alternative theories of resource allocation and corporate governance as put forth by economists.

THE SYSTEM OF SOCIAL CONDITIONS

Industrial Conditions

"Technological conditions" refer to the productive capabilities, embodied in both human and physical capital, that characterize an industry or an enterprise within an industry at a point in time. "Market conditions" refer to the existing demand (in terms of quantity, quality, and price) for an industry's products and the existing supply of factors of production. "Competitive conditions" refer to the differential ability of enterprises in an industry or the same industries in different institutional environments to transform productive resources into revenue-generating products.

Innovation entails the transformation of existing technological and/or market conditions to generate higher-quality, lower-cost products. A successful enterprise transforms the competitive conditions facing other enterprises in the industry. These new competitive conditions may or may not induce an innovative response from rivals. Challenged by an innovative enterprise, the competitor's response may entail a strategy of either *adaptation* on the basis of the preexisting technological and market conditions or *innovation* by itself seeking to transform these conditions to generate higher-quality, lower-cost products.[7]

Organizational Conditions

"Cognitive conditions" refer to the cumulated knowledge and available skill base on which an enterprise can expect to develop and utilize its productive resources. "Behavioral conditions" refer to the set of incentives that can motivate participants in the enterprise to use their knowledge and skill to develop and utilize productive resources. "Strategic conditions" refer to the enterprise's structure of control over its financial, physical, and human resources. Embodying these organizational conditions within the enterprise is a division of labor based on different functional capabilities and hierarchical responsibilities, which is itself influenced by the combination of industrial and institutional conditions in which the enterprise has evolved.

The implementation of an innovative strategy to transform technological and market conditions entails strategic choices concerning (a) whose knowledge and skill within the organization will be developed

---

[7] See Lazonick, *Business Organization*, chap. 3.

and utilized and (b) what incentives will be offered to these participants to motivate them to cooperate in the pursuit of enterprise goals. Hence, the process of transforming industrial conditions generally entails the transformation of cognitive and behavioral conditions, with the types of organizational transformations that take place depending on the competitive strategy of the enterprise.

Institutional Conditions

Financial institutions determine the ways in which a society allocates financial resources to states, enterprises, and individuals for investment and consumption, as well as the ways in which that society distributes financial returns to the holders of various forms of financial claims. Employment institutions determine how a society develops the capabilities of its present and future labor forces (and hence include education, research, and training systems), as well as how it structures the availability of employment and the conditions of work and remuneration. Regulatory institutions determine how a society assigns rights and responsibilities to different groups of people over the management of society's productive resources and how it imposes restrictions on the development and utilization of these resources.

A fundamental hypothesis that derives from the SCIE perspective is that institutional, organizational, and industrial conditions interact historically to determine a unique set of rights, responsibilities, and restrictions that characterize a particular economy and society in a particular era. This perspective hypothesizes that the historical emergence of institutional conditions related to finance, employment, and regulation reflect the changing requirements of business enterprises (and especially corporate enterprises in a society in which they dominate business activity) for the development and utilization of productive resources. Over time these financial, employment, and regulatory practices become institutionalized in laws and norms, as well as the practices of related nonbusiness organizations that play important roles in undertaking financial, employment, and regulatory functions. Insofar as they derive from the requirements of business organizations, these institutions become "embedded" in the financial, employment, and regulatory practices of these business organizations themselves. The SCIE perspective argues that, at a point in time, these social conditions determine the types of industrial transformations, and hence the types of industrial innovations, that can occur in the economy. Over time, however, the transformation of certain dimensions of these institutional and organizational conditions – in effect transforma-tions of what may be called the "political economy" – can open up new possibilities for innovative activity.

SOCIAL CONDITIONS OF INNOVATIVE ENTERPRISE

We can identify three social conditions of innovative enterprise: financial commitment, organizational integration, and strategic control. Financial commitment involves allocating financial resources to sustain the pro-cess that develops and utilizes productive resources until the resultant products can generate financial returns. The need for financial commit-ment derives directly from the cumulative character of the innovation process. Hence, a theory of innovative enterprise must show how, given the financial requirements of industrial transformation, institutions and organizations combine to provide the requisite financial commitment. Organizational integration involves creating incentives for participants to apply their skills to engage in interactive learning in pursuit of com-mon goals. The need for organizational integration derives directly from the collective character of the innovation process. A theory of innova-tive enterprise must show how institutions and organizations combine to create the necessary incentives for those who must engage in interactive learning. Entailing as it does the combination of access to financial com-mitment and influence over organizational integration, strategic control enables people within an enterprise who possess certain "visions" of how technology and markets can be transformed to generate innovation to implement those visions as enterprise practice. The need for strategic control derives directly from the uncertain character of the innovation process.

The SCIE perspective posits a dynamic historical relation between organizations and institutions. One can in principle treat the business enterprise as an independent social entity in analyzing the social condi-tions of innovative enterprise. To treat the enterprise as an independent social entity, however, would run the risk of ignoring how the insti-tutional environment proscribes and enables the enterprise to acquire certain types of knowledge bases, to structure employment incentives for participants, and to consider strategic options. Thus, the SCIE per-spective seeks to understand the dynamic interaction between business enterprises and the institutional environments in which they operate, as well as the implications of this interaction for the transformation of technological and market conditions in different industrial activities.

HISTORICAL-TRANSFORMATION METHODOLOGY

The very nature of the innovation process means that the social conditions that constrain or promote innovation change over time and vary across different productive activities. The theoretical analysis must be integrated with the historical study of the development process through an "historical-transformation methodology."

The application of this methodology requires what Schumpeter called "historical experience."[8] This experience enables the analyst to make intelligent judgments concerning which conditions must be analyzed as endogenous to the process of change and which conditions can be treated as exogenous. In my own work, I have sought this experience not only through empirical studies of innovation and development[9] but also through a critical evaluation of the efforts by other economists to integrate theory and history.[10]

A consideration of the work of Alfred Marshall (1842–1924) provides useful insights into the problems and possibilities of the two methodologies.[11] The most influential economist of his era, Marshall spent all of his adult life as a student and a professor at Cambridge University. Influenced by the concern with economic development of such classical economists as Adam Smith and John Stuart Mill, Marshall's main empirical focus was the evolution of British industry. During the third quarter of the nineteenth century, Britain had emerged as the world's leading industrial economy. After the turn of the twentieth century, with the rise of large-scale enterprise abroad, Marshall extended his study to comparisons of industrial organization in the United States, Germany, and France – nations that were challenging Britain's economic leadership.[12]

On this empirical basis, Marshall elaborated a theory of economic development that had innovative enterprise at its core. At the same time, looking forward to what would become the dominant methodological approach in economics, Marshall sought to analyze how "substitution at the margin" would determine the optimal allocation of scarce resources. The crowning achievement of Marshall's career was to combine these two

---

[8] Joseph A. Schumpeter, *History of Economic Analysis* (Oxford, 1954), 12–13.
[9] See William Lazonick, *Organization and Technology in Capitalist Development* (Aldershot, U.K., 1992).
[10] See William Lazonick, *Competitive Advantage on the Shop Floor* (Cambridge, Mass., 1990), chaps. 1 and 2; id., *Business Organization*, chaps. 4–9.
[11] See Lazonick, *Business Organization*, chap. 5.
[12] See especially Alfred Marshall, *Principles of Economics*, 9th edition (London, 1961); id., *Industry and Trade* (London, 1919).

methodological approaches – historical transformation and constrained optimization – in one book, *Principles of Economics*, a treatise that, published in eight editions between 1890 and 1920, was *the* economics textbook for two generations.

Ironically, as it turned out, the work of Alfred Marshall was central to a critical transition in the economics discipline from the broad concern of the classical economists with its focus on economic development to the narrow focus of neoclassical economists on the optimal allocation of scarce resources among alternative existing uses. At the microeconomic core of this transition was a shift in Marshall's analysis from a theory of innovative enterprise to a theory of the optimizing firm.[13] The Marshallian analysis of the firm that optimizes subject to technological and market constraints, as further elaborated by Marshall's followers, remains embedded in the economics textbooks of today, while the constrained-optimization methodology is, in the words of one well-known industrial organization economist, "mother's milk to the well-trained economist."[14] As a result, the mainstream of the economics profession has focused almost exclusively on the theory of the optimizing firm – as if it were an ideal to be pursued rather than a condition to be transformed – to the neglect of a theory of innovative enterprise. The intellectual result has been that, for the "well-trained economist," acuity in the use of the constrained-optimization methodology has been accompanied by a trained incapacity to employ an historical-transformation methodology.

These two methodologies need not be mutually exclusive – so long as it is recognized that the constrained optimization methodology cannot be used to analyze the innovation process per se. That methodology can function as a transitional analytical device for rendering tractable the complexities of historical transformation. The shift from innovative enterprise to optimizing firm can serve the purpose of providing a rigorous and relevant analysis of the "constraints" on the development and utilization of productive resources that faced enterprises at a point in time. Then one could know what conditions facing the enterprise would have to be transformed over time for economic development to occur.[15]

[13] See Lazonick, *Business Organization*, chap. 5.
[14] Richard Caves, "Industrial Organization, Corporate Strategy and Structure," *Journal of Economic Literature* 18, no. 1 (1980): 88.
[15] For an example, see William Lazonick, "Factor Costs and the Diffusion of Ring Spinning in Britain prior to World War I," *Quarterly Journal of Economics* 96, no. 1 (1981): 89–109, and the subsequent debates with Lars Sandberg in the *Quarterly Journal of Economics* 99, no. 2 (1984): 387–92; and with Gary Saxonhouse and Gavin Wright in *Economic*

On the basis of such a methodology, the static optimizing analysis with which Marshall concluded his *Principles of Economics* could have facilitated the transition to a dynamic developmental analysis comprehending the role of innovative enterprise in the ongoing structural transformation of the economy. Rather than make this *transition* from optimizing firm to innovative enterprise, however, the followers of Marshall, and subsequent generations of economists, accepted the theory of the optimizing firm as a sufficient mode of analysis of the role of the business enterprise within the economy.

Using the historical-transformation methodology, what is the unit of anaysis for understanding innovative enterprise? In nineteenth-century Britain, as Marshall recognized, innovative enterprise occurred within industrial districts rather than within industrial corporations. The sources of development were mainly external to any particular firm but internal to a particular region. Yet from the late nineteenth century on, in various places around the world, the locus of innovative enterprise shifted from the industrial district to the industrial enterprise. The transformation of innovative proprietary enterprises into managerial corporations allowed nations such as Germany, the United States, and Japan to become global economic leaders in the twentieth century.

Quite incongruously, the historical transition from industrial districts to dominant corporations as the organizational units in the developmental economy was accompanied by a theoretical transition within economics from a developmental approach to an obsession with conditions of equilibrium in general and the optimizing firm in particular. Thus economists avoided an analysis of, among other things, the historical reality and theoretical implications of the managerial revolution. This is not to say that, armed with the historical-transformation methodology, economists or historians should assume that the dominant industrial corporation is the only relevant organizational unit of analysis. To capture the full range of possibilities for innovative enterprise in the twentieth century and beyond, a relevant theory of innovative enterprise must also be able to account for, as the proponents of "flexible specialization" have sought to do,[16] innovative industries, regions, and even nations in which

History Review, 2nd ser., 40, no. 1 (1987): 87–94. See also William Mass and William Lazonick, "The British Cotton Industry and International Competitive Advantage: The State of the Debates," *Business History* 32, no. 4 (1990): 9–65; and, more generally, Lazonick, *Organization and Technology*, part 1.

[16] For a recent elaboration of the flexible-specialization approach, see Charles F. Sabel and Jonathan Zeitlin, eds., *World of Possibilities: Flexibility and Mass Production in Western*

the dominant corporate enterprise remains the exception rather than the rule.

THE MODERN CORPORATION AS
INNOVATIVE ENTERPRISE

In Edith Tilton Penrose's book *The Theory of the Growth of the Firm*, first published in 1959, the author elaborated on a theory of the operation and performance of the modern corporation as an evolving developmental organization. Penrose's now classic book contains numerous testable hypotheses for empirical investigation. Unfortunately the economics profession has largely ignored the developmental dimensions of her work[17] – a neglect that is not surprising given the intellectual hegemony of the constrained-optimization approach.

Fortunately, coming from business history rather than economics, Alfred Chandler has synthesized the historical evidence on the evolution of the modern corporation in ways that provide unprecedented insights into the characteristics of innovative enterprise in the twentieth century. Chandler has circumscribed his theoretical contribution to our understanding of the modern corporation, however, by his use of *theoretical* constructs that emphasize the utilization of productive resources to the neglect of the development of productive resources. The theoretical concepts such as "first-mover advantage" and "economies of scale and scope" that Chandler employs derive from an empirical tradition in industrial organization that has neither confronted the limits of the constrained-optimization methodology nor developed an historical-transformation methodology.

Both Penrose and Chandler placed heavy emphasis on American-style "managerial organization" as it prevailed in the 1950s.[18] In their choice

Industrialization (Cambridge, 1997). For my review of this book, see *Business History Review* 73, no. 2 (1999): 309–14.

[17] But see the special issue of *Contributions to Political Economy* 18 (2000), edited by Christos Pitelis, devoted to a consideration of Penrose's book from a developmental perspective. See also William Lazonick, "The U.S. Industrial Corporation and *The Theory of the Growth of the Firm*," in *The Growth of the Firm: The Legacy of Edith Penrose*, ed. Christos Pitelis (Oxford, 2002), 249–78, as well as the papers from the European Institute of Business Administration (INSEAD) Penrosian Legacy Conference, May 11–12, 2001 (http://www.insead.fr/events/penrose).

[18] It is worth noting that Penrose researched and wrote *The Theory of the Growth of the Firm* in the 1950s while a researcher and lecturer in the Department of Political Economy of Johns Hopkins University, the same university where Chandler was a professor in the

of subject matter and in their approaches to the study of the modern corporate enterprise, both Penrose and Chandler have created important intellectual foundations for the analysis of innovative enterprise. In different ways, the work of each of these scholars demonstrates the need for a theory of innovative enterprise that can comprehend the historical transformation of not only *industrial* and *organizational* but also *institutional* conditions in the innovation process. The analysis of the role of innovative enterprise in the historical transformation of industrial, organizational, and institutional conditions that would otherwise constrain innovation must be central to a research agenda that seeks to integrate business history into a theory of economic development.[19]

Department of History from 1963 to 1971. Nevertheless, one had little intellectual influence on the other. In the introduction to *The Visible Hand*, Chandler includes Penrose in a list of economists who "have studied the operations and actions of modern business enterprise," and in the conclusion cites *Theory* "as showing how the inability for all units in [a large, integrated industrial enterprise] to be operating at the same speed and capacity [created] constant pressure for the growth of the firm." Alfred D. Chandler, Jr., *The Visible Hand: The Managerial Revolution in American Business* (Cambridge, Mass., 1977), 5, 489. See also Alfred D. Chandler, Jr., "Scale, Scope, and Organizational Capabilities," in *The Essential Alfred Chandler*, ed. T. McCraw (Boston, 1988), 498 n, and the reference to Penrose's case study of Hercules Powder Company in Alfred D. Chandler, Jr., *Scale and Scope: The Dynamics of Industrial Capitalism* (Cambridge, Mass., 1990), 758 n. 67. In the foreword to the third edition of *Theory* (p. ix), Penrose writes: "Chandler's book [*Strategy and Structure*] was finished before *The Theory of the Growth of the Firm* appeared, but the analytical structure within which its historical analysis was cast was remarkably congruent with my own work, using much the same concepts and very nearly the same terminology at many points." Penrose notes that she "did not have access [to Chandler's research] in writing my own work," but she credits "the superb historical discussion of the growth of major American firms by Chandler" as confirming her own analysis of "the process of diversification combined with the analysis of the costs of growth on the supply side" and of making possible "the most important extensions and modifications made by others over the past few decades." Edith Penrose, *The Theory of the Growth of the Firm* (Oxford, 1995), 3rd edition, xiii. See also Edith Penrose, "The Theory of the Growth of the Firm Twenty-Five Years After," *Acta Universitatis Upsaliensis: Studia Oeconomiae Negotiorum*, no. 20, Uppsala University, 1985. For an early recognition of the importance of the Penrosian theory to business history, see Louis Galambos, "Business History and the Theory of the Growth of the Firm," *Explorations in Entrepreneurial History*, 2nd ser., 4, no. 1 (1966): 3–14.

[19] For the analysis (omitted from this essay due to space limitations) of the historical transformation of organizational conditions in the innovative enterprise, and for a related critique of the constrained-optimization methodology of Williamsonian transaction-cost economics for understanding the evolution and role of business organization in the economy, see William Lazonick, "The Theory of Innovative Enterprise," in *The International Encyclopedia of Business and Management Handbook of Economics*, ed. William Lazonick (London, 2002), 638–59. See also William Lazonick, "Innovative Enterprise and Historical Transformation," *Enterprise & Society* 3, no. 1 (2002): 3–47.

THE THEORY OF THE GROWTH OF THE FIRM

As an economist, Penrose saw her role as the elaboration of a theoretical
framework on the basis of limited empirical data so that useful hypotheses could be posed for further study. She used eclectic sources, including
business histories, to gain her theoretical insights.[20] But she did not pre-
scribe a program for systematic research on the innovative enterprise,
and remained vague about the empirical underpinnings of her own theoretical arguments.[21]

The main methodological strength of Penrose's work is her explicit
recognition of the theoretical difference between the innovative enterprise and the optimizing firm. The basis for this distinction is her understanding that a firm is a unique social entity that can engage in learning
that is both collective and cumulative.[22] She also emphasized the dynamic relation between the development of productive resources and
their utilization, and hence between the achievement of high quality and
low cost. She understood, therefore, that innovative strategies can place
the enterprise at a competitive disadvantage if the productive resources
that the enterprise develops are not sufficiently utilized.

Compared with the neoclassical theory of the firm, the main theoretical strength of Penrose's work is that she placed organizational learning
at the center of the analysis. She equated the "firm" with its managerial
organization and organizational learning with *managerial* learning.[23]
Penrose's perspective on the enterprise as managerial organization

[20] In particular, she stated in a footnote that "Charles H. Wilson's *History of Unilever* (London,
1954) is a model of what good firm histories can be. I have leaned heavily on this type of
work (and there are some others), as well as on direct discussions with businessmen, for
insights into the processes of firm growth." Penrose, *Theory*, 3.

[21] In the mid-1950s Penrose carried out a study of Hercules Powder Company, an enterprise
that had been spun off from Du Pont Chemical Company in 1907 as a result of antitrust
litigation and that, at the time of her study, ranked 165th in *Fortune* magazine's list of the
500 largest U.S. industrial companies. See Edith T. Penrose, "The Growth of the Firm – A
Case Study: The Hercules Powder Company," *Business History Review* 34, no. 1 (1960):
1–23. The study was, in Penrose's words, "originally intended for inclusion in my *Theory
of the Growth of the Firm*, but was omitted in order to keep down the size of the book."
Ibid., 1. There is no mention of the study or reference to Hercules Powder Company in
any of the editions of *Theory*, including the third edition of the book, published in 1995
with a new foreword by the author.

[22] See O'Sullivan, *Contests*, chap. 1.

[23] As Penrose puts it in the foreword to the 1995 edition of her book: "I elected to deal
with what was called the 'managerial firm' – a firm run by a management assumed to
be committed to the long-run interest of the firm, the function of shareholders being
simply to ensure the supply of equity capital. Dividends need only be sufficient to induce
investment in the firm's shares." Penrose, *Theory*, xii.

represents an important advance on economic theories of the firm in which social organization plays no role.[24]

In comparative and historical perspective, however, the main weakness of the Penrosian "theory of the growth of the firm" for building a theory of innovative enterprise is its implicit assumption that organizational learning means managerial learning. Such a perspective has difficulty explaining, for example, why most Japanese and many European enterprises in the post-World War II decades extended organizational learning to shop-floor workers and independent suppliers, and how this development and utilization of broader and deeper skill bases affected international competitive advantage and national economic performance.[25] Even at the managerial level, Penrose's theory of the growth of the firm lacks a theory of the organizational – strategic, functional, and hierarchical – integration of administrative, technical, and professional personnel into the managerial structure of the modern corporation. As a result, her perspective is ill equipped to comprehend the erosion of cohesive managerial organization in major U.S. industrial corporations that occurred in the 1980s and 1990s. The characteristic feature of this managerial "downsizing" is that the services of once-valued "human assets" are thrown on the market rather than being mobilized for the further growth of the firm or even for the strategic creation of "spin-off" firms.[26]

Penrose assumes throughout her book that the modern industrial corporation will always try to utilize the unused productive resources at its disposal. She also understands, however, that to make use of these available productive resources to enter new markets means investing in new, complementary, productive resources, including reinvestment in the productive capabilities of current personnel. But as the experience of many U.S. corporations over the past few decades has shown, internal growth may reach a point where diseconomies of growth outweigh economies, either because of a separation of strategic decision making from organizational learning or because of the emergence of new competitors with superior organizational capabilities.[27] Penrose equates the profit motive

---

[24] For the argument that Penrose's theory of the growth of the firm is a theory of innovative enterprise as I have defined it, see Lazonick, "U.S. Industrial Corporation."

[25] See Lazonick and O'Sullivan, "Organization, Finance, and International Competition"; id., "Big Business and Skill Formation."

[26] For an elaboration of this assessment of Penrose's analysis in terms of the evolution of the U.S. industrial corporation since the time she wrote her book, see Lazonick, "U.S. Industrial Corporation."

[27] O'Sullivan, *Contests*, chap. 5.

and the growth motive in determining the investment strategy of the firm.[28] But this equation holds only if those who control the allocation of corporate resources cannot or will not seek higher returns for the firm – now defined as those who remain in the enterprise's employment, including themselves – by shedding unused productive resources – that is, those human assets whose services those who exercise strategic control deem to be no longer of value.

As Penrose recognized in the Foreword to the 1995 edition of her book, writing in the late 1950s one had yet to witness the advent in the United States of the conglomeration movement of the 1960s, the subsequent divestments of the 1970s, the rise of the market for corporate control under the slogan of "creating shareholder value" in the 1980s, and the consolidation of the practice of running companies to "maximize shareholder value" in the 1990s.[29] It may be that many of these practices have reflected a tendency for established U.S. industrial corporations to favor competitive strategies that are "optimizing," or more realistically "adaptive,"[30] as opposed to those that are innovative.[31] Rather than confront new industrial, organizational, and institutional conditions by engaging in strategies to transform them, those who control corporate resources may see it as in their interests to view these conditions as constraints, and consequently may be content to optimize subject to them.

What is optimal for those who control corporate resources, however, may not be optimal for other people associated with the corporation or for the economy as a whole – thus raising the question of the relation between corporate strategy and the development of the economy, a central issue that a theory of innovative enterprise must address. One way of conceptualizing Penrose's theory of the growth of the firm is to ask how, by transforming technology and markets, a small number of innovative enterprises might be able to differentiate themselves from other firms

[28] Penrose, *Theory*, 26–30.
[29] See William Lazonick and Mary O'Sullivan, "Maximising Shareholder Value: A New Ideology for Corporate Governance," *Economy and Society* 29, no. 1 (2000): 13–35.
[30] Lazonick, *Business Organization*, chap. 3.
[31] But for an analysis of "new economy" corporations, such as Intel, Microsoft, and Cisco Systems, that emerged in the last decades of the twentieth century as innovative enterprises and that, in the speculative stock market of the late 1990s, in effect destroyed shareholder value as they used high-priced stock as a currency to accumulate innovative capabilities, see Marie Carpenter, William Lazonick, and Mary O'Sullivan, "The Stock Market, Corporate Strategy, and Innovative Capability in the 'New Economy'," INSEAD Working Paper, 2002/66/SM, April 2002.

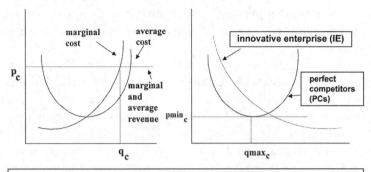

> • The innovative enterprise transforms the technological and market conditions it faces to generate higher-quality, lower-cost products.
> • There is no "optimal" output. There is no "optimal" price.

Figure 1   Transforming the conventional theory of the firm. Technological and market conditions are given by cost and revenue functions. The good manager optimizes subject to technological and market constraints. p = price; q = output; m = monopolist; c = perfect competitor; $p$min = minimum breakeven price; $q$max = maximum breakeven output.

in an industry to gain sustained competitive advantage (Figure 1).[32] It is with the economic performance of such an innovative enterprise that the optimizing firm of neoclassical theory should be compared. To do so, the theory of innovative enterprise must have an analysis of the determinants of total fixed costs, as well as the relation between average fixed costs and average variable costs during the innovation process. The task for a theory of innovative enterprise is to explain how, by changing its cost structure, a particular enterprise can emerge as dominant in its industry.

Unlike the optimizing firm, the innovative enterprise does not take as given the fixed costs of participating in an industry. Rather, given prevailing factor prices, the level of fixed costs that it incurs reflects its innovative strategy. This "fixed-cost" strategy is not dictated by indivisible technology or the entrepreneur as a fixed factor, but rather by the innovative enterprise's assessment of the quality and quantity of productive resources in which it must invest to *develop* products that are higher in quality and lower in cost than those that it had previously been capable of producing and that (in its estimation) its competitors will be able to produce, given *their* investment strategies. It is this development of productive resources within the enterprise that creates the potential

---

[32] The following arguments are developed in much more detail, including critiques of the neoclassical "monopoly model" and Williamsonian transaction-cost theory, in Lazonick, "Theory of Innovative Enterprise."

for an enterprise that pursues an innovative strategy to gain a sustained competitive advantage over its competitors and emerge as dominant in its industry.

Such development, when successful, becomes embodied in products, processes, and people with productive capabilities superior to those that had previously existed. But even the generation of superior productive capabilities will not result in sustained competitive advantage when innovative competitors have generated even superior productive capabilities and/or when the high fixed costs of the innovative strategy place the innovative enterprise at a cost disadvantage relative to less innovative, or even optimizing, competitors. An innovative strategy that enables the enterprise to generate superior productive capabilities may place that enterprise at a cost disadvantage because innovative strategies tend to entail higher fixed costs than those incurred by rivals that optimize subject to given constraints.

For a given level of factor prices, these higher fixed costs derive from the *size* and *duration* of the innovative investment strategy. Innovative strategies tend to entail higher fixed costs than those incurred by the optimizing firm because the innovation process tends to require the *simultaneous development* of productive resources across a broader and deeper range of integrated activities than those undertaken by the optimizing firm. Hence, at a point in time, the innovative enterprise must generally make a broader range of investments in fixed plant and equipment and a deeper range of investments in administrative organization than would have to be undertaken by the optimizing firm. But in addition to, and generally independent of, the size of the innovative investment strategy at a point in time, high fixed costs will be incurred because of the amount of time required to develop productive resources until they result in products that are sufficiently high in quality and low in cost to generate returns. If the size of investments in physical capital tends to increase the fixed costs of an innovative strategy, so too does the duration of the investment in an organization of people who can engage in the collective and cumulative – or organizational – learning that is the central characteristic of the innovation process.

The high fixed costs of an innovative strategy create the need for the enterprise to attain a high level of *utilization* of the productive resources that it has developed. As in the neoclassical theory of the optimizing firm, given the productive capabilities that it has developed, the innovative enterprise may experience increasing costs because of the problem of maintaining the productivity of variable inputs as it employs larger quantities of these inputs in the production process. But rather than, as in the case

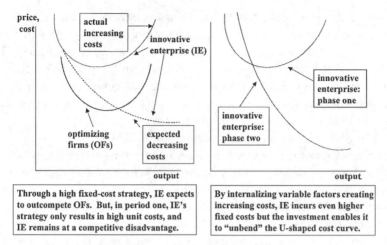

Through a high fixed-cost strategy, IE expects to outcompete OFs. But, in period one, IE's strategy only results in high unit costs, and IE remains at a competitive disadvantage.	By internalizing variable factors creating increasing costs, IE incurs even higher fixed costs but the investment enables it to "unbend" the U-shaped cost curve.

Figure 2 Industrial transformation: technology, markets, and innovative enterprise.

of the optimizing firm, taking increasing costs as a given constraint, the innovative enterprise will attempt to transform its access to high-quality productive resources at high levels of output. To do so, it will invest in the *development* of that productive resource, the *utilization* of which as a variable input has become a source of increasing costs.

The development of the productive resource adds to the fixed costs of the innovative strategy, whereas previously this productive resource was utilized as a variable factor that could be purchased at the going factor price incrementally on the market as extra units of the input were needed to expand output. Having added to its fixed costs in order to overcome the constraint on enterprise expansion posed by increasing variable costs, the innovative enterprise is then under even more pressure to expand its share of the market in order to transform high fixed costs into low unit costs. As, through the development and utilization of productive resources, the enterprise succeeds in this transformation, it in effect "unbends" the U-shaped cost curve that the optimizing firm takes as given (Figure 2[33]). By shaping the cost curve in this way, the innovative enterprise creates the possibilities for gaining a competitive advantage over its rivals.

Hence the innovative enterprise is not constrained by market demand to produce at the profit-maximizing output level where marginal cost equals marginal revenue because, over the long run, it is not subject to increasing costs. The innovative enterprise may be subject to increasing

---

[33] For a fuller theoretical elaboration of this process of sustained innovative transformation, see Lazonick, *Business Organization*, chap. 3.

costs in the short run, but by continually confronting and transforming those technological and market conditions that result in increasing costs, the innovative enterprise can generate high-quality products, the unit costs of which decline as it gains larger and larger market shares. The innovative enterprise thus not only has differentiated itself from its competitors but also has gained a sustained competitive advantage that is reinforced as it expands its level of output.

The ability of the innovative enterprise to achieve decreasing costs even as it produces larger volumes of output relative to the size of the industry's market means that the neoclassical optimizing rule that marginal cost equals marginal revenue is irrelevant to its output and pricing decisions. Constraining its level of output at a point in time is typically the presence in the industry of a small number of other innovative enterprises that compete among themselves for market share. Given the cost structure that it has put in place, the innovative enterprise can seek to increase its market share by offering buyers lower prices. But constraining such price reductions at a point in time is the need of the innovative enterprise to generate sufficient surplus revenues to reward its employees at levels above and beyond those that their labor services would fetch on the open labor market while investing in new technology, including the skills of workers, and building an organization to develop and utilize the new technology. Such investments can enable the enterprise to maintain or extend its competitive advantage in a given market or transfer some of its productive capabilities to produce output for another market that can make use of these capabilities. Insofar as the enterprise undertakes an innovative strategy in this diversification process, it will have to complement its existing capabilities with investment in, and development of, new capabilities, thus adding to the fixed costs that it must utilize to achieve low unit costs.

EXPLOITATION OF THE ECONOMIES OF SCALE AND SCOPE

As an historian, Chandler saw his role as the synthesis of the details of "a multitude of case-studies [to yield] generalizations and concepts that are not tied to a specific time and place."[34] In his three major books and many related publications written over a period of four decades, Chandler

---

[34] Alfred D. Chandler, Jr., "Comparative Business History," in *Enterprise and History*, eds. D. C. Coleman and Peter Mathias (Cambridge, 1984), 3.

integrated a massive amount of historical knowledge on the evolution of the industrial corporation, especially in the United States but also in Britain and Germany, into his "strategy and structure" framework. But he left it to, as he put it, "[the] economist, sociologist, or management scientist [to] deduce hypotheses or theorems *a priori* from an existing body of theory which is then tested with empirical data."[35]

From the perspective of the history of innovative enterprise, *The Visible Hand* is Chandler's most successful work. He brings a broad and deep familiarity with the social context of American economic development to his relentless focus on the evolution of management structure in the largest U.S. enterprises in the late nineteenth and early twentieth centuries.[36] Chandler's work has demonstrated the centrality of the "managerial revolution" to the evolution of American industrial enterprise in the twentieth century. The main weakness of his historical analysis, even for the U.S. case, is his reluctance to consider the modern business enterprise itself as a social organization. For example, in *The Visible Hand*, he states: "Modern business enterprise is easily defined.... [I]t has two specific characteristics: it contains many distinct operating units and it is managed by a hierarchy of salaried managers."[37] The only issue that Chandler raises about the social organization of the enterprise is the professionalization of management – a subject that he does not, however, analyze.[38]

On the theoretical plane, in *The Visible Hand*, Chandler emphasizes "economies of speed" in the utilization of productive resources, but he does not extend his analysis to the shop floor. In my own work, Chandler's focus on economies of speed permitted me to link my research on the development and utilization of productive resources on the shop floor with

[35] Ibid., 26.
[36] Chandler's attempt at comparative analysis in *Scale and Scope* is greatly weakened by his lack of a similar familiarity with the social conditions surrounding the evolution of British and German industrial enterprises. See William Lazonick, "The Enterprise, the Community, and the Nation: Social Organization as a Source of Global Competitive Advantage" (paper presented to the Harvard Business School Business History Seminar, December 1991); Barry Supple, "Scale and Scope: Alfred Chandler and the Dynamics of Industrial Capitalism," *Economic History Review* 44, no. 3 (1991): 500-14; and the contributions to "Scale and Scope: A Review Colloquium," *Business History Review* 64, no. 3 (1990): 690-735.
[37] Chandler, *Visible Hand*, 1.
[38] Ibid., 8-9. As Chandler states: "I have not tried to describe the work done by the labor force in these units or the organization and aspirations of the workers. Nor do I attempt to assess the impact of modern business enterprise on existing political and social arrangements." Ibid., 6.

his research on managerial organization.[39] Yet, given that in the twentieth century most U.S. industrial corporations pursued strategies of utilizing rather than developing human resources on the shop floor, it is therefore ironic that my greatest problem with Chandler's more recent attempts to place his research in a theoretical perspective revolves around his neglect of the *development* of productive resources as a source of competitive advantage. In *Scale and Scope*, published in 1990, the central analytical concept, "economies of scale and scope" (replacing his previous, more dynamic, notion of economies of speed), reflects Chandler's overemphasis on the *utilization* of productive resources as the distinctive contribution of the modern corporation to economic development.

Chandler's theoretical perspective contains no theory of innovative strategy, another irony in view of the centrality of the "strategy-structure" framework to his earlier historical research. Rather, in his view, the "capital intensity" of industries constrains enterprise strategy, as if, even within a particular industry, capital intensity were not to some extent a result of the investment strategies and organizational structures of particular enterprises. But how did these new technologies that created the potential for economies of scale and scope get developed? Once one recognizes that it is the innovative strategy of the enterprise that creates the extent of its high fixed costs, economies of scale and scope must be seen not only as a *potential* source of competitive advantage but also as a *necessity* for an innovative enterprise to attain a competitive advantage. If the enterprise does not spread the high fixed costs of developing new technology over large quantities of sold output, then the enterprise that pursues an innovative strategy will be at a competitive disadvantage, not a competitive advantage.[40] Moreover, as Penrose recognized, in diversifying its products, the innovative enterprise must invest in the development of new productive resources, so that the quest for economies of scope constantly creates a new necessity to achieve economies of scale.

Economies of scale and scope are therefore *outcomes* of the innovation process that need to be explained. To be sure, in all of his work, Chandler presents historical material that provides considerable information relevant to the development, as distinct from the utilization, of productive resources in the modern industrial corporation. The problems arise in his attempt to transform the historical research into a theoretical explanation. The shortcomings of Chandler's theorizing on the basis

---

[39] Lazonick, *Competitive Advantage*.

[40] See the previous discussion of the innovative enterprise and the theoretical analysis in Lazonick, *Business Organization*, chap. 3 and id., "Theory of Innovative Enterprise."

of his historical work are evident in his article "Organizational Capabilities and the Economic History of the Industrial Enterprise," published in *Journal of Economic Perspectives* in 1992 and directed at the economics profession.[41]

As Chandler recognizes in this article, it is the organization of the enterprise that permits it to achieve economies of scale and scope. But what does enterprise organization do? Chandler makes use of the concepts of "organizational capabilities" and "organizational learning." But what do such capabilities and learning accomplish? The internal organization of the U.S. industrial enterprise during much of the twentieth century led Chandler, like Penrose, to stress the role of the managerial organization in the learning process. For Chandler, however, managerial learning is related to the *utilization*, not the *development*, of productive resources:

> For most [industrial enterprises], the long-term continuing strategy of growth was expansion into new geographical or product markets. The move into geographically distant areas was normally based on the competitive advantages provided by organizational capabilities learned through exploiting economies of scale. Moves into related product markets rested more on capabilities developed from exploiting of the economies of scope.[42]

Chandler goes on to give a detailed summary of the sources of organizational learning that implicitly involve the development of new technologies, and he recognizes that "such learned skills and knowledge were company-specific and industry-specific."[43] Nevertheless, he constantly emphasizes that it is the utilization of resources – the achievement of economies of scale and scope, given the investments that the enterprise has made – that creates both the need for organizational learning and the context for the acquisition of skills that permit the realization of economies of scale and scope.

On the surface, Chandler closes this gap in his theoretical analysis by endowing the otherwise analytically empty concept of "first-mover advantage" (borrowed from conventional industrial organization economics) with the substance of investment in productive resources, both physical and human. As Chandler argues:

> The first firms to make the three-pronged investments in manufacturing, marketing, and management essential to exploit fully the economies of scale

---

[41] Alfred D. Chandler, Jr., "Organizational Capabilities and the Economic History of the Industrial Enterprise," *Journal of Economic Perspectives* 6, no. 3 (1992): 79–100.
[42] Ibid., 83.
[43] Ibid., 83–4.

and scope quickly dominated their industries. Most continued to do so for
decades.[44]

But the notion of a "three-pronged investment" raises more theoretical
questions than it answers. What were the capabilities that were developed by these three-pronged investments? Again, Chandler's formulation
of the source of first-mover advantage creates the strong impression
that what mattered was only skills and knowledge for the utilization of
productive resources, not for the development of productive resources.
How were these capabilities integrated strategically, functionally, and
hierarchically so that those people involved in the innovative enterprise
had the incentives to cooperate in the development and utilization of
productive resources?

Chandler is aware of the need to answer such questions. Indeed, at
the conclusion of his *Journal of Economic Perspectives* article, he poses
a number of "significant questions for study" that derive from an "evolutionary theory" of the firm:

How precisely were the learning processes carried out? How and why did
industry-specific and particularly company-specific characteristics vary? Why
were some capabilities more easily transferred to different geographic and
new product markets than others? What were the contents of the routines developed to evaluate and capture new markets and move out of old ones? Why
has functional and strategic competition in modern capitalistic economies
played a larger role in changing market share and profit than price? What are
the determinants of competitive success in national industries and national
economies?[45]

THEORY AND HISTORY

In a perceptive essay written in the mid-1980s,[46] Edith Penrose articulated the need for a methodology that integrated theory and history:

It is impossible for economic historians to select and make sense of the "facts"
of history without the aid of the theories developed by students of economic
affairs defined in the broader sense. Some of the "theory" may be little more
than dressed-up common-sense deductions from common observations and

---

[44] Ibid., 81.
[45] Ibid., 99.
[46] Edith Penrose, "History, the Social Sciences and Economic 'Theory', with Special Reference
to Multinational Enterprise," in *Historical Studies in International Corporate Business*,
eds. Alice Teichova, Maurice Lévy-Leboyer, and Helga Nussbaum (Cambridge, 1989), 7–13.

therefore not even recognized as such, but much of it has a deeper significance. Without theoretical analysis of cause and consequence one has no standard against which to appraise the significance of any given set of observations, for this significance is a question of what difference the observations make to what might otherwise have been the historical interpretation.

Yet attempts to employ, and develop, such an integrative methodology are very rare among economists or historians. I shall conclude this essay by mentioning two recent efforts – one by Richard Langlois and Paul Robertson and the other by Naomi Lamoreaux, Daniel Raff, and Peter Temin – to illustrate the distinctive hypotheses for further research that derive from the theory of innovative enterprise that I have put forth.

The effort to integrate economic theory and business history that comes closest to the perspective that I have put forward is that of Richard Langlois and Paul Robertson.[47] Focusing on the question of why two or more distinct vertically related activities that could be performed by two or more distinct firms might be integrated into one firm, Langlois and Robertson invoke a process that they call "systemic innovation." They argue that "dynamic transaction costs" solves a coordination problem in the presence of the need for a systemic change. Systemic innovation requires the simultaneous change in a number of stages of production at once, and the individual actors who need to be involved in this change would not be able or willing to make the change without coordination. As Langlois and Robertson state:

The firm overcomes the "dynamic" transaction costs of economic change. It is in this sense that we may say the firm solves a coordination problem: it enables complementary input-holders to agree on the basic nature of the system of production and distribution of the product. It provides the structure in a system of structured uncertainty.[48]

More specifically, dynamic transaction costs are, according to Langlois and Robertson, "the costs of persuading, negotiating, coordinating, and teaching outside suppliers."[49]

On the surface, it may appear that Langlois and Robertson's "dynamic transaction cost" theory is very similar to the theory of innovative enterprise that I have set out. In fact, they do not provide a theory of the

---

[47] Richard N. Langlois and Paul Robertson, eds., *Firms, Markets, and Economic Change: A Dynamic Theory of Business Institutions* (London, 1995).
[48] Ibid., 4.
[49] Ibid., 35.

relation between organizational strategy and organizational learning. As a result, Langlois and Robertson put forth a dubious explanation of organizational integration – in this case, specifically vertical integration – as a relation among previously independent firms that exogenous technology imposes on participants in a specialized division of labor.

The first problem is that Langlois and Robertson provide no theoretical perspective on how, when, and why systemic innovation appears. For them, the appearance of a systemic innovation in a particular industry simply imposes an "innovative strategy" on firms that these firms are compelled to adopt if they want to remain competitive participants in that industry. The second problem is that, given the purported necessity for firms to adopt the systemic innovation, there is no learning in the Langlois–Robertson theory that goes beyond a core firm "teaching" its outside suppliers that they can no longer remain independent firms but must join the vertically integrated firm. The assumption is that, given a choice, firms will want to remain independent of one another. As Langlois and Foss have recently written, "Langlois and Robertson (1995) build a broad theory of industrial dynamics around [the] idea" that

much vertical integration occurs not when firms venture into new areas of similar capabilities but when firms are dragged, kicking and screaming, as it were, into complementary but dissimilar activities because only in that way can they bring about a profitable reconfiguration of production or distribution.[50]

The appearance of a systemic innovation leads a firm that plays the role of systems integrator to convince independent suppliers that they must give up their independence. The implicit assumption is that when such a change in vertical relations occurs, the presumed benefits of systemic innovation will be to some extent offset by the dynamic transaction costs of overcoming the resistance of highly individualistic firms.

The desire to remain independent is a *possible* behavioral characteristic of the firm. But it is a characteristic that has to demonstrated rather than assumed. Moreover, there are large literatures on supplier relations and strategic alliances that demonstrate that innovation can occur through cooperation across legally independent firms as well as within a firm as a distinct legal entity.[51] Indeed, for a theory of innovative

[50] Richard Langlois and Nicolai Foss, "Capabilities and Organization: The Rebirth of Production in the Theory of Economic Organization," *Kyklos* 52 (1999): 201–18.

[51] See, for example, Mari Sako, "Supplier Development at Honda, Nissan, and Toyota: A Historical Case Study of Organizational Capability Enhancement," working paper, Saïd

enterprise, the biggest problem with the Langlois–Robertson perspective is that they treat the firm as if it were a unitary actor – that is, an individual – and hence do not put forth any framework or agenda for exploring the organization of individuals who occupy positions within the specialized divisions of labor within firms. The lack of such a perspective is problematic for an organization made up of only two people (think of a married couple), never mind a business enterprise with tens of thousands of employees. The willingness to see the firm as an individual reflects an individualistic bias in the analysis of "industrial dynamics" that avoids such critical issues as (a) the structure of strategic control within an enterprise and the process of strategic decision making, (b) the transformation of individual learning into organizational learning in the innovation process, and (c) the transformation of organizational learning into higher-quality, lower-cost products, thus transforming the high fixed costs of an innovative strategy into the basis for competitive advantage (see Figures 1 and 2).[52] Indeed, I would argue that an understanding of how an innovative enterprise develops and utilizes productive resources across firms as distinct units of strategic control will depend on the evolution of these capabilities within a dominant firm or firms within this network of relations.

Another important effort to link business history and economic theory is that of Naomi Lamoreaux, Daniel Raff, and Peter Temin (hereafter LRT). During the 1990s, under the auspices of the National Bureau of Economic Research, they organized a series of three conferences, all of which subsequently appeared as edited books,[53] the purpose of which was to encourage economists to build more informed theoretical models of business behavior through familiarity with the stories that business historians had to tell. LRT succeed in articulating some important lessons

Business School, University of Oxford, 1998; Yves Doz, "The Evolution of Cooperation in Strategic Alliances: Initial Conditions or Learning Processes," *Strategic Management Journal* 17 (1996): 55–83.

[52] See Lazonick and O'Sullivan, "Perspectives on Corporate Governance."

[53] Peter Temin, ed., *Inside the Business Enterprise* (Chicago, 1991); Naomi R. Lamoreaux and Daniel M. G. Raff, eds., *Coordination and Information* (Chicago, 1995); Naomi R. Lamoreaux, Daniel M. G. Raff, and Peter Temin, eds., *Learning by Doing in Markets, Firms, and Countries* (Chicago, 1999). For a summary of the lessons derived from this project, see Naomi R. Lamoreaux, Daniel M. G. Raff, and Peter Temin, "New Economic Approaches to the Study of Business History," *Business and Economic History* 26, no. 1 (1997): 57–79, which contains references to all of the papers that would subsequently appear in the third volume, published in 1999. An abridged version of this article that omits the discussion of the findings of the first two volumes in the series appears as the introduction to *Learning by Doing*.

of business history for the analysis of innovative enterprise. They do so, however, *despite* their uncritical advocacy of a theoretical model rooted in neoclassical ideology and methodology – a model that is as much if not more contradicted than supported by the lessons that they themselves draw from the work in business history that they adduce.

In terms of economic theory, LRT argue that economists have constructed new models of economic activity that are relevant to what goes on inside business enterprises. Of particular importance to business historians are "principal–agent" models that seek to understand the problems that decision makers ("principals") face in securing productive performance from subordinates ("agents") within the modern business enterprise. The key concept in the new theory is the condition of "asymmetric information" – a situation in which agents possess information that is relevant to productive performance but that is lacking to principals when they make economic decisions. Given that principals must rely on agents to inform and implement their decisions, asymmetric information can give rise to both cognitive problems of "adverse selection" (or "hidden information"), because principals are hampered by bounded rationality in choosing agents on whom to rely, and behavioral problems of "moral hazard" (or "hidden action") because agents, once chosen, can use the condition of asymmetric information to act opportunistically in the ways in which they perform services for the principal.[54]

For LRT, the introduction of the concepts of agency and asymmetry into economic models means that "business historians can turn to economic theory both for useful ideas and for the light a coherent perspective sheds on an otherwise untidy past.... The real benefit of recent theoretical developments in economics is that they enable business historians to recognize the essential unity that underlies a great number of the problems with which they are concerned."[55]

Indeed, LRT make the broad claim that the body of work of business historians that they have brought together in the three NBER volumes shows the role of "imperfect information" in the problems that firms face in their internal operations and in dealing with their external environments. Note that "asymmetric information" and "imperfect information," although often used interchangeably by LRT, should not be viewed as

---

[54] For a critical evaluation of the Williamsonian transaction-cost model, which, focusing on bounded rationality and opportunism as determinants of organizational form, represents a specific application of agency theory, see Lazonick, "Theory of Innovative Enterprise."

[55] Lamoreaux et al., "New Economic Approaches," 77.

synonymous. Asymmetric information simply means that different parties to a relation have access to different information, and does not in itself
imply superior or inferior economic performance. In contrast, imperfect
information implies a comparison with the theoretical benchmark of the
"perfect information ideal"; that is, the imperfect information inherent
in asymmetric information is being compared with the economic performance that could be achieved under conditions of perfect information.
Even if LRT and the new economic theorists whose insights they profess
to propound do not believe the perfect information story for analyzing
how the economy *actually* operates, they are still implicitly (and, for the
theorists, in many economic models explicitly) evaluating economic performance in terms of perfect information – an ideal that in conventional
economic theory is associated with the existence of "perfect markets."
That is, by asserting that asymmetric information is imperfect information, they in effect proclaim their ideological attachment to what I have
elsewhere called the "myth of the market economy" – a perspective
on resource allocation that systematically ignores the role of innovative
business organization as a determinant of the wealth of nations.[56]

Yet, notwithstanding their obeisance to conventional economic theory, if anything, the research of business historians that LRT have featured
in their volumes contributes to, and emphasizes the need for, a theoretical perspective on the social conditions of innovative enterprise and a
methodological approach to historical transformation. Indeed, in many
of their own summaries of the historical contributions, LRT themselves
inadvertently offer an interpretation of the findings that is more supportive of innovation theory than agency theory.

Innovation theory recognizes that different economic actors have differential access to information; the existence and evolution of a specialized division of labor within the enterprise are inherent in the industrial,
organizational, and institutional complexity of the innovation process. Innovation theory also recognizes the potential validity of the basic insights
of agency theory: that individuals can and do use their privileged access
to information opportunistically as a means of promoting their own interests or that a lack of complete information on the part of those making allocative decisions complicates the decision-making process. Lacking a historical-transformation methodology, however, agency theory

---

[56] Lazonick, *Business Organization*, and, for a recent restatement of this position, id., "The
Theory of the Market Economy and the Social Foundations of Innovative Enterprise,"
Economic and Industrial Democracy (forthcoming).

cannot comprehend the problems and possibilities of the innovation process; that is, agency theory has no way of incorporating the basic insights of innovation theory into its analysis. In focusing on the problematic relations between principals and agents as individual economic actors, agency theory does not ask how principals might transform the conditions that give rise to adverse selection and moral hazard.

Innovation theory, therefore, can comprehend the constrained-optimization problems of agency theory but asks how, cognitively and behaviorally, the enterprise as a collectivity overcomes these problems through a transformation of the enterprise's knowledge base. Innovation theory also recognizes that in the transformation of the enterprise's knowledge base, the new distribution of expertise among participants in the enterprise's division of labor may create new possibilities for opportunistic behavior on the part of agents or new problems of bounded rationality on the part of principals. But in contrast to the approach of agency theory, the ongoing problematic for the innovative enterprise is not to optimize subject to these conditions of information asymmetry but rather to transform the differential access to information – that is, the specialized division of labor – into a cumulative and collective learning process.

In the theory of innovative enterprise, the structure of *strategic control* within the enterprise is key to understanding the combination of financial commitment and organizational integration that enables such organizational learning to occur. The theory of innovative enterprise focuses on *how the structure of strategic control mobilizes the collective power of the skills and efforts of participants in the enterprise's specialized division of labor to transform technological and market conditions.* If one accepts that, as a field of study, business history has as its central concern such historical transformations – and, in particular, finding out why the innovation process succeeds in some times, places, and activities but not in others – then business history needs a theory of innovative enterprise and a historical-transformation methodology. Armed with such analytical tools, the business historian can then, among other things, question economists' a priori assumptions concerning who are the principals and who are the agents, or indeed, whether a division of labor between participants in the enterprise into principals and agents is useful for analyzing the issues at hand.

The intellectual problem is not one of scarce information. Over the past few decades, our useful knowledge of business history has grown by leaps and bounds – as is indeed demonstrated by much of the historical work in LRT's edited volumes. An understanding of the process of economic development, and the role of the business enterprise in it will require an intellectual revolution in economics – a transformation, so to speak, of the market to which economists sell their findings and the technologies that they use to obtain results. My hope is that the development of the SCIE perspective and the historical-transformation methodology that is needed to implement it can contribute to the achievement of these ends.

KEY WORKS

Chandler, Alfred D, Jr. "Organizational Capabilities and the Economic History of the Industrial Enterprise." *Journal of Economic Perspectives* 6, no. 3 (1992): 79-100.

Scale and Scope: The Dynamics of Industrial Capitalism. Cambridge, Mass., 1990.

The Visible Hand: The Managerial Revolution in American Business. Cambridge, Mass., 1977.

Lamoreaux, Naomi R., Daniel M. G. Raff, and Peter Temin. "New Economic Approaches to the Study of Business History." *Business and Economic History* 26, no. 1 (1997): 57-79.

Langlois, Richard N. and Paul Robertson, eds. *Firms, Markets, and Economic Change: A Dynamic Theory of Business Institutions.* London, 1995.

Lazonick, William. *Business Organization and the Myth of the Market Economy.* New York, 1991.

"The Theory of Innovative Enterprise." In *The International Encyclopedia of Business and Management Handbook of Economics*, edited by William Lazonick, 638-59. London, 2002.

Lazonick, William and Mary O'Sullivan. "Big Business and Skill Formation in the Wealthiest Nations: The Organizational Revolution in the Twentieth Century." In *Big Business and the Wealth of Nations*, edited by Alfred D. Chandler, Jr., Franco Amatori, and Takashi Hikino, 497-521. New York, 1997.

"Finance and Industrial Development, Parts 1 and 2." *Financial History Review* 4, nos. 1 and 2 (1997): 7-39, 113-34.

Marshall, Alfred. *Principles of Economics*, 9th edition. London, 1961.

O'Sullivan, Mary. *Contests for Corporate Control: Corporate Governance and Economic Performance in the United States and Germany.* Oxford, 2000.

Penrose, Edith. "The Growth of the Firm – A Case Study: The Hercules Powder Company." *Business History Review* 34, no. 1 (1960): 1-23.

"History, the Social Sciences and Economic 'Theory', with Special Reference to Multinational Enterprise." In *Historical Studies in International Corporate Business*, edited by Alice Teichova, Maurice Lévy-Leboyer, and Helga Nussbaum, 7-13. Cambridge, 1989.

The Theory of the Growth of the Firm, 3d edition. Oxford, 1995.

4

Productive Alternatives

Flexibility, Governance, and Strategic Choice in Industrial History

JONATHAN ZEITLIN

The aim of this essay is to present a brief conceptual overview of what has become known as the "historical alternatives" approach to industrial history. The notion of alternatives is central to this approach in both a historical and a historiographical sense. Historically, the hallmark of this approach has been its emphasis on the salience of alternative possibilities, contingency, and strategic choice in the development of modern industry over the past three centuries. Historiographically, this approach represents an alternative to mainstream currents in economic, technological, and business history: an alternative, in particular, to Chandlerian business history, which is focused on the economic and technological efficiency of administrative coordination and learning within large, hierarchically managed enterprises. From its origins in joint work by Charles Sabel and myself in the early 1980s, a substantial body of empirical work on European, American, and Japanese industrial history has since appeared that draws on and extends the historical alternatives approach.

At a more substantive level, the historical alternatives approach allows for the identification of flexibly specialized forms of production in the industrial past. This theoretical possibility, however, should not be confused with empirical claims about the role and importance in particular times and places of flexible specialization as an ideal-typical model of productive efficiency, based on the manufacture of a wide and changing array of customized products in short runs by skilled, adaptable workers using versatile general-purpose machinery. The historical alternatives approach can thus be used to analyze cases in which mass production – understood as the manufacture of standardized goods in high volumes by mainly unskilled labor using special-purpose equipment – predominated over more flexible forms. Recent research based on this approach has nevertheless greatly extended the historical scope of flexibly specialized production. It has also identified significant elements of flexibility even within apparently classic cases of mass production.[1]

In the interests of concision, the remainder of this essay sets out the core elements of the historical alternatives approach in the form of ten positive theses before going on to respond to five major misconceived objections that have recurrently arisen in the course of the ensuing debate.

THE HISTORICAL ALTERNATIVES APPROACH: TEN THESES

Against Teleology and Determinism

The point of departure for the historical alternatives approach is the rejection of "narrow track" models of industrialization and economic development in all their forms. In contrast to both classical economists and modern historians alike, proponents of the historical alternatives approach thus deny the existence of a unilinear logic of material progress that must be adopted by all those wishing to advance to higher levels of productivity, income, and wealth.[2] The findings of recent historical research on flexible technology and specialty manufacture confirm that neither an intrinsic logic of mechanization favoring standardization and uniformity nor an inevitable preference for mass production of the majority of the world's poor consumers have prevented firms,

---

[1] For a distinction between the flexible specialization *approach* to industrial change and the flexible specialization *thesis* – i.e., the claim that flexible specialization is becoming the dominant productive model in contemporary industry – see Paul Hirst and Jonathan Zeitlin, "Flexible Specialization vs. Post-Fordism: Theory, Evidence and Policy Implications," *Economy and Society* 20, no. 1 (1991): 1-55.

[2] For an extended critique of narrow-track models of industrialization, see Charles F. Sabel and Jonathan Zeitlin, "Historical Alternatives to Mass Production: Politics, Markets and Technology in Nineteenth-Century Industrialization," *Past and Present*, no. 108 (1985): 134-41.

regions, and even whole national economies organized along alternative lines from enjoying extensive commercial success over long periods of time.

More Than One Way to Skin a Cat: The Plasticity of Technology and Organization

A second core claim of the historical alternatives approach is that technology and organization should not be taken as fixed, given, or even latent parameters to which economic actors must adjust but rather as objects of strategic reflection and deliberate experimentation in their own right. Technological progress, in this view, should be understood as an endogenous process in which the strategies pursued by economic actors play a key part in shaping developmental trajectories. At any given moment, moreover, multiple efficient combinations of capital equipment, factor supplies, and human resources are typically possible, some more flexible than others. Thus technology and organization may be advanced not only through the pursuit of economies of scale and joint production, but also through that of economies of variety. "Economies of variety" are here understood as the capacity to adjust the volume and composition of output flexibly and to introduce new products rapidly in response to shifting demand and business strategy.[3] From this perspective, existing scale bottlenecks or indivisibilities can be overcome through deliberate innovations, such as mini-mills and thin-slab casting in steel or "process intensification" and "microreactors" in chemicals. Where process interdependencies remain fixed in the medium term, similarly, closely related phases of production such as auto body manufacture and final assembly can be combined organizationally in very different ways. This can be seen in the much lower level of vertical integration in the Japanese motor vehicle industry compared to its U.S. counterpart during the postwar period.[4] Over a longer period, the range of alternative possibilities in productive organization remains bounded only by minimal requirements for internal

---

[3] Compare Michael Storper and Robert Salais, *Worlds of Production: The Action Frameworks of the Economy* (Cambridge, Mass., 1997), 32, 313, with Alfred D. Chandler, Jr., *Scale and Scope: The Dynamics of Industrial Capitalism* (Cambridge, Mass., 1990), 17, 24–6, 28–31.

[4] For a critique of transaction-costs explanations of vertical integration under conditions of technological interdependence as applied to the canonical case of General Motors's 1926 purchase of Fisher Body, see Susan Helper, John Paul MacDuffie, and Charles F. Sabel, "Pragmatic Collaborations: Advancing Knowledge While Controlling Opportunism," *Industrial and Corporate Change* 9, no. 3 (2000): 443–88.

coherence among interdependent elements and the ability to meet the often loose performance tests of changing competitive environments.

The Mutual Constitution of Actors and Contexts

This malleability of technology and organization is only one example of a larger theoretical point regarding the mutual constitution of actors and contexts. Unlike most variants of business history, including those that celebrate the creative role of entrepreneurs and managers, the historical alternatives approach does not accept a rigid distinction between maximizing agents and constraining contexts in economic life. Economic actors, in this view, are often at least as concerned with determining, in the double sense of figuring out and shaping, the context they are in – market, technological, institutional – as with pursuing their advantage within any particular context. Self-interested adjustment to conditions taken as given therefore proceeds hand in hand with efforts to find or create a more advantageous set of constraints. Strategic action of this type thus renders moot the standard Schumpeterian distinction between adaptive and creative responses to existing constraints, whose meaning, apart from extreme cases, can rarely be determined except in long historical retrospect. Crucial to this process of strategic reflection is the capacity of economic agents to imagine and weigh alternative courses of action, connecting the present with both the future and the past through narratives that constitute their identities and interests.[5]

Uncertainty, Mutability, and Hedging Strategies

Throughout much of modern history, as is the case once again today, uncertainty, fragility, and mutability have widely been recognized as constitutive features of economic life. Under these conditions, empirical research has found, actors are frequently aware both of the complex dependence of economic organization on multiple background conditions and of the possibility of sudden and unanticipated shifts in those conditions. Hence they often seek to avoid definitive choices between polar alternatives and to anticipate in their chosen forms of economic

---

[5] For a fuller discussion, see Charles F. Sabel and Jonathan Zeitlin, "Stories, Strategies, and Structures: Rethinking Historical Alternatives to Mass Production," in *World of Possibilities: Flexibility and Mass Production in Western Industrialization*, eds. Sabel and Zeitlin (Cambridge, 1997), 5-20.

organization the need for future reconstruction in the face of changed circumstances.

Such self-reflective actors, as historical studies based on our approach show, continuously scanned foreign competitors' practices and debated the merits of alternative models while understanding the relationship between contexts and strategic choices. They could typically see, for example – even when local intellectuals or policy makers could not – the connections between foreign competitors' use of machines and their firms' organization, on the one hand, and the structure of their markets and institutional environments, on the other. The result was often judicious rejection of apparently successful foreign models, not because they were new or foreign, but because they did not fit local economic and institutional circumstances. This was matched by an equally aggressive embrace of those elements of foreign practice that served the constantly evolving definition of locally appropriate strategies. At bottom, this selective rejection and acceptance of particular elements of foreign innovations reflected a constant and permanently provisional reevaluation of local strategy. More specifically, it demonstrated an anxious effort to avoid entrapment in any given organization of production and its associated markets.

Hedging strategies of this sort might appear to observers steeped in Schumpeterian categories as passivity masquerading in the guise of prudence. Yet the historical record shows that, as such, they often led to the creation of innovative hybrids that combined indigenous with foreign practices in unforeseen but often remarkably competitive ways. Meanwhile, apparently incremental changes in industrial organization could in the aggregate amount to programs of transformation as radical in their consequences as those directly proclaimed as such.[6]

The Predominance of Hybrid Forms Over Pure Types

More generally, the process of strategic reflection and hedging against risk gives rise to a proliferation of hybrid forms of productive organization. These hybrid forms between mass production and flexible specialization can be more or less easily reconstructed and recombined in response to changing background circumstances. Hence the predominance of

---

[6] Ibid., 12–14, and Jonathan Zeitlin, "Introduction: Americanization and Its Limits: Reworking U.S. Technology and Management in Post-War Europe and Japan," in *Americanization and Its Limits: Reworking U.S. Technology and Management in Post-War Europe and Japan*, eds. Jonathan Zeitlin and Gary Herrigel (Oxford, 2000), 34–41.

hybrid, mixed, and intermediate forms of productive organization over polar types has proved to be the empirical rule rather than the exception in most times and places. Yet the notion of contrasting strategies and distinct practices remains analytically crucial, since it is economic actors' perception of the advantages and disadvantages of polar possibilities that leads them to hedge their strategies in the first place. Thus, the appreciation of the full range of possible diversity provokes the search for ever more various ways of avoiding risky bets on the extreme positions.

Economic Governance Beyond the Firm

Along with much current writing in economic sociology and political economy, the historical alternatives approach denies any ontological or epistemological privilege to the individual business firm as the key unit of analysis and economic governance. The boundaries and internal organization of the firm, in this view, must be treated as empirical variables, both in flexible and in mass production, so that autarky and internalization of activities within the enterprise become phenomena to be explained just as much as decentralization, outsourcing, and networking. While flexible and mass production, at least in their pure form, present distinctive governance problems at both the micro and macro levels, a wide – though by no means infinite – range of institutional frameworks for their solution can be observed in historical practice. Simplifying brutally, the key governance problems for flexible production are how to check opportunism and prevent free riding without stifling fluid cooperation among decentralized economic actors through institutions for the resolution of disputes and the provision of collective services. For mass production, by contrast, the crucial problem is how to balance supply and demand at different levels from individual markets and firms to national and international economies, though conflict resolution and reproduction of human resources are also significant challenges. In each case, however, these functions may be performed through a variable mix of governance mechanisms, including networks, associations, and states, as well as hierarchically managed enterprises.[7] Therefore, in both flexible

---

[7] In Sabel's recent work on "learning by monitoring," the "new pragmatic disciplines" of benchmarking, simultaneous engineering, and error detection and correction are presented as an alternative governance mechanism for flexible production based on increased information symmetry and asset redeployability among collaborating firms; see Charles F. Sabel, "Learning by Monitoring: The Institutions of Economic Development," in *The Handbook of Economic Sociology*, eds. Neil J. Smelser and Richard Swedberg (Princeton, 1994), 137–65; and Helper et al., "Pragmatic Collaborations."

and mass production – including the vast array of hybrid forms between them – firms' embeddedness in their local institutional contexts reaches far beyond a minimal dependence on clearly defined property rights and enforceable contracts.

The Historical Construction of Markets

An additional claim shared by the historical alternatives approach with other critical perspectives on the economy in contemporary social science is that there is no such thing as "the market," but only particular markets. In the real world of "actually existing" economies, social structures and institutions play a constitutive role in defining the rules and conventions governing particular markets, whether for products, raw materials, capital, or labor. Among the most important of these social and institutional influences on the construction of markets are taxes, tariffs, and income distribution; family structure and the gender division of labor; product and quality standards; competition and antitrust policies; banking and capital market regulations; and industrial relations systems. "Efficiency," moreover, can only be assessed relative to particular patterns of demand and supply. Thus mass production, as is now well known, depends on the existence of large and steadily growing markets for standardized goods. Low unit costs of production are no competitive advantage if consumers reject the product; similarly, theoretical scale economies do not yield low costs if capacity cannot be translated into sales. Precisely because managers widely understood the need to ensure a steady and predictable outlet for goods that cannot easily be turned to alternative uses, protectionism and market power played a key role in the development of mass production in the United States as well as in Western Europe and Japan. Not just mass producers but their flexible rivals as well have consistently sought to shape and respond to market demand through a variety of strategies. Prominent among these are advertising and marketing; forward and backward integration into distribution and control of raw materials; product differentiation; the creation of new niches, cartels, and alliances; lobbying; and political struggles.[8]

[8] See Henrik Glimstedt and Jonathan Zeitlin, "Constructing Markets, Shaping Production: The Historical Constitution of Product Markets in Europe and the United States" (paper presented to an international conference organized by the Institute of International Business of the Stockholm School of Economics and the Swedish Council for the Coordination and Initiation of Research [FRN], Idöborg, Sweden, July 5–6, 2002).

Neither Frictionless Adjustment Nor Path Dependency

Unlike much recent institutionalist and evolutionary work with which it shares other common ground, the historical alternatives approach rejects both frictionless adjustment and path dependency as frameworks for the understanding of economic change. Actors' strategies and decisions really matter in this view and, whatever their intrinsic merits, often exert a significant influence on the trajectory of economic development. Adjustment to changing market or technological conditions is thus far from automatic. Yet in contrast to the claims of evolutionary theorists, deliberate adaptation typically predominates over natural selection in economic adjustment. Actors are rarely so "locked in" by institutions and history as path dependency models contend. Hedging strategies, "learning by monitoring," and continuous, provisional reevaluation of existing practice can thus be understood as pragmatic mechanisms for routinely questioning firms' routines without undercutting their use as templates for everyday activity.

Similarly, technological hybrids such as converters and transformers in electric power systems, flexible transfer machinery composed of standard recombinable units, or programmable automation can likewise be viewed as conscious devices for avoiding and overcoming potential lock-in. At a still deeper level, even quite stable institutional arrangements, like technologies and production models, may be reconfigured through apparently marginal modifications to operate quite differently under new environmental conditions. Thus continuing relationships or network ties between institutions may belie a deep transformation in the ways actors conceive of themselves, their mission, and their strategic possibilities. History, in this view, surely matters, but its consequences may often be to facilitate rather than to obstruct economic adjustment by serving as a cognitive and practical resource for self-reflective actors responding to external challenges.[9]

Orientations Rather Than Epochs

The interpenetration of strategies and practices within industries and national economies at any one time casts inevitable doubt on the possibility

[9] See Sabel and Zeitlin, "Stories, Strategies, and Structures," 8–11; Charles F. Sabel, "Intelligible Differences: On Deliberate Strategy and the Exploration of Possibilities in Economic Life," *Rivista Italiana degli Economisti* 1, no. 1 (1996): 55–80; Zeitlin, "Introduction: Americanization," 13–14, 19–20.

of drawing sharp distinctions between epochs or periods such as the "age of Fordism" or the "era of flexibility." From this vantage point, it seems more useful to distinguish historical epochs according to changing orientations toward those political and economic ideas regarded as normal or paradigmatic rather than to divide history into periods where social life was thoroughly organized according to one or another master principle. This idea of a continually changing orientation toward paradigmatic or normal ideas faithfully conveys both a sense of changing constraints on historical actors and that of the continuing scope of localized strategic choice. Ideas of normality tend to magnify and thus to increase the importance of dominant conceptions without reflecting or constraining anything like the totality of behavior they purportedly characterize.[10]

Contingency and Strategic Choice as the Mainsprings of Economic Change

Without a teleological and deterministic model of material progress, contingency and strategic choice become the mainsprings of economic change and thus the core theme of industrial history. Nor is the significance of such choices, as we once thought, concentrated at rare moments of historical openness – evolutionary branching points, punctuated equilibria, or industrial divides. Although great events such as wars, revolutions, or radical reforms are undoubtedly critical to economic change, small everyday choices and incremental innovations may cumulatively exert a profound influence on the industrial development of individual firms, regions, and whole national economies. Hence industrial history should be written in a narrative form attentive to the relationship between economic actors' self-understanding and strategic calculations, on the one hand, and the consequences of their decisions, both intended and unintended, on the other. Such narratives will involve typically a variety of devices, such as flashbacks, polyphony, and multiple retellings of the same tale as a means for the representation of action as a process of deliberative choice among an open (though not, of course, infinite) set of alternative possibilities. At the same time, they will also seek to avoid narratives that abuse hindsight to recount events as if their outcome were predetermined and could be used to judge the choices of

[10] For an elaboration of these claims, see Sabel and Zeitlin, "Stories, Strategies, and Structures," 4–5, 29–33.

historical actors, irrespective of what the latter could realistically have been expected to know at the time.[11]

FIVE MISCONCEIVED OBJECTIONS

The historical alternatives approach to industrial history has aroused a storm of critical debate. Some of the objections raised in this debate were, of course, well founded, and contributed to a rethinking of the historical alternatives approach by Charles Sabel and myself in our introduction to *World of Possibilities: Flexibility and Mass Production in Western Industrialization*. But other objections, by contrast, are based on a series of recurrent misconceptions about the argument, to the most common of which the remainder of this essay responds.[12]

The Size of the Firm Is Not a Determining Variable

Contrary to widespread assumptions, the historical alternatives approach is not a "small is beautiful" argument about the inherent superiority – whether economic, social, or political – of small over large firms. Flexible specialization, in this view, can be pursued within industrial districts or geographically localized networks of small and medium-sized enterprises; it can take place within large, decentralized, or federated firms. It can occur as well in a variety of intermediate forms between the two. Even in mass production, as has been argued in the sixth thesis, the boundaries of the corporation may be fluid and variable, especially when the possibilities of hybrid production strategies are taken into account. Forms of coordination and the relationships between economic units, rather than formal ownership or even managerial structure, are thus the key variables in industrial organization. In the historical alternatives approach, the argument about firm size is instead really a negative claim: namely, there are no intrinsic barriers preventing networks of small firms from being economically efficient, technologically innovative, and commercially successful. Meanwhile, large size and vertical integration may have as much to do with struggles for market control as with any efficiency or coordination advantages.[13]

---

[11] For fuller discussion and examples of narrative practice, see ibid.,15-20, and Zeitlin, "Introduction: Americanization," 21-2.

[12] For a discussion of the closely related debate over flexible specialization, see Hirst and Zeitlin, "Flexible Specialization."

[13] See Naomi R. Lamoreaux, *The Great Merger Movement in American Business, 1895-1904* (Cambridge, 1985), and William G. Roy, *Socializing Capital: The Rise of the Large*

Industrial Sectors Are Not a Determining Variable

Contrary to another widely held claim, the intrinsic characteristics of industrial sectors – markets, technologies, factor supplies, and so on – do not determine the boundaries between mass production and flexible specialization. In particular, it is not the case that flexible production can be successfully pursued only in light, labor-intensive industries (Franco Amatori, "Reflections on Global Business and Modern Italian Enterprise by a Stubborn 'Chandlerian'," *Business History Review* 71, no. 2 [1997]: 309-18).[14] Although industrial sectors do, of course, have distinctive economic and technological characteristics at any given time, within each sector there are typically a range of firms pursuing different strategies marked by varying degrees of flexibility and specialization. Examples of this include fine versus commodity chemicals, specialty versus basic steels, platform technologies versus therapeutics in biotechnology, and customized information technology services versus standardized software products (Steven Casper, Mark Lehrer, and David Soskice, "Can High-Technology Industries Prosper in Germany? Institutional Frameworks and the Evolution of the German Software and Biotechnology Industries," *Industry and Innovation* 6, no. 1 [1999]: 5-24).[15] Such

Industrial Corporation in America (Princeton, 1997) on the importance of market power as opposed to pure efficiency considerations in the determinants of the great U.S. merger wave at the turn of the twentieth century, and Giovanni Dosi, "Organizational Competences, Firm Size, and the Wealth of Nations: Some Comments from a Comparative Perspective," in *Big Business and the Wealth of Nations*, eds. Alfred D. Chandler, Jr., Franco Amatori, and Takashi Hikino (Cambridge, 1997), 465-79, on the absence of any correlation between the size distribution of industrial firms across national economies and variations in their growth rates.

[14] The claim that the modern corporation clustered in sectors whose technological characteristics permitted the exploitation of potential scale and scope economies through managerial coordination is a recurrent feature of Chandlerian analysis. For the most recent formulation, see Alfred D. Chandler, Jr., and Takashi Hikino, "The Large Industrial Enterprise and the Dynamics of Modern Economic Growth," in Chandler et al., *Big Business*, 24-57.

[15] Even within a given market segment, "comparisons of closely matched firms in the same country (e.g., Federal Express and UPS or McKinsey and Boston Consulting Group) have shown that there is more than one path to success ... with direct competitors pursuing very different organizational and human-resource strategies." Peter Cappelli and Anne Crocker-Hefter, "Distinctive Human Resources Are Firms' Core Competencies," *Organizational Dynamics* 24, no. 3 (1996): 7-21, quoted in David Finegold and Karin Wagner, "The German Skill-Creation System and Team-Based Production: Competitive Asset or Liability?" in *The German Skills Machine: Sustaining Comparative Advantage in a Global Economy*, eds. Pepper D. Culpepper and David Finegold (New York, 1999), 124, which makes a similar point about standardized, assembled-to-order, and customized pump manufacturing in Germany and the United States.

divergent strategies can in time transform the commercial and technological characteristics of the sector itself. The result can be the reduction of minimum efficient scales of production along with an increase
in the fragmentation and specialization of demand. Mini-mills in steel,
combined-cycle power plants in electricity supply, and Japanese flexible
production and product development techniques in motor vehicles all
are examples of this impact (Gary Herrigel, "Varieties of Collective Regeneration: Comparisons of the German, Japanese and American Steel
Industries since the Mid-1970s" [paper presented to the IIB–FRN conference on "Constructing Markets, Shaping Production," Idöborg, Sweden,
July 5–6, 2002]; Richard F. Hirsh, *Technology and Transformation in
the American Electrical Utility Industry* [Cambridge, 1989], chap. 13;
Kim B. Clark and Takahiro Fujimoto, *Product Development Performance:
Strategy, Management, and Organization in the World Auto Industry*
[Boston, 1991]).

Governance structures and thus the effective boundaries of the firm
likewise vary widely within the same sector. This variation appears not
only across countries (J. Rogers Hollingsworth, Philippe C. Schmitter,
and Wolfgang Streeck, eds., *Governing Capitalist Economies: Performance and Control of Economic Sectors* [Oxford, 1994]), but even
within different regions of the same country, as in the case of autarkic
versus decentralized industrial orders in German mechanical engineering (Gary Herrigel, *Industrial Constructions: The Sources of German
Industrial Power* [Cambridge, 1996]). Many large German, Japanese,
and even American steel, machinery, and electrical manufacturing companies turn out to have been extensively engaged in more or less flexible
and specialized forms of production throughout much of their history
(Herrigel, *Industrial Constructions;* id., "American Occupation, Market
Order, and Democracy: Reconfiguring the Steel Industry in Japan and
Germany after the Second World War," in *Americanization and Its Limits: Reworking U.S. Technology and Management in Post-War Europe
and Japan*, eds. Jonathan Zeitlin and Gary Herrigel [Oxford, 2000],
340–99; Mark W. Fruin, *The Japanese Enterprise System: Competitive
Strategies and Cooperative Structures* [Oxford, 1994]; Philip Scranton,
*Endless Novelty: Specialty Production and American Industrialization,
1865–1925* [Princeton, 1997]). The Chandlerian claim that large modern
corporations became concentrated in certain industries but not others
fails to take adequate account of aggregation problems within sectors,
diversity among large firms, and variations in the significance of the top
200 industrial firms within individual national economies (see Fruin,

Japanese Enterprise System, or Youssef Cassis, *Big Business: The European Experience in the Twentieth Century* [Oxford, 1997] on Britain).

Strategic Action as Hyperrationality?

The emphasis that the historical alternatives approach puts on the role and sophistication of strategizing actors is sometimes accused of representing a form of hyperrationality. According to this criticism, the approach imposes unrealistic demands on the information-processing and computational powers of actual economic agents and thereby inadvertently mirrors neoclassical rational actor models, complete with all their well-known weaknesses. Whatever its superficial plausibility, such an interpretation constitutes a clear misreading of the historical alternatives approach. Strategic reflection, as Sabel and I explicitly acknowledge, is a necessary but not sufficient condition for competitive success. Well-informed contemplation of alternatives can in extreme cases lead to paralysis through familiar paradoxes such as Hegel's vortex of bad infinity and the dilemma of Buridan's ass (Charles F. Sabel and Jonathan Zeitlin, "Stories, Strategies, and Structures: Rethinking Historical Alternatives to Mass Production," in *World of Possibilities: Flexibility and Mass Production in Western Industrialization*, eds. Charles F. Sabel and Jonathan Zeitlin [Cambridge, 1997], 14–15). Like much behavioral and evolutionary economics, the historical alternatives approach recognizes volatility, uncertainty, and incomplete information as fundamental obstacles to economic optimization.

But unlike other nonstandard perspectives, the historical alternatives approach regards unreflective dependence on "satisficing" routines such as standard operating procedures, rules of thumb, and accounting conventions as myopic and potentially dangerous solutions to the underlying problems of incomplete information and unanticipated change. "Bounded rationality," in this view, is not a second-best approximation of rationality itself under adverse conditions, but rather an oxymoron, since no rational means are available to determine the optimal limits of search activity and thus the appropriate scope of any particular set of routines. Hedging strategies, "learning by monitoring," and hybrid, recombinable organizational and productive forms can thus be seen as superior responses to volatility and uncertainty. These pragmatic mechanisms enable economic actors to expose their existing beliefs and practices piece by piece to possible challenges without plunging into a paralyzing state of complete self-doubt. No assumption of optimality or maximization is entailed by this "practically reasonable" conception of economic action, so-called because agents are typically capable both of giving provisional reasons for their actions in any given situation and of reciprocally adjusting ends and means in light of their practical experience with particular courses of action.[16] In this view, economic actors do not always make the "right" choices, but their decisions nonetheless are often broadly consequential.

Power, Exploitation, Conflict

Another frequently raised charge against the historical alternatives approach is that it systematically neglects the "dark side" of power, exploitation, and conflict within industrial districts or flexible regional economies. Critics claim that empirical studies of individual districts and regions such as Birmingham, Sheffield, St. Etienne, or Cholet typically find greater evidence of hierarchy and power imbalances than is acknowledged by proponents of the historical alternatives approach. These critics charge the historical alternatives approach with neglecting the weight of medium-sized and even large firms in their industrial structure, the role of credit and marketing relations in the subordination of formally independent small producers, and reliance on sweated labor and exploitation to sustain competitiveness. These critics likewise suggest that a greater incidence of overt conflict – in the form of strikes and other types of disputes, on the one hand, and industrial secrecy and other failures of local cooperation, on the other – challenges the characterization of these districts or regions in the historical alternatives literature.[17]

---

[16] For this pragmatist or "practically reasonable" conception of economic action, see Sabel, "Learning by Monitoring"; Helper et al., "Pragmatic Collaborations"; and from a slightly different theoretical perspective, Robert Salais, Elisabeth Chatel, and Dorothée Rivaud-Danset, eds., *Institutions et conventions: La réflexivité de l'action économique* (Paris, 1999).

[17] For examples of these criticisms, see Maxine Berg, "Small Producer Capitalism in Eighteenth-Century England," *Business History* 35, no. 1 (1993): 17–39; id., *The Age of Manufactures, 1700-1820*, 2nd edition (London, 1994); Lars Magnusson, *The Contest for Control: Metal Industries in Sheffield, Solingen, Remscheid and Eskilstuna during Industrialization* (Oxford, 1994); Clive Behagg, "Myths of Cohesion: Capital and Compromise in the Historiography of Nineteenth-Century Birmingham," *Social History* 11, no. 3 (1986): 375–84; Alan White, " '... We Never Knew What Price We Were Going to Have Till We Got to the Warehouse': Nineteenth-Century Sheffield and the Industrial District Debate," *Social History* 22, no. 3 (1997): 307–17; Ronald Aminzade, "Reinterpreting Capitalist Industrialization: A Study of Nineteenth-Century France," *Social History* 9, no. 3 (1984): 329–50; and Tessie P. Liu, *The Weaver's Knot: The Contradictions of Class Struggle and Family Solidarity in Western France, 1750-1914* (Ithaca, N.Y., 1994).

Some of these criticisms are based on confusions about the role of firm size and scale in the historical alternatives approach discussed earlier. Others, by contrast, ignore the attention within this approach devoted to internal cleavages and the scope for conflict within flexible regional economies, arising both from contention for place among individuals and social groups and from the potentially disruptive impact of hybridizing experimentation on the existing institutional order. At issue thus is not the existence or potential for such internal conflicts but rather the institutions and governance mechanisms through which they were handled and resolved. In most successful flexible economies, empirical studies confirm that collective wage-setting institutions, dispute adjudication procedures, and other regulatory institutions have played a crucial part in balancing cooperation and competition among decentralized economic actors. When flexible regional economies face difficult adjustments to external shifts in markets and technology, the fact is that social stalemate, deregulation, and decline are always possible outcomes. But so too is the regeneration of innovative capabilities and competitiveness through collective deliberation and institutional reform. What is crucial is whether or not internal conflicts over the challenges posed by economic change can be resolved by reinforcing collaborative governance mechanisms that equitably distribute the burdens and benefits of adjustment among the actors concerned.[18]

What, finally, of the relationship between social power and economic choices? Doesn't the emphasis on the role of power in shaping the outcome of struggles over the evolution of markets, technology, and industrial organization undercut the role of contingency and choice by reintroducing an underlying structural logic – based now on social interests rather than efficiency?[19] Here again, this superficially plausible conclusion proves misleading for a number of well-grounded theoretical and empirical reasons. The first such reason concerns the inherent uncertainty surrounding all strategic calculations. In a world in which actions often have unintended consequences, the distribution of power resources does not necessarily determine the outcome of economic and political struggles. The second reason lies in the structural ambiguity

---

[18] For historical examples of both possible outcomes, see Sabel and Zeitlin, *World of Possibilities*.

[19] See, for example, the discussion of power-based explanations of industrial change in Roy, *Socializing Capital*; Margaret Levenstein, review of William G. Roy, *Socializing Capital: The Rise of the Large Industrial Corporation in America*, August 1997, available from H-Business (electronic bulletin board).

of social interests themselves, together with their frequently observed redefinition through the making and breaking of alliances with other actors in the course of pursuing particular economic or political strategies (Charles F. Sabel, *Work and Politics: The Division of Labor in Industry* [Cambridge, 1982]; Susan Helper, John Paul MacDuffie, and Charles F. Sabel, "Pragmatic Collaborations: Advancing Knowledge While Controlling Opportunism," *Industrial and Corporate Change* 9, no. 3 [2000]: 443–88). The third reason lies in the ongoing significance of small, everyday decisions and microalternatives – in addition to the more obvious large-scale battles and industrial divides – in shaping the productive trajectories of firms, regions, and entire national economies. This recurrent salience of small-scale choices belies the idea of an underlying logic of economic and technological development based on the putatively decisive role of social power in determining collective choices at key turning points.

Utopian Romanticism: History in the Optative Mood?

Nor, finally, can the historical alternatives approach be fairly dismissed as "history in the optative mood," an exaltation of ideologically desirable but unrealistic alternatives with little empirical relevance (David S. Landes, "Small Is Beautiful. Small Is Beautiful?" in Fondazione ASSI/Istituto per la storia dell'Umbria contemporanea, *Piccola e grande impresa: Un problema storico* [Milan, 1987], 15–28). For as the growing body of research inspired by it testifies, the historical alternatives approach has already yielded a substantial empirical payoff as both a positive and a negative heuristic.[20] As a positive heuristic, the historical alternatives approach has drawn attention to neglected but historically significant forms of productive organization, both pure and hybrid. The most important such positive finding has been the rediscovery of flexible production as a pervasive feature of industrial history prior to its contemporary resurgence since the 1970s. This rediscovery has come in industrial districts dominated by small and medium-sized enterprises, large internally decentralized or federated firms, and intermediate combinations between the two. Some of these flexible production systems have continued to thrive for long periods of time down to the present. Others were large

---

[20] For a similar argument about the flexible specialization approach in the context of contemporary debates about the analysis of industrial change, see Hirst and Zeitlin, "Flexible Specialization," 25–6.

and successful in their day but eventually declined or were transformed into something different, whether for internal or external reasons. But the same could be said of many mass-production firms and regions. The survival of any particular economic unit over a specific time period has no direct bearing on the viability of the broader productive model on which it is based. The key point emerging from recent research is that at no stage did flexible production die out altogether, or even fall into a clearly subordinate relationship to mass production, despite the latter's ascendancy as a technological and economic paradigm during the mid-twentieth century.[21]

The historical alternatives approach also serves as a negative heuristic, drawing attention to what might have happened but did not, thereby giving rise to different and richer accounts of the course of industrial history. Causal explanations in history, as is widely recognized, implicitly depend upon counterfactual arguments; but plausible counterfactual arguments must, in turn, be grounded in possibilities that were realistically open to historical actors at the time.[22] In this area, too, there is now a growing body of work that traces the role of political struggles, technological paradigms, and strategic choices in shaping trajectories of industrial development. Perhaps the most important findings of this strand of research concern the impact of national institutions and policies on the reproduction or decline of flexible regional economies. Among the most important such factors highlighted by this research are the degree of administrative centralization as opposed to local government autonomy, the effectiveness of state rationalization and concentration policies, the form and intensity of antitrust regulation, the extent of political tolerance of associational governance, the relative concentration of retail distribution, and the territorial structure of banking and finance systems.[23] Here, too, national cases of flexible production that initially

---

[21] For the incomplete dominance of mass over flexible production in mid-twentieth-century industry, see Jonathan Zeitlin, ed., "Flexibility in the 'Age of Fordism'": Technology and Production in the International Automobile Industry," special issue of *Enterprise and Society* 1, no. 1 (2000); Zeitlin and Herrigel, *Americanization and Its Limits*; Steven Tolliday and Jonathan Zeitlin, eds., *Between Fordism and Flexibility: The Automobile Industry and Its Workers*, 2nd edition (Oxford, 1992).

[22] For this view of the role of counterfactual arguments in historical explanation, see Jon Elster, *Logic and Society: Contradictions and Possible Worlds* (New York, 1978), chap. 6; Geoffrey Hawthorn, *Plausible Worlds: Possibility and Understanding in History and the Social Sciences* (Cambridge, 1991); and Paul Ricoeur, *Time and Narrative*, vol. 1, trans. Kathleen McLaughlin and David Pellauer (Chicago, 1984), chap. 6.

[23] For discussion of national institutional and political influences on the fate of flexible regional economies in Britain and the United States, see Jonathan Zeitlin, "Why Are There No

appeared as exceptional deviations from the mainstream of historical development have increasingly come to be understood as the result of variations on a common theme.[24] Thus small differences in the outcome of similar struggles can eventually yield large cumulative divergences in economic governance and productive organization.

But the historical alternatives approach offers a normative as well as an empirical payoff. By expanding our understanding of the range of organizational and productive forms in the past, and by enriching our understanding of the reasons for and outcomes of earlier decisions about economic governance, the historical alternatives approach can improve the quality of public debate about the range of strategic choices open to us in the present and the future. This is arguably a legitimate, even a necessary, role for industrial history at the beginning of the new millennium if it is to contribute to public problem solving rather than to ossify into a purely scholastic activity.

KEY WORKS

Berk, Gerald. *Alternative Tracks: The Constitution of American Industrial Order, 1865-1917*. Baltimore, 1994.
Helper, Susan, John Paul MacDuffie, and Charles F. Sabel. "Pragmatic Collaborations: Advancing Knowledge While Controlling Opportunism." *Industrial and Corporate Change* 9, no. 3 (2000): 443-88.
Piore, Michael J. and Charles F. Sabel. *The Second Industrial Divide: Possibilities for Prosperity*. New York, 1984.
Sabel, Charles F. "Learning by Monitoring: The Institutions of Economic Development." In *The Handbook of Economic Sociology*, edited by Neil J. Smelser and Richard Swedberg, 137-65. Princeton, 1994.
Sabel, Charles F. and Jonathan Zeitlin, "Historical Alternatives to Mass Production: Politics, Markets and Technology in Western Industrialization." *Past and Present*, no. 108 (1985): 133-76.
"Stories, Strategies, and Structures: Rethinking Historical Alternatives to Mass Production." In *World of Possibilities: Flexibility and Mass Production in Western Industrialization*, edited by Charles F. Sabel and Jonathan Zeitlin, 1-33. Cambridge, 1997.
    eds. *World of Possibilities: Flexibility and Mass Production in Western Industrialization*. Cambridge, 1997.

Industrial Districts in the United Kingdom?" in *Small and Medium-Size Enterprises*, eds. Arnaldo Bagnasco and Charles F. Sabel (London, 1995), 98-114; Gerald Berk, *Alternative Tracks: The Constitution of American Industrial Order, 1865-1917* (Baltimore, 1994).

[24] For a key case in point, see Peer Hull Kristensen and Charles F. Sabel, "The Small-Holder Economy in Denmark: The Exception as Variation," in Sabel and Zeitlin, *World of Possibilities*, 344-78.

Scranton, Philip. *Endless Novelty: Specialty Production and American Industrialization, 1865–1925*. Princeton, 1997.

Zeitlin, Jonathan and Gary Herrigel, eds. *Americanization and Its Limits: Reworking U.S. Technology and Management in Post-War Europe and Japan*. Oxford, 2000.

PART II

Area Patterns

5

Business History in the United States at the End of the Twentieth Century

WILLIAM J. HAUSMAN

Business history in the United States at the end of the twentieth century and the beginning of the twenty-first is simultaneously thriving and struggling with its identity. There are clear signs of vigor, including a rising membership in the major professional organization in the field, the Business History Conference (BHC). The membership of the organization has more than doubled to around 550 over the past decade, and interest in presenting papers at its annual meeting has intensified. There were 103 papers proposed for the 1998 annual meeting and more than 200 for the 2000 meeting. The organization recently launched a new quarterly professional journal, *Enterprise & Society*, the successor to its proceedings volume, *Business and Economic History*. A second professional organization, the Economic and Business Historical Society, established in 1974 as an offshoot of the Western Economics Association, also thrives. It has around 200 members, meets annually, and publishes a proceedings volume, *Essays in Economic and Business History*. But there also are some signs of stress (or excitement), including a growing debate among business historians over the future direction of the field.

I would like to thank the following for their comments on an earlier draft of this essay: Richard John, Sally Clarke, Mira Wilkins, Angel Kwolek-Folland, Mansel Blackford, David Sicilia, Stanley Engerman, Pat Denault, and participants at the conference in Milan. The usual disclaimer applies.

Business history has grown tremendously in recent years, not only in terms of the number of scholars interested in the subject but also in academic stature. This is in no small part due to the creative work of a single individual, Alfred D. Chandler, Jr. By virtually any measure, Chandler has dominated the field over the past several decades. Chandler has stimulated an outpouring of work that extends, amends, explicitly rejects, but rarely ignores his basic approach and conclusions. One reason for the tremendous impact of Chandler's work is its appeal to a very broad audience.

Business history, of course, is more than Chandler. But, though business historians are doing exciting new work, there is no consensus about which way the field will or should be headed in the twenty-first century.[1] This "identity crisis" stems in part from the inherently interdisciplinary nature of the field, with business history practitioners distributed among departments of history, economics, or business, each with its own culture and constituencies. Of the president (2000–1), president-elect, and thirteen immediate past presidents of the BHC, five are in history departments, five are in schools of business, four are in economics departments, and one has a joint appointment in history and economics. Of the 411 members in the organization's database whose professional affiliation could be identified, 30 percent were in history departments, 22 percent were in business schools, 18 percent were in economics departments, 7 percent were in departments or programs in business, technological, or economic history, and 23 percent were in other departments, programs, or related occupations (including, for example, law, government agencies, and archives).

Trends in each of these fields are having an impact on research in business history, as well as on the views that individual business historians articulate regarding the future of the field. One possible outcome of this process is fragmentation of the community of business historians, a result that must be avoided for the long-term health of the field. Frank and vigorous interdisciplinary discussion may be the best means of thwarting this danger. In a recent article, Lamoreaux, Raff, and Temin assert pessimistically that there is "little communication today between economists and historians or even between economic historians (who are largely economists by training) and business historians (who typically

---

[1] For example, Richard R. John, "Elaborations, Revisions, Dissents: Alfred D. Chandler, Jr.'s, *The Visible Hand* after Twenty Years," *Business History Review* 71 (Summer 1997): 151–200.

come out of history departments)."[2] The Economic History Association (EHA) lists 1,242 members, over twice the membership of the BHC. There are 158 members in common, meaning that 25 percent of BHC members also belong to the EHA. Whether or not this is sufficient overlap to foster communication remains an issue.

Debate over what constitutes the essence of business history is not new. Business historians have always tried to define themselves and their field, and have endeavored to convince their colleagues to move in certain directions. From the intellectual battle between Edwin F. Gay and N. S. B. Gras at the Harvard Business School in the 1920s and 1930s, through the first meeting of the BHC in 1954, to a 1997 conference at the Hagley Museum and Library on the "Future of Business History," scholars who identify themselves as business historians often have paused to question what they are doing and ask where they should be headed.

To examine the state of business history in the United States at the end of the twentieth century, we must get down to basics and ask a few fundamental questions about business history. Where have we come from? What are its practitioners saying about the future of business history? Who is currently doing business history, and what are they doing? I sought to provide a quantitative foundation for answers where possible. As I started working on answers, another important question, relevant to the debate about where business history is headed, emerged: To what extent did Chandler dominate the field at the end of the twentieth century? To obtain a sense of that, I performed a citation-based analysis, using past presidents of the BHC as a reference. Nobody will be shocked by the results, but I think a few insights about the market for business history were obtained in the process. To gain a sense of who is doing business history and what they are doing, I analyzed articles published over recent five-year periods in the *Business History Review* and *Business and Economic History*. Again, there are few surprises in the type of work actually getting published, but some new trends are emerging.

A HISTORY OF BUSINESS HISTORY IN THE UNITED STATES: FROM THE 1920S TO CHANDLER

Several recurrent themes appear in the debates regarding the proper focus of business history. These themes, which should be familiar to

---

[2] Naomi R. Lamoreaux, Daniel M. G. Raff, and Peter Temin, "New Economic Approaches to the Study of Business History," *Business and Economic History* 26 (Fall 1997): 57.

those currently debating the future of business history, can perhaps best
be expressed as questions: What is the relationship between economic
history and business history? Should a particular theory form the basis of
analysis in business history? Should business history focus on the internal
organization and policies of the firm or should it be expanded to include
study of the social context of business?

Although both economic and business history trace their roots to
German and English scholarship in the nineteenth century, business history as a distinct area of study was born at the Harvard Business School in
the mid-1920s. From the beginning, the economic historian Edwin F. Gay
and his student, N. S. B. Gras, the first Straus Professor of Business History at the school, quarreled over the purpose and definition of the field:
"Gay and other economic historians at the time believed that business
history should contribute to the synthetic view of economic history they
were trying to construct.... Gras, on the other hand, had little use for
the type of theorizing that characterized the more established field. He
was an inductive thinker who believed that business behavior should be
studied for its own sake...."[3] The feud had real consequences. Because
they could not agree on editorial policy, the journal they had founded
in 1928 and coedited, the *Journal of Economic and Business History*,
folded within three years.

There is no question that Gras believed strongly that there was one best
way to engage in business history, a view he discussed in an address to the
Business Historical Society in 1949.[4] The Business Historical Society was
created in 1925 as part of the expansion of the Harvard Graduate School
of Business Administration into new areas, including business ethics and
human relations. Dean Wallace B. Donham and George Woodbridge,
a Boston journalist and Harvard fund-raiser, were believers in the utility of business history in business education and were instrumental in
forming the society. One of the society's tasks was to collect books and
manuscripts for the newly established Baker Library, and the society's
members, many of whom were businessmen, also served as consumers
of the research being done on business history. When it came to discussing the *Journal*, published jointly by the society and the School of
Business, Gras was to the point: "The editor, Professor Gay, insisted on

[3] Ibid., 58-9.
[4] N. S. B. Gras, "Past, Present, and Future of the Business Historical Society," *Bulletin of the
Business Historical Society* 24 (March 1950): 1-12.

keeping business history out of the *Journal*, and I insisted on putting it in."[5]

After discussing the substantial fluctuations in the membership of the Business Historical Society through the Depression, World War II, and the immediate postwar years, Gras considered where future support for the organization might be obtained. Businessmen and librarians were first on the list, but he also considered the prospects among the various academic disciplines. Historians were an obvious source of potential support because they "are always looking for new themes and new sources of study. Business can be put alongside politics, religion, education, and recreation as component parts of life." Gras sensed, however, that they would not be interested. The prospect of attracting the interest of economists was not good "for the simple reason that few economists have any interest in business or the business man, and therefore none in business history." Economic historians, of course, were not much better than economists, because "the economic historian often takes his clue from the economist and therefore has no clear vision of the importance of the business man, though he does play with the metaphysical concept of the entrepreneur." That left merely the "little band of business historians which, though small, may grow." The appeal of business history might be broadened, Gras argued, if it were to encompass all of the following: "The economic history of business. The political history of business. The social history of business. The legal history of business. The business interpretation of general history." But he feared that such expansion would just lead to "the time-honored neglect of administration and the business man."[6] At around the time these words were written, Alfred Chandler was working on his dissertation. He, along with several other graduate students, consulted Gras on how to write business history: "Gras was pleased to instruct us, but he made it clear that there was only one way to write business history, his way.... After our discussion I almost decided not to become a business historian."[7]

---

[5] Ibid., 4.

[6] Ibid., 7-10.

[7] Alfred D. Chandler, Jr., "Presidential Address, 1978: Business History – A Personal Experience," *Business and Economic History* 7 (1978): 2-3. Fortunately, Chandler was asked to participate in the Research Center for Entrepreneurial History that had been organized by Joseph Schumpeter and Arthur Cole in 1948. He described the several years spent there as "intellectually the most stimulating in my life." Ibid., 3.

Henrietta Larson published the bibliographical *Guide to Business History* (Cambridge, Mass.), in 1948. The general introduction to the volume contains her views on the meaning and development of the field, which – like so many other commentators – she noted was still in its formative stage: "To many persons it is not yet clear how business history differs from economic history."[8] A few pages later, she argued that Gras viewed business history as a new and separate field, descended from economic history but "not a branch of economic history."[9]

Larson at first outlined a very broad and inclusive definition of the subject, one that is particularly interesting in light of today's debate because it stressed social context: "Whatever the form of the business unit or of the system in which a given unit operates, business is a social institution. This is an essential concept that must never be overlooked. As a functional division of society, the division that supplies the material needs and a broad range of services, business is part of a large network of relationships of individuals and groups within society. In the highly complex and integrated society of today, these relationships include administrators, owners, laborers, business suppliers and customers, consumers, and the general public particularly as represented by government."[10] She also acknowledged that business operated in a world of ideas: "What business can or cannot do, as well as the way in which it must operate, is determined in part by the predominating concepts or theories in the society in which it exists."[11] She continued in this very rich vein, arguing that the fundamental subject of study was actually quite complex: "The business historian recognizes the business man as more than an economic man; all sides of his nature have a bearing on business and should be considered by the historian. Moreover, the business man works, as he lives, within his business, material, social, political, and cultural environment, an environment which is in a constant state of flux, cyclical and otherwise, and which is marked by conflicts, rigidities, contradictions, cultural lags, and brilliant creativeness. . . ."[12] But when it came time to consider "the flow of influence in the past from business to contemporary political, social, and American cultural life," an obviously important subject, she backed off: "This is, however, a subject which the student of those other fields of history should handle. The business historian hopes

[8] Henrietta M. Larson, *Guide to Business History* (Cambridge, Mass., 1948), 6.
[9] Ibid., 17.
[10] Ibid., 4.
[11] Ibid., 5.
[12] Ibid., 18.

that by providing facts and generalizations he will help political, social, and cultural historians to write more intelligently about business and business men as these touch their various fields. He should not attempt to do this himself."[13]

There were continued attempts to define the field in the 1950s. The first meeting of what was to become the BHC was held at Northwestern University (which had a Department of Business History) in February 1954, with eighteen people in attendance. Those attending included seven faculty from several departments at Northwestern (Howard Bennett, Joseph W. Ernst, Gene Lavengood, Kenneth H. Myers, Richard C. Overton, Charles Slater, and Harold F. Williamson), six from other midwestern universities (Donald Kemmerer and William Woodruff from Illinois, Robert Eckles from Purdue, Orange A. Smalley from Loyola, Albert K. Steigerwalt from Michigan, and William Fredrickson from North Park College), Joe B. Frantz from the University of Texas, Ralph Hidy from New York University, Donald McNeil from the Wisconsin Historical Society, and Eric Waugh, an international fellow from the University of Dublin. Papers were not read at the first meeting. There was a morning session devoted to a discussion of the teaching of business history and an afternoon session devoted to the writing of business history. But as Donald Kemmerer, who presided at the morning session, noted, "It was soon apparent that one man's business history is another man's economic history and still another's business management course with materials from the recent past. We spent the morning talking not about Business History Teaching so much as what Business History was."[14]

In 1958 Ralph Hidy organized a conference at the Harvard Business School to be devoted to a discussion of "the range and content of the

---

[13] Ibid., 31.

[14] Donald L. Kemmerer, diary comments on business history meeting, BHC Archives (currently in possession of the secretary-treasurer at the Hagley Museum and Library, Wilmington, Del.). Another participant at the meeting, Albert K. Steigerwalt, wrote in a letter to Kemmerer after the meeting, "I came away from the meeting impressed with the 'ferment' in the field of business history – or whatever we shall come to call it when it finally becomes differentiated from economic history." Steigerwalt to Kemmerer, April 7, 1954, BHC Archives. A second meeting in November 1954 at the University of Michigan drew thirty-four participants. All were from the Midwest with the exception of Ralph Hidy, soon to be appointed to the Straus Professorship at Harvard. There was no meeting in 1955, but the group met again in April 1956 at Indiana University in Bloomington, where for the first time substantive papers were delivered and discussed. The organization has met annually since then.

history of American business."[15] It followed lines similar to those of the
first BHC, which Hidy had attended. The morning session was devoted
to defining the subject, and the afternoon session was devoted to the
teaching and writing of business history. One of the premises of the
conference was that it was time the field moved beyond production of
company histories and toward some attempt at synthesis.[16] Following
some prepared remarks by Hidy and Thomas Cochran in the morning
session, the floor was opened for discussion, and "from that point on . . .
any previous appearances of unanimity on the scope and nature of business history disappeared."[17]

The Harvard group organized another conference in 1961, this time to
discuss "Business History as a Teaching Challenge." The discussion among
the fifty participants, however, quickly moved to the broader topic of "the
appropriate subject matter of business history, past accomplishments,
and future possibilities."[18] According to Arthur Johnson, it was agreed
that business history was not just company history, although it was essential that "the institutions, instruments and processes of business, the
firm or the businessman, defined in broad terms and many relationships"
remain a focal point. Company history was deemed to be quite useful
to others, as Gras and Larson had predicted. At the same time, "the conference put considerable emphasis on the need for comparative studies,
the use of tools from other disciplines, and the requirement to examine business in its total environment." Cochran commented that in order
to recruit first-class business historians, it was necessary to make "the
history of business an integral part of general history."[19] Finally, Arthur
H. Cole argued for an open approach: "It appears to me that business
history, if properly developed, holds numerous enticing opportunities
for research and writing – in a rather diverse rainbow of relationships

[15] Hidy to Kemmerer, October 1, 1958, BHC Archives. The conference was attended by
eighty people, nine of whom went on to become presidents of the BHC. A list of those
who attended is in the BHC Archives.

[16] Arthur M. Johnson, "Conference on the History of American Business," *Business History
Review* 33 (Summer 1959): 205. Hidy, Thomas Cochran, and others had been asked to
write a four-volume history of business in the United States, and another rationale for
holding the conference was to obtain ideas for this project, which was never completed.
R. C. Overton to Kemmerer, October 9, 1958, BHC Archives.

[17] Ibid.

[18] Arthur M. Johnson, "Where Does Business History Go from Here?" *Business History Review* 36 (Spring 1962): 11.

[19] Thomas C. Cochran, "Comment," *Business History Review* 36 (Spring 1962): 54.

and themes."[20] Forty years later, we are once again debating very similar issues – but with one significant difference. We debate them – explicitly or implicitly – in relation to the work of Alfred D. Chandler, Jr.

CHANDLER ENTERS

Chandler began giving conference presentations and publishing articles on the rise of big business in the mid-1950s and published *Strategy* and *Structure* in 1962. By 1967, Louis Galambos noted, in the first of several historiographical essays, that Chandler (with whom he was working on a project at the time) was pursuing "another new approach" to research in the field. Chandler provided "some new and important generalizations about the shifting forms of business organization and administration in the American economy. . . . His manner of analyzing the changing structure of business organizations and the related changes in strategy gave business historians the guidelines for a new synthesis. . . . For several reasons, future business historians will probably follow Chandler's lead and form their histories in terms of basic business strategies."[21] Among the reasons given by Galambos were the ability of business historians subscribing to this approach to use existing company histories and biographies (the strength of the Grasian tradition), the ability to draw on the ideas and research of the entrepreneurial school (thus making a connection to economic history), the ability to share ideas with behavioral scientists (especially sociologists and most specifically the Parsonian structuralist-functionalists), and the ability to "join hands with" the economists interested in the theory of the growth of the firm. This turned out to be an astutely accurate prediction of the course of business history. Several years later, in his second historiographical article, Galambos elaborated on what came to be known as the "organizational synthesis."[22] The *Visible Hand* was published in 1977, and in 1983 Galambos wrote that this book had "revitalized business history, in part by generating fruitful intersections between the subdisciplines and the history of technology, the analysis of economic growth, and the

---

[20] Arthur H. Cole, "What Is Business History?" *Business History Review* 36 (Spring 1962): 106. Cole especially called for comparative studies across nations and for examination of the relationship between business and the economic growth of nations. Ibid., 103.

[21] Louis Galambos, *American Business History* (Washington, D.C., 1967), 27–8.

[22] Louis Galambos, "The Emerging Organizational Synthesis in American History," *Business History Review* 44 (Autumn 1970): 279–90.

economics of the firm."[23] From there, Chandler's reputation continued to grow, to the extent that "non-Chandlerian approaches to the history of American business came to seem out-of-date."[24]

TO WHAT EXTENT DOES CHANDLER DOMINATE BUSINESS HISTORY? A CITATION-BASED APPROACH

Nobody familiar with the field would challenge Galambos's recent and straightforward statement that "the dominant paradigm in business history has for many years been the synthesis developed by Alfred D. Chandler, Jr."[25] No matter how it is measured or assessed, Chandler's work has been widely recognized both within and outside the field of business history.[26]

A very thoughtful historiographical assessment of Chandler by Richard R. John was published in the *Business History Review*.[27] John's purpose was to assess the impact of Chandler's *The Visible Hand* on scholarship in American history, but he actually went well beyond this, explicating Chandler's methodological approach, relating his personal background to that approach, and examining how those he terms "champions," "critics," and "skeptics" have used, expanded, or attacked Chandler's methods and conclusions. The article is an excellent survey of business history today, with comments on some of the directions in which it might be headed in the future. In terms of Chandler's impact, John concludes that it would be "hard to exaggerate" his influence on business history and that his work can be said to have shaped the "intellectual agenda"

---

[23] Louis Galambos, "Technology, Political Economy, and Professionalization: Central Themes of the Organizational Synthesis," *Business History Review* 57 (Winter 1983): 473.

[24] John, "Elaborations," 169.

[25] Louis Galambos, "Global Perspectives on Modern Business," *Business History Review* 71 (Summer 1997): 287.

[26] Galambos's comment was made in his capacity as chair of a session at the Organization of American Historians in 1997 devoted to Chandler's work. His work was also the subject of an "A" session at the Eleventh International Economic History Congress in Milan in 1994. This resulted in publication of Alfred D. Chandler, Jr., Franco Amatori, and Takashi Hikino, *Big Business and the Wealth of Nations* (Cambridge, 1997), which one reviewer described as a "mega-international revisiting of Chandler's analysis in *Scale and Scope* [which demonstrates] that Chandler's analysis survives period-stretching and geographical widening to a considerable extent." Roy Church, "Review of Chandler, et al.," *Business History* 40 (July 1988): 167.

[27] John, "Elaborations." The article was the subject of a forum on the listserv H-Business in February 2000: http://cs.muohio.edu/Archives/h-business/feb-2000/date.php

of business historians for the past several decades. John finds, however, that Chandler's influence on American history in general "may well be more limited than many business historians might wish or assume." This latter effect John attributes to the course of American historiography, where, he asserts, "cultural studies" have become the dominant tradition of scholarship. And, in fact, business history itself is moving in that direction – perhaps the primary reason for the current debate about the future of the field.

One method of assessing the impact of a particular scholar, or of a field of study such as business history, is to look at both how often and, very importantly, where work is cited. My original purpose in embarking on this exercise was to use journal citations as a rough quantitative measure of the extent to which Chandler's work dominated the field at the end of the twentieth century. Citations are a crude measure of impact, and comparisons can be invidious.[28] There are plenty of reasons to be wary, not the least of which is that a citation count may impart a false sense of precision: twenty citations does not imply twice the impact of ten citations. A citation is merely an unweighted count; a negative or critical citation counts just as much as a positive one, and a casual or perfunctory citation counts just as much as a citation to work that has had a profound impact on the author's own scholarship. Indeed, a work does not even have to be read to be cited. As Galambos noted in his introduction to the "Global Perspectives" session, "for some years, it was customary to perform a ritual bow toward [Chandler's] work in the first or second paragraph of any article appearing in the *Business History Review*." The implication is that the bow was made whether or not the article actually had anything to do with Chandler's work, but it still would appear to magnify the importance of that work. There is one other major caveat. The most readily available citation indexes include only journals, and books are more important than journal articles to historians. However, unless there is reason to believe that citation patterns would differ substantially and systematically between books and journal articles, and so long as care is used in their interpretation, journal citations can be used as a rough measure, however imperfect and imprecise, of impact. Journal editors certainly are aware of the role played by citations. In

[28] One can think of other quantitative measures of impact; book sales, for example, or number of syllabi on which the author's work appears, or number of graduate students produced. All of these, however, are more difficult to measure than journal citations.

his introduction to the issue containing John's article, Thomas McCraw touted its likely importance by stating, "It will doubtless be cited for many years to come."[29]

John, in fact, used the Arts and Humanities Citation Index as one measure to assess the relative impact of *The Visible Hand* in American history. He searched for citations to *The Visible Hand* in major history journals, including the *Journal of American History*, the *American Historical Review*, and *Reviews in American History*. He found that it was cited twenty-six times in these journals between 1978 and 1994, a total exceeding that of "most other works in business and economic history that had been published at roughly the same period."[30] He specifically listed only one other book that could strictly be called business history, Thomas Cochran's *Frontiers of Change: Early Industrialization in America* (New York, 1981),[31] which was cited six times. The other works mentioned were in economic and social history, and no one book dominated the others in terms of number of citations. The range for the books mentioned was twelve to forty-seven citations over the fifteen-year period.

Considering business history at the end of the twentieth century, I was interested in assessing the current impact of Chandler and, of necessity for comparison, selected others.[32] I performed a combined search of the (ISI) Arts and Humanities Citation Index and the ISI Social Science

[29] In "Note from the Editor," *Business History Review* 71 (Summer 1997).

[30] John, "Elaborations," 173–4. He also tabulated citations to *The Visible Hand* in the *Journal of Economic History* and found that it has been cited forty-two times over the same period. P. 167.

[31] In his article speculating on why Cochran's legacy in business history has been so modest, David Sicilia compared citations to Cochran versus Chandler in the *Social Science Citation Index* over the period 1966–85. While citations to Cochran remained stable over those years, citations to Chandler's work escalated to the point where there was a substantial difference. David B. Sicilia, "Cochran's Legacy: A Cultural Path Not Taken," *Business and Economic History* 24 (Fall 1995): 37.

[32] Robin Pearson recently conducted a citation-based study for the (British) Association of Business Historians. He considered all articles published between 1981 and 1990 in *Business History* and *Business History Review* and searched the online Bath Information and Data Services (BIDS) International Bibliography of the Social Sciences for citations to articles in those journals in the years 1981–96. For the *Business History Review* he found that just over a quarter of the articles were never cited and that there were an average of 3.2 citations to those that were. About 75 percent of the citations were in history journals, with 17 percent being in the journal itself. These results should make it clear that citations to articles are relatively rare and that a single citation is valuable. Robin Pearson, "Business History Citation Survey," *Business History News*, no. 11 (March 1996): 1–5.

Citation Index for the years 1996 and 1997.[33] I searched for citations to Chandler and to past presidents of the BHC (1987–98), as well as several others. The results may surprise no one: using citations as a measure of impact, Chandler dominates the field. His work was cited in 466 articles published in those two years; this was 6.4 times the next highest count and 1.6 times the number of articles citing the work of all eleven past presidents combined. This may not be news, but a closer examination of the citation patterns suggests why Chandler's impact has been so great. First, Chandler has produced a large body of work that has developed and elaborated a consistent theme. No single work dominates the pattern of citations. *The Visible Hand* (1977) was cited most frequently, but *Strategy and Structure* (1962) was close behind, with *Scale and Scope* (1990) a bit further behind.[34] Citations to these three books comprised roughly 65 percent of the total number of citations to Chandler's work. Four of his journal articles were very actively cited: his recent (1992) discussion of theory in the *Journal of Economic Perspectives*, his 1972 *Business History Review* article on anthracite coal and the industrial revolution, and two articles published in 1980 and 1984 that anticipated the arguments in *Scale and Scope*.

What is truly impressive is the range of journals containing articles that cite Chandler's work. They include, of course, all of the major business and economic history journals (*Business History, Business History Review, Journal of Economic History, Economic History Review*, and *Explorations in Economic History*). They also include journals in technological, military, agricultural, and regional history (*Technology and Culture, Agricultural History*, and *California History*, for example); major economics journals (*American Economic Review, Rand Journal of Economics, Economic Journal, Journal of Finance, Cambridge Journal of Economics, Public Choice*, etc.); management and organizational behavior journals (*Strategic Management Journal, Management Science, Journal of Marketing, Administrative Science Quarterly*, etc.); law reviews (*California, Texas, Cornell, Pittsburgh, Notre Dame*, etc.); and journals in sociology, political economy, and public administration. The only possibly relevant journals missing in the two

---

[33] I thank Pat Denault for searching ISI's combined online database. This search procedure was checked by consulting the printed version of the *Social Science Citation Index* and a different online version of the Arts and Humanities Citation Index. Although there were some differences in the articles identified, the orders of magnitude were quite similar.

[34] This part of the analysis is based on the total number of citations over the period 1988–98 to those works cited in 1996 and 1997.

years considered are the general history journals mentioned in John's analysis.

The purpose of this exercise was not to rank business historians; nevertheless, the data do warrant a few additional comments based on the citation patterns to the work of past presidents of the BHC. Chandler abstracted and generalized the experience of individual firms, even though he wrote several business biographies himself. As useful as they may be for other purposes, they are rarely cited by the authors of journal articles; case studies of single firms do not appear to have a large academic audience. Furthermore, although business history is an inherently interdisciplinary subject, individual business historians appeal to slightly different constituencies, to the extent that this can be inferred from the types of journals in which their work has recently been cited. Business historians trained as historians and residing in history or economics departments, such as Louis Galambos, Mansel Blackford, K. Austin Kerr, Edwin Perkins, and Mira Wilkins, tend to have their work cited by their colleagues in business history and in a wide variety of other history journals, but they are cited much less frequently in business and economics journals. Thomas McCraw and Richard H. K. Vietor, who maintain the strong presence of business history at the Harvard Business School, tend to have their work cited in business, management, law, and, to a lesser extent, sociology, public policy, and economics journals; they tend to be cited less frequently in history journals. William Lazonick and Leslie Hannah, both critics of the neoclassical model but with training in economics, tend to have their work cited in a blend of history, economics, and, to a lesser extent, sociology and business journals. These patterns may reflect very real differences in the potential audience for business history and should be considered carefully by those who strongly advocate moving the field in a particular direction. It is very clear, however, that taken as a group, the work of business historians is being used by a wide and diverse audience, which is quite encouraging and confirms the vibrancy of the field.

THE FUTURE OF BUSINESS HISTORY

Louis Galambos predicted in "Global Perspectives" in 1997 that Chandler's paradigm "has been so completely absorbed that we will in future years spend less time praising, bashing, modifying, or explicating it" – a persuasive prediction but one that, as Galambos's own work shows, has yet to be realized. His introductory comments to a series of papers on "Global Perspectives on Modern Business" and Richard John's historiographical examination of business history appeared in the same issue of *Business History Review* and suggest the same conclusion. Even as many business historians attempt to define their work and their field as distinct from Chandler's, his work still holds a firm grip on the way business historians do their work. Even business historians less explicitly indebted to Chandler, like Philip Scranton and Roger Horowitz in their summation of trends at the Hagley's "Future of Business History" conference, implicitly use his work as a point of departure.[35] And the last decade or so of presidential addresses at the annual BHC suggest that, even as the field becomes increasingly contested – particularly by what Galambos terms "cultural criticism" – business historians continue to define themselves in accordance with, in defiance of, but always in relation to Chandler's paradigm.

Richard John focuses his attention on the "many imaginative historians who have adopted, revised, or rejected Chandler's managerial thesis." He divides these into "champions" who elaborate on and share Chandler's basic approach, "critics" who probe anomalies between Chandler's framework and their own, and "skeptics" who challenge Chandler's basic assumptions and reject his argument. Champions include "several of his students and a number of colleagues and former colleagues at the Harvard Business School ... [as well as] historians of technology interested in the relationship of modern business enterprise to industrial research." They include scholars such as W. Bernard Carlson, David Hounshell, John Kenly Smith, Leonard Reich, William H. Becker, Richard Tedlow, Thomas McCraw, and Richard H. K. Vietor. Critics of Chandler "have fixed the spotlight on anomalies in his account" and are a varied group. Scholars such as Edwin Perkins, for example, have found Cochran's analysis more compelling than Chandler's for the early national period of American history. John considers that his own work on the post office falls into this category. Other scholars John places in this group include, for various reasons, Colleen Dunlavy, Charles W. McCurdy, Gavin Wright, Olivier Zunz, Martin Sklar, James Livingston, William Lazonick, and Louis Galambos. Skeptics, according to John, have a deeper quarrel with Chandler. He was either too easy on the modern industrial corporation from a moral standpoint or left too much out of the story (e.g., batch producers, small business, women, minorities). John includes in this list

[35] Philip Scranton and Roger Horowitz, " 'The Future of Business History': An Introduction," *Business and Economic History* 26 (Fall 1997): 1–4.

of scholars Michael J. Piore and Charles F. Sabel, John Ingham, Mansel
Blackford, Philip Scranton, and Gerald Berk, and argues that "From their
[the skeptics'] standpoint, it was morally indefensible to treat politics,
culture, and the environment as mere background factors that business
historians could in good conscience leave for others to explore." In
sum, John could not identify a consensus on the future of the field, but
argued, "it seems not only likely but also desirable that, in the future,
business historians will devote more attention to the wider political,
cultural, and social context in which American business has evolved.
In so doing, business historians can be expected to build on concepts
and insights drawn from cultural studies, semiotics, and other currently
influential approaches. But they would miss an opportunity for creative
synthesis if they abandoned the comparative institutional approach to
historical change that lies at the core of the Chandlerian tradition."[36]

Louis Galambos's introduction to the "Global Perspectives" session
actually is a brief historiographical essay. There he identifies what he
sees as five "post-Chandlerian lines of analysis."[37] Two of these are fundamentally Chandlerian and three are not. The two Chandlerian lines
include scholarship on the process of innovation (including here his
own work on Merck) and studies of the globalization of business in the
post–World War II era (including, for example, the work of Lazonick).
Although focused on Chandlerian firms or rooted in Chandlerian analysis, this recent work tends to be more textured and more appreciative
of the "rich matrix of cultural values, institutions, and social groups"
involved with innovation and globalization. The three non-Chandlerian
strands include one that attempts to bring politics back into our understanding of modern enterprise, one that refocuses attention on small
and medium-sized firms (the work of Philip Scranton, for example), and,
finally, one that he broadly terms "cultural studies," which, according
to Galambos, "clearly deserve[s] more attention than [it has] received."
Galambos sees changes in American historiography as the driving force
behind the increased attention being given in business history to "the cultural components of business behavior, to the social construction of business concepts, and to the gender elements in business that have been long
unexamined. . . ."

[36] John, "Elaborations," 176, 177, 180, 193–5, 198, 199–200. His last words, however, were
that if "present trends" continue, the "contextualist" approach will become "a dominant
mode of inquiry for business historians in the United States." P. 200.
[37] Galambos, "Global Perspectives," 287.

Although John and Galambos use different categories and employ different criteria to determine whose work falls into those categories, both measure the work of business historians in relation to Chandler's paradigm, whether their work uses the paradigm, tries to modify it, or attempts to shift business history away from it. Even where work is not defined explicitly in terms of Chandler, he remains a strong presence. Philip Scranton and Roger Horowitz detected four broad themes in the papers presented at the "Future of Business History" conference. The first theme considered entrepreneurial dynamics: "Some papers sought to extricate historical analysis of American business from a conventional attention to center firms and corporate research, envisioning a broader canvas for sketching other elements of the business enterprise."[38] This means that those formerly marginalized – women and African Americans, for example – can now be analyzed as economic agents. The second theme was culture: "The tendency, already eroding, to wall off enterprises, strategies and structures from their cultural surrounding received a resounding critique."[39] The third theme was the exploration of the boundaries of the firm. Formerly, the firm was the subject of study, but firms, as the argument goes, have played with their own boundaries, thus blurring what is private and what is public. The final theme was an intense interest in finding a more compelling theory (whether based on economics or sociology) upon which business historians could draw in the future. Scranton and Horowitz do not define their categories as faithful or unfaithful to Chandler; however, his presence – as "conventional attention" or a "tendency already eroding" or the less compelling theory – is manifest.

Every year, the president of the BHC delivers an address devoted more or less to the health and future of the field. Not surprisingly, these remarks over the past decade have touched on the same sorts of conflicts that John, Galambos, and Scranton and Horowitz describe in their historiographical work. Also not surprisingly – especially since presidents tend to be relatively senior and so trained during Chandler's heyday – Chandler's shadow looms large. Nevertheless, if the field were in fact steadily moving away from Chandler's paradigm, one might expect the most recently elected presidents to be increasingly skeptical about its value. But such is not the case. For the most part, the presidents remain largely within John's critical category: John identifies only one – 1997 president

---

[38] Scranton and Horowitz, "The Future," 2.
[39] Ibid., 3.

Mansel Blackford – as a skeptic. But the presidents' positions relative to
Chandler's work have not grown increasingly radical – "recursive" might
be the better word.[40] Blackford's immediate predecessor was Chandler's
student, William Becker, a champion in John's typology. What a review of
the last decade of presidential addresses reveals is not so much that the
field is moving beyond Chandler, but that his position in it is still hotly
contested.

Mira Wilkins (BHC president 1988), Wayne Broehl (1989), and Thomas
McCraw (1990) propose relatively conservative modifications to the
Chandlerian tradition. Wilkins was particularly concerned to define business history as a distinct field, one that should no longer be considered
a "stepchild" of economic history. Clearly inspired by Chandler's work
and concerned particularly with the global nature of business, she argued
that big firms were the key actors and called for an international, comparative "study of the growth and development of business as an institution."
Echoing Gras and Larson, she argued for keeping an explicitly internalist
view: ". . . we must not write for other audiences. If our work is excellent,
others will use it."[41] The following year, Wayne Broehl argued against the
focus on big firms. Following his own interest in individual firms, and
particularly family-owned enterprises (some of which are nevertheless
quite large, like Cargill, whose history he wrote), he called for further
"comparative research on family companies."[42] He argued that such studies would address such important questions as whether family firms are
more oriented toward the long run, are more entrepreneurial, or have a
different culture of labor relations. In 1990, Thomas McCraw – consistent
with his interest in business and public policy – focused on the need to
explore ideas about competition and competition policies, calling for
more comparative work across both industries and countries.[43]

Wilkins, Broehl, and McCraw found that, to varying degrees,
Chandler's work still unifies and defines the field, although each exposed
areas where the paradigm needs to be modified – to take into account,
for example, increasing globalization or the effects of public policy. The

[40] This is partly determined by the fact that the nominating committee for the president-
elect is composed of the three previous presidents. The trustees of the BHC have recently
adopted a revision of the by-laws that provides for an elected nominating committee
chaired by the president.

[41] Mira Wilkins, "Business History as a Discipline," *Business and Economic History* 17
(1988): 7.

[42] Wayne Broehl, "The Family Business," *Business and Economic History* 18 (1989): 10.

[43] Thomas K. McCraw, "Ideas, Policies, and Outcomes in Business History," *Business and
Economic History* 19 (1990): 2.

work of 1991 BHC president William Lazonick, on the other hand, marked a fairly radical departure from Wilkins's insistence on self-sufficiency. Lazonick called instead for making the field more interdisciplinary in order to broaden its appeal and its efficacy. Lazonick averred that neo-classical economics is in a "sorry state"[44] for several reasons: economists see markets before social relations, while the opposite should be the case; modern economists' obsession with static equilibrium means that they are not good at studying economic development; and, as Gras had argued many years before him, economists have great difficulty comprehending what goes on inside the firm. Obviously impressed, however, by Schumpeter, Marx, and Galbraith, he engaged in a study of the cotton textile industry in order "to do a detailed case study that could reveal the dynamic interaction of organization and technology in capitalist development."[45] He argued that business historians can help economists understand how the economy works, but said that "if business history is to have an impact on economics, our comprehension of history needs to be diffused to economists."[46] However, he was pessimistic about the prospects for such diffusion because economics departments are no longer requiring economic history, let alone offering business history. Nor did he believe that business history is being offered in many history departments. He noted that "the other possibility for the teaching of business history, and one that offers more scope than history departments for integrating business history with economic analysis, is business schools,"[47] an idea he claimed the Harvard Business School has been important in fostering; however, he questioned the amount of diffusion of business history from that base. Finally, he applauded the fact that "the Business History Conference has brought together academics from different disciplines and with different perspectives.... Increasingly, research in business history has become well-integrated with research in labor history, history of technology, history of science, political history, intellectual history, and even economic history."[48]

Like Lazonick, 1992 BHC president Louis Galambos argued that the future of business history would depend on its ability to build on its

---

[44] William Lazonick, "Business History and Economics," *Business and Economic History* 20 (1991): 1.

[45] Ibid., 7.

[46] Ibid., 11.

[47] Ibid., 12. He mentioned that we do not know, in fact, where business history is being offered. This is still the case.

[48] Ibid.

interdisciplinary nature, particularly as it made room for cultural studies. Galambos was quite aware that increased interdisciplinarity would
move the field away from Chandler, arguing, in fact, that while Chandler's
success allowed business historians to gain self-confidence, it also made
them oblivious to new trends: "Chandler emphasized construction, not
deconstruction. Instead of opening the field toward culture, he narrowed
the scope of business history while greatly increasing its analytical depth
and intellectual significance. His opening, as it turned out, was toward
economics, organizational analysis, and comparative institutional history,
instead of cultural history."[49] Nevertheless, Galambos – much more explicitly than Lazonick – values the center that Chandler provides. At
the same time that he recognizes "deconstruction ... [as] philosophi-
cally akin to the new emphasis upon history as culture"[50] – an emphasis
he believes business history must adopt if it is to "weave the findings
of business history into the fabric of general American history"[51] – he
also maintains that deconstruction, combined with increasing specialization, has tended to fracture knowledge and make impossible the kind of
Chandlerian synthesis that made business history viable. But Galambos
remains confident that a new general synthesis is obtainable, although it
will necessitate "reach[ing] out beyond the confines of our subdiscipline
as it is currently understood. We will no longer be able to avoid dealing
with the question of power, its changing distribution, and in particular
the impact of business' power upon American society."[52] This means
incorporating "the best work being done by deconstructionists and by
cultural and gender historians ... without shifting our primary focus from
institutions to culture."[53] If reforms are accepted, if business historians
learn "from some of those who hold our work in greatest contempt,"[54]
then they will be capable of making important contributions to history
("our profession") and to society.

If Galambos's emphasis on synthesis can be seen as a cautionary step
back from Lazonick's embracing of a broader interdisciplinary approach,
K. Austin Kerr's 1993 address can be construed as almost reactionary. Ac-
knowledging that "business history connects to the rest of history, and

[49] Louis Galambos, "What Makes Us Think We Can Put Business Back into American History,"
   Business and Economic History 21 (1992): 2.
[50] Ibid., 6.
[51] Ibid., 2.
[52] Ibid., 7.
[53] Ibid., 8–9.
[54] Ibid., 11.

we should be proud of our roles in developing large subjects of understanding,"[55] Kerr warned against giving business history over too much to academic fashion: "Business history is rooted intellectually in the social sciences, including of course economics but also in sociology and political science, and to some extent this is disconnected from some of the now fashionable intellectual traditions in the humanities, including deconstruction."[56] Identifying two traditions within business history, one "focus[ing] on the firm and the patterns of development of the firm . . . [t]he other . . . ha[ving] more to do with the environment of the firm, of how society acts upon the firm and vice versa,"[57] he praised the "compelling" work being done that connects the development of business firms with the broader American society in which they operate. His own study, with Mansel Blackford, of BFGoodrich "leads me to think that there is much exciting work to be done in the history of the firm, work that connects our fragmented fields into 'social and economic history.' "[58] But he insisted that any incorporation of cultural studies into business history take place firmly on business history's own terms, lamenting that those now in "power" in the humanities hold business history in contempt "because race, class, and gender are not the only variables of our central concern."[59]

Like Kerr, Edwin Perkins (1995) expressed the concern that certain forms of cultural studies might be inimical to business history: ". . . business history has become increasingly marginalized in the broader scheme of things. Gender, class, and ethnicity are all the rage. With few exceptions, most historians' attitudes toward our capitalist system and the majority of its business leaders are hostile and suspicious."[60] Perkins argued that all history is "one immense and unending case study, and that our task is to sift through the mountains of evidence and figure out what is really important within a given context or in response to a given question."[61] One of Chandler's critics, according to John, Perkins urged business historians to pay more attention to the colonial and early national period, where there was substantial growth before industrialization, and he stressed the importance of institutions, like banks, for economic development. But he strongly averred that business history

---

[55] K. Austin Kerr, "Connections," *Business and Economic History* 22 (Fall 1993): 2.
[56] Ibid.
[57] Ibid., 3.
[58] Ibid., 6.
[59] Ibid.
[60] Edwin J. Perkins, "Banks and Brokers," *Business and Economic History* 24 (Fall 1995): 6.
[61] Ibid., 1.

must defend its own interests and methods, noting that the popularity of cultural studies might ironically turn out to be good for the discipline: "by rejecting us and forcing us to stick to our knitting, the broader historical profession has prompted economic and business historians to make enormous strides over the last quarter century in virtually every topic area."[62]

The 1996 president, William Becker, was a student of both Chandler and Galambos. According to John, Becker is a champion of the Chandlerian paradigm. He has been engaged in a study of big business in the twentieth century – a synthesis "designed to examine the political and social, as well as the economic and organizational, dimensions of large-scale enterprise. . . ."[63] Nevertheless, he too has "become interested in what business historians might learn from those engaged in, broadly speaking, cultural studies."[64] He quite clearly saw a need to add further dimensions to the structural functional conception of the large firm: "While structural functionalism has great explanatory power, it is nevertheless rooted in a limited behavioral model of enterprise development that, in the interest of methodological rigor, has left out politics, society, and culture."[65] He notes that not everyone will agree that business history should go in this direction, since current trends in American historiography are controversial. But he sees an opportunity for business historians to contribute to the debate over the role of government in the post–World War II economy, especially in relation to the "boundaries" of the firm in high-tech industries.

Mansel Blackford, 1997 president and a skeptic in John's terms, nevertheless acknowledged the role Chandler's *Strategy and Structure* played in getting him interested in business history. Having written a number of company histories, he thinks they "remain a fruitful way to approach business history and, indeed, American history."[66] However, he stresses that "business historians need to consider seriously the context of business – that is, business in its social, political, and cultural settings, for business decisions are not made in a vacuum."[67] While Blackford expressed the belief that business history is very much alive and is moving in exciting

---

[62] Ibid., 6.

[63] William H. Becker, "Managerial Culture and the American Political Economy," *Business and Economic History* 25 (Fall 1996): 4.

[64] Ibid.

[65] Ibid.

[66] Mansel Blackford, "Business History and Beyond," *Business and Economic History* 26 (Winter 1997): 284.

[67] Ibid.

new directions, he simultaneously worried that "our field is in trouble."[68] He argued that it is still not fully accepted in the academy, remains too insular, and speaks too narrowly to its own practitioners and not enough to the rest of the world.

What the presidents' addresses thus point to is not steady movement away from Chandler's work; instead, their remarks reflect the continuing influence of that work even as they evidence the general restlessness in the field and the concern that business history may be becoming too fragmented. However, if these addresses are any indication, it would appear that when this sense of fragmentation is high, business history as a discipline responds by moving back toward what still unifies it – the Chandlerian paradigm. In fact, it seems that a wholesale movement away from Chandler may be less likely than the development of some new synthesis of the type that Galambos explicitly and Becker and Blackford implicitly seek – one that would seek to understand institutions in the broader context of the complicated political and social forces that affect them.

WHAT IS GETTING PUBLISHED IN BUSINESS HISTORY JOURNALS?

In addition to books,[69] the major outlets for work in U.S. business history are refereed journals and conference proceedings volumes. The leading U.S. journal in the field has been the *Business History Review*, but business history can be found in economic history journals and journals in related fields, such as the history of technology, women's studies, management, accounting, and finance. Articles on U.S. business history have been published frequently in the British journal *Business History*. The BHC proceedings volume, *Business and Economic History*, is the leading venue for publication of conference papers.

In order to get a sense of what type of work is being presented and getting published, I examined the articles in two journals over a five-year period: 1993-7 in the case of *Business and Economic History* and 1992-6 in the case of *Business History Review*.[70] The articles in

[68] Ibid., 285.
[69] A recently published bibliography lists just over 4,400 books in business history. Francis Goodall, Terry Gourvish, and Steven Tolliday, eds., *International Bibliography of Business History* (London and New York, 1997).
[70] Review essays, a list of the founding dates of Fortune 500 companies, and an article describing the holdings of the Pennsylvania Historical Society were excluded from consideration.

Business History Review are refereed. The articles in *Business and Economic History* are not refereed, but they have been screened in a variety of ways over the years.[71] I categorized all articles by nationality of author and subject (presented in Table 1, Part 1). I excluded non-U.S. scholars writing on non-U.S. topics from further consideration and categorized the remaining articles (all either on U.S. subjects or written by U.S. scholars) by broad topic and subject type (Table 1, Parts 2 and 3). Finally, if an article had a particular emphasis or was a cross-national comparison, I recorded that as well (Table 1, Part 4). Although most articles could be categorized fairly easily, judgment was needed in some cases.

There were 55 articles from *Business History Review* and 199 articles from *Business and Economic History* published over the respective five-year periods that were analyzed. The first thing I examined was the nationality of authors[72] and the subjects about which they wrote. The BHC has increasingly considered itself to be an international association and has encouraged international participation. The *Business History Review* has always been receptive to work by international scholars. The numbers and percentages for *Business and Economic History* are slightly skewed toward international participation and subjects because the 1997 annual meeting was held jointly with the Association of Business Historians in Glasgow, Scotland. Both journals appear to be open to work on countries other than the United States, with roughly a quarter to a third of the work published focusing on business history in other countries (Table 1, Part 1).[73]

---

[71] For example, between 1993 and 1996, articles published in the second issue each year went through a competitive process in which a committee selected them from among papers submitted about two weeks prior to the meetings. An annual dissertation session, where summaries of recently completed dissertations are presented, has been very competitive in recent years. The dissertation summaries are included in the analysis. The other papers are screened at the proposal stage by the president-elect, who serves as program chair, but are not refereed. Some of the papers are invited. About three-quarters of the papers presented at the meeting are subsequently published in the proceedings volumes. Presidential addresses were excluded from this analysis.

[72] When nationality was in doubt, I used the location of the university with which authors were affiliated. The small number of papers with a U.S. and a non-U.S. coauthor were placed in the U.S. category. It is perhaps unfortunate that cross-national collaboration of this kind is rare.

[73] This includes the relatively small number of papers that were comparative. See the figures under "Special Emphasis" in the table. Over the period 1993–7, slightly over 10 percent of the articles in the British journal *Business History* were on U.S. subjects.

Table 1. Summary of Journal Article Characteristics

	BHR 1992–6		BEH 1993–7	
	#	%	#	%
Part 1				
Nationality of Scholar and Topic				
U.S. on U.S. (or comparative)	34	62	115	58
Foreign on U.S. (or comparative)	7	13	14	7
U.S. on foreign (or comparative)	8	14	28	14
Foreign on foreign	6	11	42	21
TOTAL	55	100	199	100
Part 2				
Sector (U.S. Subjects or Scholars)				
Industry/manufacturing	25	51	57	36
Mining/agriculture/fishing/oil exploration	2	4	8	5
Service (banking, transport, medical, utilities)	5	10	35	22
Retail/wholesale	2	4	8	5
Entertainment	2	4	6	4
General business (including theory)	8	17	40	26
Other	5	10	3	2
TOTAL	49	100	157	100
Part 3				
Subject type				
Single firm or entrepreneur	14	29	39	25
Single industry	14	29	62	39
U.S. multinational abroad	3	6	3	2
Foreign multinational or investor in U.S.	0	0	2	1
Management or accounting history	3	6	8	5
Theoretical or methodological	1	2	20	13
Multiple industries, sectors, or regions	11	22	23	15
Other	3	6	0	0
TOTAL	49	100	157	100
Part 4				
Special emphasis[a]				
Technology, research & development	3	6	12	8
Public policy, government	7	14	28	18
Gender	1	2	7	4
Ethnicity or race	2	4	5	3
Comparative (cross-national, excluding multinationals)	0	0	9	6
TOTAL	13	26	61	39

[a] Percentages are relative to the total number of articles and do not total 100%.

The next step was to examine the types of subjects studied (Table 1, Part 2).[74] The articles were categorized along two dimensions, sector of the economy and subject type. It is evident that the study of industry or manufacturing dominates the attention of U.S. business historians, although this is more prevalent in the *Business History Review* than in *Business and Economic History*. This is not surprising given that Chandler's paradigm stresses the rise of big business and managerial capitalism, and that manufacturing industries played a crucial role in the transformation Chandler and others discuss (even though railroads were the nation's first businesses to adopt modern management structures). Furthermore, the *Business History Review* has been closely associated with the work of Chandler, and this may have created some self-selection in terms of manuscripts submitted to the journal, possibly contributing to the larger proportion of articles on manufacturing. Services have been receiving slightly more attention in *Business and Economic History*, and some have argued that more work should be done in this area.[75]

Articles were also categorized by subject type. The striking finding here is the extent to which work in U.S. business history still focuses on a single firm or entrepreneur or on firms in a single industry. If multinationals are included with these, roughly two-thirds of the articles published in both journals combined fall into these categories. Of course, studies of firms or industries provide the raw data for broader or synthetic studies. Space limitations in articles also may preclude presentation of broader, comparative, or synthetic work. However, it may be the case that most business historians, whether taking a traditional approach or a cultural approach, still focus on the study of one business or one industry at a time because, when well conceived, that remains the best approach to advancing understanding.[76]

Two differences in publication patterns between the two journals are worthy of comment. The *Business History Review* has published a

---

[74] Foreign authors writing on foreign subjects were excluded from this analysis. The vast majority of these were European authors writing on European subjects, with fewer articles on Asia and very few on any other area of the world.

[75] In an article critical of the disproportionately large effect attributed to manufacturing (by Chandler and others) in explaining American economic growth in the twentieth century, Les Hannah argued that "it is in the service sector that the distinctive nature of the twentieth-century American productivity miracle must principally be sought.... There is a critical lesson here for U.S. business history." Leslie Hannah, "The American Miracle, 1875–1950, and After: A View in the European Mirror," *Business and Economic History* 24 (Winter 1995): 202–3.

[76] I thank Richard John for emphasizing this point in e-mail correspondence.

slightly greater proportion of articles covering multiple industries, whole sectors of the economy, or the role of business in regional development. An examination of the yearly trend indicates that these types of articles have increased in number in the most recent years, which may indicate a movement away from the single-firm, single-industry emphasis.[77] On the other hand, the annual meeting of the BHC in recent years has been the site of several vigorous methodological discussions focusing on where the discipline is headed. In addition, the first issue of the journal in 1997 contained papers from the Hagley conference on the "Future of Business History," resulting in a greater proportion of papers on theoretical or methodological subjects.

Table 1, Part 4 presents my attempt to categorize articles along several other dimensions. Business history is intimately related to technological history (a crucial component of Chandler's model) because it is the mechanism by which technical changes are implemented. Furthermore, business does not operate in a political vacuum; it is both affected by and shapes public policy. In recent years, issues of gender, race, and ethnicity have attracted the interest of business historians. If an article had a definite emphasis on one of these areas, I placed it in the appropriate category. Finally, articles that used cross-national comparisons were noted. A large minority of articles published had one or another of these attributes, a policy dimension being the most common. A relatively small proportion of published articles in business history have dealt with issues of gender, race, and ethnicity.

CONCLUSION

It is quite likely that while business historians will continue to pose their own particular questions, they will increasingly incorporate issues of culture and society into their work. Certainly, changes in that direction have been called for and occasionally warned against – not just recently, but over the entire history of the field – prompting some concerns about where the field is headed. At this point, however, publications in major journals and presentations at major conferences suggest that the field may be more unified than some of its practitioners perceive it to be. Despite business historians' diverse attitudes toward Chandler's work – whether, to use John's categories, they are champions, critics, or skeptics – that

---

[77] The numbers are small enough that this might be a random fluctuation.

work continues to provide a focus and, just as important, an appeal and a usefulness to a very broad audience.

Business historians must remain aware of the danger of fragmentation that besets any interdisciplinary field, especially one containing as much diversity as business history. As business historians respond to the specific trends in their constituent fields, they must be aware that if they respond only to those fields, they risk narrowing their audience and stifling the open, challenging, and broad-based cross-disciplinary discussions that kept the field vital, expanding, and responsive at the end of the twentieth century. It is imperative that these discussions be continued in books, in articles, and at conferences as business historians elaborate the Chandlerian paradigm or search for a new paradigm capable of creating an even more meaningful synthesis.

KEY WORKS

Chandler, Alfred D., Jr. *The Visible Hand: The Managerial Revolution in American Business*. Cambridge, Mass., 1977.

Cochran, Thomas C. *Frontiers of Change: Early Industrialization in America*. New York, 1981.

Galambos, Louis, "Global Perspectives on Modern Business." *Business History Review* 71 (Summer 1997): 287–90.

Gras, N. S. B. "Past, Present, and Future of the Business Historical Society." *Bulletin of the Business Historical Society*, 24 (March 1950): 1–12.

John, Richard R. "Elaborations, Revisions, Dissents: Alfred D. Chandler, Jr.'s, *The Visible Hand* after Twenty Years." *Business History Review* 71 (Summer 1997): 151–200.

Lamoreaux, Naomi R., Daniel M. G. Raff, and Peter Temin. "New Economic Approaches to the Study of Business History." *Business and Economic History* 26 (Fall 1997): 57–79.

Larson, Henrietta M. *Guide to Business History*. Cambridge, Mass., 1948.

6

British and Dutch Business History

GEOFFREY JONES AND KEETIE E. SLUYTERMAN

This essay compares the business history literatures of Britain and the Netherlands. Although these two European countries are geographically – and, some would argue, culturally – proximate and share a similar commercial and colonial past, their historians have often looked elsewhere, especially to Germany and the United States, when making international comparisons. Moreover while U.S. and other foreign scholars have made substantive contributions to the British literature – and have often compared Britain unfavorably with their own countries – the business history of the Netherlands has been largely ignored by the rest of the world. This essay will identify both the commonalities and differences in the business histories of the two countries and how they have been interpreted.

There can be little dispute that the central research agendas in the two countries have been predominantly national. Although British business history research covering the past 100 years is extensive and rich, it has a strong preoccupation with the theme of "failure." The origins of Britain's industrial decline have been firmly placed as far back as at least the late nineteenth century, when the nation was slow to develop the new industries of electrical engineering and dyestuffs. For each successive generation, failure and missed opportunities have been relentlessly examined. Only since the 1980s have business historians begun to show

that this theme has been overdone and have moved on to new preoccupations.[1] The Dutch have had similar "failure" debates, to which business
historians have made substantial contributions both for the eighteenth
century and to explain why the Netherlands was so slow to industrialize
in the nineteenth century.[2] In contrast, since the Dutch business sector
performed well for much of the twentieth century, Dutch business historians have not been haunted by the specter of failure that has hung over
their British counterparts.

Both British and Dutch business history developed in a highly empirical fashion. Commissioned company histories were the main research vehicle. However, the British also produced more general studies and have
been more prone to engage in debates with one another. Moreover, the
British, despite their deep attachment to empiricism and their inherent
suspicion of abstract generalizations, have proved more willing than the
Dutch to provide syntheses. Leslie Hannah, inspired by Chandler's work
in the United States, published the first modern-style British business
history, *The Rise of the Corporate Economy* (London, 1976). Revised in
1983, Hannah's book described the growth of big business in the United
Kingdom. The 1990s saw the publication of textbooks by Maurice Kirby
and Mary Rose, John Wilson and David Jeremy, which have drawn the
field together. In contrast, there remains no general history of Dutch business, although there are a number of industry-level studies, often written
as dissertations.

THE INSTITUTIONAL FRAMEWORK

A brief survey of the institutional setting of business history explains
some of the differences in the nature of the British and Dutch literatures.
Business history as a separate discipline is young in the Netherlands, even
though the tradition of writing business monographs is long-standing
and the wider economic history community has always concerned
itself with issues now regarded as business history. The Netherlands
Economic History Archives (NEHA), founded in 1914, played an active
role in preserving company archives. However during the postwar
decades, the overall preoccupation of Dutch economic historians was

[1] Barry Supple, "Fear of Failing: Economic History and the Decline of Britain," *Economic History Review* 47, no. 3 (1994): 441–58.

[2] Richard Griffiths, "Backward, Late or Different?" In *The Economic Development of the Netherlands since 1870*, ed. Jan Luiten van Zanden (Cheltenham, 1996), 1–22.

macroeconomic. Company histories were written mainly by journalists or writers, which often resulted in readable books with limited scholarly depth.

In the mid-1970s, Johan de Vries began to promote business history as a special field of interest for the academic world. He brought foreign, especially American, trends and debates to the attention of the Dutch audience.[3] From the 1980s on, the number of academics interested in business history increased, and an informal Dutch association of business historians was set up, the Werkgroep Bedrijfsgeschiedenis (Business History Study Group), later relaunched as Stichting Bedrijfsgeschiedenis (Business History Foundation) in 1994. There followed a new publication venue that was a yearbook on the history of business and technology. After the merger with the Neha yearbook, the new title of the periodical became *Neha-Jaarboek voor economische, bedrijfs- en techniekgeschiedenis*. Nevertheless the institutional foundations of business history in the Netherlands remain fragile, although there are centers at Rotterdam and Utrecht that are active in writing commissioned research.

The two main sources of new research in the Netherlands are the dissertations published by Ph.D. students – some of whom leave the academic profession – and company histories. Spin-offs of both types of research find their way into articles and conference papers. The commissioned histories have included many business sectors, as well as the interaction between external circumstances and internal development of the companies. Well-known companies such as ABN-AMRO, Philips Electronics, Hoogovens (Corus after 1999), CSM, and Heineken have been objects of study. Dissertations often deal with branches as a whole, such as the beet sugar, machine-building, and textile industries or the cigar and brickmaking industries. Others touch on specific themes such as entrepreneurship, company financing, technological developments, social policy or privatization, and state support for failing industries.[4]

---

[3] Johan de Vries, "De stand der bedrijfsgeschiedenis in Nederland," *Economisch- en Sociaal-Historisch Jaarboek* 37 (1974): 1–22.

[4] For more extensive references to the works of Dutch business historians, see Keetie E. Sluyterman, "Nederlandse bedrijfsgeschiedenis: De oogst van vijftien jaar," *Neha-jaarboek voor economische, bedrijfs- en techniekgeschiedenis* 62 (1999): 350–87. This article is available online at www.neha.nl. For further research into Dutch business history literature, two bibliographies are available: Ard Kramer (compiler), *Bibliografie voor de bedrijfsgeschiedenis* (Rotterdam, 1993), and Mieke van Baarsel (compiler), *Supplement op de bibliografie 1993* (Rotterdam, 1999).

In Britain, business history was also slow to establish itself as a separate discipline, but it became strongly entrenched in the numerous economic history departments that became a distinctive feature of that country's university system. By the 1970s, the first dedicated university post in business history – a lectureship at Glasgow University – had been established. Subsequently, many business historians held and continue to hold established posts in economic history, history, and economics departments, and since the 1990s the discipline has also flourished in some business schools. The result is that a substantial number of business historians hold permanent university posts in Britain, even though perhaps fewer than a dozen posts have the name "business history" in their titles.

As in the Netherlands, the subject has also built up the infrastructure of a separate discipline in Britain. Interest in business history was formalized early, in 1934, when the Business Archives Council was established by a group of academics and business leaders. This society made (and makes) a major contribution by registering business records and holding annual conferences. A journal, *Business History*, initially edited at the University of Liverpool, was founded in 1958, but a society, the Association of Business Historians, followed only in 1990. The past decade saw a number of new journals launched to cover niche areas, including *Accounting, Business and Financial History*, and the *Journal of Industrial History*. From the late 1970s on, a number of research centers in business history were also founded at British universities. The pioneer was the Business History Unit at the London School of Economics, established in 1978. Later, other centers were established at such universities as Glasgow, Leeds, Nottingham, and Reading.

The different institutional setting of business history in the Netherlands and Britain has affected the nature of the literature. The subject is much more entrenched in universities in the United Kingdom, which has permitted its practitioners to develop business history far more extensively away from the format of commissioned histories. It may also have permitted the British a more critical assessment of business, insofar as literature largely based on commissioned histories is necessarily biased toward established and successful firms.

MANAGERIAL AND FAMILY CAPITALISM

British and Dutch business historians have shared the general preoccupation of their colleagues elsewhere of explaining the growth of large firms and the rise of professional managers. In the British case, the study of this subject long predated the influence of Chandler's work. The publication of Charles Wilson's pioneering study of the Anglo-Dutch company Unilever in 1954 was followed by a host of other substantive scholarly studies of major manufacturing and service firms that mapped out the reasons behind their growth and explored their internal structures.[5] These studies represent the first, classic generation of modern British business history, and they remain standard works of reference.

The company studies produced in this era were often wide-ranging, covering topics from marketing to labor relations, and it was only with the impact of Chandler's work that a more narrow focus on the relationship between corporate size, strategy, and internal organization began to emerge in the literature. Britain was the first country Chandler systematically compared to the United States. In 1980 he published a key article contrasting the much slower growth of modern managerial enterprise in Britain to the rapid rise in the United States. In this article, Chandler explored the continuance of family firms in Britain and the slower appearance of managerial hierarchies, which he dated only to the 1930s. The upshot was that British firms were slower to take up mass production and mass distribution. As a result, they fell behind the Americans in a swath of industries. At the same time, a reluctance to employ professional and trained managers produced an amateurish managerial cadre far from equipped to compete in industries such as chemicals, machinery, and electrical equipment.[6]

Ten years later, Chandler's critique of British business was deepened and extended in *Scale and Scope* (Cambridge, Mass., 1990). It was in Britain that Chandler found the most striking contrasts to the developments he had analyzed in the United States before 1945. The British failed to make the three-pronged investment in production, marketing, and management. As a result, they failed to become the "first movers" in the new industries of the Second Industrial Revolution. Although the

---

[5] Charles Wilson, *The History of Unilever*, 2 vols. (London, 1954); T. C. Barker, *Pilkington Brothers and the Glass Industry* (London, 1960); A. E. Musson, *Enterprise in Soap and Chemicals, Joseph Crosfield & Sons Ltd, 1815-1965* (Manchester, 1965); Peter Matthias, *Retailing Revolution* (London, 1967); D. C. Coleman, *Courtaulds: An Economic and Social History*, 2 vols. (London, 1969); W. J. Reader, *Imperial Chemical Industries: A History*, 2 vols. (Oxford, 1970, 1975); Barry Supple, *The Royal Exchange Assurance* (Cambridge, 1970); B. W. E. Alford, *W. D. & H. O. Wills and the Development of the U.K. Tobacco Industry, 1786-1965* (London, 1973).

[6] Alfred D. Chandler, Jr., "The Growth of the Transnational Industrial Firm in the United States and the United Kingdom: A Comparative Analysis," *Economic History Review* 33, no. 3 (1980): 396-410.

British caught up in some industries, such as chemicals and petroleum, during the interwar years, many weaknesses remained. The blame for the situation lay with "personal capitalism." This was partly associated with the continuing prominence of family-owned firms, but the concept was widened by Chandler to include personal styles of management. These styles hindered the creation of large firms, leaving many sectors of British industry dominated by small, highly specialized companies with very thin managerial hierarchies. At the same time, these British personal capitalists had a strong preference for short-term income rather than long-term growth in assets.

An extension of Chandler's interpretation came in William Lazonick's *Business Organization and the Myth of the Market Economy* (Cambridge, 1991). He argued that British "proprietary capitalism" in localized industrial regions, where economies were external rather than internal to the firm, became inappropriate when international competitive advantage shifted toward capital-intensive and technologically sophisticated production.

The consequences of British "personal" or "proprietary" capitalism have been widely debated over the past twenty years. In general, British scholars have agreed that British companies had a variety of failings; however, they have difficulty accepting the generalization that personal capitalism was the root cause of them. Roy Church, in his "The Limitations of the Personal Capitalism Paradigm" (*Business History Review*, 1990), argued that Britain did not have more family firms than the United States or Germany before 1945 and that British personal capitalists did not have a systematic bias toward short-term income over long-term growth in assets. D. C. Coleman stressed (*Business History*, 1987) that one of the most noticeable "failings" of British firms – their slow response to the need for change – was as apparent in managerial firms as in family firms. Most other authors have similarly found it difficult to correlate business strategies with managerial or personal capitalism, suggesting that the nature of the British business culture, rather than ownership form per se, may be the most appropriate unit of analysis. From another perspective, recent research on the profitability of Lancashire cotton textile spinners and weavers has questioned Lazonick's blanket critique of the specialized and family-run nature of the industry.[7]

---

[7] Geoffrey Jones, "Great Britain: Big Business, Management, and Competitiveness in Twentieth Century Britain," in *Big Business and the Wealth of Nations*, eds. Alfred D. Chandler, Jr., Franco Amatori, and Takashi Hikino (Cambridge, 1997), 102–38; J. S. Toms, "The Finance

Partly in response to the Chandlerian critique, a much richer and more complex picture of British family firms has emerged in recent literature. The so-called Buddenbrooks syndrome has been widely criticized, not so much because of the well-known examples of dynamic, long-lived British family firms, but because of the low survival rate of family firms. In part because of the difficulties of arranging generational succession, very few firms survived for more than a single generation in nineteenth-century Britain. If family firms contributed to any failure in late-nineteenth-century Britain, the problem was a slowing in the rate of formation of new firms. At the same time, Mary Rose and others have reexamined the strategies of British family firms, stressing not their failure to build U.S.-style diversified and vertically integrated corporations, but their strategic evolution within the context of the local communities in which they operated. This has given rise to a rich literature on the role of informal networks in which facilitated information flows have provided alternatives to internalization and shaped diversification strategies. Rose's *Firms, Networks and Values* (Cambridge, 2000) explores these themes in the case of the cotton textile industry in a wide-ranging Anglo-American comparative study.

The Chandlerian synthesis regarding Britain has been criticized or qualified in other respects. It has been shown that whatever the situation in manufacturing, large British firms did emerge in the service sector. In a major revisionist study, "The Anatomy of Big Business: Aspects of Corporate Development in the Twentieth Century" (*Business History*, 1991), Peter Wardley demonstrated the importance of service-providing companies in the British corporate economy. He based his findings on revised estimates of the fifty largest British companies (by market capitalization) in 1904–5, 1934–5, and 1985.

Moreover, the weak performance of the British economy after the Second World War coincided with changes that brought it much closer to U.S. managerial capitalism. Merger waves, especially in the 1960s and 1980s, resulted in the most concentrated economy in Europe.[8] Personal capitalism and family ownership were swept away. Britain became a classic big-business economy, with unusually unimportant small and medium-sized sectors, where ownership was separated from control. In their

and Growth of the Lancashire Cotton Industry, 1870–1914," *Business and Economic History* 26, no. 2 (1997): 323–9.

[8] Derek F. Channon, *The Strategy and Structure of British Enterprise* (London, 1973); George A. Luffman and Richard Reed, *The Strategy and Performance of British Industry* (London, 1987).

major study of the strategies and structures of large British, French, and German firms from the 1950s to the 1990s, Whittington and Mayer found no clear correlation between performance and the business system.[9]

There is a continuing debate on the extent to which British business was actually "Americanized" after 1945. A considerable number of scholars have argued that the British manufacturing industry was resistant to the adoption of American management and production techniques, and that this contributed to Britain's poor postwar business performance.[10] However, in a study of the engineering sector, Zeitlin has shown how often hybrid production forms were developed by British companies in the first postwar decade. The subsequent transfer and adoption on a larger scale of American techniques coincided with British firms' growing difficulties with competitiveness.[11]

Generalizations about post-1945 British business history are now increasingly testable because of the growing number of corporate histories covering the period. The 1980s saw a cluster of excellent commissioned histories of the nationalized industries, such as W. Ashworth's work on the coal industry and T. R. Gourvish's work on British Railways.[12] Critical archivally based studies of British private sector companies covering the postwar decades are also accumulating. A pioneer was Coleman's study of Courtaulds between 1945 and 1965, *Courtaulds: An Economic and Social History*, volume 3 (Oxford, 1980), which tracked the adoption of a hybrid form of holding company and then a more radical managerial reorganization after an unsuccessful takeover bid from ICI in 1961. Over the following two decades, many different corporate sectors have been examined. T. R. Gourvish and R. G. Wilson provide substantive insights on Britain's once highly successful brewing industry in the context of their wider study, *The British Brewing Industry, 1830-1990* (Cambridge, 1994). Recently there has been an impressive study by R. Fitzgerald of Rowntree before 1969 focused on the marketing capabilities of this

[9] Richard Whittington and Michael Mayer, *The European Corporation* (Oxford, 2000).
[10] Stephen N. Broadberry, *The Productivity Race: British Manufacturing in International Perspective 1850-1990* (Cambridge, 1997); Jim Tomlinson and Nick Tiratsoo, "Americanization Beyond the Mass Production Paradigm: The Case of British Industry," in *The Americanisation of European Business, 1948-1960*, eds. Matthias Kipping and Ove Bjarnar (London, 1998), 115-32.
[11] Jonathan Zeitlin, "Americanizing British Engineering?" in *Americanization and Its Limits*, eds. Jonathan Zeitlin and Gary Herrigel (Oxford, 2000), 123-52.
[12] William Ashworth, *1946-1982: The Nationalised Industry*, vol. 5 of *The History of the British Coal Industry* (Oxford, 1986); Terence R. Gourvish, *British Railways, 1948-73: A Business History* (Cambridge, 1986).

chocolate company. Another impressive example is G. Tweedale's pioneering work on Turner & Newall and its role in making lethal asbestos, based on corporate archives that came into the public domain as a result of American litigation.[13]

Business historians have published studies of both Britain's successful and unsuccessful sectors and firms. Among the former, there is now available plentiful information on Britain's highly successful pharmaceutical industry. There is a two-volume study of Glaxo, R. P. T. Davenport-Hines and Judy Slinn's *Glaxo: A History to 1962* (Cambridge, 1992), and Edgar Jones's *The Business of Medicine* (London, 2001). J. H. Bamberg's history of British Petroleum, *The History of the British Petroleum Company*, volumes 2 and 3 (Cambridge, 1994 and 2000), now extends to1975, and the research for the fourth volume up to 2000 is underway. The Anglo-Dutch company Unilever is also covered in several studies that will shortly reach 1990.[14] However, the number of studies of large corporations remains limited. There are no histories covering the past half century of such major food and drink companies as Cadbury Schweppes or Diageo, or of very-fast-growing firms such as Vodafone and Rentokil.

Turning to Britain's poor performers, there have been studies of the British computer industry, and the reasons for its failure and the demise of the British-owned automobile industry.[15] In the latest major study of the latter by Whisler, the author argues that all the actors in the industry – management, labor, and government – were locked into a set of beliefs and institutions that were incompatible with the high-volume production of highly engineered products. British firms could succeed only in the labor-intensive production of low-volume distinctive semispecialist models.[16]

In the Netherlands, as in Britain, the rise of large corporations has been the object of study, but the influence of Chandler has been surprisingly

[13] Robert Fitzgerald, *Rowntree and the Marketing Revolution 1862-1969* (Cambridge, 1995); Geoffrey Tweedale, *Magic Mineral to Killer Dust* (Oxford, 2000).

[14] Charles Wilson, *Unilever, 1945-1965* (London, 1968); David K. Fieldhouse, *Unilever Overseas* (London, 1978); id., *Merchant Capital and Economic Decolonisation* (Oxford, 1994). Geoffrey Jones is writing a history of Unilever from 1965 to 1990.

[15] Martin Campbell-Kelly, *ICL: A Business and Technical History* (Oxford, 1989); John Hendry, *Innovating for Failure* (Cambridge, Mass., 1990); Geoffrey Tweedale, "Marketing in the Second Industrial Revolution: A Case Study of the Ferranti Computer Group, 1949-1963," *Business History* 34, no. 1 (1992): 96-122; Roy Church, *The Rise and Decline of the British Motor Industry* (Cambridge, 1994); James Forman-Peck, Sue Bowden, and Alan McKinlay, *The British Motor Industry* (Manchester, 1995).

[16] Timothy R. Whisler, *The British Motor Industry, 1945-94* (Oxford, 1999).

limited. The histories of both Royal Dutch/Shell and Unilever were written before Chandler's influential work appeared in the 1960s. In fact, those two Anglo-Dutch companies were among the first to be honored by multivolume scholarly studies, though in the case of Royal Dutch/Shell, the story did not extend further than 1922.[17] Not until Chandler himself compared the American experiences with those in Britain and Germany in *Scale and Scope* was his work scrutinized in the Netherlands. Ivo Blanken, writing the history of Philips Electronics, found Chandler's three-pronged approach to be the perfect model for describing Philips's successful entrance into the radio business in the 1920s. However, he did not discuss how Chandler's criticism of the family firm related to the Philips Company, which was then a listed limited company still headed by Anton Philips. Was it so successful because it was a family firm or despite it?[18]

The European comparison in *Scale and Scope* inspired many researchers, including Dutch ones, to draw up lists of the largest 100 companies in their country. Lists ranging from 1913 to 1973, with additional material about 1990, were assembled by Erik Bloemen, Jan Kok, and Jan Luiten van Zanden.[19] This work was done not to evaluate the importance of investment in managerial capabilities, but to study the importance and the mobility in the top 100 industrial companies. Their conclusion was that while the top five or six companies were very stable indeed, the rest were not. There had been a great deal of change (sometimes by merger) over the past eighty years; in fact, the authors found greater mobility in this stratum than Chandler theorized. The importance of the top 100 companies for the Dutch economy was relatively large, and it increased until 1970 but stabilized after 1973. The importance of the top hundred supports Chandler's theories, but the lack of growth after 1973 less so, especially as part of this lack can be explained by disintegration and closing down. Recently, Jan Luiten van Zanden analyzed the rise of the Dutch managerial enterprise in the Chandlerian framework, which

[17] F. C. Gerretson, *History of the Royal Dutch* (Leiden, 1953); the period 1914–22 was only covered in two additional volumes in Dutch of F. C. Gerretson, *Geschiedenis der "Koninklijke,"* vols. 4 and 5 (1973).

[18] Ivo J. Blanken, *De ontwikkeling van de N. V. Philips' Gloeilampenfabrieken tot elektrotechnisch concern,* vol. 3 (Leiden, 1992). Volume 4 covers the sensitive period of the Second World War: Ivo J. Blanken, *Onder Duits beheer,* vol. 4 (Zaltbommel, 1997).

[19] Erik Bloemen, Jan Kok, and Jan Luiten van Zanden, *De top 100 van industriële bedrijven in Nederland 1913–1990* (The Hague, 1993).

he considered very helpful to explain Dutch developments up to the 1970s.[20]

Keetie Sluyterman and Hélène Winkelman studied another aspect of Chandler's rich work. Based on a list of the top 100 companies for 1930, they evaluated the importance of family firms, especially in the sectors of the Second Industrial Revolution.[21] They concluded that the Netherlands resembled Britain in the enduring influence of the family firm and personal relationships. It contrasted as a country with Germany, in that cartels and entrepreneurial agreements did not become important in the Netherlands before the 1930s. However, personal capitalism was not synonymous with failure. Though large, integrated companies were rare in the Netherlands, this did not mean that the smaller companies lacked efficiency or competitiveness. Many personal and sometimes financial links between firms worked to a large extent as an alternative to integration or diversification. Many of the small Dutch firms competed successfully in foreign markets. There is no evidence that family firms extracted more profits from the business than listed companies. If anything, the opposite was the case. These conclusions would support the hypothesis that it was the nature of the British business culture rather than ownership form per se that caused the British problem.

Economists and sociologists discussed the family firm during the 1950s and 1960s, mostly in a negative way. They criticized the privileged position of members of the family and their inherited wealth, which appeared out of place in a democratic society. Members of the family were considered less professional than outside managers, and it was claimed that family companies hindered economic growth because they were inclined to keep expansion within the boundaries of the family resources. However, from the 1980s on, appreciation for the family firm began to rise in the Netherlands.

The unfavorable situation in the Dutch cotton industry, the traditional stronghold of the family firm, contributed to the negative image of the family firm. The persistence of the family firm was held at least partially responsible for the poor economic performance of this sector. In his study on the textile manufacturer Van Heek & Co, the historian Van Schelven argued in 1984 that it was typical for the family firm to place the interest

[20] Jan Luiten van Zanden, *The Economic History of the Netherlands 1914-1995* (London and New York, 1998).
[21] Keetie Sluyterman and Hélène Winkelman, "The Dutch Family Firm Confronted with Chandler's Dynamics of Industrial Capitalism, 1890-1940," *Business History* 35 (1993): 152-83.

of the family – its wealth, its social status, and the continuation of its social position – above the firm's goal of profit maximization. In periods of prosperity this attitude stimulated the growth of the company, but in economic downturns it had a restraining and negative effect.[22] The slow decline of the textile industry in the 1960s seemed to illustrate his point. However, it does not seem entirely fair to blame the family firm for the blind-alley situation of the textile industry. In another study of a family firm in the textile industry, Henk Muntjewerff highlighted the conflict between the economic interests of the firm and the social interests of the family. He came to the conclusion that it was in the well-understood interest of the family to divest in the 1960s, which ultimately led to the closure of the company. Muntjewerff did not discuss the question of whether it was also right from a general economic point of view to withdraw funds from a losing industry and put them into more promising ventures. If this was the case, which seems very likely, the family supported the economy in the right way while at the same time serving their own best interests. Though his study was published in 1993, Muntjewerff did not go into the debate following Chandler's critique of British personal capitalism.[23]

Going beyond the debate on the quality of family management or the persistence of the family firm, Doreen Arnoldus compared the internal and external strategies of six family firms in the Dutch food industry. She concluded that only the capital strategy was strongly related to the internal strategies of the family; the strategy with regard to labor, raw materials, and marketing had no evident relationship with the internal strategy. The capital, raw materials, and marketing strategy, however, had moderate to strong relationships with the social network of the family.

Interestingly, the labor strategy seemed to have no connection with either the internal strategies or the social network.[24] Recently, Karel Davids has pointed out that in the whole discussion of change and continuity within the family firm, business historians have overlooked the changes in the family itself, in the norms and values of family life and its place in society. Tacitly, they have assumed that the family remained unchanged. In his view, this is untrue. As elsewhere in Europe, in the Netherlands

---

[22] Arnout L. van Schelven, *Onderneming en familisme. Opkomst, bloei en neergang van de textielonderneming Van Heek & Co te Enschede* (Leiden, 1984).

[23] Henk A. Muntjewerff, *De spil waar alles om draaide. Opkomst, bloei en neergang van de Tilburgse familie-onderneming Wolspinnerij Pieter van Dooren 1825-1975* (Tilburg, 1993).

[24] Doreen Arnoldus, *Family, Family Firm and Strategy. Six Dutch Family Firms in the Food Industry 1880-1970* (Amsterdam, 2002).

a process of individualization took place, which had important implications for the family structure and culture. People married less often,
divorced more frequently, and attached less importance to their marriage.
These trends affected the coherence and continuity of families. Through
frequent remarriage, the nucleus of the family became more diffuse.[25]
Though individualism is a slippery concept to define and date, Davids
sees the loosening of family ties as a rather recent – at least postwar –
phenomenon. In this context, it would also make sense to study the
changing nature of parent–child relationships. We assume that relationships became somewhat less hierarchical and authoritarian after the Second World War. Children gained more freedom in making vocational
choices. These changes must have had a bearing on the management
of the family firm, which might be included in future discussions of the
family firm.

Both Britain and the Netherlands developed very large firms, especially after 1945, which, as in the United States, accounted for a growing
share of economic activity. Also, as in the United States, they were professionally managed. However, in both countries, other types of business
enterprise, especially family-owned firms, continued to be important,
and business historians have shown that they were by no means automatically inferior to large managerial firms.

INNOVATION AND HUMAN RESOURCES

A central feature of the large American corporations that developed in
the late nineteenth century was their willingness to invest in innovation, especially with the foundation of industrial research laboratories,
and in management. In both areas there were contrasts with European
companies.

There was until recently a widespread assumption that Britain lagged
in industrial research and development (R&D) and that this lag was directly correlated with the lag in the appearance of large U.S.-style corporations. In *Scale and Scope*, Chandler argued that the personally managed firms, such as Courtaulds and Pilkingtons, "chose to pay dividends
rather than to re-invest in R&D." Even the more dynamic firms in automobiles and electrical equipment "invested less in research," leaving "the

---

[25] Karel Davids, "Familiebedrijven, familisme en individualisering Nederland, ca. 1880–1990.
Een bijdrage aan de theorievorming," *Amsterdams Sociologisch Tijdschrift* 24 (1997):
527–54.

development of new products and processes to be carried on primarily in the U.S. and Germany."[26]

The extent to which this generalization holds true has been challenged, especially in the work of D. E. H. Edgerton. Edgerton has challenged the dismissal of British industrial investment in R&D before 1945, pointing to the limited evidence on which others have generalized.[27] He and S. M. Horrocks have demonstrated that British chemical and electrical engineering firms before 1945 were substantial employers of R&D staff, and that they invested as much in R&D as all but the largest U.S. corporations. Edgerton suggests that British firms may have put too much emphasis on R&D in this period and later become disillusioned.

Certainly in the immediate post-1945 decades, Britain was the world's second largest investor in R&D after the United States During the late 1940s and 1950s, scientists and engineers seem to have acquired growing influence on the boards of leading British companies. Thereafter, the spread of U.S. management methods and the growing pressure for shareholder value appear to have converted many British managers to the view that R&D was a cost rather than an investment. High dividends left little money for R&D spending, which languished with the exception of a few sectors, such as pharmaceuticals.

A wider problem for innovation in post-1945 Britain was the allocation of R&D spending. Spending was heavily concentrated in nuclear electricity, civilian aircraft, and defense – all areas where the returns were low, either because the British competed directly with the Americans but lacked their resources or because their investment was inefficient. British governments poured money into defense in their ever more futile attempt to remain a great power. In the mid-1950s total British R&D expenditure was the highest in Western Europe; 63 percent of the total was spent in defense, while two-thirds of private industry research was related directly to defense contracts. From the early 1970s on, the proportion of total British R&D spent on defense rose, perhaps in response to the continual ebbing of the country's standing and reputation in the world and to the perceived threat of European integration.[28]

---

[26] Alfred D. Chandler, Jr., *Scale and Scope* (Cambridge, Mass., 1990), 390-1.

[27] D. E. H. Edgerton, "Science and Technology in British Business History," *Business History* 29, no. 4 (1987): 84-103; id., "British Industrial R&D, 1900-1970," *Journal of European Economic History* 23, no. 1 (1994): 49-67; Sally M. Horrocks, "Enthusiasm Constrained? British Industrial R&D and the Transition from War to Peace, 1942-51," *Business History* 41, no. 3 (1999): 42-63.

[28] David Edgerton, *England and the Aeroplane: An Essay on a Militant and Technological Nation* (London, 1991).

However many uncertainties remain about the nature of innovation in British business.[29] Existing fragmentary studies only point to the complexity of the situation. T. C. Barker has examined the intriguing case of the postwar invention of float glass by Pilkington, a family company until 1970. The inventor of float glass was recruited and promoted in the firm after 1945 because he had the family name, even though the two branches of the family had separated at least fifteen generations previously.[30] In contrast, M. Campbell-Kelly has identified the weak management structures within the computer company ICL that led to its inability to control R&D costs and contributed to its near-bankruptcy in 1981.[31] This would support the argument that if British business had a long-term problem with innovation, it was less that it spent too little on R&D than it often spent inefficiently.

In the Netherlands, the literature on technology and innovation has taken a different approach and focus, with especially fertile collaboration between business historians and historians of technology. The collaboration has existed since the early 1980s and was underlined by the jointly published Dutch yearbook on the history of technology and business. Initially the engineers focused on the diffusion of technology, especially in the nineteenth century. This research linked perfectly well with the interest of business historians in the earlier-mentioned late industrialization of the Netherlands and the question of whether economic circumstances or entrepreneurial lack of initiative were to blame. Both interests resulted in studies of the relative merits of the use of steam or wind energy, with the conclusion that using windmills was often quite sensible as long as output was low. Researchers began to look in more detail at new production processes, the moment of introduction, and the kinds of processes used. The conclusion was that even imitation often required quite a lot of creativity, because the new technologies had to be adapted to local production circumstances and local raw materials. This research also shed new light on the themes of innovation and entrepreneurship.[32]

---

[29] Edgerton, "Science and Technology," 85.

[30] T. C. Barker, "Business Implications of Technical Development in the Glass Industry, 1945–1965: A Case Study," in *Essays in British Business History*, ed. Barry Supple (Oxford, 1977), 187–204.

[31] M. Campbell-Kelly, "ICL: Taming the R&D Beast," *Business and Economic History* 22, no. 1 (1993): 169–80.

[32] Martijn Bakker, *Ondernemerschap en vernieuwing. De Nederlandse bietsuikerindustrie 1858–1919* (Amsterdam, 1989); Giel van Hooff, *In het rijk van de Nederlandse vulcanus. De Nederlandse machinenijverheid 1825–1914. Een historische bedrijfstakverkenning* (Amsterdam, 1990); Geert Verbong, *Technische innovaties in de katoendrukkerij en -ververij in Nederland 1835–1920* (Amsterdam, 1988).

Under the driving force of Harry Lintsen, professor of the history of technology at Eindhoven and Delft Universities, these preliminary case studies were included in a big project on technological developments in the Netherlands in the nineteenth century. This project resulted in the publication of six volumes dealing with modernization and the interaction between technological and societal developments. The starting point was the belief that technicians, craftsmen, local and national authorities, scientists and entrepreneurs, and the everyday users of technology were all involved in the process of shaping technology. Therefore, the contribution of all these actors needed to be analyzed, as well as the larger technological, economic, and social environment. This comprehensive approach invited the participation of many scholars, including business historians, who both contributed to the series and profited from the results.[33] When the project was evaluated in 1995, the organizers were justifiably proud of what had been achieved, as well as aware of the fact that their theoretical points of view had changed in the process. From the discussions concerning the late industrialization of the Netherlands, the project had moved toward the processes of shaping technology itself and the societal consequences. The influence of sociological theories had grown during the project. Having published six volumes on the nineteenth century, the group of researchers has now advanced to the twentieth century, and their new project covers the period between 1890 and 1970.[34] This project is even more ambitious than the first one. It strives to write not only a contextual history of technology, but also a history that attempted to recognize the role of technological innovation in historical development and to contribute to the development of the discipline by using and advancing the sociology and economics of technology. The three volumes that have appeared thus far are particularly relevant for business historians, with discussions on office technology, the coal and oil industry, the chemical industry, and the food sector.

The British business history literature has much to say about human resource management, which is not surprising since there is widespread agreement that inadequate investment in human capital was a root cause of poor productivity in that country. This problem had several dimensions. Before the 1950s, British firms rarely employed university

---

[33] Harry W. Lintsen et al., eds., *Geschiedenis van de techniek in Nederland: De wording van een moderne samenleving 1800-1890*, 6 vols. (Zutphen, 1992-5).

[34] Three volumes have appeared since 1998: Johan W. Schot et al., *Techniek in Nederland in de twintigste eeuw* (Zutphen, 1998-2001).

graduates as managers and had a special dislike of any form of management education. When graduates were recruited as future senior managers, the preferred educational background through the 1950s remained a liberal arts degree from either Oxford or Cambridge, preferably combined with attendance at one of Britain's fee-paying public schools. During the 1960s, Britain's first business schools were established and graduate recruitment to management on a large scale increased. Nevertheless, British managers continued at least until the 1980s to be "undereducated" compared to those of other European countries, the United States, or Japan. They were notably lacking in an engineering background, while curiously, many of them had professional qualifications in accounting. Once recruited, managers were given little subsequent training inhouse until the 1970s.[35]

It seems that the average British manager in the postwar period was less capable than his or her counterparts in the Netherlands or elsewhere in Western Europe or in the United States. In his 1987 survey of twelve prominent British company histories, D. C. Coleman found that all levels of management in British industry were plagued by poor decision making.[36] During the postwar decades, the British managerial cadre often appeared short on technical competence and motivation, prone more to interdepartmental politics than aggressive competition, and hobbled by short time horizons. Mary Rose has shown that British firms in the 1950s had a distinct preference for internal leadership succession, a tendency that might have preserved inward-looking attitudes.[37] However, such generalizations disguise major distinctions between a handful of large companies and the rest. Kenneth Brown's study of the collapse and demise of the British-owned toy industry during the 1970s and early 1980s, *The British Toy Business* (London, 1996), provides a distressing indictment of complacent and incompetent British managers. In contrast, during the postwar decades, a number of firms such as BP, Unilever, and ICI attracted excellent young managers who trained well, thus serving as "quasi-business schools" for the other British industries. An interesting question is why some British firms were able to recruit and retain high-quality management, while so many others could not.

---

[35] Shirley Keeble, *The Ability to Manage* (Manchester, 1992); Derek Matthews, M. Anderson, and J. R. Edwards, "The Rise of the Professional Accountant in British Management," *Economic History Review* 50, no. 3 (1997): 407–29.

[36] Donald C. Coleman, "Failings and Achievements: Some British Businesses, 1910–1980," *Business History* 29, no. 4 (1987): 1–24.

[37] Derek F. Channon, *The Strategy and Structure of British Enterprise* (London, 1973).

Meanwhile, the legendary reluctance of British firms to train their work forces continues to attract the attention of business historians. In part because of the legacy of the Industrial Revolution, in part because of the class system, and in part because of the atomistic governance structures of many industries, British business trained its workers less than the United States and Germany even before 1914. Until the mid-1960s, British governments also denied all responsibility for training. British educational policy after 1945 focused resources on educating an academic elite, consigning three-quarters of all its pupils to so-called secondary modern schools, where they received neither a proper education nor vocational training.[38] Vocational training in the postwar decades was largely in the hands of the traditional apprenticeship system, but this began to collapse in the 1970s and was fatally undermined during the Thatcher administration in the following decade.[39]

The low skill levels of British workers have been widely and convincingly shown to have been a major explanation of low British labor productivity in a series of studies extending over the past three decades. There is, however, disappointingly little business history research on firms, especially for the period since the Second World War, to establish precisely why British managers took the view that training their workforce was not necessary, despite all the evidence from elsewhere to the contrary. E. Lorenz, in his study of the British cotton, shipbuilding, and automobile industries after 1945 (in *Industrial and Corporate Change*, 1994), takes the "institutional rigidities" approach, suggesting that these businesses were so committed to traditional systems of training that it would have been costly for them to establish separate training programs. Keith Burgess shows that, for the 1930s and 1940s, the intention of large firms in "new" industries to improve technical education and training was thwarted by smaller firms in "old" industries, which among other things did not like the expense.[40] Most business historians who have addressed the issue seem eventually to throw up their hands and conclude that the fundamental problem lay in some irrational failure within the British culture. N. Tiratsoo has noted the great emphasis placed in the

---

[38] M. Sanderson, "Education and Economic Decline, the 1890s–1980s," *Oxford Review of Economic Policy* 4 (1988): 38–50.

[39] Mary B. Rose, "Investment in Human Capital and British Manufacturing Industry to 1990," in *Business Enterprise in Modern Britain*, eds. Maurice W. Kirby and M. B. Rose (London, 1994), 339–71.

[40] Keith Burgess, "British Employers and Education Policy, 1935–45: A Decade of 'Missed Opportunities'?" *Business History* 36, no. 3 (1994): 29–61.

postwar British management culture on "character" rather than competence and "leadership" rather than skill training.[41] It might be speculated that the parochial nature of the post-1945 British culture – itself puzzling given their imperial past, the international usage of the English language, and the internationalized business sector – handicapped managers from benchmarking their policies on training with those elsewhere in Europe.

Unlike the British, Dutch companies generally saw the merits of well-educated managers and well-trained workers. This provides one of the great contrasts between the two countries and probably explains much of the productivity gap that opened up between them in the postwar decades. Nevertheless, studies evaluating the educational background of Dutch managers generally have not yet appeared. Another factor may have been important in understanding the productivity gap: the largely positive attitude of the Dutch labor unions toward scientific management from the 1920s on. The unions were confident that the rise in labor productivity would result in higher wages. This attitude becomes clear from Bloemen's study on the reception of scientific management in the Netherlands. Hellema and Marsman take the story on management consultancy further into the 1960s and also touch on the Americanization debate. The management consultant B. W. Berenschot was one of the most active promoters of U.S. management techniques. Studying the influence of the postwar U.S. productivity drive in the Netherlands and particularly the study visits to the United States, Frank Inklaar highlighted how the American managerial ideas and methods were studied and talked about eagerly in the Netherlands. However, it was more difficult to assess the effect on individual companies. In trade and industry, the study visits seem to have been particularly valuable for ambitious companies of some magnitude. For smaller companies, the American practice was not as relevant. Big companies had their own means of remaining up-to-date. Management consultants undoubtedly benefited most from the whole productivity drive. The U.S. influence on management consulting and education continued into the 1960s. The mid-1960s also saw the founding of new business schools attached to the university.[42] On the level

---

[41] Nick Tiratsoo, "British Management, 1945–64: Reformers and the Struggle to Improve Standards," in *Japanese Success? British Failure?* eds. Etsuo Abe and Terence R. Gourvish (Oxford, 1997), 77–98.

[42] Erik Bloemen, *Scientific Management in Nederland, 1900–1930* (Amsterdam, 1988); Peter Hellema and Joop Marsman, *De organisatie-adviseur. Opkomst en groei van een nieuw vak in Nederland 1920–1960* (Boom, 1997); Frank Inklaar, *Van Amerika geleerd. Marshall-hulp en kennisimport in Nederland* (The Hague, 1997); Huibert de Man and

of the individual company, Mel van Elteren analyzed corporate policy on industrial accommodation processes among workers in the industrial complex of Hoogovens and did similar work on Océ-van der Grinten.[43]

ENTREPRENEURS, BANKS, AND GOVERNMENTS

While Chandler helped focus the research agenda of U.S. business history for two generations on organization and big business, these never became dominant preoccupations in Europe. Entrepreneurs, banks, and governments – all of them found in but not at the heart of the Chandlerian world – have continued to feature prominently in the British and Dutch literatures.

Entrepreneurs – and their alleged failure from the late nineteenth century – long lay at the center of debates in British history. This view of entrepreneurial failure subsequently became a major area of contention when new economic historians in the United States such as D. N. McCloskey challenged the subjective nature of the methodology used by traditional historians and sought to argue that any failure was "rational." Lazonick, and W. Mass and Lazonick, in turn, found failure in the Lancashire cotton industry in particular, but pointed the analysis toward the structure and organization of firms rather than the behavior of entrepreneurs.[44] Chandler himself subscribed to the entrepreneurial failure hypothesis in the sense that British entrepreneurs failed to make the necessary three-pronged investment in production, marketing, and management.

The theme of "attitudes" or "culture" reappears in much of the discussion of British entrepreneurial failure. Proponents of the failure hypothesis have often blamed it on some wider catastrophic failure within the British culture since the late nineteenth century. Coleman addressed this

Luchien Karsten, "Academic Management Education in the Netherlands," in *Management Studies in an Academic Context*, eds. L. Engwall and E. Gunnarsson (Uppsala, 1994), 84–115.

[43] Mel van Elteren, *Staal en arbeid: Een sociaal-historische studie naar industriële accomodatieprocessen onder arbeiders en het desbetreffend bedrijfsbeleid bij Hoogovens IJmuiden, 1924–1966* (Leiden, 1986); Mel van Elteren, "Tussen verlicht paternalisme en functioneel-zakelijk management," in *Van boterkleursel naar kopieersystemen. De ontstaansgeschiedenis van Océ-van der Grinten, 1877–1956*, ed. Harry van den Eerenbeemt (Leiden, 1992), 268–342.

[44] William Lazonick, *Competitive Advantage on the Shopfloor* (Cambridge, Mass., 1990); William Mass and W. Lazonick, "The British Cotton Industry and International Competitive Advantage: The State of the Debates," *Business History* 32, no. 4 (1990): 9–65.

in a seminal article, "Gentlemen and Players" (*Economic History Review*, 1973). In 1981 the "cultural failure" hypothesis was given widespread currency by M. Weiner's *English Culture and the Decline of the Industrial Spirit* (Cambridge, 1981), which analyzed the "anti-industrial" spirit that caused Britain's alleged competitive collapse. Weiner's work was widely criticized within the history profession.

These debates about the competence and motivation of British entrepreneurs have been largely waged at the macro or industry level of analysis and have remained rather disconnected from studies of particular firms or entrepreneurs. This is rather disappointing in some ways, as the multivolume *Dictionary of Business Biography*, edited by David Jeremy and published in the 1980s, was a pioneering attempt to assemble the collective biographies of leading British businesspeople in such a way as to provide for a systematic analysis. There exists as well a companion volume, *Dictionary of Scottish Business Biography*, edited by Tony Slaven. In practice, it has proved hard to use these collective studies in a rigorous fashion, and to some extent debates about British entrepreneurs continue on rather familiar lines, but with some tendency to exonerate them from the worst allegations of failure. This seems to be the general thrust of the large literature on the pre-1940 British coal industry, whose entrepreneurs were once treated as among the worst failures.[45]

During the 1990s, perhaps the most innovative British business history research in the area of entrepreneurship concerned the role of "networks" of finance, information, and trust in influencing and shaping entrepreneurial strategies. In studies of the nineteenth century, these networks have been examined as alternatives to firms, but they have been treated as equally important in the twentieth-century corporate economy. This research has explicitly drawn inspiration from the growing interest in networks by institutional economists and organizational theorists. Fine recent examples of the application of network theory include G. Cookson's work on textile engineering in Yorkshire, G. Tweedale's study of Sheffield's steel firms, and G. H. Boyce's work on the pre-1919 British shipping industry.[46]

[45] Michael Dintenfass, *Managing Industrial Decline; The British Coal Industry between the Wars* (Columbus, Ohio, 1992); David Greasley, "Economies of Scale in British Coalmining between the Wars," *Economic History Review* 46, no. 1 (1993): 155-9; Judith M. Wale, "Entrepreneurship in an Industry Subject to External Shocks: British 'Coalowners', 1900–1946," *Management Decision* 39, no. 9 (2001): 729–38.

[46] Gillian Cookson, "Family Firms and Business Networks," *Business History* 39, no. 1 (1997): 1-20; Geoffrey Tweedale, *Steel City: Entrepreneurship, Strategy and Technology in*

In contrast to Britain, the Netherlands has no dictionary of business biographies. Entrepreneurial biographies appear from time to time, such as the study by Chantal Vancoppenolle on the entrepreneur C. J. Honig. She shows how Honig's social entrepreneurship was situated between the nineteenth-century tradition of paternalistic care and the 1960s functional management. M. Dierikx's biography of Anthony Fokker, the airplane pioneer nicknamed the "Flying Dutchman," is another example.[47] Dutch efforts in entrepreneurial history were recently reviewed by Ferry de Goey in an article comparing the Netherlands and Belgium with the United States.[48] De Goey concludes that the Dutch never made a sharp distinction between business history and entrepreneurial history, as occurred in the United States in the 1950s. Though there was some discussion about the question of whether the two fields needed separate attention, in practice the entrepreneur and the firm were researched together and at the same time. Though theories were used only sparsely, Schumpeter's approach of the true entrepreneur as the source of innovation through "Neue Combinationen" has inspired researchers to such an extent that there is some danger that all business leaders will become Schumpeterian entrepreneurs. Recent times have witnessed a revival in the entrepreneurial history of the seventeenth and eighteenth centuries. Most of the historians involved would not term themselves business historians, and indeed, this essay would stretch too much if we tried to include the seventeenth- and eighteenth-century literature and debates. However, it is worth noting that a research project "Entrepreneurship and Institutional Context in a Comparative Perspective," started in 1999, intending to bring both groups of scholars together, while at the same time including research on Asian entrepreneurs. In their recent book on Dutch international trading companies, Joost Jonker and Keetie Sluyterman have covered the period from the sixteenth century to the present, analyzing the position of merchant

Sheffield, 1743-1993 (Oxford, 1995); Gordon H. Boyce, *Information, Mediation and Institutional Development: The Rise of the Large-Scale Enterprise in British Shipping, 1870-1919* (Manchester, 1995).

[47] Chantal Vancoppenolle, *Tussen paternalistische zorg en zakelijk management. C. J. Honig als eindpunt van persoonsgericht sociaal ondernemersgedrag in een Zaans familiebedrijf (1930-1957)* (Amsterdam, 1993); Marc Dierikx, *Dwarswind. Een biografie van Anthony Fokker* (The Hague, 1997).

[48] Ferry de Goey, "Ondernemersgeschiedenis in Amerika, Nederland en België (1940-1995): Trends in vraagstellingen, onderzoekmethoden en thema's: Een overzicht," *Neha-jaarboek voor economische, bedrijfs- en techniekgeschiedenis* 59 (1996): 21-65. This article is recommended because it contains a wide-ranging review of the literature.

houses in business, the nature of their work, and how it evolved over four centuries.[49]

The revival of the entrepreneur is partially inspired by the desire to personalize history and move away from the structures and the macroeconomic figures. One result of the present preoccupation in the Netherlands is the discovery of the importance of networks of family, friends, and business relations. At least three authors have analyzed the network of interlocking directorships in Dutch and colonial Dutch companies in the period before the Second World War. They used slightly different sources and collected information from different years, ranging from 1886 to 1939. Yet, their conclusions are remarkably similar: banks and shipowners had an important place in the network of interlocking directorships, with traders figuring largely in the period before 1914 and directors of plantation companies in the interwar period. Manufacturers had only a modest position in the network. The similarity in the results is all the more striking as Schijf concentrated on the Dutch companies in the Netherlands and Bossenbroek and Taselaar on the Dutch companies working in colonial Indonesia.[50]

The subject of entrepreneurship raises the question of culture. The Dutch sociologist Geert Hofstede's seminal study of the impact of national cultures on corporate organization and strategy inspired management consultants, but few Dutch business historians have tried to use or discuss his findings.[51] One reason for their reluctance might stem from a hesitance to use Hofstede's results, based on data for 1968-72, for a different historical period. Ad van Iterson used Hofstede for his study of the entrepreneur Petrus Regout in the years 1834-70. However, as Van Iterson himself admits, and as Hofstede warned, statements about culture are not statements about individuals.[52] Van Iterson's results have not convinced historians of the usefulness of Hofstede in historical research, though the importance of cultural differences is undeniable. As such,

---

[49] Joost Jonker and Keetie Sluyterman, *At Home on the World Markets. Dutch International Trading Companies from the 16th Century Until the Present* (Montreal, 2000).

[50] Martin Bossenbroek, *Holland op zijn breedst. Indië en Zuid-Afrika in de Nederlandse cultuur omstreeks 1900* (Amsterdam, 1996); Huibert Schijf, *Netwerken van een financieel-economische elite. Personele verbindingen in het Nederlandse bedrijfsleven aan het einde van de negentiende eeuw* (Amsterdam, 1993); Arjen Taselaar, *De Nederlandse koloniale lobby. Ondernemers en de Indische politiek, 1914-1940* (Leiden, 1998).

[51] Geert Hofstede, *Culture's Consequences: International Differences in Work-Related Values* (London, 1984).

[52] Ad van Iterson, "*Vader, Raadgever en Beschermer," Petrus Regout en zijn arbeiders 1834-1870* (Maastricht, 1992).

the work of Hofstede has opened new perspectives. The importance of national cultures in international mergers was analyzed by René Olie in his study on three German–Dutch mergers, two of which were failures. Cultural differences played a part in the failures, but they were not the only factor.[53]

In both countries there is a considerable literature on financial services. In Britain, banks were among the very first business enterprises to commission scholarly histories, a trend going back to the interwar years with the pioneering history of Midland Bank by Wilfred E. Crick and John E. Wadsworth, *A Hundred Years of Joint Stock Banking* (London, 1936). The 1940s and 1950s saw further first-rate studies, and in more recent times, outstanding company histories have continued to be written, especially of the merchant or investment banks. Richard Roberts's study of Schroders, *Merchants and Bankers* (London, 1992), is an impressive example. At the same time, banks have long been established as actual players in the British "decline" literature. From well before the Second World War, British banks have been criticized for failing British industry by not lending long term, a contrast to the (often stereotyped) German model. Although a wholly separate issue, the criticism of British banks has often been merged into a wider critique of the City of London within British business. It has been argued that the City was concerned more with international business than with domestic industry – and certainly knew more about it – and that the City was able to influence British government policy making over the long term in ways detrimental to British business.

Regarding the banking system and its alleged failure, the literature now suggests a number of agreed-upon points and a number of continuing debates. It was widely accepted that there was a major structural change in British banking between the mid-nineteenth century and 1914 involving a shift from hundreds of separate banks to a concentrated and oligopolistic system. Coincidentally, most researchers accept that British banks probably became more risk averse over time and less inclined toward industrial finance. After the First World War, the banks lent very heavily to industry but continued to emphasize their role as suppliers of short-term credit. This subject remains controversial. The Bank of England and the commercial banks were involved in supporting and sometimes reconstructing a large number of firms in the troubled cotton, steel, and other industries. However, Steve Tolliday's study of the steel industry, *Business,*

[53] René Olie, *European transnational mergers* (Maastricht, 1996).

Banking and Politics (Cambridge, Mass., 1987), and James Bamberg's research on the cotton industry suggest that the banks were reluctant to, and largely incapable of, taking broad responsibility for industrial restructuring and were rather narrowly concerned with safeguarding their own interests. More recent research by Katherine Watson, Duncan Ross, and others has again stressed the flexibility of bank lending policies, given their position within a specialist financial system.[54]

In the postwar period, recent historians have suggested, the banks were more flexible than was often suggested. However, British governments, anxious to achieve banking stability and to enforce monetary policy, tightly controlled bank lending through qualitative and quantitative controls and froze the oligopolistic banking structure. While there may have been problems with diseconomies of scale and of other low-quality management after 1945, government controls effectively ruled out any entrepreneurial action or innovation in the sector.[55] Few researchers on the post-1945 period (or earlier) now believe that shortage or the high price of capital was a critical problem for British industry, whatever the defects of the banks. The British tradition was for industrial finance to come from internal sources. It remains plausible that banks might have intervened more to discipline inefficient management. They can be criticized for not taking this responsibility or indeed – as the evidence of the interwar British steel, automobile, and cotton industries might suggest – for doing the opposite by providing exit barriers for inefficient management and firms. However, there remains little evidence that British bankers had the competence to serve as "visible hands." This whole area needs further investigation. Whatever the outcome of this and other research, British banks proved remarkably stable over the course of the twentieth century, and the country suffered none of the traumas of bank failures seen in the United States and several European countries.

---

[54] Michael Collins, *Money and Banking in the U.K.* (London, 1988); id., "The Banking Crisis of 1878," *Economic History Review* 42, no. 4 (1978): 504–27; James Bamberg, "The Rationalisation of the British Cotton Industry in the Interwar Years," *Textile History* 19 (1988): 83–102; Katherine Watson, "Banks and Industrial Finance: The Experience of the Brewers, 1880–1913," *Economic History Review* 49, no. 1 (1996): 58–81; Duncan Ross, "Commercial Banking in a Market-Oriented Financial System: Britain Between the Wars," *Economic History Review* 49, no. 2 (1996): 314–25; Forest Capie and Michael Collins, "Industry and Finance, 1880–1914," *Business History* 41, no. 1 (1999): 37–62.

[55] Geoffrey Jones, "Competition and Competitiveness in British Banking, 1918–1971," in *Competitiveness and the State*, eds. Geoffrey Jones and Maurice W. Kirby (Manchester, 1991), 120–40.

The debates on the structure and efficiency of the British capital markets also continued, though they have somewhat changed in substance in recent years. During the 1980s, there was a heated discussion about whether pre-1914 British capital markets failed British industry by being biased toward overseas investment, a reasonable supposition given the scale of British overseas lending in this period. However, this argument, advocated by William P. Kennedy in *Industrial Structure, Capital Markets and the Origins of British Economic Decline* (Cambridge, 1987), has been undermined by the acceptance that a substantial proportion of Britain's capital exports before 1914 took the form of foreign direct investment (FDI) rather than portfolio investment. The different causes and consequences of the two types of investment makes such a failure case much harder to sustain.

In the interwar years, the British capital market was reoriented toward the domestic market, though British industry continued to rely upon other sources for most of its capital. Contemporaries found that small and medium-sized firms found raising capital very costly – the "Macmillan Gap" – and the scale of this gap continues to be debated. In general, however, as Leslie Hannah has shown, the growth of the capital market and the emergence of a market for corporate control provided the basis for the mergers and growth of large firms in the interwar years. Subsequently, the British capital markets grew in sophistication and depth. In the 1950s and 1960s, the British pioneered hostile takeover bids, which became a prominent feature of the British business system. In *Rise*, Hannah casts this development in a positive light, as permitting further concentration and providing "a major pressure on the directors of industrial firms."[56] A later generation of British business historians was more inclined to view the emergence of this market for corporate control in Britain as a mixed blessing, contributing to the chronic "short-termism" that was subsequently to bedevil British firms.[57]

Complaints about a failing banking system were frequently voiced in the Netherlands, especially with regard to the late industrialization of the country in the nineteenth century. Did the banks delay industrialization by their refusal to give industry necessary long-term credit? The debate started with the argument that the banking system was old-fashioned, as the Netherlands lacked the industrial banks typical of

---

[56] Leslie Hannah, *The Rise of the Corporate Economy*, 2d ed. (London, 1983), 150.
[57] Richard Roberts, "Regulatory Responses to the Rise of the Market for Corporate Control in Britain in the 1950s," *Business History* 34, no. 1 (1992): 183–200.

Germany and France. The next step was to blame the Dutch investor, who behaved in a conservative and risk-adverse fashion. A new point of view was introduced with the suggestion that the attractive opportunities for investment were simply too limited. Research in the archives of manufacturing companies then demonstrated that, by and large, these companies had no difficulty in finding financial resources to start or expand, because the combination of self-finance and short-term loans from banks and other sources covered their needs sufficiently.[58]

In his study of the Amsterdam money market Joost Jonker concluded that the Amsterdam money market worked differently, but not necessarily less flexibly and responsively than its foreign counterparts. If investors were wary of some of the publicly floated issues, as indeed they were, they had good reasons to be. However, it is possible that provincial businesses experienced some difficulties in finding sufficient financial means. There may have been bottlenecks, but no severe shortages, let alone consistent market failure.[59] Also, Dutch investors liked to take a financial gamble occasionally, as August Veenendaal has demonstrated. Despite mixed successes, the Dutch were keen financiers of American railways in the nineteenth century.[60] Many Dutch banks as well as insurance companies commissioned serious books on their history. A useful review of the history of Dutch banking, including many references to company histories, appeared in 1999.[61]

The role of government has been a further area of research for both British and Dutch business historians. Although British governments have been perhaps even more committed to liberal laissez-faire beliefs than those of the United States, British governments have had a major impact on business. In 1914 the acquisition of 51 percent of the Anglo-Persian Oil Company provided the basis for the emergence of BP, one of Britain's largest twentieth-century firms. Interwar governments helped reorganize the chemical industry by encouraging the formation of ICI;

---

[58] A good survey of the whole debate can be found in Joost Jonker, "Sinecures or Sinews of Power? Interlocking Directorships and Bank–Industry Relations in the Netherlands, 1910-1940," *Economic and Social History in the Netherlands* 3 (1991): 119-32.

[59] Joost Jonker, *Merchants, Bankers, Middlemen: The Amsterdam Money Market During the First Half of the 19th Century* (Amsterdam, 1996).

[60] August Veenendaal, *Slow Train to Paradise* (California, 1996).

[61] Johan van der Lugt, "Het commerciële bankwezen in Nederland in de twintigste eeuw. Een historiografisch overzicht," *Neha-jaarboek* 62 (1999): 388-421. For the insurance industry and its clients, see the wide-ranging collection by Jacques van Gerwen and Marco van Leeuwen, eds., *Studies over zekerheidsarrangementen, risico's, risicobestrijding en verzekeringen in Nederland vanaf de middeleeuwen* (Amsterdam, 1998).

by establishing the National Grid, they transformed the productivity of British electricity generation; and in the 1930s, they created a modern passenger transport system for London. These policies have been widely praised by their historians. Moreover, between the 1940s and the 1970s, large segments of British industry were nationalized.

Leaving aside the wider debates about the competence and direction of British economic policy as a whole, a number of more business-specific aspects of government policy have been debated. Perhaps the most general thesis was proposed by Bernard Elbaum and William Lazonick, who argued in *The Decline of the British Economy* (Oxford, 1987) that governments should have acted as a "visible hand" to reorganize and modernize British industry in the twentieth century. This argument rests on the central supposition that institutional rigidities were the main problems for British industry. It also assumes that – as in the parallel argument with banks – governments possessed the competence to improve matters rather than make them worse. This seems unlikely, especially after 1945. The general thrust of British industrial policy for much of the twentieth century was a drive for stability and security. Collusive agreements and arrangements were not only permitted but encouraged. In the case of the nationalized industries, British government took its suspicion of competition to the logical conclusion by taking over and merging together all the firms in an industry. Consequently, it was public policy itself in all likelihood that raised the barriers that ultimately coddled inefficient British firms and industries. This point is argued by John Singleton in his analysis of the post-1950 Lancashire cotton industry, *Lancashire on the Scrap Heap* (Oxford, 1991).

The extent to which governments facilitated or encouraged the growth of big business in Britain has also been a subject of debate. Helen Mercer has argued, in Kirby and Rose's *Business Enterprise in Modern Britain* (London, 1994), that from the interwar years and later, governments sought to encourage the growth of large firms with the general aim of improving industrial efficiency. They were rather more successful in the first aim than the second. Part of the problem was the distinctive nature of British competition policy after 1945, which largely avoided investigation of large firms and rarely intervened to block mergers.

In contrast, business historians have done much to bolster the reputations of British nationalized industries. After considerable reorganization problems in the 1950s, their management functioned well, at least when allowed to by interventionist governments, and kept adjusting corporate goals. By the 1960s, dynamic chief executives were reorganizing their large businesses and introducing new management methods. James

Foreman-Peck and Robert Millward, in *Public and Private Ownership of British Industries, 1820–1990* (Oxford, 1994), have confirmed that the productivity of the British publicly owned sector compared favorably to that of British privately owned manufacturing and to that of equivalent American industries in the period between the 1950s and the 1970s.

Several aspects of the relationship between business and government in the Netherlands have been examined in recent years. Firstly, the state-as-entrepreneur figured in the histories of the closure of the Dutch state mines and the privatization of the PTT (postal, telegraph, and telephone services). The interaction with local or regional government was paramount in several histories of electricity companies and the Schiphol Airport.[62] Though most of the authors comment on the special position of their companies in relation to central or local government, a debate on the pros and cons of state enterprises similar to that in Britain has not been waged so far. Secondly, some attention has been given to the issue of the government's industrialization policy. In particular, the mercantilistic policy of King Willem I in the beginning of the nineteenth century has been subject to study. There appeared to be considerable skepticism with regard to the possibility and wisdom of government support for individual companies, but the positive effects of investment in infrastructure such as canals and railways are acknowledged.[63] The Dutch policy of industrialization in the 1950s and 1960s met with success, though it is hard to decide whether government support itself or the favorable economic circumstances were responsible for this result. Dutch government support for weak companies during the 1970s was clearly unsuccessful, as a number of studies pointed out.[64] The British experience was equally negative.

Lastly, the governmental attitude toward cartels is a promising but still largely ignored field. It is generally supposed that the Dutch government

[62] Frans Messing, *Geschiedenis van de mijnsluiting in Limburg. Noodzaak en lotgevallen van een regionale herstructurering, 1955–1975* (Leiden, 1988); Mila Davids, *De weg naar zelfstandigheid. De voorgeschiedenis van de verzelfstandiging van de PTT in 1989* (Hilversum, 1993); Geert Verbong, "Naar aanleiding van: Drie boeken over electriciteitsbedrijven," *Neha-bulletin* 8 (1994): 93–100; Marc Dierikx and Bram Bouwens, *Building Castles of the Air: Schiphol Amsterdam and the Development of Airport Infrastructure in Europe, 1916–1996* (The Hague, 1997).

[63] Rudolf Filarski, *Kanalen van de koning-koopman. Goederenvervoer, binnenscheepvaart en kanalenbouw in Nederland en Belgie in de eerste helft van de negentiende eeuw* (Amsterdam, 1995); Ben Gales and Reiner Fremdling, "IJzerfabrikanten en industriepolitiek onder koning Willem I: De enquete van 1828," *Neha-jaarboek* 57 (1994): 287–347.

[64] Gerard J. Wijers, *Industriepolitiek. Een onderzoek naar de vormgeving van het overheidsbeleid gericht op industriële sectoren* (Leiden, 1982); Cornelis de Voogd, *De neergang van de scheepsbouw en andere industriële bedrijfstakken* (Vlissingen, 1993).

was lenient toward cartels, even to the point of encouraging them before the Second World War. Frans van Waarden's study of the organization of entrepreneurs in the textile industry between 1800 and 1940 makes clear the power of the textile cartel in its relation both to its employees and to the government. Recent research has also drawn attention to the fact that European cartels turned out to be more enduring after the Second World War than has often been supposed.[65]

INTERNATIONAL BUSINESS

The extensive literature on the history of multinationals is reviewed in detail by Jones in this volume. Nevertheless, it needs to be mentioned here that the British and Dutch business histories are especially active in this field, reflecting the great importance of multinational enterprise in both of these countries.

Both economies were major multinational investors over the past 100 years. Together with the United States, Britain and the Netherlands composed a trio of major and persistent multinational investors. Britain was the world's largest direct investor until 1945 and has remained the second largest after the United States up to the present. After the loss of virtually all German FDI as a result of the First World War, the Netherlands became the world's third largest direct investor and retained that position until around 1980. While the Germans, French, and Italians preferred exporting to direct investment in the "miracle" years of the 1950s and 1960s, the Dutch, like the British, engaged in substantial multinational investment. In 1967 the stock of Dutch FDI was equal to that of Germany, France, and Italy combined. This situation continued until about 1980, when the stock of Dutch FDI was surpassed by that of Germany.

In both countries, the propensity to invest abroad can be firmly traced back to the colonial empires and the various chartered trading companies of the early era. In the case of Britain, there is a formidable literature on the chartered companies that, more recently, has discussed their similarities to modern multinationals.[66] As the chartered trading companies began

[65] Frans van Waarden, *Het geheim van Twente. Fabrikantenverenigingen in de oudste grootindustrie van Nederland, 1800-1940* (Amersfoort/Leuven, 1987); Wendy Asbeek Brusse and Richard Griffiths, "The Management of Markets: Business, Government and Cartels in Post-War Europe," in *Business and European Integration Since 1800. Regional, National and International Perspectives*, ed. Ulf Olssen (Göteborg, 1997), 162-88.
[66] K. N. Chaudhuri, *The Trading World of Asia and the English East India Company 1660-1760* (Cambridge, 1978); A. M. Carlos and S. Nicholas, " 'Giants of an Earlier Capitalism':

to give way to private sector merchant houses, their strategies in the Atlantic, Asia, and elsewhere received much attention.[67] A number of studies have traced the subsequent evolution of these merchant houses during the nineteenth century and up to the present day.[68]

In the Netherlands, a major subject is the history of the Dutch East India Company as a business enterprise and its impact – usually described as marginal or highly negative – on the development of the colony. A similar debate is in progress on the Cultivation System (1830–70) and its mainly negative influence on the development of Java. In recent years, researchers have argued for a greater dynamic in Java's agrarian development. An endlessly debated theme has been the character of Dutch imperialism. This was especially relevant for the Outer Provinces, which were integrated into the colonial empire at the end of the nineteenth century, when Western business was highly interested in the economic exploitation of agrarian plantations and mineral resources.[69] In his company history *Koninklijke Paketvaart Maatschappij*, Joep à Campo showed how the KPM, by offering transport and communication, strengthened state formation and economic infrastructure. In the KPM and its board of directors, all communicating lines of the colony came together. Economic and political interests were closely intertwined.[70]

The political risks involved in foreign direct investment are highlighted by Frans-Paul van der Putten in his study of Dutch companies in China in the early twentieth century. Comparing the experiences of eight firms, he concludes that companies with strong local involvement and a long-term strategy were most willing to accommodate the interests of local governments. This policy was particularly visible in the two Anglo-Dutch multinationals, Royal Dutch/Shell and Unilever. These companies

The Chartered Trading Companies as Modern Multinationals," *Business History Review* 62 (1988): 398–419.

[67] David Hancock, *Citizens of the World* (Cambridge, 1995).

[68] Charles Jones, *International Business in the Nineteenth Century* (Brighton, 1987); Stanley Chapman, *Merchant Enterprise in Britain* (Cambridge, 1992); Geoffrey Jones, *Merchants to Multinationals* (Oxford, 2000).

[69] J. Thomas Lindblad, "The Economic History of Colonial Indonesia: An Historiographical Survey," *Economic and Social History in the Netherlands* 1 (1989): 31–48; an important volume on the economic and business history of Indonesia is J. Thomas Lindblad, ed., *Historical Foundations of a National Economy in Indonesia, 1890s–1990s* (Amsterdam, 1996); for a survey on the imperialism debate, see Maarten Kuitenbrouwer, "Het imperialisme-debat in de Nederlandse geschiedschrijving," *Bijdragen en Mededelingen betreffende de geschiedenis der Nederlanden* 113, no. 1 (1998): 56–73.

[70] Joep à Campo, *Koninklijke Paketvaart Maatschappij. Stoomvaart en staatsvorming in de Indische archipel, 1888–1914* (Hilversum, 1992).

had the added advantage of being able to look to both the Dutch and British governments for protection. The fact that Britain was at that time a world power might have had a considerable impact on their policies.[71]

In both Britain and the Netherlands, there has been research on the "free-standing" firms, which accounted for so much of their foreign direct investment before the First World War, if not later. Building on the earlier work of Wilkins on the British case, Ben Gales and Sluyterman concluded that in the Dutch case, the free-standing company was especially vigorous in the colonial context. There the free-standing companies were embedded in a comfortable community of trading houses, merchant banks, and an active community of Dutchmen and other Europeans. The phenomenon ended when colonialism came to an end.[72]

The growth of modern-style multinationals in Britain and the Netherlands, as noted in Jones's essay, has received considerable attention. In the British case, there are general surveys of its historical growth as well as many specific studies.[73] In the Netherlands, many company histories dealing with the period after the Second World War discuss the theme of internationalization, but they seldom reflect on the issue in general. An interesting aspect of the Dutch internationalization process is that even relatively small companies set up foreign subsidiaries. In other small countries, a comparable willingness to engage in foreign direct investment is noticeable.[74] A number of studies written primarily by economists provide historical insights on Dutch multinationals. In *Multinational Enterprises from the Netherlands*, edited by Roger van Hoesel and Rajneesh Narula (London and New York, 1999), the Dutch experiences in the past three decades are consistently compared with those in other countries.

[71] Frans-Paul van der Putten, *Corporate Behavior and Political Risk; Dutch Companies in China, 1903-1941* (Leiden, 2001).
[72] Ben Gales and Keetie Sluyterman, "Dutch Free-Standing Companies, 1870-1940," in *The Free-standing Company in the World Economy, 1830-1996*, eds. Mira Wilkins and Harm Schröter (Oxford, 1998), 293-322.
[73] Geoffrey Jones, "British Multinational Enterprise and British Business since 1850," in *Business Enterprise in Modern Britain from the Eighteenth to the Twentieth Centuries*, eds. Maurice W. Kirby and Mary B. Rose (London, 1994), 172-206.
[74] Ben Gales and Keetie Sluyterman, "Outward Bound: The Rise of Dutch Multinationals," in *The Rise of Multinationals in Continental Europe*, eds. Geoffrey Jones and Harm Schröter (Aldershot, 1993), 65-98. Harm Schröter included the Netherlands in his study on multinationals from small countries before 1914. Harm G. Schröter, *Aufstieg der Kleinen: Multinationale Unternehmen aus fünf kleinen Staaten vor 1914* (Berlin, 1993).

A highly distinctive feature of British and Dutch business has been their joint ownership of two of the world's largest multinationals, Shell and Unilever. Three of the most important Dutch multinationals were the result of cross-border mergers that took place between 1907 and 1929, two of them Anglo-Dutch. The merger between DAF and the truck division of British Leyland, however, was one of the less successful Anglo-Dutch mergers. During the 1990s other Anglo-Dutch firms were formed, including Reed Elsevier in publishing and Corus in steel.

Both Britain and the Netherlands were major recipients of foreign direct investment. There is extensive research on the impact of foreign multinationals on Britain. While Britain was one of the world's great multinational investors in the twentieth century, it has also been a leading host economy. During the 1850s, Britain received its first inward manufacturing FDI, from U.S. firms such as Colt and J. R. Ford and from the German company Siemens. By 1914 foreign-owned companies were very important in such industrial sectors as dyestuffs and electrical goods. Much greater numbers of foreign firms arrived in the interwar years and still more in the 1950s, clustered in chemicals, mechanical and electrical engineering, metal goods, motor vehicles, and food products. Britain became and has stayed the world's second largest host economy. By 2002, one-quarter of British manufacturing output and one-half of all British exports were from foreign-owned firms. These firms continued – as seems to have been the case throughout the twentieth century – to have much higher productivity than their domestically owned counterparts.

The growth of U.S. multinational investment in Britain – the United States has always been Britain's largest inward investor – was the subject of a pioneering study by John H. Dunning, *American Investment in British Manufacturing Industry* (London, 1958). Dunning, later to become the doyen of economists of the multinational, traced the growth of U.S. multinationals in Britain from the nineteenth century and then undertook a systematic investigation of their impact in the 1950s. Thereafter, the study of the history of foreign multinationals in Britain languished. However, the interest of Dunning and many others in contemporary developments was awakened in the 1980s by the arrival of large-scale Japanese investment in automobiles and electronics.[75] So far, the Dutch

---

[75] John H. Dunning, *Japanese Participation in British Industry* (London, 1986); Geoffrey Jones, "Foreign Multinationals and British Industry before 1945," *Economic History Review* 41, no. 3 (1988): 429–53; Frances Bostock and Geoffrey Jones, "Foreign Multinationals in British Manufacturing, 1850–1962," *Business History* 36, no. 1 (1994): 89–126.

experience with foreign companies has been studied primarily by economic geographers.[76]

CONCLUDING REMARKS

This essay has examined the business history literatures of Britain and the Netherlands, highlighting the common themes pursued by scholars, as well as the differences in approach and conclusion. It therefore forms part of a growing trend, seen in the books by Cassis and Whittington and Mayer, to place the national experiences of individual countries in a wider European comparative context. One result is that some apparently startling differences from the United States can be seen as in reality a general European phenomenon.

The business histories of Britain and the Netherlands show many similarities. The two countries were imperial powers and later shared the experience of decolonization. In the post–Second World War period, both countries' economies became highly concentrated and dominated by large firms. However, family business remained important and was more successful than the Chandlerian model might suggest. Networks of firms and families have been significant forces in both British and Dutch business histories. In both countries the service sector became especially prominent, and both business cultures are noted for their mercantile outlook. Both countries shared a long-term and persistent tendency to engage in foreign direct investment. They shared ownership of two of the world's largest multinational corporations, Shell and Unilever. In other words, many distinctive features of British and Dutch business history turn out to be part of a wider pattern for countries with shared historical patterns of development, geographical positions, and cultural orientations.

The sharpest contrasts seem to be found in their respective managerial cultures. The Dutch emphasis on managers possessing an engineering or technical background contrasted with the historic British preference for character and "gentlemen amateurs" when selecting managers. This would appear to be one major explanation for Britain's poorer productivity performance compared to that of the Netherlands after the Second

---

[76] N. J. Kemper and Marc de Smidt, "Foreign Manufacturing Establishments in the Netherlands," *Tijdschrift voor economische en sociale geografie* 71 (1980): 21–40; Marc de Smidt, "Foreign Industrial Establishments Located in the Netherlands," *Tijdschrift voor economische en sociale geografie* 57 (1966): 1–19.

World War. However, the complementary managerial cultures of Britain and the Netherlands may form part of the explanation for their ability to create, and sustain, large jointly owned multinational corporations.

KEY WORKS

Cassis, Youssef. *Big Business. The European Experience in the Twentieth Century*. Oxford, 1997.

Hannah, Leslie. *The Rise of the Corporate Economy*. London, 1983.

Hoesel, Roger van and Rajneesh Narula, eds. *Multinational Enterprises from the Netherlands*. London and New York, 1999.

Jeremy, David J. *A Business History of Britain, 1900-1990s*. Oxford, 1998.

Jones, Geoffrey. *The Evolution of International Business*. London, 1996.

    "Great Britain: Big Business, Management and Competitiveness in Twentieth Century Britain." In *Big Business and the Wealth of Nations*, edited by Alfred D. Chandler, Jr., Franco Amatori, and Takashi Hikino, 102-38. Cambridge, 1997.

Jonker, Joost and Keetie Sluyterman. *At Home on the World Markets: Dutch International Trading Companies from the 16th Century until the Present*. Montreal, 2000.

Kirby, Maurice W. and Mary B. Rose, eds. *Business Enterprise in Modern Britain*. London, 1994.

Whittington, Richard and Michael Mayer. *The European Corporation*. Oxford, 2000.

Wilson, John F. *British Business History, 1720-1994*. Manchester, 1995.

Zanden, Jan Luiten van. *The Economic History of the Netherlands, 1914-1995: A Small Open Economy in the "Long" Twentieth Century*. London, 1998.

7

Scandinavian Business History at the End of the 1990s

Its Prior Development, Present Situation, and Future

HÅKAN LINDGREN

BUSINESS HISTORY AS ECONOMIC HISTORY

In the Scandinavian countries, business history has its roots in economic history. The relationship between the two has developed into a true symbiosis. Today business history is recognized as an important branch of economic history, and the old controversies of the 1960s and 1970s between "macro" and "micro" approaches, between econometric model-oriented, "aggregative" economic historians and the more inductive, qualitatively oriented business historians, appear to have disappeared. The incorporation of business history as a recognized subdiscipline of economic history has not yet resulted in any business history independence movement, in contrast to developments in the United States and Britain. In fact, business historians have not raised any demands for upgrading their discipline by establishing academic chairs or departments of their own.[1]

There are at least two main reasons for the accommodative relationship between business history and economic history in the Scandinavian

---

[1] The strong conviction that business history is an integrated part of economic history in Scandinavian academia is illustrated by the Swedish business historian Kersti Ullenhag. In her comments on Rolv Petter Amdam's paper at a seminar on "Theory and Methods in Financial and Business History" at Stockholm University in 1994, she relates the "shocking

countries. To begin with, developments in the social sciences, especially in economics, during the past two decades have weakened the methodological boundaries between macro- and microanalyses. The removal of these walls has had an obvious connection with the changes that have taken place in economic science since the 1970s. Stagflation and crises, as well as the absence of enduring growth in the underdeveloped countries despite massive capital transfers, caused many economists of the late 1970s to doubt the ability of Keynesian theory to provide the relevant analytical tools. The use of very broad aggregates as analytical concepts had proven unsuitable for explaining the mechanisms of economic fluctuation and growth, and an intense search for the microfoundations of macrovariables was undertaken. One result was the revival of Austrian, Schumpeterian, and institutional economics, which had earlier been placed in quarantine by a nearly unanimous body of Scandinavian economists.

A new social science discipline, business economics or business administration, grew strongly during the 1980s at Scandinavian universities. The new subject soon proved to be a real dynamo of the academic world. Measured by the number of students and teachers, business administration emerged within a couple of decades as the largest discipline in the social science faculties, as well as the core subject in the growing number of business schools that were established at or spun off from universities. Within the new subject, the scientific management literature grew broadly and contributed strongly to increased research on the conditions of business' operations and resource-creating abilities. This research had an inductive character and a clear empirical direction, and was based often on case studies of individual firms. It constituted an opportunity as well as a challenge for business history. The most important development for business history, however, was the increasing legitimacy of "microstructure" studies, which was a result of the establishment of large, influential departments of business administration within social science faculties.

The methodological renewal in the economic social sciences also had a counterpart in the humanities and in general history. This implies that the change in the type and level of approach might be part of a

experience" of "hearing participants discuss whether business history has anything in common with economic history" at the Erasmus University Conference on Business History some weeks earlier. See H. Sjögren, ed., *Aspekter på näringslivets historia (Aspects of Business History)*, Research Report, no. 5 (Stockholm, 1995).

more general scientific renewal, constituting a reaction against the pronounced theoretical and aggregative dominance of research (the "tyranny
of aggregation") during the 1960s and 1970s. As early as 1991, Rolf
Torstendahl, professor of history at Uppsala University, noted in an article that anthropologically oriented, historical mentality studies were in
the process of squeezing out the quantitative social history that previously had totally dominated research in history. Today, scarcely a decade
later, microhistory is the height of fashion in history departments. When
placed in a broader perspective, this "new" research has even been en-
dowed with a new name, "mezzo" history.[2]

   It is perfectly clear that these developments in scientific methodology also have affected the content of economic history research. The
increased acceptance of microstudies in economic history is undoubtedly an important factor in explaining the convergence of economic and
business history in recent decades. The change in perspective, which in
some regards is reminiscent of a Kuhnian paradigm shift, has permitted
a number of theoretical impulses to grow and prosper. These range from
institutionally oriented theories to entrepreneurial, networking, and evolutionary, so-called neo-Austrian, theories. The competition among alternative approaches has resulted in an experimental and creative research
environment. Cumulatively, this situation has contributed to strengthening the position of business history research within the field of economic
history, the entire academic community, and even society in general.

   But even research developments within business history itself contributed to dissolving the old value conflicts between individual events
and lawlike behavior, between the narrative description of unique events
and theory-tied abstractions at higher aggregate levels. A new generation
of business historians had grown up, demonstrating a very different and
much greater understanding of theoretical approaches. The lively discussions in methodological issues during the second half of the 1960s
and during the 1970s, which displayed characteristics similar to those of
the great "Methodenstreit" in the economic sciences at the end of the
nineteenth century, had the positive result that arguments were sharp-
ened and new knowledge was established. For the relatively few younger
researchers in economic history who had devoted themselves to business
history research with scientific ambitions, the debate involved justifying
their existence and their survival in a harsh academic environment.

----

[2] B. Odén, *Leda vid livet: Fyra mikrohistoriska essäer om självmordets historia* (Lund,
1998), 11. See also Rolf Torstendahl's article in *Svenska Dagbladet*, September 2, 1991.

EARLY PROFESSIONALIZATION AND CONTROVERSIES

Business history as a scientific research field already had a strong base in Sweden by the 1950s. The early professionalization coincided with the strong standing of iron processing in Swedish business life, both before and after the Industrial Revolution. Well-preserved source materials from Swedish iron mills in the public central archives and private company archives formed the bases for the new research field that was designated economic history and whose introduction in Sweden and Scandinavia is inseparably associated with Eli F. Heckscher's name. In 1950 Heckscher published a strong plea for business history as an important research field for economic historians in his paper entitled "On Swedish Business Companies and their Historical Treatment."[3]

Both in Norway and in Sweden, large research projects served as the starting point for the expansion of business history research. The 1950s marked a breakthrough in Sweden. The first academic chairs in economic history at Swedish universities were inaugurated at this time, and the so-called first-generation professors in economic history – Artur Attman (Gothenburg), Oscar Bjurling (Lund), Karl-Gustaf Hildebrand (Uppsala), and Ernst Söderlund (Stockholm) – established themselves as significant business historians. A broad-based research project on the history of the Fagersta iron works during the 1950s brought together nearly all the professional economic historians in Sweden. In the five thick volumes on the history of the Fagersta Company, published in 1957–9, different approaches were united, and totally different types of archive materials served as the bases for a presentation with clearly broad and contextual ambitions. This voluminous work treated the history of Swedish iron processing as a totality, and it set the norms for how professional business history with scientific ambitions would be conducted in Sweden.[4]

In Norway at the end of the 1960s, several young historians and economic historians produced a major three-volume work on the wood-processing firm Mathiesen Eiswold Verk. Their interest lay in treating firms as central actors in the economy. One of them was Francis Sejersted, in 1972 appointed to a post as Professor of Economic History at the University of Oslo. During the 1970s, Sejersted supervised a large research project that analyzed the economic crises of the interwar period using a

---

[3] E. F. Heckscher, "Om svenska företag och deras historiska behandling," *Nordisk Tidskrift*, no. 3 (1950): 213–35.

[4] E. Söderlund, K.-G. Hildebrand, A. Attman, et al., *Fagerstabrukens historia*, 5 vols. (Stockholm, 1957–9).

business history approach. He also actively participated in the scholarly
discussion concerning the role of business history. In 1972, in a now
classic article published in the then leading Swedish historical journal,
Historisk Tidskrift, he defended traditional historical writing against the
so-called New Economic Historians and their claims of greater abstraction
and higher levels of generalization.[5]

The development of research on business history in Denmark is closely
tied to Kristof Glaman, who became the first holder of a professorship in
economic history at the University of Copenhagen in 1960. During the
1960s, in cooperation with, among others, the statistician and economist
Svend Aage Hansen, he built up a special institute for economic history
at the university. Published in 1950, his early book on the organizational
evolution of the Danish tobacco industry constitutes, especially in its
problem formulation, an exemplary work. His monograph on the Danish
brewing industry, published in 1962, quickly became a standard work
for Scandinavian business historians. Following in Glaman's footsteps,
Hans Christian Johansen, Professor of Economic and Social History at the
University of Odense, has written widely in the field of business history.
Among his works are corporate monographs on the Albani Breweries
and the Danfoss Concern, one of Denmark's major international firms in
the engineering field.[6]

The problem of preserving archival material and making it available
for business history research was solved early on in Denmark through
the establishment of a national archival center. In cooperation between
the city government and the newly founded University of Århus, an independent institution to collect and preserve separate firm archives, the
Erhvervsarkivet, was founded in 1948. The yearbook it has published
annually since 1949 not only provides good information concerning the
archives' holdings and their growth, but also constitutes a historiographically very interesting account of developments within Danish business
history research.[7] As is usual with such projects, the contributions of

[5] F. Sejersted, "Apologi for den gammeldagse ökonomiske historie," *Historisk Tidskrift*
(Swedish), no. 4 (1972): 461–73. Sejersted's main contribution to the Mathiesen Eidsvold
project was *Den gamle bedrift og den nye tid: 1842–1895* (Oslo, 1979).
[6] K. Glaman, *75-foreningen. Den danske tobaksindustris organisatoriske utvikling 1875–
1950* (Copenhagen, 1950); id., *Bryggeriets historie i Danmark indtil slutningen af det
19. Århundrede* (Copenhagen, 1962); P. Boje and H. C. Johansen, *Alltid på vej ... Albani
Bryggeriernes historie, 1859–1984* (Odense, 1989); id., *En ivaerksaetter: Historien om
Mads Clausen og Danfoss* (Odense, 1994).
[7] "Erhvervsarkivet 1948–1998. Udvikling og positioner," *Erhvervsarkivets Årbog 1997*
(Århus, 1997), 5–48.

individuals were of crucial importance. Vagn Dybdahl made the Århus archives a model for the other Scandinavian countries as its long-serving director. Later, Dybdahl became the head of the Danish National Archives.

In Finland during the 1950s and 1960s, the major firms began to utilize scholarly competence to produce good-quality company histories. Until the mid-1970s there was only a single professorship in economic and social history in the country – at Helsinki University. It was therefore only natural that the first generation of business historians was mainly recruited either from among historians (e.g., Eino Jutikkala, Oscar Nikula, Vilho Annala, and Keijo Alho) or from among economists interested in history (e.g., Nils Meinander and Hugo Pipping).[8] The pioneering work in Finland was Pipping's two-volume history of the Bank of Finland, followed in 1972 by Jorma Ahvenainen's book on the large forest industry concern, Kymmene.[9]

The discussion in Sweden and Norway during the 1950s and 1960s concerning the scholarly role of business history had a Finnish counterpart, with the younger generation of scholars actively participating. Already in 1965, Sven-Erik Åström, Professor of Economic History at Helsinki University, had drawn an emphatic distinction between business history as a scholarly enterprise and shallow corporate histories designed for public relations and anniversary celebrations. In 1975, Erkki Pihkala asserted that business history had a special role to play concerning phenomena that are ignored by economic theory, including especially the origin and evaluation of innovations. A decade later, against the background of increasing skepticism concerning Keynesian macrotheory that arose in the 1970s, Per Schybergson delightedly reported on the new demand for empirical business research emanating from economists' increased interest in innovations and entrepreneurial behavior. Nonetheless, Schybergson doubted that business history could – or even should – be reoriented in a more economic theoretical direction.[10]

---

[8] Eino Jutikkala, a well-known social historian, held a professorship in economic and social history at Helsinki University until 1954. That year he transferred to a chair in Finnish history.

[9] H. E. Pipping, *Från pappersrubel till guldmark: Finlands Bank 1811–1877* (Helsinki, 1961); id., *I guldmyntfotens hägn: Finlands Bank 1878–1914* (Helsinki, 1969); J. Ahvenainen, *Från pappersbruk till storföretag: Kymmene Aktiebolag 1918–1939* (Helsinki, 1972).

[10] S.-E. Åström, "Företagshistoria eller företagshistorik: Vetenskap eller reklam?" (Business History or Company History: Scholarship or Public Relations?), *Ekonomiska Samfundets Tidskrift* 18, no. 3 (1965): 195–201; E. Pihkala, "Katsauksia, Taloushistoria tutkimuksen kentässä" (Chronicles: An Economic History Research Field), *Historiallinen*

Placing this Nordic debate in its methodological and political context is of interest. From the late 1960s through the 1970s, business history increasingly was subjected to criticism from two different directions. To begin with, economic historians with leftist sympathies maintained that business history amounted to no more than a collection of commissioned works, produced on terms established by the corporations being studied. Business history, therefore, was by definition not objective scholarship. Instead, it concentrated on success stories while sweeping important problems, such as the contradiction between capital and labor, under the proverbial rug.

Criticism of business history written without political overtones was also leveled by "generalizers" in economic history. Influenced by deductive economics in general and Keynesian growth theory in particular, the generalizers believed in structural explanations at higher aggregate levels. In the hunt for general law-determined behavior that could explain macroeconomic development, there was no room for the individual and the unique, and business history was accused of being narrative, without theory, and overly concerned with singular events. Business history lost ground in the environment of this academic discourse, and with the generational change that took place in economic history in Sweden during the 1970s, the major chairs in the subject became occupied by generalists and structuralists who worked from a Marxist or Keynesian perspective.

BUSINESS HISTORY GETS ORGANIZED

This attack on two fronts forced the younger economic historians with business history research ambitions to take a conscious position and search for a balance between empiricism and theory in research. Almost three decades after the publication of Heckscher's programmatic plea for business history in 1950, the Swedish *Historisk Tidskrift* published a special issue on business history in 1979. A comparison with Heckscher's article illustrates in a very dramatic way both the expansion of the research field since 1950 and the greatly increased presence of theory in business history. The 1979 thematic issue on business history in *Historisk Tidskrift* had great significance for the subsequent renaissance in research in the 1980s and 1990s and therefore warrants closer attention.

aikakauskirja, no. 4 (1975): 313–15; P. Schybergson, "Företagshistoria: Empirisk arsenal för ekonomisk teori" (Business History: An Empirical Supply Depot for Economic Theory?), *Historisk Tidskrift för Finland* 71, no. 1 (1986): 139–43.

The issue contained a well-conceived defense for what could be termed the "traditional business history monograph" and pleaded for a contextual business history focusing on industry and systems levels along with new, theoretically more conscious methods in business history research.

For Heckscher, in 1950 business history was synonymous with commissioned company histories, monographic histories, or case studies of a business organization in its entirety. In his article in the *Historisk Tidskrift's* special issue of 1979, Ulf Olsson, Professor of Economic History at the University of Umeå, labeled this way of doing business history the "organic" approach, aiming at a complete description of the historical development of a company. In line with Francis Sejersted's 1972 article, Olsson defended the study of individual processes in its entirety, convincingly arguing that an organically structured company history is quite different from a simple narrative, "wall-to-wall carpeting" of description, provided that the study is done by a professional academic scholar.

Olsson's basic argument was that no description of reality can be made at a scale of 1:1. The professional judgment of a well-trained academic scholar is needed to organize the empirical material in a way that renders the firm's history interesting, readable, and analytically rigorous. When writing a company history, even the most ardent believer in history as *l'art pour l'art* or as a chain of unique events must decide what aspects, what strategic decisions, or what periods in the history of a firm are more important than others. Moreover, to understand why certain strategic decisions were made or why certain things happened, the writer must know the value systems of the time period under study. And to develop a more generalized approach, the writer must know what happened in the world outside the firm under study.

Olsson presented a purely functional selection method in contrast to the traditional company monograph approach. By "functional selection" Olsson meant a deliberate, conscious choice of certain aspects of a company or of business relations in order to illuminate and give specification to general issues or theories at the micro level. The danger, for example, of illuminating different aspects or testing different theories in various articles in a company anthology is, of course, that the presentation tends to be fragmented. "It can be difficult to explain at the end how the firm once lived and functioned as an organic entity, which after all is not unimportant in the context."[11]

---

[11] U. Olsson, "Företagshistoria som ekonomisk historia" (Business History as Economic History), *Historisk Tidskrift* (Swedish), no. 3 (1979): 243.

Two other articles appeared in the *Historisk Tidskrift*'s special issue, one by Kersti Ullenhag and the other by Erik Dahmén. Both argued for a renewal of business history research in a more consistent theoretical direction. In her contribution, "Business History and its Renewal," Ullenhag, Associate Professor of Economic History at Uppsala University, emphasized the desirability of renewal in two directions. One direction concerned the extent of small business activity and its conditions. Despite technical difficulties in research, such as deficiencies in official statistics and undeveloped archival awareness among small businesses, Ullenhag argued that significantly more research should be brought to bear on small and midsized companies, which were hopelessly underrepresented in the population of subjects for serious business history research. Renewal was also demanded to develop the explanatory value of business history studies in the general sociohistorical development and to link the results with established theory. Through her exemplification of achieved results, Ullenhag hinted that she had primarily Joseph Schumpeter's growth and business cycle theories in mind, in which the entrepreneurial function plays a decisive role.[12]

Erik Dahmén's contribution undoubtedly received the greatest attention from the younger generation of business historians. He was the most renowned of the contributors: since 1957 he had been Professor of Economics with Economic and Social History at the Stockholm School of Economics and Director of its Institute for Research in Economic History. For several decades, he had acted as special adviser to both Marcus Wallenberg, one of Sweden's most famous entrepreneurs of the twentieth century, and Stockholm's Enskilda Bank, the industrial bank of the Wallenberg family. Dahmén had developed a system of thought in the 1950s and 1960s that was influenced by Joseph Schumpeter and the Swedish economist Johan Åkerman at Lund University in the 1930s and 1940s. This was mostly referred to as "Dahménianism" or the "Dahménian approach to economics," which in Sweden became a major intellectual force paving the way for the breakdown of the hegemonic Keynesian macromodels in the 1970s and 1980s.[13]

In his 1979 article, Dahmén convincingly showed in what ways business history research could advance and develop economic theory. He used examples to demonstrate the fallacies of aggregative thinking when

---

[12] K. Ullenhag, "Företagsforskning och förnyelse" (Company Research and Renewal), *Historisk Tidskrift* (Swedish), no. 3 (1979): 270-1.

[13] The importance of Erik Dahmén in establishing a Schumpeterian tradition in Swedish social science is developed by R. Swedberg, "Joseph Schumpeter in Sweden," *Scandinavian Economic History Review* 45, no. 2 (1997): 113-30.

approaching certain (important) questions relating to transformation processes and industrial dynamics. This was most obvious when analyzing the determinants of supply. With the slogan "Macrotheory needs microfoundations," Erik Dahmén made a strong plea for increased multidisciplinary cooperation between economic historians, business economists, and economists. The shared objective was to develop a new business history, focused on the character and role of the firm's operations, with the power not only to use or "consume" established theories, but also to produce new theories.[14]

In 1976, three years before the special issue of *Historisk Tidskrift*, Dahmén and Gert Nylander, Chief Archivist of the Stockholms Enskilda Bank, had reorganized the Institute for Research in Economic History (EHF) at the Stockholm School of Economics. The EHF had originally been founded by Eli F. Heckscher in 1929. In 1976, the institute was reorganized as an interdisciplinary organization, combining economic, historical, and social research with special applications to business and industry. The revived EHF Institute was designed to act as an intermediary between business and research, organize commissioned research, and thereby guarantee the scientific integrity of the business historian in relation to the sponsor. At the same time, the EHF Institute was provided with its own research resources, sufficient to actively initiate, organize, and promote scholarly research in the field of business history research.

The EHF Institute at the Stockholm School of Economics, with its creative interdisciplinary organization, proved to be a good example of farsighted planning to propel business history into the front line of research. With such professors as Dahmén, Johan Myhrman, and Ulf Olsson in its management, the institute has earned a solid reputation for its qualitatively superior and advanced business history research. The institute's monograph series has produced twenty-six works, starting with *Banking in Pioneer Times: A. O. Wallenberg in Swedish Banking Policy 1850–1856*, which was published in 1981 by Göran B. Nilsson. In 2001 the series brought out Mats Larsson's analysis of corporate governance, succession strategies, and corporate culture in the Bonnier family business group, *Bonniers: A Media Family. Publishing House, Conglomerate and Media Group, 1953–1990.*[15]

---

[14] E. Dahmén, "Kan den företagshistoriska forskningen bidra till den ekonomiska teoriens utveckling?" (Can the Business History Research Contribute to the Development of Economic Theory?), *Historisk Tidskrift* (Swedish), no. 3 (1979): 261–4.

[15] G. B. Nilsson, *Banker i brytningstid: A. O. Wallenberg i svensk bankpolitik, 1850–1856* (Stockholm, 1981); M. Larsson, *Bonniers: En mediefamilj. Förlag, konglomerat och mediekoncern, 1953–1990* (Stockholm, 1991).

In addition to the monograph series, the EHF Institute began publishing research reports in 1991. The aim of this series is twofold: first, to quickly publish the results of research pursued at EHF and, second, to publish surveys of the current state of research in various fields. The latter come frequently in the form of reports on conferences or seminars organized by EHF. An example is report No. 10, an essay by Michael Bordo of Rutgers University and the National Bureau of Economic Research (NBER) entitled "Currency Crises (and Banking Crises) in Historical Perspective." Recently, the Stockholm School of Economics, supported by EHF, has instituted a Ph.D. program in economic history intended to ensure the development of a new generation of scholars, especially in financial and business history.

The Norwegian example demonstrates that the creation of an organizational base for operations, preferably with its own research resources, facilitates a successful academic establishment. I am not just being courteous, due to my association with the Stockholm School of Economics and its EHF Institute, when I emphatically maintain that the academic legitimization of business history in the Scandinavian countries has been most successful in Norway. As in other contexts, it was personal initiative and enterprise that had decisive significance. Even Lange was one of the younger researchers who collaborated with Francis Sejersted in the previously mentioned Mathiesen Eidsvold project on the Norwegian forest industry. He was responsible for the Centre for Business History, which was established at the Norwegian National Archives in 1979, the same year as the business history counteroffensive that materialized in Sweden with the publication in *Historisk Tidskrift* of the special issue on business history.

Although there was only one permanent position at the Centre for Business History until 1988, an impressive series of ten commissioned business history projects were published in the 1980s. Among these were *Bjölsen Valsemölle A/S and the Development of the Norwegian Flour Industry, 1884–1984*, edited by Helge Nordvik (1984); *Christiania Glasmagasin and the Norwegian Glass Industry 1739–1989*, written by Rolv Petter Amdam, Tore Jörgen Harnisch, and Ingvild Pharo (1989); and *Technology in Practice: Mechanical Engineering Industries in Norway since 1840*, edited by Even Lange (1989).

As a concrete expression of the successful academic legitimization process of business history in Norway, the Centre for Business History was transferred from the National Archives to the Norwegian School of Management BI as an Economic History Unit in 1989. The old designation in English – Centre for Business History – was retained, however. In connection with the move to BI, a professorship in economic history was created, and the department received an additional three permanent research positions in business history. Under Professor Even Lange's leadership, the research organization expanded rapidly during the 1990s, and the Oslo Centre for Business History became the most important business history research location in Scandinavia. By the end of 1997, the number of permanent research positions had increased to six, and Rolv Petter Amdam was appointed to a second professorship at the Oslo Centre.

With the support of a favorable Norwegian oil business cycle, commissioned research projects from the state and business flowed. The productivity of research as well as its breadth at the BI Centre for Business History is impressive. Among the widely divergent projects that were successfully completed during the 1990s were projects on the Norwegian pharmaceutical industry (Nyegaard & Co.), Norwegian industrial policy (Norges Industriforbund), the growth of formalized economic education in Norway, the Norwegian tanning industry, and the expansion of hydroelectric power. The latest in a line of published company histories is the history of Kreditkassen, one of the most important actors in the Norwegian financial markets in the twentieth century. This was published for the bank's 150-year jubilee in May 1998. Among the ongoing larger research efforts is the history of the Norwegian Telephone Company, a broad-based study of telecommunications and society over 150 years, and a three-volume study on the history of Norsk Hydro, a work involving several research students.[16]

In order to strengthen research and instruction in business history, in May 1999 the Copenhagen Business School established a Centre for Business History. A three-year plan of action, to be followed by an evaluation procedure, has been laid out. The Centre is associated with the Institute for International Business and Management, and it has business internationalization as a priority research field. In conjunction with the founding of the Centre, there has been a major expansion of business history research at the Copenhagen School of Business. This has resulted in the creation of Scandinavia's first chair in pure business history. The

---

[16] R. P. Amdam, "Oppdragsresearch som akademisk disiplin: Trekk ved norsk foretagshistorisk research" (Commissioned Research as an Academic Discipline: Features of Norwegian Business History Research), in *Aspekter på näringslivets historia*, ed. H. Sjögren, Research Report no. 5 (Stockholm, 1995), 33–46; *Årsmedling Avdelning for ökonomisk historie* (Handelshöyskolen BI, 1994–7).

first appointed occupant is Ole Lange, previously associate professor in
the same subject at the school.

TOWARD A BROADER DEFINITION OF
BUSINESS HISTORY

The position of business history in Scandinavia as an integrated part of
economic history explains why methodology has focused on the contextual aspects of business history from the very beginning. A criterion for
qualitatively good business history has always been that the company is
analyzed in relation to its surroundings.

The striving for generalization became even more evident during the
rapid expansion of this research area in the 1980s and 1990s, regardless
of what aspects of the firm and its activities were studied. Even if the
individual firm is the focus, the study is now closer in character to a
sector monograph, with analyses of different types of "business systems,"
rather than a pure company monograph. Trends in business organization
and business cultures are analyzed, as are the educational system and the
curricula of business schools. Technology and innovations are studied in
an ideological, cultural, economic, and societal context. Finally, the "rules
of the game," especially those involving state industrial and economic
policies, receive significantly greater attention than before.

Contextual efforts also characterize to a high degree business history
research in Finland and Denmark, which did not develop the same organized forms as those in Norway and Sweden. However, individual researchers such as Per Boje, Hans Christian Johansen, and Ole Lange in
Denmark, as well as Jorma Ahvenainen, Markku Kuisma, Antti Kuusterä,
and Per Schybergson in Finland, have made significant efforts to develop
a more synthesized business history.[17]

Several attention-drawing studies recently published in Denmark exemplify the renewal of business history research that has occurred in
Scandinavia. One of these is Per Boje's *Ledere, ledelse og organisation* (Odense, 1997). The book is a clear, problem-oriented presentation

---

[17] H. C. Johansen, *Fra monopol til konkurrence: P&Ts historie efter 1960* (Copenhagen,
1993); J. Ahvenainen, *Enso-Gutzeit Oy, 1872–1992*, 2 vols. (Jyväskylä, 1993); M. Kuisma,
Kylmä sota, kuuma öljy: Neste, Suomi ja kaksi Eurooppaa, 1948–1979 (Porvoo, 1997);
A. Kuusterä, *Pelisäännöt: Helsingin rahamarkkinakeskuksen lyhyt historia* (Helsinki,
1998); P. Schybergson, *Työt ja päivät: Ahlströmin historia, 1851–1981* (Vammala, 1992).
The Schybergson study has also been published in Swedish with the title *Verk och dagar:
Ahlströms historia, 1851–1981* (Vammala, 1992).

related to a specific theme: ownership, business leadership, and firm organization in Danish industry from 1870 until the end of the golden years of economic growth in the early 1970s. In an exemplary fashion, Boje relates general trends in key areas (e.g., ownership and management structures, incorporation and company formation, the recruitment and training of executives, leadership, and control) to concrete reality. The many well-chosen examples bear witness not just to his being well read, but also to his ability to not "let the forest obscure the trees." From a methodological perspective, the success of the book's strictly thematic organization demonstrates the power of the functional approach to business history discussed earlier.[18]

Ole Lange demonstrates in his book on the Lauritzen shipping companies that it is possible to combine the readability required of an anniversary volume – the book was written for J. Lauritzen Holding's centenary celebration – with high scholarly standards in contextual and theoretical underpinnings. A wide-ranging 1996 doctoral thesis on the Danish banking system during the interwar period by Per H. Hansen serves as a good example of the benefits that occur when business historians widen their research beyond business archives. Making good use of the abundant public material contained in the archives of the State Bank Inspection (the Banktilsynet), his problem-oriented and systematic study clearly brings out the connections between politics and economics.[19]

Another excellent example of the increasing emphasis on the analysis of the interplay between companies and society in Scandinavian business history research is Antti Kuusterä's book on the Finnish savings banks. This is more than a treatment of the savings banks in a narrow sense. Kuusterä also provides a broad social description of the savings bank movement in Finland – its German and British origins, its populist tendencies, and the degradation that led inevitably to the Finnish savings bank catastrophe in the financial crisis of the 1990s.[20]

The contextual approach of the business history of the 1990s is, of course, one answer to criticisms from the generalists of the 1970s. This is a development that has been advocated in most programmatic

---

[18] P. Boje, *Ledere, ledelse og organisation: Dansk industri efter 1870*, tom 5 (Odense, 1997).

[19] O. Lange, *Logbog for Lauritzen, 1884–1995: Historien om Konsulen, hans sønner og Lauritzen Gruppen* (Copenhagen, 1995); Per H. Hansen, *På glidebanen til den bitre ende. Dansk bankvaesen i krise, 1920–1933* (Odense, 1996).

[20] A. Kuusterä, *Aate ja raha: Säästöpankit suomalaisessa yhteiskunnassa, 1822–1994* (Helsinki, 1996). Also published in Swedish with the title *Idé och pengar: Sparbankerna i den finländska samhället, 1822–1994* (Helsinki, 1996).

articles on business history as a research field since the 1970s, not only in Scandinavia but elsewhere as well.[21] The development is, however, not entirely unproblematic. To clarify the problematic character of the generalist approach in business history, I will refer to two standard textbooks on the subject, one American and one British, that today are widely used in business history courses in Scandinavia.

In their classical textbook *Business Enterprise in American History*, intended for students in both history and business schools, Blackford and Kerr have chosen two main topics or themes to describe U.S. business history: the development of the firm and the development of government–business relations. In their introduction, these themes are used to define the scope of business history.[22] It appears to me that the definition is successful in one respect and less successful in another. It is successful in that *the business firm is stressed as the core of business history analysis*. The path dependence of our research field provides a strong motivation to define business history in a strictly operational sense, stressing the focus of historical research on the firm as one of the key actors of industrial society.

The weakness of the Blackford–Kerr delimitation of the contents of business history can be seen in the second part of their definition. It seems to me difficult to justify why government–business relations alone should be given the same weight as the study of the firm. And why should the relation between business and government be more interesting than in-depth studies of, for example, the relationship to "systems" of business culture, business education and training, or technological innovation?

John F. Wilson, of the University of Manchester, has developed in his textbook *British Business History, 1720–1994*, the modern and more generalized approach to business history. He defines four key themes as central to business history research: the business culture and society's attitudes toward it; labor; businesses and financial institutions; and business and the state.[23]

---

[21] Besides the Swedish *Historisk Tidskrift* issue of 1979, referred to earlier, see, for example, E. Lange, "Business history som innfallsvinkel til ökonomisk historie" (Business History as an Insight to Economic History), *Historisk Tidsskrift* (Norwegian), no. 3 (1988): 261–4; K. Sogner, "Recent Trends in Business History," *Scandinavian Economic History Review* 45, no. 1 (1997): 58–69.

[22] M. G. Blackford and K. A. Kerr, *Business Enterprise in American History*, 3d ed. (Boston, 1994), 1–2.

[23] J. F. Wilson, *British Business History, 1720–1994* (Manchester, 1995), 1–3.

The approach of British business history fits well into the Scandinavian pattern of development, and Wilson's book has become popular in this region. In its well-motivated and legitimate ambitions there is, however, a danger that the very core of our research field – the firm – will come to occupy an obscure place and that the multifaceted contents will be interpreted as reflecting a lack of consensus on the object of research in our subject. Also, especially in relation to economic history, there is a tendency for the broad definition of Scandinavian business history to be understood as reflecting imperialistic ambitions of our subject. In dealing with, for example, value systems of society or business systems, the question of where a business history approach starts and where it ends seems quite legitimate.

A simple answer to that question is that the individual (entrepreneurial or firm) and general (institutional) approaches must be combined in business history research if we want to develop our subject on a solid scientific basis. The perspective of the firm is fundamental, and regardless of the nature of the issue, the firm is and remains the central object of analysis. Therefore, I maintain that business history comprises all historical research that seeks answers to different questions *at the level of the firm*. The nature of these questions can be very different. Business history is about everything from issues of ownership and leadership functions, power and influence, principal–agent problems, and information asymmetries to issues of technology, organizational innovations, and power over work and the work environment. But without the perspective of the firm, there is no business history.

All business research, like business history research, is ultimately inspired by the fact that a significant number of the economic decisions of society are made within firms. In the firm, production and information resources are constantly organized in new combinations, both in conflict and in collaboration with different individuals and groups. New decisions are constantly made regarding R&D efforts, implementation of new technologies for solving organizational, marketing, or production problems, and whether coordination is to occur inside, or outside the firm, using the market mechanism. Since these decisions are of great significance for local communities, for nation-states, and, with the increasing scale of business enterprises, for international relations and the global economy, it is not difficult to justify the utility of business history by this traditional scope of inquiry.

When the decision making of firms is placed at the center of business history research, it becomes necessary to apply process or dynamic analyses as the main methodological approach. Basically, dynamic analyses are historical analyses, which search for causal relationships with time series analyses and attempt to explain events by linking individual behavior to structural phenomena by means of successive abstraction.[24] Decision making is itself a process, during which many choices are made under constantly changing conditions, both internal and external to the organization. The firm – or rather those decision makers within the firm – reacts to impulses and signals. In dealing with exchange and transactions, neoclassical theory has isolated the price signals as the fundamental explanatory variable. In reality, however, the importance of price varies greatly in different markets. In industrial markets, for example, technical, operative, and, not least, social impulses have been shown to be of much greater importance than prices in explaining transactions.[25]

But the decision makers are also creating new firm-specific assets or increasing the firm's command of existing resources in their struggle for survival and growth in more or less competitive markets. All these decisions at the firm level have implications for the overall social and economic organization of society: for work organization, work content, and work intensity; for efficiency in production and distribution; and for innovations, industrial transformation, and economic performance.

BUSINESS HISTORY AND THEORY

With the results in hand, it is quite obvious that an important part of the program for a renewal of Scandinavian business history, which was launched in the 1979 special issue of *Historisk Tidskrift*, has been realized. This conclusion applies especially to the plea for a more contextual business history. The efforts to achieve generalization, however, have also had a positive effect on theory consciousness among Scandinavian

[24] Applied to the theory of foreign direct investments, this way of combining microevents with macro or structural explanations is further developed in my paper "Business History, Historical Economics and Economic Theory," read at the Business History Conference in Athens, 1990, organized by Professor Margarita Dritsas and published in her conference report, *L'Entreprise en Grèce et en Europe XIXe–XXe siècles* (Athens, 1992).

[25] The view that factors other than prices are important in shaping the behavior of the firm is a fundamental part of the so-called network approach, elaborated in the 1980s by the Swedish business economists Håkan Håkanson, Jan Johanson, and Lars-Gunnar Mattsson; see, for example, Håkansson, *International Marketing and Purchasing of Industrial Goods: An Interaction Approach* (Chichester, 1982); and Johanson and Mattsson, "Internationalisation in Industrial Systems: A Network Approach," in *Strategies in Global Competition*, eds. N. Hood and J.-E. Vahlne (New York, 1988), 287–314.

business historians, and there is a clear tendency toward increased *theory consumption* in both economic and social theory. It is above all institutional theory, with its consideration of social and political influences, that has attracted business historians, just as it has attracted economic historians in general.

The major problems with institutional economic theory and institutional economic history involve the operationalization of the concept of institutions and the determination, based on reliable experience or reasonably accepted theory, of which rules of the game can be expected to have significance for the reality under study. Since "institutions" are usually given a very broad interpretation, the question arises of what actually *separates* institutional theory from the ordinary economic-historical approach. For example, Douglass North – who has had significant influence in Scandinavia and has inspired the 1990s generation of younger business historians and economic historians – defines institutions as all the "constraints," formal and informal, that are created to facilitate human interaction. This is a very broad determination of the concept.

The designation "institutional theory" is an expression of a theoretical concept that will eventually become superficial and watered down. It is increasingly confused with scientific method in meaning "approach," "view," or "perspective," which reminds me of the Swedish saying that a loved child has many names. From an analytical perspective, how theory is defined is not an insignificant issue. If the theory concept is reduced to assumptions, hypotheses, or structures, that the researcher chooses or constructs to impart meaning to empirical statements, there is little or no demand for empirical support. A theory worthy of the name should be anchored in empirical experience that is based on recurrent observation (repetitive phenomena). An empirical link in one direction facilitates, of course, links in the opposite direction. In my view, a theory should be amenable to testing against reality so that its ability to generalize can be established.[26]

Based on this specification of demands, there does not exist a general institutional development theory but rather a set of basic methodological principles for structuring and focusing research work. These principles

---

[26] A convincing plea in English for a clear demarcation between methods in terms of basic methodological principles from which research is planned, and theory as a system of well-defined concepts and their internal relationships, has been made in Scandinavia by the science historian J. Witt-Hansen, *Historical Materialism: The Method, the Theories* (London, 1960). As the title indicates, this is a study of historical materialism and Marxist theory, but the conclusions have direct relevance for the analysis of institutional theory.

concern general concepts that are scarcely amenable to unequivocal definition. Consequently, they are difficult to operationalize. The institutional
approach puts transactions – the distribution – at the center of analysis,
and defines problems in terms of how markets are created and made to
function. The major concepts are transaction costs, property rights, institutions, and organizations; this includes the state as a superorganization
at the national level, rendering the public sector important both for the
allocation of given resources and for the creation of new resources.

What is missing in these attempts to apply institutional analysis in business history research, at least in the Scandinavian countries, is explicit
empirical testing of the theoretical connections that can be constructed
and operationalized when a specific institutional approach is used. In
business history, it is possible to empirically test the interest-group theory of competition for property rights; likewise, the Williamson theory
of governance and market solutions depending on transaction costs can
be tested, as well as the principal–agent theory at the level of the firm.
These are only a few of the partial *middle-range* theories in the institutional methodological framework.

A more theoretically conscious mode of research work would increase
our knowledge of the conditions of business activities, provide nuances
to the existing theoretical understanding, and, above all, contribute to the
development of new and better theories. This applies not only to neoinstitutional economic theory, but also to other theories: Schumpeterian
growth theories, the Dahménian theory of development blocks, and the
social and cultural theories of economic action, which are advocated by,
among others, economic sociologists like Mark Granovetter and Richard
Whitley.

Moreover, there is another, more crass and discipline-centered reason why business history should be more explicitly tied to economic
theory. Regardless of what we think about it, economists and business
economists today set the agenda in the current social science debate. In
the Scandinavian countries, it is above all economists who have established a near monopoly in defining the problems and setting the agenda
for public debate. Conscious exploitation of economic theory in business history research would give the subject a more prominent position
in the academic discourse and would represent a large step forward in
the scientific legitimization of business history in all these countries.

Modern economic theory is entirely different from the neoclassical
theory that I was taught and that is still dominant in undergraduate economics textbooks. Ronald Coase has elevated the firm to an analytical

unit, economic theory has incorporated parts of institutional theory, and a significant interest exists today in what has come to be called "neoinstitutional economics." I.O., a widely used abbreviation for "industrial organization," is a research area that developed rapidly during the 1990s. The firm is analyzed as a nexus of contracts; principal–agent relations in the firm become the focus of research interests, and game theories have gained importance in explaining the behavior of firms in oligopoly markets.

In these areas, business history can definitely make important contributions to economic theory and develop in a *theory-producing* direction. This necessarily means that only certain aspects of the firm's behavior are treated with the purpose of illuminating and giving substance to theoretical conceptions. In other words, in this conception, business history as a conscious functional selection is prioritized over the "organic methodology," to use Ulf Olsson's terminology from his 1979 *Historisk Tidskrift* article.

I want to stress that my plea for a conscious rapprochement toward economic theory does not mean that I find it in any way desirable for business history to develop as a branch of economics. The demarcation line is plainly visible. Business history, like economic history, is an empirical, inductive science, firmly rooted in the historical method that includes both traditional source criticism, process analysis, and attempts to connect unique observations with more abstract development trends in a scientifically convincing manner. My modest advocacy is that the application of modern economic theory should be made more explicit and be performed more actively than is currently the case. This would strengthen the position of business history in the research society and develop the subject in stride with the other social sciences.

BUSINESS HISTORY AS A BRIDGE BUILDER

In a decentralized market, a number of decisions are made at the same time; some of these reinforce each other, while others are conflicting. In our attempts to abstract from an apparently chaotic reality, that is, to generalize or make conclusions at the macrolevel, it is the outcome or effects of the field of forces that are relevant for abstractions. In the giant international corporations of the modern world, decisions have immediate implications not only at micro- or mesolevels, but also in defining the framework for monetary and fiscal policy at national levels and, ultimately, the degree of national independence.

Thus company decisions at the microlevel have an immediate bearing
on the overall organization of society. For business history, the key task,
however, is to understand the role of economic and social change, in
which business firms play a vital part. By exposing the premises of decision making in the firm and the effects of company behavior, business
history bestows greater realism on aggregates and general assumptions.
To refer back to the Swedish Schumpeterian economist Erik Dahmén:
business history provides the necessary microfoundation to macrotheory. By focusing on the dynamics of structural change, it may contribute
to the development of new theories of growth rooted in the traditions
of institutional economics and based on states of disequilibrium rather
than equilibrium analysis.[27]

But if we want to use modern economic theory, the level of competence must be raised significantly among those researchers who, at least
in Scandinavia, devote themselves to general economic history and those
who specialize in business history. The next generation of Scandinavian
business historians must receive significantly better education in modern
economic and business economic theories than the present one. Doctoral
programs in both economic history and business history are still dominated by the history-humanist education tradition, with large reading
courses and insignificant training in economic theory and methodology.
As department heads, it is our responsibility to ensure that research education in the subject takes partly another direction, with significantly
larger elements of interdisciplinary courses in methodology and theory
as well as training in quantitative methods. The problem is that it takes a
long time before a curriculum revision in this direction reaches fruition
in research production.

One possible approach to quickly increasing competence and raising
the level of theoretical knowledge is to organize research projects and
create research environments in which established business economists,
economists, and economic historians can work together and learn from
each other. Business history, in particular, is well suited for such collaborative efforts. In recent years, the EHR Institute at the Stockholm School has
striven to encourage interdisciplinary research leading to the Ph.D. in financial and business history. The supervisory committees in the doctoral
program deliberately include representatives of various subdisciplines

[27] In English, his views in this respect are most clearly expressed in E. Dahmén, "Entrepreneurial Activity, Banking and Finance. Historical Aspects and Theoretical Suggestions," in *Markets for Innovation, Ownership and Control*, eds. R. Day, G. Eliasson, and
C. Wihlborg (Stockholm and Amsterdam, 1993), 17–27.

within economic science. Among these are business economics, organizational analysis, economic history, economic sociology, finance, and regular economics. The EHF Institute also organizes research projects involving collaboration among economists, business economists, and economic historians.

All too often, business historians take for granted the availability of good corporate archives. The Danish Erhvervsarkivet in Århus, which in the other Scandinavian countries has been admired for many decades and cited as an example to be emulated, represents a centralized archival solution on the national level. A similar approach was taken in Finland when the Central Archives for Business Records in Mikkeli was established in the 1970s. Sweden, like Norway, has gradually developed a more regionally based archival system. Modern information technology, with its enhanced digital searching capability, makes it likely that this structure will endure. In Sweden, a step-by-step expansion of the regional business and popular movements archives is currently occurring in association with the new regional university campuses. In addition, large quantities of business archival material can be found in the Swedish government archives, which for a long time have willingly accepted private archival donations.

The firms themselves, however, have made the most important contribution, both to maintaining the archives and to providing service to scholars. The major firms, especially the banks, have adopted a policy of preserving their historical archives, which by international standards, are admirable in their extent. This includes maintaining the archives of many other firms and banks that have been acquired through purchase or merger over the years. In Sweden and Norway, there is an especially strong tradition among major firms of providing access to, and assistance with, documentary material for serious scholarly research. The ease with which firm archives can be accessed often surprises foreign guest scholars. By the same token, access problems frequently have arisen when Swedish firms have been sold abroad and control has shifted to foreigners. This difference in attitude may well be a serious omen for the future as the market for corporate control becomes increasingly international and corporate leadership more subject to replacement. It is the dominant open attitude of firms that has permitted the emergence of animated business history research. The slogan "Without business archives, no business research" contains much truth.

What is required for the future is both the professional administration of firm archives and a business history research agenda based on solid theoretical foundations. These conditions, viewed in conjunction with the methodological and theoretical evolution of the social sciences that has proceeded during recent decades, creates a future scenario of rapidly growing interest in business archives by the scholarly community. The long-term intellectual shift away from macrotheory and the "tyranny of aggregation" toward a greater emphasis on microstructures and microhistory will result in an increased demand for sound empirical underpinnings. The fact derived from business archives thus will play an even more important role in supporting theory-building in the social sciences and the humanities in the future than is the case today.

The crucial task of building bridges between the fields of economics and history is a challenge for business history. Whether or not business historians, in Scandinavia or elsewhere, are ready to meet this challenge, however, is another question. New interdisciplinary research groups should be organized and new academic institutes created. These would act as intermediaries between the business and scholarly communities. It is important that the scholarly legitimacy of these business history institutes be strengthened by endowing them with an independent research capability, while at the same time integrating them into the academic environment.

Moreover, a comparative, problem-oriented business history approach is indispensable if business history is to fulfill its mission as a bridge builder. This approach needs to be exploited much more systematically. Business history is still too often identified with the production of case studies that provide the full record of the development of single firms. My experience has been that business history will not win full scientific respect until its practitioners gain the opportunity to work in interdisciplinary groups, brought together by a shared interest in projects with specific, clearly defined research problems. And – need I add? – these projects and research problems are, of course, to be defined by the researchers, not by the granting authorities or sponsors.

KEY WORKS

Ahvenainen, Jorma. *Enso-Gutzeit Oy, 1872–1992*. 2 vols. Jyväskylä, 1993.
Boje, Per. *Ledere, ledelse og organisation: Dansk industri efter 1870*. Tom 5. Odense, 1997.
Dahmén, Erik. "Entrepreneurial Activity, Banking and Finance. Historical Aspects and Theoretical Suggestions." In *Markets for Innovation, Ownership and Control*, edited by R. Day, G. Eliasson, and C. Wihlborg, 17–27. Stockholm and Amsterdam, 1993.
Hansen, Per H. *På glidebanen til den bitre ende: Danskt bankevaesen i krise, 1920–1933*. Odense, 1996.

Lange, Ole. *Logbog for Lauritzen, 1884-1995: Historien om Konsulen, hans sønner og Lauritzen Gruppen.* Copenhagen, 1995.

Larsson, Mats. *Bonniers: En mediefamilj. Förlag, konglomerat och mediekoncern, 1953-1990.* Stockholm, 1991.

Lindgren, Hakån. "Business History, Historical Economics and Economic Theory." In *L'Entreprise en Grèce et en Europe XIXe-XXe siècles,* edited by Margarita Dritsas, 25-40. Athens, 1992.

Nilsson, Göran B. *Banker i brytningstid: A. O. Wallenberg i svensk bankpolitik, 1850-1856.* Stockholm, 1981.

Schybergson, Per. *Työt ja päivät: Ahlströmin historia, 1851-1981.* Vammala, 1992.

Sogner, K. "Recent Trends in Business History." *Scandinavian Economic History Review* 45, no. 1 (1997): 58-69.

8

Business History in German-Speaking States at the End of the Century

Achievements and Gaps

HARM G. SCHRÖTER

For decades German business history not only took place in the shadow of economic history, but its value and its methods were sometimes questioned by economic and other historians. However, during the 1990s, there came a remarkable change. It is illustrated by the fact that outstanding and highly respected general historians, such as Lothar Gall, president of the Historiker-Verband (Germany's history association), who previously had rarely taken an interest in economic history, suddenly declared their commitment to business history. Writing business history became not only respected but, as new questions arose regarding how to approach it – particularly in light of political pressure on firms whose behavior was questioned during the Nazi period – a challenge.

In this context both terms, "German" and "business history," need definitions. "German" is used in the widest sense: It encompasses the German-speaking part of the world, which includes Austria and two-thirds of Switzerland. The reasons for using this term are not only the common language and an exchange of personnel, but a couple of common

I want to thank the following persons for information and advice: Dr. Hartmut Berghoff, Dr. Christian Kleinschmidt, Dr. Franz Mathis, Dr. Margrit Müller, Dr. Werner Plumpe, Dr. Hans Pohl, Dr. Manfred Pohl, Andrea Schneider, Dr. Jakob Tanner, Dr. Thomas Welskopp, and above all, Dr. Wolfram Fischer. Of course, all errors are the fault of the author.

institutions as well. For example, scholars of all German-speaking states take part in the Verein für Socialpolitik, founded by Gustav Schmoller in 1872; all institutes, organizations, and persons of the German-speaking region are included in one single *vademekum*, a central reference book for historical researchers. However, in spite of a fairly regular exchange of representatives, distinctions remain between the historical communities of the three states, which imply deficits of information, especially between Switzerland and Germany.

Furthermore, we take into account contributions written on German business history but published abroad, for example the book *Patrons d'Allemagne: Sociologie d'une élite industrielle 1933–1989* (Paris, 1996) by Hervé Joly from Lyon, as well as works by members of the German-speaking community who publish on the business history of other states, such as Hartmut Berghoff's work on British entrepreneurs. And, of course, the activities of multinational companies in connection with these three states are included as well.

Defining "business history" is more complicated since business history itself has changed over time. Today the comprehensive definition by Hans Pohl can be agreed upon: "Business history deals with all private and public owned enterprises and mixed forms thereof. In this context the firm is understood as a social and economic construction."[1] Especially since the 1990s, the social embeddedness of firms has been underlined. While economic history has been in decline since the beginning of the 1990s – indications of this downturn are seen in the declining number of students and professorships, which indicates a decrease in demand by society and colleagues – we are not so sure about the trend in business history. On the one hand, the decline of economic history affected business history; on the other hand, new topics and the tendency of economic historians to become more interested in business history than before may turn the tide.

HISTORICAL AND ORGANIZATIONAL DEVELOPMENT

The earliest German business history we know of was published in 1825 by Johann Trautscholdt on heavy industry. It described the first hundred years of the Eisenwerk Lauchhammer, which suggested more such

---

[1] Hans Pohl, "Betrachtungen zum wissenschaftlichen Standort von Wirtschafts- und Unternehmensgeschichte," *Vierteljahrschrift für Sozial- und Wirtschaftsgeschichte* 73, no. 3 (1991): 329 (previous contributions are mentioned in the footnotes there).

anniversaries to come; and in fact, Lauchhammer remained a site of the machine building industry well into the twentieth century. Jubilee books became a substantial source of income, mainly for journalists, as very few historians took part in this process. Journalists were quicker and more adaptable, and within the so-called *Zunft* (guild) of historians, commissioned work traditionally had been questioned as unhistorical. Only very recently have highly ranked German historians come to share the view that it is possible to write commissioned books on a scholarly basis. By comparison, the Scandinavian states have a much longer and more positive tradition in this respect.

Economic and business history have the same origins: they have developed out of the work of economists as well as that of historians. In this respect, the comparatively late development of German business history is strange. Both branches of scholarly work had been very well established in the nineteenth century, and there have been substantial incentives to care about business history. The very influential economist Gustav Schmoller (1838–1917) was an advocate of history, and Josef Alois Schumpeter (1883–1950) was an advocate of entrepreneurs. Schmoller was German and Schumpeter Austrian.

In writing history, social and economic issues came under pressure after the so-called Lamprecht-Streit (dispute) before the First World War. Since then and up to the 1960s, political history prevailed, which left little room for business history. Social and to a certain extent economic history were carried out primarily on a regional basis, and by anthropologists. In 1967, by revealing the economic aims of industry in connection with the First World War, Fritz Fischer changed the paradigm.[2] During the 1970s, together with social and economic history, business history became an interesting field for many historians, and some professorships were founded.

Within the German development of economics, Gustav Schmoller and his so-called historical school made their influence felt for a long period even after his death. But after 1945 things changed. In the West, economists thought more in terms of models than in terms of developments. Still, they kept economic history – often combined with social history – as a general commitment and expanded it when, during the 1960s and 1970s, the whole university sector grew. However, today, neither history nor economic departments employ a professor of business

---

[2] Fritz Fischer, *Griff nach der Weltmacht: Die Kriegsziele des kaiserlichen Deutschland, 1914/18* (Düsseldorf, 1967).

history. Some scholars have specialized in this field, such as Hans Pohl of Bonn or Alois Mosser of Vienna, to mention only two. Others have taken a strong interest in this field, such as Hansjörg Siegenthaler of Zurich or Wolfram Fischer and Jürgen Kocka, both of Berlin. But there is neither a chair in one of the three states for business history nor even a substantial official commitment to business history. However, it seems that since the 1960s, the younger generations of economic historians in all three states have taken a deeper interest in business history than their teachers did. To what extent this growth is based on intensified international exchange of ideas, or on the impact of English-language works, or even on an Americanization can only be guessed.

Some important exceptions have to be mentioned. Around the turn of the twentieth century, Conrad Matschoss started to publish on business history. His writings provided a lot of information, especially on technical matters. At that time there was generally a great trust in technical development. This gave Matschoss the resources to start a yearbook on technical history in cooperation with the Verein Deutscher Ingenieure, the professional engineers' society. Out of this initiative the periodical *Technikgeschichte (History of Techniques)* emerged. Thus, the first initiative for business history was channeled through technical history. Some outstanding books emerged, for example the work on Bosch by Theodor Heuss, who later became president of West Germany.[3] In spite of their high quality, however, these volumes remained single events.

It took quite some time before the next initiative succeeded. In 1956 Wilhelm Treue founded the periodical *Tradition, Zeitschrift für Firmengeschichte und Unternehmerbiographie (Journal for Business History and Biographies of Entrepreneurs)*, which later became *Zeitschrift für Unternehmensgeschichte (ZUG)*. One of the most important contributions during its early period came from Fritz Redlich, who had emigrated to the United States and had been publishing on German business history at least since 1952. The general political mood after the Second World War and, though in decline, still widespread during the 1950s, questioned the legitimacy of entrepreneurs in the West. Not only social democrats and the labor unions, but groups of conservatives, too, preferred state and cooperative ownership. Thus, the foundation of a journal concerned with entrepreneurship ran contrary to the political trend of the period. Further, many historians thought that the journal would not maintain the highest standards of scholarship, and

[3] Theodor Heuss, *Robert Bosch: Leben und Leistung* (Tübingen, 1946).

its founder, Wilhelm Treue, the author of two commissioned volumes on Thyssen, sometimes had to face problems of acceptance within the historic community.

In 1962 the journalist Erich Achterberg founded the Archiv für Bankengeschichtliche Forschung, a bank-related archive, as a private enterprise. In 1969 it became the Institut für bankhistorische Forschung (Institute for Banking History). The main activities of this institute are the publication of a journal, *Bankhistorisches Archiv*, and the organization of national and international historical colloquia. It initiated several books on banking and financial history such as *Europäische Bankengeschichte* (Frankfurt, 1993) and Hans Pohl's (ed.) volume *Geschichte der deutschen Kreditwirtschaft seit 1945* (Frankfurt, 1998).

The next important step was taken not in Germany but in Austria. In 1971 a society for business history was founded. Due to its long and complicated name, it was soon referred to as the Langnamen-Verein, the "Long-Name Society." Consequently its name was changed to Österreichischen Gesellschaft für Unternehmensgeschichte (Austrian Society for Business History), or ÖGU, in 1987.[4] According to its founder, Alois Brusatti, the foundation was to be understood not only in a scholarly context but in a political one as well. ÖGU tried to promote issues in three main fields by writing business history on a scholarly basis, by helping to correct the distorted picture of entrepreneurs, and by offering case studies for the training of students of business administration. Especially in the last area American influence can be seen, since this point had been stressed in U.S. business history since the interwar period. Besides historians, distinguished managers were elected to its board. Scholarly cooperation focused primarily on institutes for economic history at universities. In 1971 the postwar reconstruction of the European economy already was history, but the postwar boom had not yet ended. However, student revolts were just one expression of a leftist trend in society, which challenged the role of private enterprise and ownership. Though this was an overall European trend, Austria was a special case. In Austria the state sector was directly and indirectly more involved in the economy than in Germany or Switzerland. Socialist tendencies toward large firms were much more pronounced on all political levels. In this climate, the foundation of the ÖGU was understood to be a reaction. In the following years the political paradigm changed, and by the end of the 1980s, the

---

[4] Its original name was Verein der wissenschaftlichen Forschung auf dem Gebiete der Unternehmerbiographie und Firmengeschichte.

role of the entrepreneur was valued highly. In 1997 Alois Brusatti commented with satisfaction that the ÖGU had contributed to this process.
"With this the ÖGU carried out an important task for the whole society."[5]

How did the ÖGU achieve its ends? The financial means came from
firms, some of which ordered their histories to be written. The focus
was on *historical works analysis* (*historische Betriebsanalyse*), which
was divided into four fields. A system of enterprise analysis was agreed
upon; this provided scholarly criteria for writing enterprise history and
at the same time a basis of comparison. Next, social history was taken
into account. Third, microeconomic history was suggested to economists
as a supplement to their teaching. Finally, historical works analysis was
offered to managers as an auxiliary tool for long-term decisions. Interestingly, public relations and corporate identity were discussed only later, in
spite of the fact that most firms' archives were held in those departments.
With their catalog the ÖGU's founders tried to establish microeconomic
history on an equal footing with the traditional macroeconomic history.

The ÖGU tried to tackle issues that were both scholarly and widely discussed in society. When private ownership of large firms was questioned,
the ÖGU not only discussed the role of entrepreneurs but additionally
that of "capitalists without capital" – the managers. When during the
1970s inflation became a threatening problem within Austria, the ÖGU
contributed to the discourse by providing the historical dimension. It
did not refrain from throwing itself into politically troubled waters. At
the request of the prince of Liechtenstein, it carried out an evaluation
of the losses that his house had suffered when its vast properties in
Bohemia were confiscated by socialist Czechoslovakia after the Second
World War. In doing so, the ÖGU provided the basis on which the state of
Liechtenstein has demanded its old properties from the Czech Republic,
an international diplomatic case that has not been settled to this day.

Swiss business historians did not follow the Austrian pattern of founding their own society. Here, organized business history takes place within
the Schweizerische Gesellschaft für Wirtschafts- und Sozialgeschichte
(Swiss Society for Economic and Social History), which since 1981,
in typically Swiss understatement, has annually edited so-called book-
lets (*Hefte*) of more than 500 pages. In 1996 a circle for business history (Arbeitsgruppe für Unternehmensgeschichte) was founded at the

---

[5] Alois Brusatti, "Zur Geschichte der Österreichischen Gesellschaft für Unternehmensgeschichte (21 Jahre: 1971–1992)," in *Historische Betriebsanalyse und Unternehmer:
Festschrift für Alois Mosser*, ed. H. Matis (Vienna, 1997), 24–32.

University of Zurich, which is intended to act as a nucleus for a larger
organization yet to be founded. For decades the Verein für wirtschaftshistorische Studien (Study Group for Economic History) has focused
on publishing biographies of Swiss entrepreneurs, while the Verein für
Bankengeschichte has covered banking history.

Recent political events caused the foundation of an independent
commission (the *Unabhängige Expertenkommission Schweiz Zweiter
Weltkrieg*), which was set up to inquire into the behavior of about forty
Swiss banks, insurance companies, and industrial firms during the Second World War. In 1998 this commission employed no fewer than forty
people, which made it probably the biggest team set up for business
history, at least in the German-speaking part of the world. Twenty-five
volumes have been published, which perhaps turn Switzerland into the
best-researched country concerning the relationship with Germany and
the Axis powers. Still, relations with the Allies are omitted.

A special form of enterprise history (*Betriebsgeschichte*) emerged in
the socialist German Democratic Republic (GDR) in eastern Germany in
the early 1950s. In many places, the development of a certain factory was
discussed and published. Works history was specifically a tool of ideological influence. For example, Comrade Banisch, secretary for *Agitation
und Propaganda* at the Buna plant, wrote in the foreword of the first
volume of his factory story: "The most important task of historical research in this respect is to augment the efficiency of political-ideological
work, which means, by presenting a vivid picture of the history of the
factory, to underline the socialistic consciousness and to develop new
initiatives by the workers."[6] During the following years, works histories
were written for nearly all important firms and parts thereof, in most
cases by grass-roots historians. About 2,000 such volumes were published, but their historical value is mostly quite limited. However, since
many firms broke down and a considerable amount of archival material
has been lost, these books sometimes remain as one of the few sources
of available information.

In the GDR, for ideological and personal reasons, economic history was important. Its foremost promoter, Jürgen Kuczynski, personally had access to the highest political decision makers, including Erich
Honnecker. Though Kuczynski himself concentrated on economic history, he encouraged the writing of business history in his institute at the

---

[6] *Über Buna wehen rote Fahnen: Geschichte der Arbeiterbewegung des Kombinates VEB
Chemische Werke Buna*, 1: 4 (Schkopau, ca. 1975).

Academy of Science. The eighth Communist Party conference in 1971 encouraged economic historians to take part in works history. Scholarly standards often clashed with the political aims of firm histories, but in the end, historians succeeded in raising their quality.[7]

During the 1970s, the emphasis was on German big business and its relation to the Nazis. The ensuing publications and editions of sources[8] had a considerable impact on West German historians. These, in turn, confronted the Marxist interpretation of state-monopoly capitalism with an alternative model, called "organized capitalism." But with Gossweiler's interpretation of state-monopoly capitalism, that concept became over-stretched and soon lost its attraction even for socialist students in the West. Of course, historians in the GDR writing business history were Marxists, but in most cases this did not distort their empirical findings; on the contrary, their practical work sometimes caused differences with the official party line. Later GDR historians gave up focusing on the period between 1914 and 1945, losing their special impact on their colleagues in the West. However, as far as was politically tolerated by the GDR, many of them remained scholars who were sought internationally. The volumes on multinational enterprise that Helga Nussbaum edited with Alice Teichova and Maurice Lévy-Leboyer provide but one example.[9] After the unification of Germany in 1990 positions in economic and business history in the former GDR were reduced considerably. However, most of the distinguished scholars found employment elsewhere or retired.

There are certain similarities in West German and Austrian business history development patterns; therefore in the following I shall concentrate on the deviations. In contrast to its later success, failure and a threatening crisis occurred at the beginning of the first West German society for business history, the Gesellschaft für Unternehmensgeschichte (GUG). In 1972 a working group was initiated at the Institut der Deutschen Wirtschaft that was intended to act as a scholarly advisory committee to

---

[7] Wolfram Fischer and Frank Zschaler, "Wirtschafts- und Sozialgeschichte," in *Wissenschaft und Wiedervereinigung: Disziplinen im Umbruch*, eds. Jürgen Kocka and Renate Mayntz (Berlin, 1998), 385ff.; as an example, see the various contributions of Jörg Roesler.

[8] See the so-called anatomy volumes: Dietrich Eichholtz and Wolfgang Schumann, eds., *Anatomie des Krieges* (Berlin, 1969), and Gerhard Hass and Wolfgang Schumann, eds., *Anatomie der Aggression* (Berlin, 1972), or Hans Radant, ed., *Fall 6: Ausgewählte Dokumente und Urteil des IG Farben-Prozesses* (Berlin, 1970).

[9] Alice Teichova, Maurice Lévy-Leboyer, and Helga Nussbaum, eds., *Historical Studies in International Corporate Business* (Cambridge and Paris, 1989); id., eds., *Multinational Enterprise in Historical Perspective* (Cambridge and Paris, 1986).

the Verein der Wirtschaftsarchivare (Society of Economic Archivists) in
the preparation of a society for business history. However, this promising
initiative failed. Even worse, due to lack of finances, the journal *Tradition* was heading toward its demise in 1973. However, Wilhelm Treue,
Hans Pohl, and Manfred Pohl, the archivist of Deutsche Bank, succeeded
not only in raising money for *Tradition* but also in raising a commitment
and funds for the foundation of the GUG in 1976. Thus not only was the
crisis mastered, but a new horizon was opened.

The political context and intentions were similar to those in Austria,
focusing on a historical dialogue between historians and industry. This
was achieved by two types of annual events in which both sides took part.
On the one hand, small symposia were held for specialists; on the other,
comprehensive lectures were presented for a much wider audience. GUG
edited three directories covering virtually all enterprise archives.[10] These
directories not only created incentives to do business history, but they
reduced the traditional uneasiness of many historians, who perceived
firms to be a black box, especially in respect to their archives. Like ÖGU,
GUG focused on the legitimacy of entrepreneurship, especially during
its initial years.

By its design, GUG was financed by companies, including Deutsche
Bank, which, through its membership, had a decisive say in the society.
However, business did not influence the historical program of GUG. The
purpose of GUG was – and is – to promote the exchange between history and economic life. GUG never was reduced to a useful instrument in
the public relations activities of industry. Historical expertise was added
through an advisory board, of which Hans Pohl became the chairman.
This chairman turned out to be extremely dynamic, with an influence
much greater than appeared on paper. To a large extent, the success of
GUG during that time is due to him, and, at least as viewed from outside, Hans Pohl became the personification of business history in West
Germany. For eighteen years he remained the driving force of GUG until
he retired from his chairmanship in 1994 in a process of overall change.
Today, GUG describes itself as "a service institution for enterprises, especially for historical consultation." It helps to promote business history in
historical sciences. It has standing circles for banking, insurance, transport history, and, additionally, one on the role of firms during the Nazi
period. Thus GUG does not circumvent critical issues.

[10] Gesellschaft für Unternehmensgeschichte, ed., *Deutsche Wirtschaftsarchive*, 3 vols.
(Stuttgart, 1988–94).

GUG, together with the newly founded Society for European Business History and the European Association for Banking History, form the Center for European Business History. GUG boosted its membership to 237 in 1999. Since Ulrich Wengenroth became chairman of the historic advisory board, closer cooperation with the society for technical history, the Gesellschaft für Technikgeschichte, has been established, because he is the chairman of that organization, too.

Atypical of Germany, a second, competing society for enterprise history emerged in 1989, the Arbeitskreis für kritische Unternehmens-und Industriegeschichte (AKKU). Its basic idea is to explore a stricter theoretical approach, and it is opposed to any glossing over of business history. AKKU was founded at the University of Bochum, and it is still situated there. It edits a regular leaflet, *AKKUMULATION*, for its membership of about seventy. Sources of finances are similar to those of GUG, through membership fees, fund-raising, and the like. In contrast to GUG, the members of AKKU are much younger; most of them are neither professors nor institutional members. Consequently, AKKU has less funds. It certainly does not consider itself a consulting group for firms. Its regular conferences, compared to those of GUG, are a little less professional but, perhaps because of its younger members, much more vivid. AKKU has begun to discuss demanding and modern topics such as ethics in business history. Similar to ÖGU at its beginning, AKKU stresses the demand for theory in order to promote business history. Macroeconomic theories do not meet the demand of microeconomic history. Consequently, AKKU proposes to try multidisciplinary approaches from sociology to microeconomics and from ethnic to gender history in order to reach a better, theory-led writing of business history. Its annual conference in 1999 was on methods and reflections of writing business history.

Germans are not accustomed to several competing institutions that try to do the same job. Against this mental background, GUG, of course, felt embarrassed by the founding of AKKU, which certainly is a challenge for GUG in various ways. Offering a helping hand as a consultant while acting as a scholarly body was the challenge that GUG had to face from its beginning. This is reflected in the leaflet by which GUG introduces itself: "The GUG aids its membership at historical exhibitions and in designing the historical part of enterprise-jubilees. Furthermore it looks after independent research projects, that is, writing critical business history." Up to now, the mostly unspoken competition between GUG and AKKU has helped to improve the standards of writing business history substantially and in nearly all quarters.

Besides the two general societies for business history, some special ones exist. The society for banking history has already been mentioned but more specific is the Arbeitskreis für Bayerische Sparkassengeschichte (Circle for Savings Banks History) founded in 1981. This society, with its stronghold in Bavaria and neighboring parts of Austria, has edited a journal since 1987, the *Zeitschrift für Bayerische Sparkassen-Geschichte*, including *Beihefte*, as well as the journal *GeschichtsWelt*. As is often the case, this initiative rested mainly on the shoulders of its founders, Manfred Pix from the financial side and the late Josef Wysocki from the historical side. Even more specialized are initiatives or museums with a regional, branch of industry, or local focus. There is a circle on industrial history within the working group for the history of chemistry, to mention only one. A special case is the Verein der Wirtschaftsarchivare (Society of Enterprise Archivists) in Germany and similar organizations in Switzerland and Austria, which sometimes have overlapping memberships.

Two different points of view exist in Germany with respect to business history. Some historians include it in economic history, while others see it as an entity in itself, parallel to economic history. In the first case, business is understood as one of several factors of the economy. In the second case, innovation carried out by enterprises is valued so highly that business history develops its own status in addition to economic history. Considerable theoretical and practical efforts have been made to establish microeconomic history parallel to the already established macrohistory. Success in this respect would offer opportunities not only in teaching and research, but in terms of institutions and personnel as well. The departments of business administration were once one of the largest branches of teaching in many universities, while history departments are at most of medium size. However, historical case studies usually are not included in teaching students of business administration, and managers usually do not look to history in order to find advice for their decision making. At the same time, the majority of historians are not as interested in economic and social history as they were during the 1970s and early 1980s; today they are more interested in topics such as behavior, gender, and culture. Until now, business history has not felt compelled to explain its competence in these fields. Consequently, German universities have not seen particular value in business history, which is reflected by the fact that there is no chair in business history in German universities. Schumpeter's view of the entrepreneur as the driving force in capitalist economies has not been honored in its historical dimension, either in departments of economy or in departments of history, both of which usually harbor economic history. GUG and AKKU both deplore this situation.

THE STATE OF THE ART AT THE END OF THE CENTURY

After the foundation was laid in the 1970s and much progress was made during the 1980s, the 1990s saw a further spurt in the quantity and quality of written business history. Particularly in the second half of the 1990s, business history achieved substantial success in German-speaking areas. For historians it generally emerged as a serious and special partner. Many economists still do not see what it is good for, beyond testing economic models with historical information. In contrast, more and more firms understand the dimensions of business history for their own purpose. Many have opened their archives for external research, which, of course, has increased the trust of historians. Most important, opinion makers such as Daimler-Benz and Deutsche Bank have ended the tradition of distributing triumphant brochures written by journalists. Instead they have begun employing historians, who sometimes have dealt critically with the past of the firms. Though firms are sometimes still afraid of their own courage, this has enhanced trust both inside and outside the firm. The Deutsche Bahn (German railways) is an example in this respect. Whereas in 1988 its book on the past decades was written by engineers, the 1999 volume was commissioned at GUG.

Nearly all major fields of business history have been worked on. Particular achievements have been made in studying problems in the relationship between the state, banks, and private enterprise and economic concentration. Research on cartels can be claimed to be superior to that of most other countries.[11] To a certain extent this may be no surprise, because problems in these fields used to be widespread in Germany. Up to 1945 Germany was very much a cartel economy, and on the international level it had tried to organize as much trade by cartels as possible. The special cooperative relationship within the three German-speaking economies, which Alfred D. Chandler, Jr., characterized as "cooperative capitalism," even created words with special meanings – which is one

[11] The volumes edited by Barjot, Kudo, and Takahashi are not as comprehensive as those edited by Pohl (Dominique Barjot, ed., *International Cartels Revisited* [Caen, 1994]; Akira Kudo and Terushi Hara, eds., *International Cartels in Business History* [Tokyo, 1992]; Hans Pohl, ed., *Kartelle und Kartellgesetzgebung in Praxis und Rechtsprechung vom 19. Jahrhundert bis zur Gegenwart* [Stuttgart, 1985]; id., ed., *Wettbewerbsbeschränkungen auf internationalen Märkten* [Stuttgart, 1988]).

of the best proofs for Chandler's thesis. For example, there is no appropriate English word for *Sanierung*, which means making a firm viable again, usually through the help of banks or the state. It seems that there are national "path dependencies." With this expression, we are already in the area of deficits of business history. Path dependencies can be defined only on an internationally comparative level. Despite the political incentive that the European integration has generated for decades, there are still only very few studies comparing business history internationally.[12] The results of work by sociologists have not been sufficiently taken into account. The economic role of intermediate institutions, such as those of arbitration, has attracted relatively little attention. Globalization, one of the most pressing problems today, has still attracted little attention. Only a handful of scholars have devoted attention to this field. Furthermore, while English-speaking world organizations have emerged for the historical evaluation of financial systems such as bookkeeping, these issues are almost totally neglected. Though the history of industrialization was the center of research in writing economic history for twenty years or so, some historians still understand the entrepreneur, as well as the firm, as one of several "aspects" and not as the key to industrialization. There is no overview of business history from the gender perspective. Certain special but substantial parts of business history, such as accounting or controlling, have hardly been taken up. Our list could be extended; however, in the end, it is more interesting to point out achievements than gaps.

---

[12] See Paul Erker, "The Choice between Competition and Cooperation: Research and Development in the Electrical Industry in Germany and the Netherlands, 1920-1936," in *Innovations in the European Economy between the Wars*, eds. François Caron, Paul Erker, and Wolfram Fischer (Berlin and New York, 1995), 231-54; Martin Fiedler, "Betriebliche Sozialpolitik in der Zwischenkriegszeit: Wege der Interpretation und Probleme der Forschung im deutsch-französischen Vergleich," *Geschichte und Gesellschaft* 22 (1996): 350-75; Hervé Joly, "Die Säuberung der wirtschaftlichen Eliten in Frankreich und Deutschland in der Nachkriegszeit: Der Versuch eines Vergleichs," in *1945-50 Jahre danach: Aspekte und Perspektiven im deutsch-französischen Beziehungsfeld*, eds. Thomas Höpel and Dieter Thiemann (Leipzig, 1996), 130-52; Gerhard Kümmel, *Transnationale Wirtschaftskooperation und der Nationalstaat: Deutsch-amerikanische Unternehmensbeziehungen in den 1930er Jahren* (Stuttgart, 1995); Harm G. Schröter, *Aufstieg der Kleinen: Multinationale Unternehmen aus fünf kleinen Staaten vor 1914* (Berlin, 1993); id., "Continental European Free-Standing Companies: The Case of Belgium, Germany, and Switzerland," in *The Free-Standing Company in the World Economy, 1830-1996*, eds. Mira Wilkins and Harm Schröter (Oxford, 1998), 323-43; Thomas Welskopp, *Arbeit und Macht im Hüttenwerk: Arbeits- und industrielle Beziehungen in der deutschen und amerikanischen Eisen- und Stahlindustrie von den 1860er bis zu den 1930er Jahren* (Bonn, 1994).

During the past few years, many new books have been published, some of which try to shed new light on business history. They cluster around certain clearly identifiable topics, including competition and regulation; the Nazi period; banks and enterprises (which already have a long publishing history); innovation and rationalization; elites; industrial relations; ecology; commercialization and networks; and regional business history. In the following, only a few examples each of this recent research will be mentioned.

For about two decades, German writing on competition and cooperation has been influenced by Chandler. Many scholars have used his theory directly, such as Franz Mathis in his *Big Business in Österreich* (Vienna, 1987) or Harm Schröter in his article on small nations and European cartels in Chandler's *Big Business and the Wealth of Nations* (Cambridge, 1997). Others, like Margrit Müller or Richard Tilly, applied it indirectly or contradicted it.[13] Compared to the English-speaking world, research on multinational firms still is underdeveloped in the German-speaking states, but some new books reveal a growing interest.[14] State and private enterprise is a traditional topic in German business history. Some general reflections on it were published by Volker Berghahn, and there is a comprehensive case study on a state-owned firm by Manfred Pohl.[15] The most interesting research in this field was done on the Nazi period.

The Nazi period has been studied only in the past few years. It took West Germany about twenty years until people were ready to discuss the burning questions of the Nazi period critically without being pressed from abroad. It took another twenty years until enterprises were ready to study their involvement in this part of the past. After the confrontation with the Marxists on this question – which flourished during the

---

[13] Margrit Müller, ed., *Structure and Strategy of Small- and Medium-Sized Enterprises since the Industrial Revolution* (Stuttgart, 1994); Richard Tilly, "Grossunternehmen: Schlüssel zur Wirtschafts- und Sozialgeschichte der Industrieländer? Literaturbericht," *Geschichte und Gesellschaft* 19 (1993): 530–48.

[14] Antje Hagen, *Deutsche Direktinvestitionen in Grossbritannien, 1871–1918* (Stuttgart, 1997); Anne von Oswald, *Die deutsche Industrie auf dem italienischen Markt* (Frankfurt, 1996); Hans Pohl, ed., *Der Einfluss ausländischer Unternehmen auf die deutsche Wirtschaft vom Spätmittelalter bis zur Gegenwart* (Stuttgart, 1992); Toru Takenaka, *Siemens in Japan: Von der Landesöffnung bis zum Ersten Weltkrieg* (Stuttgart, 1996).

[15] Volker R. Berghahn, ed., *Quest for Economic Empire: European Strategies of German Big Business in the Twentieth Century* (Providence and Oxford, 1996); Manfred Pohl, *VIAG Aktiengesellschaft 1923–1998: Vom Staatsunternehmen zum internationalen Konzern* (Munich, 1998); Christopher Kopper, *Zwischen Marktwirtschaft und Dirigismus: Bankenpolitik im "Dritten Reich," 1933–1939* (Bonn, 1995).

1970s and early 1980s – was over, books such as Peter Hayes's *Indus-try and Ideology: IG Farben in the Nazi Era* (Cambridge, 1987) paved the way for a deeper understanding. In the second half of the 1980s, Daimler-Benz asked GUG to write its business history during the Nazi period, which included researching the firm's involvement in forced and slave labor.[16] This was, of course, a highly controversial issue, and it en-tailed the question of financial compensation to the persons involved. Now it was not only outstanding anniversaries, but the Nazi question too, that caused enterprises such as Deutsche Bank or Volkswagen to order business histories written by distinguished and critical scholars. In 1998, Dresdner Bank, which was assumed to have had a greater role in the Nazi period than the other major banks, began paying a group of historians for several years. This group, which is under the supervision of the Hannah-Ahrendt Institut für Totalitarismusforschung, scrutinizes the Nazi past of the bank and has started to publish.[17] Of course, much more needs to be done. While in 1998 the Swiss banks came under heavy pressure from Jewish organizations and the U.S. media, one year later it was the German industrial firms under scrutiny for their use of slave labor. In reaction to the public debate on firms involved in the use of slave labor, some firms, such as Diehl, recently have agreed to compensate in-dividual former "employees." For instance, Volkswagen in the summer of 1998 set up a fund for this purpose after having denied individual compensation for years. The topic of *Arisierung*, the expulsion of Jews from German business life, was taken up again only recently, as well as the question of entrepreneurial behavior from a less ideological point of view.[18]

Innovation and rationalization are traditional fields in German business history, but a lot remains to be done. In R&D, historical organizations are often studied,[19] but the process, as well as the factors promoting and

---

[16] Beate Brüninghaus, Stephanie Habeth, and Hans Pohl, *Die Daimler-Benz AG in den Jahren 1933 bis 1945* (Stuttgart, 1986).

[17] See Johannes Bähr, *Die Goldgeschäfte der Dresdner Bank im Zweiten Weltkrieg* (Frankfurt, 1999).

[18] Again, only two books can be mentioned: Helmut Genschel, *Die Verdrängung der Juden aus der Wirtschaft im Dritten Reich* (Göttingen, 1966), and Johannes Ludwig, *Boykott, Enteignung, Mord: Die "Entjudung" der deutschen Wirtschaft* (Hamburg, 1989). A non-ideologic point of view is, of course, impossible.

[19] See the contributions in Caron et al., *Innovations*; Christian Kleinschmidt, *Rational-isierung als Unternehmensstrategie: Die Eisen- und Stahlindustrie des Ruhrgebiets zwischen Jahrhundertwende und Weltwirtschaftskrise* (Essen, 1993); *Zeitschrift für Un-ternehmensgeschichte* 41, no. 2 (1996), special issue on rationalization.

retarding it, are less well covered.[20] The question of the extent to which crises promote innovation and rationalization is another traditional issue. In most cases, single enterprises are not at the center of the respective research, but are used to exemplify macroeconomic history.[21]

The history of elites has been approached recently and in terms of social as well as business history. Though individual biographies still dominate, some general books and collective biographies have been published.[22]

The field of industrial relations was formerly dominated by social historians, who, since the mid-1980s, developed differently from economic historians. But in this instance, some trespassing has been welcome on both sides.[23] Apart from the typical East German *Betriebsgeschichte*

---

[20] Such aspects are covered by Gert K. von Oheimb-Loup, "Technischer Fortschritt und Unternehmerverhalten am Beispiel der württembergischen Kammgarnspinnerei Merkel & Wolf, 1830-1870," in *Unternehmer und technischer Fortschritt*, ed. Francesca Schinzinger (Munich, 1996), 283-300; Tony Travis, Harm G. Schröter, and Ernst Homburg, eds., *Determinants in the Evolution of the European Chemical Industry, 1900-1939* (Dordrecht, 1998).

[21] Friedrich W. Henning, ed., *Krisen und Krisenbewältigung vom 19. Jahrhundert bis heute* (Frankfurt, 1998).

[22] Hartmut Berghoff, *Englische Unternehmer, 1870-1915* (Göttingen, 1991); Paul Erker, *Industrie-Eliten in der NS-Zeit: Anpassungsbereitschaft und Eigeninteresse von Unternehmern in der Rüstungs- und Kriegswirtschaft, 1936-1945* (Passau, 1993); Gerald D. Feldmann, *Hugo Stinnes: Biographie eines Industriellen, 1870-1924* (Munich, 1998); Natalie Fryde, *Ein mittelalterlicher deutscher Grossunternehmer: Terricus Teutonicus de Colonia in England, 1217-1247* (Stuttgart, 1998); Hervé Joly, *Patrons d'Allemagne: Sociologie d'une élite industrielle, 1933-1989* (Paris, 1996); Ulrich Pfister, "Entstehung des industriellen Unternehmertums in der Schweiz, 18.-19. Jahrhundert," *Zeitschrift für Unternehmensgeschichte* 43, no. 1 (1997): 14-38; Toni Pierenkemper, "Deutsche Unternehmer im 19. Jahrhundert als Elite," in *Eliten in Deutschland und Frankreich im 19. und 20. Jahrhundert*, eds. Rainer Hudemann and George H. Soutou, vol. 1 (Munich, 1994), 119-35; Paul Erker and Toni Pierenkemper, eds., *Deutsche Unternehmer zwischen Kriegswirtschaft und Wiederaufbau: Studien zur Erfahrungsbildung von Industrieliten* (Munich, 1998); Astrid Gehrig, *Nationalsozialistische Rüstungspolitik und unternehmerischer Entscheidungsspielraum: Vergleichende Fallstudien zur württembergischen Maschinenbauindustrie* (Munich, 1996); Mark Spoerer, "From Paper Profits to Armaments: The Profitability of German Industrial Stock Corporations, 1925-1941," in *Business and European Integration since 1800: Regional, National, and International Perspectives*, ed. Ulf Olsson (Göteborg, 1997), 429-40.

[23] Karl Lauschke and Thomas Welskopp, eds., *Mikropolitik im Unternehmen: Arbeitsbeziehungen und Machtstrukturen in industriellen Grossbetrieben des 20. Jarhunderts* (Essen, 1994); Hans Pohl, ed., *Mitbestimmung und Betriebsverfassung in Deutschland, Frankreich und Grossbritannien seit dem 19. Jahrhundert* (Stuttgart, 1996); Dorothea Schmidt, *Massenhafte Produktion? Produkte, Produktion und Beschäftigte im Stammwerk von Siemens vor 1918* (Münster, 1993); Harm G. Schröter, "European Integration by the German Model? Unions, Multinational Enterprise and Labour Relations since the 1950s," in Olsson, *Business and European Integration*, 85-99.

(history of the plant), much less was been published on industrial relations in the GDR. This is understandable, since *Betriebsgeschichte* was
a tool of political control, and some experts in this field had employment problems after reunification.[24] Right after reunification, the consequences of division and unification of business were discussed on a
business history level, too. A DFG project focused on this field, but the
main activity had already ended in 1998.[25]

It would have been strange if the special German concern about ecology had not been reflected in business history. Indeed, several volumes
have been published on this problem. They are usually critical, revealing
the undeniable shortcomings of industry. However, it would be instructive to learn not only how problems emerged, but also how they were
perceived and manipulated in history.[26]

The history of small and medium-sized firms has been studied –
especially in the small states of Austria and Switzerland. The focus was
on the change from nonmarket relations to market-centered processes,
and on the general commercialization of society on the one hand and
networks of firms and survival strategies on the other.[27]

Last, though not least, there is a variety of business histories with
a local and regional focus. These works, often edited by organizations
such as museums or chambers of commerce, sometimes are of very high
quality. The problem is that only in exceptional cases have they been

---

[24] The volume on uranium mining is but an introduction to this field; see Rainer Karlsch
and Harm G. Schröter, eds., *"Strahlende Vergangenheit": Studien zur Geschichte des
Uranbergbaus der Wismut* (St. Katharinen, 1996).

[25] Johannes Bähr and Dietmar Petzina, eds., *Innovationsverhalten und Entscheidungsstruk-
turen: Vergleichende Studien zur wirtschaftlichen Entwicklung im geteilten Deutsch-
land, 1945–1990* (Berlin, 1996); Wolfram Fischer, Uwe Müller, and Frank Zschaler, eds.,
*Wirtschaft im Umbruch: Strukturveränderungen und Wirtschaftspolitik im 19. und 20.
Jahrhundert* (St. Katharinen, 1997); Peter Hefele, *Die Verlagerung von Industrie- und
Dienstleistungsunternehmen aus der SBZ/DDR nach Westdeutschland* (Stuttgart, 1998);
Dietmar Petzina and Lothar Baar, eds., *Deutsch-deutsche Wirtschaft 1945 bis 1990, Struk-
turveränderungen, Innovationen und regionaler Wandel. Ein Vergleich* (St. Katharinen,
1999).

[26] Werner Abelshauser, ed., *Umweltgeschichte: Umweltverträgliches Wirtschaften in
historischer Perspektive* (Stuttgart, 1994); Arne Andersen, *Historische Technikfolgen-
abschätzung am Beispiel des Metallhüttenwesens und der Chemieindustrie, 1850–
1933* (Stuttgart, 1996); Ulrike Gilhaus, *"Schmerzenskinder der Industrie": Umweltver-
schmutzung, Umweltpolitik und sozialer Protest im Industriezeitalter in Westfalen,
1845–1914* (Paderborn, 1995); Hans Pohl, ed., *Industrie und Umwelt* (Stuttgart,
1993).

[27] See various contributions in Matis, *Historische Betriebsanalyse*, and Margrit Müller,
Organisationsformen und wirtschaftliche Entwicklung (Bern, 1991).

related to the general perspectives of the respective branch of industry, the nation, or the world economy.[28]

PERIOD OF REORIENTATION: NEW DIRECTIONS IN GERMAN BUSINESS HISTORY

The perceived need for a new quality in writing business history has provoked action by individual authors as well as by the various societies mentioned earlier. They all share the desire for improvement. Of all the initiatives that have emerged during the past few years in breaking new paths in business history, three will be explained in detail. All three have several things in common. First, all of the works have been written by young but experienced historians. All three are the *habilitation*, which in the German academic context is the second major book after the publication of the Ph.D. thesis. The *habilitation*, which traditionally opens the door to a professorship, is therefore regarded not only as a work of supreme importance, but also as an indication of the direction of research and writing in which the author is headed for the coming years. All three authors – Hartmut Berghoff, Christian Kleinschmidt, and David Gugerli – on reflecting upon the state of business history, decided to write something new.

First is Hartmut Berghoff's *Zwischen Kleinstadt und Weltmarkt: Hohner und die Harmonika, 1857–1961* (Stuttgart, 1997). In our context, Berghoff's subtitle, *Unternehmensgeschichte als Gesellschaftsgeschichte (Business History as History of Society)*, is even more important than the main heading. Berghoff embarked on the task of portraying the whole of society, or at least decisive parts of it, by presenting the firm of Hohner. Hohner is a small to medium-sized firm – with maximum sales of about $100 million a year – that manufactures musical instruments. In many ways, this enterprise is representative not only of the southwestern part of Germany but of Austria and Switzerland, too. It is rather small, is oriented to craftsmanship, and falls within a special niche, but in this niche it is a world market leader. Even more interesting in light of Berghoff's thesis is how Hohner is rooted in society. Berghoff presents

[28] Examples are Johannes Bähr and Wolfram Fischer, eds., *Wirtschaft im geteilten Berlin, 1945–1990: Forschungsansätze und Zeitzeugen* (Munich, 1994); Industrie und Handelskammer zu Berlin, ed., *Berlin und seine Wirtschaft: Ein Weg aus der Geschichte in die Zukunft: Lehren und Erkenntnisse* (Berlin, 1987); Landesmuseum für Technik und Arbeit in Mannheim, ed., *Tradition und Umbruch: 40 Jahre Wirtschaft in Baden-Würtemberg* (Mannheim, 1992).

not only the firm's economic development but also the social differences, the geographical structures, the political intertwinings, and the firm's embeddedness in the local culture. He draws from the traditional theory of locations of enterprises and enlarges it at the same time with additional dimensions. Berghoff's attempt to understand and present the business history of Hohner as a history of society is convincing. It is a new and extremely comprehensive way of understanding business history, and his book suggests more studies of this kind. However, there are doubts about the concept too. It has been shown to be a valid and exciting one, but the preconditions were exceptionally well suited for this case study: Hohner focuses on producing consumer goods – it sells harmonicas all over the world – while generally speaking, German firms are more famous for their production of investment goods. Hohner surely is rooted more deeply in both the local society and the world market than a saw mill, for example. And, of course, "society" in Berghoff's context means not the society of the state or even a substantial part of it, but a very small town, the name of which even many Germans have never heard of before. But if we can understand that Berghoff's intention is not to portray a whole nation, but rather how a business is deeply rooted in a certain location and simultaneously able to act worldwide, we can see its utility perfectly.

Christian Kleinschmidt's work is *Der produktive Blick: Wahrnehmung amerikanischer und japanischer Management- und Produktionsmethoden durch deutsche Unternehmer, 1950-1985* (Berlin, 2001). In it Kleinschmidt attempts to present new insights reflecting the recent trend toward mental and cultural history. He looks for signs of Americanization and Japanization in ten large German firms after the Second World War. By "Americanization" and "Japanization" he means not only the transfer of machinery but also of schemes, ways of organization, management approaches, quality control, and so on. Indeed, there was a lot of transfer. During the 1950s it was from the United States that the world could learn how to build and sell cars. Since we have no comprehensive theory on how managers learn and decide, Kleinschmidt borrows mainly from Gidden's model of structuring. At the same time, he suggests that the authors of business history should present their findings in what he called "moduls," which are to be combined easily with other studies. Whether this last suggestion can be achieved or not, his findings present a new way of writing that pays more attention to what Hofstede called the "mental program" of decision making, whereas many more traditional writers have concentrated on hard facts, such as turnover or

technology. Surely such soft facts should generally be paid more attention to in the future. The second impressive aspect of Kleinschmidt's
work is a theory-led comparison of several firms, a task that often has
been claimed to be necessary but rarely achieved. Kleinschmidt concen-
trates on big enterprise and defined subquestions (moduls). Thus his
findings may be more easily applied in discussing other firms' histories
than Berghoff's approach of writing not only about the enterprise but
also about its setting in society and culture.

Our third innovator, David Gugerli, is from Switzerland and writes
on its electrification in *Redeströme: Zur Elektrifizierung der Schweiz,
1880–1914* (Zurich, 1996). His approach is radical. He denies the importance of entrepreneurial initiatives, financial institutions, and technical
facts in comparison with interaction. "Streams of talking" would perhaps be the best translation of the key words in his title. His book takes
an extreme linguistic turn. Of course, Gugerli is right when he claims
that the visions of electrification in Switzerland had to be hammered
out through confrontations with nature, consideration of financial possibilities, and massive logistical planning, all of which was carried out by
oral and written interaction. However, in the end, Swiss firms fortunately
stopped talking and started to do things. Gugerli is right in stating that
the decision-making process is interesting and should be part of every
business history. But in contrast to his presentation, this is not the whole
story. Plans are changed by nature, technical innovations, and men – in
other words, by realities. Because Gugerli's approach is one-sided, I do
not consider it as a major contribution to the future of writing business
history.

OUTLOOK

The 1990s saw a search for reorientation in writing business history. To
begin with, there was a strong political demand for business history.
This development came as a surprise to the historians and archivists
concerned, in spite of the fact that business history always was to a certain extent understood as a political issue. The international demand for
an historical account of the enterprises was new, because it came from
outside, from the public, which started to question firms about their
behavior during the Nazi period. Public pressure became so strong that
firms had no choice but to stand up and answer. Beyond all considerations of justice and the fact that firms have to say something concerning their past, this demand for business history may represent German

business history's second big chance. Large firms especially now value their archives and the work of business historians much more highly than before. Of course, the possibility exists that once enterprises have their business histories written by historians, they will want to end the discussion and consequently close all archives. But optimists point to the momentum of institutions and to a stabilization in the demand for such information.

What is the future of business history within the German-speaking community? With new topics, new methods, new scholars, institutional deepening, greater competition, and an enhanced reputation, there should be new possibilities. The new approaches should find a place within investigations that understand firms as a field of social interaction by defined actors. Since outside relations of enterprises ought to be included, it is obvious that such research is of particular importance in understanding history in general as well as our world today. It seems that these possibilities of business history will be situated closer to history than to economics. This fact is reflected by both German business history societies. In a 1997 editorial *ZUG* argued for focusing on history without economy. AKKU from the beginning has concentrated on historians.

However, when the new topics and methods have proved their attractiveness and reliability, undoubtedly economists will understand the usefulness of business history, especially as some economists of business management have begun to look into organizational culture and now understand the political potential of business history. Thus, in spite of institutional stress and financial cutbacks, and perhaps in some contrast to economic history, the future of business history seems to be brighter than before. Whether the old dream of business historians – to establish microeconomic history parallel to macroeconomic history – will come true, perhaps the next decade will show us.

KEY WORKS

Berghoff, Hartmut. *Zwischen Kleinstadt und Weltmarkt: Hohner und die Harmonika, 1857–1961*. Stuttgart, 1997.

Eichholtz, Dietrich and Wolfgang Schumann, eds. *Anatomie des Krieges*. Berlin, 1969.

Gall, Lothar, et al. *Die Deutsche Bank, 1870–1995*. Munich, 1995.

Gugerli, David. *Redeströme: Zur Elektrifizierung der Schweiz, 1880–1914*. Zurich, 1996.

Hass, Gerhard and Wolfgang Schumann, eds. *Anatomie der Aggression*. Berlin, 1972.

Hayes, Peter. *Industry and Ideology: IG Farben in the Nazi Era.* Cambridge, 1987.

Kleinschmidt, Christian. *Der produktive Blick: Wahrnehmung amerikanischer und japanischer Management- und Produktionsmethoden durch deutsche Unternehmer, 1950-1985.* Berlin, 2001.

Mathis, Franz. *Big Business in Österreich.* Vienna, 1987.

Pohl, Hans. "Betrachtungen zum wissenschaftlichen Standort von Wirtschafts- und Unternehmensgeschichte." *Vierteljahrschrift für Sozial- und Wirtschaftsgeschichte* 73, no. 3 (1991): 326-43.

Radant, Hans, ed. *Fall 6: Ausgewählte Dokumente und Urteil des IG Farben-Prozesses.* Berlin, 1970.

9

Business History in France

YOUSSEF CASSIS

Economic backwardness had been the dominant theme in French business history, especially according to American scholars, until the 1960s. Explanations were found in, among other places, France's business organization – in particular the persistence of the medium-sized family firm. Following the reassessments of the "revisionist" school, the concept of "backwardness" was almost totally discarded in the analyses of French economic performance and replaced by that of "difference" or, more recently, "specificity."[1] However, with the loss of its backwardness, France might have lost most of its appeal to foreign, particularly American, business historians and analysts. The notion of specificity does not fit easily into the general categories cherished by social scientists: Britain is a better example of early start, world dominance, and decline. Germany

I should like to thank Patrick Fridenson for his helpful comments on an earlier draft of this essay.

[1] See in particular Jean Bouvier, "Libres propos autour d'une démarche révisionniste," in *Le capitalisme français 19e-20e siècle. Blocages et dynamismes d'une croissance*, eds. Patrick Fridenson and André Straus (Paris, 1987), 11–27; Rondo Cameron and Charles E. Freedman, "French Economic Growth: A Radical Revision," *Social Science History* 7, no. 1 (1983): 3–30; Maurice Lévy-Leboyer, "Le patronat français a-t-il été malthusien?" *Le mouvement social* 3 (1974), 3–49.

provides a better example of a bank-dominated economy. Japan is a better example of state-induced economic prowess, and so on.

As a result, France has become somewhat marginalized in international business history comparisons. One cannot criticize Alfred Chandler for not including France in *Scale and Scope*, especially as he originally intended to do so but was discouraged by the restrictive practices of some business historians and company archivists. Dealing with Great Britain and Germany, in addition to the United States, was enough of an achievement.[2] The position attributed to France in the recent *Big Business and the Wealth of Nations* is more contentious.[3] Together with Italy and Spain, France is ranked among the "followers in Western Europe." The "prime movers in Western Europe" are not only Great Britain and Germany, but also an array of small countries including Belgium, Denmark, Finland, Luxembourg, the Netherlands, Norway, Sweden, and Switzerland. The implications of this choice cannot be fully discussed here. France was a pioneer of modern industrialization, and its gross domestic product (GDP) per capita was higher than that of Germany throughout the nineteenth century.[4] The question of the emergence of large industrial enterprises and the development of organizational capabilities that is at the heart of Chandler's argument needs to be taken into account. In light of a number of recent appraisals, it appears that France was not far behind Britain and Germany, with strong positions in iron, steel, glass, rubber, automobiles, and aeronautics. More important, the differences among the three countries, especially between France and Germany, were not very significant.[5] In addition, France obviously had many more opportunities to develop large industrial enterprises than its smaller European neighbors. We will come back to the theme of the

---

[2] Alfred D. Chandler, Jr., *Scale and Scope: The Dynamics of Industrial Capitalism* (Cambridge, Mass., 1990).

[3] Alfred D. Chandler, Jr., Franco Amatori, and Takashi Hikino, eds., *Big Business and the Wealth of Nations* (Cambridge, 1997).

[4] Angus Maddison, *Dynamic Forces in Capitalist Development: A Long-Run Comparative View* (Oxford, 1991), 6.

[5] See Michael Smith, "Putting France in the Chandlerian Framework: France's 100 Largest Industrial Firms in 1913," *Business History Review* 72, no. 1 (1998): 46–85; Patrick Fridenson, "France: The Relatively Slow Development of Big Business in the Twentieth Century," in Chandler et al., eds., *Big Business and the Wealth of Nations*, 207–45; Youssef Cassis, *Big Business: The European Experience in the Twentieth Century* (Oxford, 1997); Bruce Kogut, "Evolution of the Large Firm in France in Comparative Perspective," *Entreprises et Histoire*, 19 (1998): 113–51.

large enterprise in a subsequent section. What can be said at this stage is that the position of France in international business history appears somewhat misjudged.

The same problem can be approached from another perspective: for example, the number of entries in the recent *International Bibliography of Business History*.[6] Out of 4,247, only 181 are devoted to France. What significance should be given to this figure? The overwhelming number of entries relate to the United Kingdom and the United States for reasons of both language and influence over the discipline. France's number of entries is almost identical to Germany's (182), though both are far behind Japan (388), which can be partly explained by publishing factors. However imperfect, this rough indicator would suggest that, despite a relative neglect in the international literature, business history has been as dynamic in France as in Germany and Japan, the two countries most commonly included in international comparisons alongside the United States and the United Kingdom. In the following sections, I will examine whether such a claim can be substantiated by France's actual research output.[7]

How far ahead are the United Kingdom and the United States? A precise answer is difficult to provide. The gap is undoubtedly still substantial in quantitative terms as well as in the range of subjects dealt with. But it is at the theoretical and methodological levels that the American and British domination is most striking. The only significant contributions by French authors to the section on "Approaches to Business History" are by Henri Fayol, Jean-Jacques Servan-Schreiber, Michel Lescure, and Maurice Lévy-Leboyer. This is rather poor by comparison with a good thirty British and American names, including Alfred Chandler, Leslie Hannah, William Lazonick, Mark Casson, Ronald Coase, John Dunning, John Kenneth Galbraith, Albert Hirschman, Oliver Williamson, Peter Drucker, John Kay, and Michael Porter. One of the questions to be addressed is to what extent French business historiography has been following international trends and to what extent it has developed a specific approach that could prove a valuable contribution to the discipline.

[6] Francis Goodall, Terry Gourvish, and Steven Tolliday, eds., *International Bibliography of Business History* (London, 1997). Both the total number of entries and those for France include cross-referencing; the 174 entries related to "General Sources" have been deducted from the total.

[7] For a recent bibliography of French business history, see Alain Beltran, Jean-Pierre Daviet, and Michèle Ruffat, *L'histoire des entreprises en France. Essai bibliographique*, Les Cahiers de l'IHTP, 30 (Paris, 1995).

ISSUES AND DEBATES

For the past three decades, thematic approaches of business history have been dominated in France by four main issues: the rise of the large corporation; business leaders; science, technology, and innovation; and the role of the state. However, other areas have also been at the top of the agenda, in particular profits and profitability; international business and multinationals; business culture; and industrial and commercial policies.

Following Alfred Chandler's enormous influence, the major debates in business history have centered on the emergence, development, and role of the large company. One of the first questions to be answered was, which were the largest firms? Lists of the 50, 100, or 200 largest companies in the United States, Britain, and Germany were duly published in the 1970s and 1980s. Surprisingly, no such lists were published in France, even though a number of the country's largest companies were used in various studies, in particular by Maurice Lévy-Leboyer.[8] One could, however, make use of the lists established by Houssiaux in the 1950s.[9] In recent years, however, American scholars have started to compile comparable lists for France.[10]

The main question confronting France has been the late emergence of the large corporation. It has been approached from three points of view. The first one, mostly adopted by Maurice Lévy-Leboyer in the early days of the Chandlerian debate, has been to look for explanations of this phenomenon. Reasons were found in market conditions, managerial attitudes, and institutional factors: in particular, the prevalence of holding companies. In addition, the severity of the depression of the 1930s, followed by war and occupation, delayed the country's modernization. Nevertheless, on the whole, French firms were found to have responded adequately to their environmental constraints.[11] A second point of view has been to play down the importance of the Chandlerian

---

[8] Maurice Lévy-Leboyer, "Le patronat français, 1912–1973," in id., *Le patronat de la seconde industrialisation* (Paris, 1979), 137–85; id., "The Large Corporation in Modern France," in *Managerial Hierarchies: Comparative Perspectives on the Rise of the Modern Industrial Enterprise*, eds. Alfred D. Chandler, Jr., and Hermann Daems (Cambridge, Mass., 1980), 117–60.

[9] Jacques Houssiaux, *Le pouvoir de monopole* (Paris, 1956).

[10] Smith, "Putting France in the Chandlerian Framework"; Kogut, "Evolution of the Large Firm in France."

[11] Lévy-Leboyer, "The Large Corporation in Modern France"; id., "La grande entreprise française: Un modèle français?," in *Entre l'Etat et le marché. L'économie française des années 1880 à nos jours*, eds. Maurice Lévy-Leboyer and Jean-Claude Casanova (Paris, 1991), 365–410.

model and to rehabilitate the family firm.[12] The emphasis on family capitalism has been a traditional feature of French business history[13] and has found a new legitimacy with the growing consensus on the persistence of family control within large European companies as well as the positive role played by family firms in Europe's economic development.[14] This point has been reinforced by the existence, in several industries, of clusters based on personal links or other subtle forms of control.[15] In the same way, the role of small and medium-sized companies has been seen as a permanent feature of French business organization, featuring interdependence between firms of different sizes and a certain division of labor between large firms and small and medium-sized enterprises.[16] Finally, the third, and most recent point of view, has been to study in context France's lack of large firms in the first phase of the corporate age, without, however, entirely shelving the issue. Large French companies tended to be smaller than their British and German counterparts. However, significant differences were limited to a few sectors, while sectorial distribution followed the same patterns as in other industrialized countries, including the United States.[17]

The study of business leaders is of equal interest to business historians and social historians. Social historians have been mostly concerned

[12] See, for example, Emmanuel Chadeau, "The Large Family Firm in Twentieth Century France," *Business History* 35, no. 4 (1993): 184–205; Daniel Henri, "Capitalisme familial et gestion industrielle au XIXe siècle," *Revue française de gestion* 70 (1988): 141–50.

[13] See, for example, Louis Bergeron, *Les capitalistes en France (1780–1914)* (Paris, 1978).

[14] See Geoffrey Jones and Mary B. Rose, "Family Capitalism," and Roy Church, "The Family Firm in Industrial Capitalism: International Perspectives on Hypotheses and History," both in *Business History* 35, no. 4 (1993), special issue on family capitalism.

[15] Fridenson, "France"; Ginette Kurgan van Hentenryk and Emmanuel Chadeau, "Structure et stratégie de la petite et moyenne entreprise depuis la révolution industrielle," in *Debates and Controversies in Economic History*, eds. Hermann Van der Wee and Erik Aerts (Leuven, 1990), 167–91; Alain Cottereau, "The Fate of Collective Manufactures in the Industrial World: The Silk Industries of Lyons and London," in *World of Possibilities*, eds. Charles Sabel and Jonathan Zeitlin (Cambridge, 1997), 67–83.

[16] Emmanuel Chadeau, "La permance des petites et moyennes entreprises en France au XXème siècle," in *Structure and Strategy of Small and Medium-Size Enterprises since the Industrial Revolution,* ed. Margrit Müller (Stuttgart, 1994), 21–37.

[17] The title of Patrick Fridenson's contribution to the volume on *Big Business and the Wealth of Nations* is significant in that respect: "France: The *Relatively* Slow Development of Big Business in the Twentieth Century" (my emphasis). This third point of view is developed by Cassis, *Big Business*; Kogut, "Large Firm in France"; Smith, "Putting France in the Chandlerian Framework"; see also J. R. Kinghorn and J. V. Nye, "The Scale of Production in Western Economic Development: A Comparison of Official Industry Statistics in the United States, Britain, France, and Germany, 1905–1913," *Journal of Economic History* 56, no. 1 (1996): 90–112.

with businessmen as social elites.[18] This approach can be of direct use to business historians in their assessment of the sociocultural determinants of business performance. However, the French tradition has been to integrate the economic, social, political, and cultural dimensions of the subject, making wide use of the prosopographical method. Despite this emphasis on the human factor, the project of a dictionary of business biography has so far been limited to the period of the Second Empire (1852–70). Its initiators favored coverage encompassing all geographic regions rather than restricted to the national business elite.[19] As elsewhere, historians have been interested in the social origins of business leaders and the extent to which the group has been open to newcomers. A broad consensus has emerged from the various inquiries undertaken in the past thirty or forty years in both Europe and the United States about the social origins of business elites. The overwhelming majority came from a middle- or upper-middle-class background.[20] Maurice Lévy-Leboyer, however, has challenged the view of a closed elite and argued that the widening of the recruitment basis of business leaders, with a fair proportion of sons of engineers, army officers, academics, and so on, especially in the new industries, has been concealed by aggregate statistical figures.[21]

In a similar context, the rehabilitation of the family firm has revived interest in business dynasties. Particular attention recently has been paid to the reality of their existence, the reasons that could explain the persistence of family ownership and control beyond the third generation, and the family's effects on economic and business performance.[22] The results show that business dynasties have exerted a far greater fascination on historians than is warranted by their actual weight in the business world. On the whole, family control has proved limited from the fourth generation on, though a proportion of 17 to 20 percent for the business leaders active between 1885 and 1935 could be interpreted as a sign

---

[18] See in particular Christophe Charle, *Les élites de la République (1880–1900)* (Paris, 1987).

[19] *Les patrons du Second Empire.* 1. *Anjou-Normandie*, ed. Dominique Barjot (Paris, 1991); 2. *Bourgogne*, ed. Philippe Jobert (Paris, 1991); 3. *Franche-Comté*, ed. Claude-Isabelle Brelot (Paris, 1991); 4. *Bordeaux et la Gironde*, ed. Hubert Bonin (Paris and Le Mans, 1999).

[20] See Hartmut Kaelble, "Long-Term Change in the Recruitment of Business Elites: Germany Compared to the U.S., Great Britain and France since the Industrial Revolution," *Journal of Social History* 13, no. 3 (1980): 404–23.

[21] Lévy-Leboyer, "Le patronat français."

[22] See the special issues of *Le mouvement social* 132 (1985) and *Entreprises et Histoire* 9 (1995) and 12 (1996) on this theme.

either of entrepreneurial change (by Lévy-Leboyer) or of dynastic per-
petuation (by Crouzet). There were, however, regional variations. Michel
Hau detected exceptional firm longevities in Alsace as a result not only
of religious factors, but also of the importance families attached to the
education of their members.[23] Interestingly, Crouzet found that business
dynasties appear to have been stronger in France than in Britain, though
they mostly gave way after the Second World War.[24]

Education and training is the second constituent part of the history of
business leaders and, as in the case of recruitment, includes a social as
well as a business side, though the two can be reconciled in the concept
of business culture. In France, three interrelated issues have been at the
heart of the debate: the influence of the *grandes écoles*, the role of engineers, and the career pattern of French top managers. Discussions about
French business leaders' education has been less concerned about their
level of education, which was the highest in Europe – over 70 percent had
a university or other type of higher education before 1914 – than about
its content. The majority of French business leaders have been educated
at one of the *grandes écoles*. Several of them are engineering schools,
including the most famous of them, the Ecole Polytechnique. There have
been mixed appraisals of the *grandes écoles*, both in France and abroad.[25]
On the one hand, there is no doubt that they have been admired for turning out a scientifically trained elite of engineers. But they have also been
criticized, above all the Ecole Polytechnique, for being too theoretical and
indifferent to the practical application of their teaching. The effects of the
selective entrance examination (the *concours*) have also been judged to
be negative. More recently, the *grandes écoles* have been accused of producing administrators and bureaucrats rather than businessmen. To what
extent these critics are justified remains a matter of contention, though
the current orthodoxy in business history would concur and favor the
German model of business education.[26] In any case, the weight of the
grandes écoles, including lesser engineering schools such as the *écoles*

[23] M. Hau, "La longévité des dynasties industrielles alsaciennes," *Le mouvement social* 132
(1985): 9–25.

[24] François Crouzet, "Les dynasties d'entrepreneurs en France et en Grande-Bretagne,"
Entreprises et Histoire 9 (1995): 25–42.

[25] See, for example, Ezra N. Suleiman, *Elites in French Society: The Politics of Survival*
(Princeton, 1978), and Pierre Bourdieu, *La noblesse d'Etat: Grandes Ecoles et esprit de
corps* (Paris, 1989).

[26] See, for example, Robert Locke, *The End of the Practical Man: Entrepreneurship and
Higher Education in Germany, France and Great Britain, 1880-1940* (Greenwich,
Conn., 1984).

d'arts et métiers, which have mostly catered to middle management, has aroused more interest for *"ingénieurs"* in France than in any other country.[27] Their socioprofessional status together with their conception of discipline and authority, and their natural bent for technology rather than marketing, have long been considered major influences on French business development in the first third of the twentieth century. Indeed, as the essays in A. Thépot's *L'ingénieur dans la société française* (Paris, 1985) demonstrated, the extent of engineers' involvement in business enterprises has come to be seen as the main criterion of French industrial development in the age of the Second Industrial Revolution.

Top managers in large companies have traditionally been recruited from the higher ranks of the civil service.[28] Such moves from the public to the private sector are not unique to France. It is rather the extent of the phenomenon, known as *pantouflage*, that sets French business leaders apart.[29] The effects of this recruitment pattern on France's business performance remain uncertain, and the debate still goes on. Common sense would suggest that professional experience acquired in the business world might be better suited to the responsibilities of running a large company than that gained in the state service. However, one should avoid the pitfall of giving too much importance to a single determinant of business performance; old established traditions are usually adapted to a national context. The grip of the members of the *grands corps* on top business positions has increased in the past thirty years, with the Ecole Nationale d'Administration (ENA) gaining ground over all other institutions, including the Ecole Polytechnique as well as the newly formed, or modernized, business schools. As in the rest of Europe, the business schools themselves have aroused renewed interest among business historians in the past few years. Three different educational models have coexisted in France: the management schools created under the pressure of the business world from the late nineteenth century on (Ecole des hautes études commerciales [HEC], Ecole supérieure des sciences économiques et commerciales [ESSEC]); the university system,

---

[27] It should be remembered that the words "engineer" and *ingénieur* do not have the same meaning in English and French: whereas in England the notion usually extends to manual workers, in France it is reserved for middle managers, or *cadres*.

[28] See Christophe Charle, "Le pantouflage en France, vers 1880–vers 1980," *Annales E.S.C.* 42, no. 5 (1987): 1115–37.

[29] See in particular Michel Bauer and Bénédicte Bertin-Mourot, *"Les 200" en France et en Allemagne: Deux modèles de détection-sélection-formation de dirigeants de grandes entreprises* (Paris, n.d. [1992]).

which has grown considerably since the 1960s; and, more recently, the American-style business school, Institut européen d'administration des affaires (INSEAD).[30] The approach, however, has been mainly institutional. The influence of business education on French senior managers remains to be assessed.

French historiography has kept pace with the growing international interest in the themes of science, technology, and innovation. Their importance has not only been discussed within the wider context of economic history, but has also been approached at the level of the firm. The development of scientific knowledge in France has attracted a fair amount of interest, especially on the part of British and American writers.[31] The training of engineers and the development of engineering schools are two other related areas that have been directly connected to business history.[32] Technological innovation has been approached through company monographs, especially in the science-related industries. In that respect, the massive interest in the history of electricity in the past twenty years has had positive effects. At a more general level, the work of François Caron, particularly *Les deux révolutions industrielles du XXe siècle* (Paris, 1997), has endeavored to provide a general explanatory framework for the process of technological innovation in the twentieth century, not only in France but internationally. It is based on the concept of technical systems, that is, "the close interdependence of technology's various components at a given moment in history." In Caron's analysis, in which business enterprises play an integral part, the domination of coal and steam was questioned in the 1880s by the emergence of new technological fields, such as electricity, the combustion engine, and organic chemistry. These fields flourished, forming an original technical system from which originated mass civilization. In France, a recurrent subject of national soul-searching has been the innovative capacity of the country's industry, reflecting a psychological complex, first about Britain and later about Germany. Most historical analyses, however, have

---

[30] Good overview of recent research in *Entreprises et Histoire* 14–15 (1997) devoted to the theme "Former des gestionnaires."

[31] See in particular Robert Fox and George Weisz, eds., *The Organization of Science and Technology in France 1808–1914* (Cambridge, 1980).

[32] Terry Shinn, *Savoir scientifique et pouvoir social: L'école Polytechnique 1794–1914* (Paris, 1980); John H. Weiss, *The Making of Technological Man: The Social Origins of French Engineering Education* (Cambridge, Mass., 1982); André Grelon, "Training Electrical Engineers in France, 1880–1939," in *Management and Business in Britain and France*, eds. Youssef Cassis, François Crouzet, and Terry Gourvish (Oxford, 1995), 147–58.

taken a positive view of the achievements of French industrial companies in this respect.[33] Another important recent development has been the study of science, technology, and innovation within the context of business history, which has mainly been done by analyzing the research and development activity of major firms.[34]

State intervention is a more contentious issue, one that is readily associated with the French model of capitalism after the Second World War. Several analyses have emphasized the role of the state in the modernization of the French economy after 1945.[35] As far as business enterprises are concerned, there is no doubt that they benefited from economic planning, especially as far as their investments were concerned, and a climate of reduced uncertainties. One of the original aspects of the relationship between business and government in France has been the constant flow of senior civil servants into the major banking and industrial companies referred to earlier. This ensured a certain degree of intimacy between the two spheres. The active part played by the state in a number of industries in the interwar years, such as oil (with the formation of the Compagnie Française des Pétroles in 1924) or electricity, has been discussed in numerous studies. Others have underlined the negative effects of state policies on entrepreneurial activities, especially in the aeronautical industry.[36] The postwar nationalizations have been approached largely from a political rather than a business point of view[37] and, unlike in Britain, for example, there have been no general assessments of the performance of state enterprises. Attention has instead focused on the policy of national champions, whether in private or – after 1981 – public ownership, with mixed appraisals of its success.[38]

Among other themes of interest, the analysis of profits and profitability has played a more significant role in France than in other European

[33] See a survey of the issue in Jean-Jacques Salomon, "La capacité d'innovation," in *Entre l'Etat et le marché*, eds. Lévy-Leboyer and Casanova.

[34] Philippe-Jean Bernard and Jean-Pierre Daviet, eds., *Culture d'entreprise et innovation* (Paris, 1992); Muriel Le Roux, *L'entreprise et la recherche: Un siècle de recherche industrielle à Pechiney, 1886-1996* (Paris, 1998); François Jacq, "Pratiques scientifiques, formes d'organisation et conceptions politiques de la science dans la France d'après-guerre (1944-1962)" (Ph.D. diss., Ecole des Mines, 1996).

[35] See in particular Richard F. Kuisel, *Capitalism and the State in Modern France: Renovation and Economic Management in the Twentieth Century* (Cambridge, 1981).

[36] Emmanuel Chadeau, "Schumpeter, l'Etat et les capitalistes: Entreprendre dans l'aviation en France (1900-1980)," *Le Mouvement social* 145 (1988): 9-39.

[37] See Claire Andrieu, Lucette Le Van, and Antoine Prost, eds., *Les nationalisations de la Libération. De l'utopie au compromis* (Paris, 1987).

[38] Good overview in Fridenson, "France."

countries. The approach has changed in the thirty years separating two major studies of the subject. In *Le mouvement du profit en France au XIXe siècle* (Paris, 1965) J. Bouvier, F. Furet, and M. Gillet were primarily interested in the growth of profit in nineteenth-century France, as measured by a sample of companies in three sectors: iron and steel, banking, and coal mining. Methodological problems related to the real meaning of published profits were discussed at length. And while the performances of individual enterprises were given due consideration, the emphasis was on the general trend of the period. Next, in the volume edited by J. Marseille, *Les performances des entreprises françaises au XXe siècle* (Paris, 1995), the focus was on the performance of French enterprises in the twentieth century, as measured by the published balance sheets of most publicly traded French companies since the 1930s. One of the objects of the study was to determine which have been the most competitive French companies. One of its findings was the strong results of a number of small and medium-sized companies in industries such as wine, luxury goods (haute couture, perfumes), retailing, and services. Despite an excessive concern for ranking winners and losers, this analysis put performance at the core of business history.[39] This is an important corrective to recent studies, which have tended to be more interested in the factors explaining business success or failure rather than in business performance itself.

The history of multinational enterprises has attracted growing interest in the past fifteen years, with old assumptions being questioned by new estimates of the respective share of direct and indirect investment.[40] However, French historiography has remained on the margins of this movement, though a number of case studies have documented the multinational expansion of the major companies[41] as well as France's direct investment in its colonial empire and zones of influence.[42] Otherwise,

[39] For a comparison of the performances of the leading French companies with their counterparts in Britain and Germany in the twentieth century, see Cassis, *Big Business*.

[40] For a recent survey see Geoffrey Jones, *The Evolution of International Business. An Introduction* (London, 1996).

[41] In addition to the company histories already referred to, see the French contributions to Alice Teichova, Maurice Lévy-Leboyer and Helga Nussbaum, eds., *Multinational Enterprise in Historical Perspective* (Cambridge, 1986); Peter Hertner and Geoffrey Jones, eds., *Multinationals: Theory and History* (Aldershot, 1986); Geoffrey Jones and Harm Schröter, eds., *The Rise of Multinationals in Continental Europe* (Aldershot, 1993).

[42] Jacques Marseille, *Empire colonial et capitalisme français. Histoire d'un divorce* (Paris, 1984); René Girault, *Emprunts russes et investissements français en Russie 1887-1914* (Paris, 1973); Jacques Thobie, *Intérêts et impérialisme français dans l'empire ottoman (1895-1914)* (Paris, 1977).

growth in the 1990s was away from the big questions and toward more detailed analysis of the working of the firm, the use of management tools, and the elaboration of industrial and commercial policies. Recent issues of *Entreprises et Histoire* have been devoted to themes such as "resorting to the social sciences," "communication in large enterprises," "management tools," and "safety in industry," all of which are closely related to management studies.[43] This trend reflects to a large extent the work of young researchers.

MAJOR WORKS IN FRENCH BUSINESS HISTORY

So far, there has been no attempt to write a general history of French business.[44] One reason might be that such a synthesis would be premature in the current state of research. Another complementary reason could be the absence of a general framework of analysis outside the Chandlerian model. As in other countries, French business history has developed mainly along sectoral and thematic lines. The closest thing to a general business history has been the recent publication of two histories of French industry. The first is an individual effort by Denis Woronoff, *Histoire de l'industrie en France, du XVIe siècle à nos jours* (Paris, 1994), that goes back to the sixteenth century and seeks to identify a French model of industrialization. Woronoff singles out four determining factors: energy resources, the share of the agrarian economy, cultural values, and state intervention. The second, edited by Maurice Lévy-Leboyer, *Histoire de la France industrielle* (Paris, 1995), is a collective work by the country's leading specialists covering the years 1700 to 2000. While far more detailed and systematic than the previous volume, it obviously lacks the unity of purpose that can only derive from single-authored works.

At the sectoral level, French business historiography has been particularly strong in three main areas: banking and finance, the motor industry, and energy, especially electricity. Major works have dealt with other sectors but have remained fairly isolated. While the service industry appears the most promising growth area, its extreme diversity and connections

[43] *Entreprises et Histoire* 7 (1994), "Le recours aux sciences sociales"; 11 (1996), "La communication de la grande entreprise"; 13 (1996), "Les outils de gestion"; 17 (1997), "La sécurité dans l'industrie."

[44] One should mention, however, an early and still useful attempt to deal with the French business world, past and present: Jacques Boudet, *Le monde des affaires en France* (Paris, 1952).

with most business activities make it difficult to pigeonhole as a single homogeneous sector.

Banking history has had a long tradition in France. Scholars such as Jean Bouvier and Maurice Lévy-Leboyer were among the founding fathers of the discipline in the 1960s, alongside Rondo Cameron and David Landes in the United States and Leslie Presnell in Great Britain. In *Les banques européennes et l'industrialisation internationale dans la première moitié du XIXe siècle* (Paris, 1964), Lévy-Leboyer reassessed the role of the banks in the early industrialization of France and in the continental powers, combining economic insight and historical sensitivity while relying on an extremely wide range of sources. In many respects, banking history has been the forerunner of business history, as it was concerned not only with issues related to the provision of credit but also with the analysis of the working of business organizations. This was particularly the case with *Le Crédit Lyonnais de 1863 à 1882* (Paris, 1961), Bouvier's detailed account of the formative years of the Crédit Lyonnais, one of the first French joint stock banks, which was to become the country's, and indeed one of Europe's, largest. His early essay on the history of French banking from the mid-nineteenth century to the 1960s remains a thought-provoking introduction to the field.[45] The tradition has continued, even though banking history is no longer at the forefront of French business history. Alain Plessis's detailed and scholarly history of the Banque de France during the Second Empire added a social dimension to the economic analysis of the bank's policy.[46] More recent publications include Eric Bussière's short but serious history of the Banque de Paris et des Pays-Bas, France's leading *banque d'affaires*, followed by a business biography of Horace Finaly (1871–1945), its legendary leader in the interwar years.[47] Other examples are Michel Lescure's pioneering study of the financing of small and medium-sized companies in the 1920s, which reappraises the respective roles of local banks and semipublic institutions,[48] and Hubert Bonin's monumental history of French banks in the

---

[45] Jean Bouvier, *Un siècle de banque française. Les contraintes de l'Etat et les incertitudes du marché* (Paris, 1973).

[46] Alain Plessis, *La Banque de France et ses deux cents actionnaires sous le Second Empire* (Geneva, 1982); id., *Régents et gouverneurs de la Banque de France sous le Second Empire* (Geneva, 1985); id., *La politique de la Banque de France sous le Second Empire* (Geneva, 1985).

[47] Eric Bussière, *Paribas, l'Europe et le monde 1872–1992* (Antwerp, 1993), and *Horace Finaly, banquier 1871–1945* (Paris, 1996).

[48] Michel Lescure, *PME et croissance économique* (Paris, 1996).

interwar years, which will prove a mine of information, especially on the relationships between banks and industry as well as on the development of banking practices.[49] There has been a steady flow of archive-based studies on the automobile industry since the early 1970s, dealing both with the history of individual companies and with the industry as a whole. Here the pioneering work is Patrick Fridenson's history of Renault's first forty years, a thoroughly modern, archive-based company monograph dealing with all sides of the business and underlining the dynamism of French entrepreneurship.[50] The two other leading manufacturers, Peugeot and Citroën, have also been the subjects of scholarly studies. In his history of Peugeot, Jean-Louis Loubet discussed how the most provincial of the "big three" reconstructed itself after the Second World War, first around a strategy of a single model and later, from the mid-1960s, of a large range of cars, showing a remarkable capacity for change and adaptation.[51] Citroën, which went bankrupt in 1934 and was taken over by Michelin, has been addressed by Sylvie Schweitzer through a biography of its brilliant founder, André Citroën, as well as through close attention to the production processes and the labor relations of the company.[52] At a more general level, though firmly anchored in the historical experience of individual firms, James Laux analyzed the development of the French automobile industry before 1914, whose production was second only to that of the United States before 1904 and which continued to lead Europe until the early 1930s.[53] For his part, Jean-Louis Loubet dealt with the strategic choices in terms of products, marketing, exports, multinational expansion, alliances, and mergers and acquisitions made by the leaders of the major firms from the 1930s to the 1990s – in other words, the determinants of a motor company's activities and development.[54] As

---

[49] Hubert Bonin, *Les banques françaises de l'entre-deux-guerres.* Vol. 1, *L'apogée de l'économie libérale française (1919-1935);* Vol. 2, *Les banques et les entreprises (1919-1935);* Vol. 3, *Les métiers financiers des banques françaises à l'époque de l'économie libérale (1919-1935)* (Paris, 1999).

[50] Patrick Fridenson, *Histoire des usines Renault. 1. Naissance de la grande entreprise 1898-1939* (Paris, 1972).

[51] Jean-Louis Loubet, *Automobiles Peugeot. Une réussite industrielle 1945-1974* (Paris, 1990).

[52] Sylvie Schweitzer, *André Citroën* (Paris, 1992); id., *Des engrenages à la chaîne. Les usines Citroën 1915-1935* (Lyon, 1982).

[53] James M. Laux, *In First Gear. The French Automobile Industry to 1914* (Liverpool, 1976).

[54] Jean-Louis Loubet, *Citroën, Peugeot, Renault et les autres. Soixante ans de stratégie* (Paris, 1995).

elsewhere, the automobile industry has proved a fertile ground for the discussion of more wide-ranging themes such as the strategy and structure of the firm, work organization, the innovation process, industrial relations, and so on. To automobiles must be added airplanes, another industry where entrepreneurs in France played a pioneering role. This story has been told by Emmanuel Chadeau, whose sectoral approach skillfully combines a detailed study of the main firms and their leaders with a discussion of the responsibility of the state in the shortcomings of the industry as a whole.[55]

Compared with banking and the automobile industry, electricity is a relative newcomer in French business history, one that has enjoyed nonetheless impressive growth since the foundation in 1982 of the Association pour l'histoire de l'électricité en France. The most notable publication on this subject is the three-volume history of electricity in France, *Histoire générale de l'électricité en France* (Paris, 1991–6), edited by François Caron, Fabienne Cardot, Maurice Lévy-Leboyer, and Henri Morsel. This collective work, resulting from nearly two decades of research, provides a global approach to the sector's historical development, with discussions of economic, social, political, cultural, and technical issues concerning both electricity supply and electrical engineering. In addition, the supply of gas and electricity, until their nationalization in 1946, has been discussed in several regional studies incorporating the history of major energy companies in Paris,[56] the southwest,[57] and especially the Rhône region.[58]

[55] Emmanuel Chadeau, *L'industrie aéronautique en France 1900–1950. De Blériot à Dassault* (Paris, 1987). See also *Le Mouvement Social* 145 (1988), special issue on "La France et l'aéronautique," ed. Patrick Fridenson.

[56] Alain Beltran, "L'énergie électrique dans la région parisienne entre 1878 et 1946," unpublished doctorat d'Etat, University of Paris IV, 1995 (Compagnie Parisienne de Distribution d'Electricité, Union d'Electricité); J.-P. Willot, "La Compagnie Parisienne d'éclairage et de chauffage par le gaz," unpublished doctoral thesis, University of Paris IV, 1995.

[57] Christophe Bouneau, *Modernisation et territoire. L'électrification du grand Sud-Ouest de la fin du 19ème siècle à 1946* (Bordeaux, 1997) (Union des Producteurs d'Electricité des Pyrennées Occidentales).

[58] Denis Varaschin, *La Société Lyonnaise des Forces Motrices du Rhône (1892–1946). Du service public à la nationalisation* (La Luiraz, 1996); Anne Dalmasso, "Nationalisation et exploitation de la production hydro-électrique en Savoie des années 1930 aux années 1970," unpublished doctoral thesis, University of Lyon II, 1994; Alexandre Giandou, "Histoire d'un partenaire régional de l'Etat: La Compagnie nationale du Rhône (1933–1974)," unpublished doctoral thesis, University of Lyon II, 1997; Catherine Vuillermot, " 'L'energie industrielle': D'une société à un groupe de production-distribution," unpublished doctoral thesis, University of Lyon II, 1997.

Other sectors have mostly been connected with the work of a single scholar. Transport, especially railway companies, is a case in point, being dominated by François Caron's history of the Chemin de fer du Nord. This major study, which analyzes the role of government, sources of capital, management of costs, rates, relations with suppliers, and the effects of the company on the wider economy, was an epoch-making work for French business history.[59] Similarly, the building industry has been thoroughly investigated by Dominique Barjot. Though his monumental *thèse d'Etat* has so far remained unpublished, his many publications have substantially documented the subject.[60] Major industries such as textiles, iron and steel, chemicals, and engineering have, of course, attracted a great deal of interest, though the record is mixed.

In iron and steel, for example, despite a number of important case studies, the country's two largest companies and the only ones of European proportions – Schneider and De Wendel – still require a proper academic history, while at the industry level, general studies are confined to the early nineteenth century.[61] However, Jean-Marie Moine's collective biography of the steel masters of Lorraine, France's main steel production region since the perfecting of the Thomas process in 1879, is a good example of the global approach, integrating the economic, social, political, and cultural dimensions.[62] In recent years, interest has mostly centered on the postwar era, with formation of the European Coal and Steel Community (ECSC) and the reorganization of the industry in a European context. Philippe Mioche's unpublished *thèse d'Etat* describes the decline of the French steel companies and their relationship to the state.[63] Eric Godelier's thesis on Usinor, France's largest iron and steel concern from its inception in 1948, investigates the formation of the firm's identity through mergers, technological innovation, and globalization.[64] Matthias

[59] François Caron, *Histoire de l'exploitation d'un grand réseau. La Compagnie du Chemin de fer du Nord (1846–1937)* (Paris, 1973); id., *Histoire des chemins de fer en France*, t. I: *1740–1883* (Paris, 1997).

[60] Dominique Barjot, "La grande entreprise française de travaux publics (1883–1974)," unpublished doctorat d'Etat, University of Paris IV, 1989.

[61] See Denis Woronoff, *L'industrie sidérurgique en France pendant La Révolution et l'Empire* (Paris, 1984).

[62] Jean-Marie Moine, *Les barons du fer. Les maîtres de forges en Lorraine du milieu du XIXe siècle aux années trente. Histoire sociale d'un patronat sidérurgique* (Nancy, 1988).

[63] Philippe Mioche, "La sidérurgie et l'Etat en France des années 1940 aux années 1960," unpublished doctorat d'Etat, University of Paris IV, 1992.

[64] Eric Godelier, "De la stratégie locale à la stratégie globale: La formation d'une identité de groupe chez Usinor (1948–1986)," unpublished doctral thesis, EHESS, 1995.

Kipping has highlighted the importance of economic reasons and business interest groups behind the French proposal to create an ECSC, made by the French foreign minister, Robert Schuman, on May 9, 1950.[65] The history of another metal industry, aluminum, is currently enjoying steady growth through the support of Pechiney, with Ludovic Cailluet's analysis of the company's strategy and structure, Muriel Leroux's discussion of its R&D policy, and Florence Hachez-Leroy's study of the aluminum cartel.[66]

The chemical industry has been approached mainly through the history of two leading firms: Saint-Gobain, the famous glass and chemicals company, studied by Jean-Pierre Daviet, and Rhône-Poulenc, France's largest chemical and drug company since the Second World War, studied by Pierre Cayez.[67] Pharmaceuticals have recently attracted a great deal of attention, with Michèle Ruffat's commissioned history of Synthélabo, and the two unpublished doctoral theses of Michael Robson and Sophie Chauveau.[68] Electrical engineering has benefited from the huge interest in the history of electricity with, in particular, another weighty unpublished *thèse d'Etat*, Pierre Lanthier's study of the major multinational groups established in France. There is also a high-quality commissioned history of the Compagnie Générale d'Electricité (now Alcatel), the largest French company in electronics, by Albert Broder and Felix Torres.[69]

---

[65] Orginally published by Matthis Kipping in German as *Zwischen Kartellen und Konkurrenz. Der Schuman-Plan und die Ursprünge der europäischen Einigung, 1944-1952* (Berlin, 1996), it is now also available in a revised French translation, *Intégration économique et compétitivité internationale. La France et les origines de la construction européenne* (Paris, 2000).

[66] Ludovic Cailluet, "Stratégies, structures d'organisation et pratiques de gestion de Pechiney des années 1880 à 1971," unpublished doctoral thesis, University of Lyon II, 1995; Le Roux, *L'entreprise et la recherche*; Florence Hachez-Leroy, *L'aluminium français. L'invention d'un marché 1911-1983* (Paris, 2000).

[67] Jean-Pierre Daviet, *Un destin international: La Compagnie de Saint-Gobain de 1830 à 1939* (Paris, 1988) and *Une multinationale à la française: Saint-Gobain 1665-1989* (Paris, 1989); Pierre Cayez, *Rhône-Poulenc: Contribution à l'étude d'un groupe industriel* (Paris, 1988).

[68] Michèle Ruffat, *175 ans d'industrie pharmaceutique française. Histoire de Synthélabo* (Paris, 1996); Michael Robson, "The Pharmaceutical Industry in Britain and France, 1919-1939," unpublished Ph.D. thesis, London School of Economics, 1993; Sophie Chauveau, "Politique de la pharmacie et du médicament, entreprises et marchés. L'industrie pharmaceutique en France des années 1920 à la fin des années 1970," unpublished doctoral thesis, University of Paris IV, 1997.

[69] Pierre Lanthier, "Les constructions électriques en France: Financement et stratégie de six groupes industriels internationaux de 1880 à 1940," unpublished doctorat d'Etat, University of Paris X, 1988; Albert Broder and Felix Torres, *Alcatel-Alsthom: Histoire de la Compagnie Générale d'Electricité* (Paris, 1992); see also the three volumes of the *Histoire de l'électricité en France*.

The most important contributions to the history of the textile industry have been concerned with the early nineteenth century. To begin with, there is Serge Chassagne's collective biography of the cotton masters, *Le coton et ses patrons, 1760-1840* (Paris 1991). However, recent company monographs, notably by Jean-Claude Dumas and Pierre Vernus, have recounted the rise and eventual fall, in the early 1970s, of significant family firms in cloth manufacturing and the silk industry.[70]

The past decade or so has witnessed a renewed interest in the service industries. The main development has been the sheer variety of business activities discovered, or rediscovered, by historical research. In a traditional field such as retail trade, attention first concentrated on department stores, most notably in Michael Miller's classic study of the Bon Marché, which linked the rise of department stores to bourgeois culture, and François Faraut's ethnographical approach to the Belle Jardinière.[71] More recently, the retail trade has been studied by Laurence Badel from the perspective of its lobbying organizations and their position toward European integration.[72] At the same time, attention has shifted to mass retailing, which, as underlined by Emmanuel Chadeau, underwent tremendous change after the Second World War.[73]

Other activities, old and new, can only be mentioned in passing: insurance, long neglected by financial historians, is enjoying a revival at Michèle Ruffat's instigation.[74] In newspapers and the media, the archive-based business history of the newspaper *Le Monde*, by Patrick Eveno, and that of the news agency Havas, by Pascal Lefebvre, have been worthy additions to Francine Amaury's pioneering history of the *Petit Parisien*, one of the world's largest newspapers at the turn of the century.[75] Advertising

---

[70] Jean-Claude Daumas, *L'amour du drap. Blin et Blin, 1827-1975* (Besançon, 1999); Pierre Vernus, "Bianchini Férier, fabricant de soierie à Lyon, 1888-1973," unpublished doctoral thesis, University of Lyon II, 1997.

[71] Michael Miller, *The Bon Marché. Bourgeois Culture and the Department Store* (Princeton, 1982); François Faraut, *Histoire de la Belle Jardinière* (Paris, 1987).

[72] Laurence Badel, *Un milieu libéral et européen. Le grand commerce français 1925-1948* (Paris, 1999).

[73] See Emmanuel Chadeau, "Mass Retailing: A Last Chance for the Family Firm in France, 1945-1990?" in Cassis et al., *Management and Business*, 52-71.

[74] Michèle Ruffat, E.-V. Caloni, and B. Laguerre, *UAP et l'histoire de l'assurance* (Paris, 1990); Marc Auffret, "Histoire d'un groupe d'assurances: Les Mutuelles du Mans, 1828-1946," unpublished doctorat d'Etat, University of Paris X, 1991.

[75] Patrick Eveno, *Le Monde, 1944-1995: Histoire d'une entreprise de presse* (Paris, 1996); Pascal Lefebvre, *Havas et l'audiovisuel 1920-1986* (Paris, 1998); Francine Amaury, *Histoire du plus grand quotidien de la IIIe République: Le Petit Parisien, 1876-1914* (Paris, 1972).

has been the subject of two recent fine studies, one by Marc Martin, taking a long-term view, the other by Marie-Emmanuelle Chessel, concentrating on the interwar years.[76] And in professional services, consultants have already attracted their historians.[77] This undoubted vitality, especially in the past ten years, has made France one of the most vibrant places in Europe for the study of business history.

THE ORGANIZATION OF BUSINESS HISTORY IN FRANCE

As a discipline, business history in France has acquired in the past fifteen years an organizational structure similar to that now found in other European countries. This broadly consists of chaired professorships, specialized research centers, an association, a learned journal, formal and informal links with business enterprises and business schools, and greater accessibility to business archives.

There is one chair of business history in France. It was established in 1985 at the Ecole des Hautes Etudes en Sciences Sociales and has been held since then by Patrick Fridenson. Otherwise, business history is mostly taught and researched in history departments as part of the broader field of economic and social history. In many respects, however, business history has now overtaken economic history as the dominant partner, and it is present in most French universities. Most French professors of economic history have been involved to some extent in business history research. The links with business schools remain rather tenuous, as none of the leading French institutions (HEC, ESCP, ESSEC, INSEAD) so far has established a formal teaching and research program in business history. Within the universities, however, departments of management studies have shown an increasing interest in the subject. A number of business historians have been appointed in the past few years – at Paris VIII, Toulouse I, and Evry – with the aim of starting or reinforcing business history. On the other hand, some specialists of business and management studies have devoted their attention to the history of their own disciplines in Brest, Orléans, and Poitiers.

---

[76] Marc Martin, *Trois siècles de publicité en France* (Paris, 1992); Marie-Emmanuelle Chessel, *La publicité* (Paris, 1998).

[77] Odile Henry, "Le conseil, un espace professionel autonome?" *Entreprises et Histoire* 7 (1994): 37–58; Matthias Kipping, "Consultancies, Institutions and the Diffusion of Taylorism in Britain, Germany and France," *Business History* 39, no. 4 (1997): 67–83; Antoine Weexsteen, "Le conseil aux entreprises et à l'Etat en France: Le rôle de Jean Milhaud (1898–1991) dans le CEGOS et dans l'ITAP," unpublished doctoral thesis, EHESS, 1999.

The relationships between business history and management studies appear nonetheless one of the main characteristics in the recent institutional development of business history in France. These relationships may well have gone further in France than in other European countries, with the possible exception of Great Britain. This is particularly visible in the composition of the French business history association (Association française pour l'histoire des entreprises), whose membership includes a fair proportion of specialists of business and management studies. This cooperation is reflected in the journal *Entreprises et Histoire*, published three times a year by the association. *Entreprises et Histoire* was founded in 1992, filling a gap that had existed since the demise of *Histoire des entreprises*, a journal published almost singlehandedly by Bertrand Gille between 1958 and 1965.

Three main features differentiate *Entreprises et Histoire* from other business history journals. First, all issues are thematic. Second, it is published in partnership with specialists of business and management studies. And third, it is open to the business world, mostly in the form of interviews and round tables gathering businessmen and academics. Apart from *Entreprises et Histoire*, journals such as *Histoire, Economie et Société* and *Le Mouvement Social* are also concerned with themes directly or indirectly related to business history, while management journals, for example the *Revue française de gestion*, have been interested in historical issues.[78] Public history has also caught on in France, with *Public histoire*, led by Felix Torres; *Clio Média*, led by Pierre Dottelonde; and *Créapress*, led by Catherine Malaval.

The relationship with businesses is another notable aspect of French business history. The commissioning of established academics to write corporate histories has not yet reached the same scale as in Britain, but it is firmly on the increase, as witnessed by the recent studies of Alcatel-Alsthom, Rhône-Poulenc, Paribas, Elf, and others.[79] French companies are not as collectively involved in a business history association, as in the German Gesellschaft für Unternehmensgeschichte. However, there is in France the systematic support given to historical research by a number of large and usually state-owned institutions. The most impressive achievement has been the history of electricity, with the foundation in 1982 of the Association pour l'Histoire de l'Electricité en France (AHDEF),

[78] *Revue française de gestion* 70 (1988), special issue on "Les racines de l'entreprise."
[79] Broder and Torres, *Alcatel-Alsthom*; Cayez, *Rhône-Poulenc*; Bussière, *Paribas*; Alain Beltran and Sophie Chauveau, *Histoire du groupe Elf-Aquitaine depuis 1939* (Paris, 1999).

sponsored by Electricité de France (EDF), the National Electric Enterprise. Under its aegis, a journal, the *Bulletin d'histoire de l'électricité*, has been published, several colloquia organized, their proceedings published, and the publication of a massive three-volume history of electricity in France completed. In addition, the association has supported through small grants countless Ph.D. theses and master's dissertations on all aspects of the history of electricity, thus creating a large pool of researchers in the field. Such a project obviously goes far beyond the scope of business history. However, most of the issues upon which it touches – science and technology, state intervention, and so on – are of prime interest to the business historian, while others, especially those involving business undertakings, are directly in its domain.

Other institutions have encouraged historical research in similar fashion. Examples abound. Pechiney founded an institute for the history of aluminum, the Institut pour l'histoire de l'aluminium (IHA), in 1986, which publishes the biannual *Cahiers d'histoire de l'aluminium*. The French national railways company (SNCF) in 1987 founded a French railways history association, the Association pour l'histoire des chemins de fer en France (AHICF), and the publication of the *Revue d'histoire des chemins de fer*. The savings banks have recently followed suit. Their association was founded in 1995, and the *Cahiers pour l'histoire de l'épargne* commenced publication in 1999. The iron and steel industry also has its association, the Académie François Bourdon, established in 1985 and based in Le Creusot. The Banque de France set up a history group in 1995, with the aim of sponsoring research in monetary, banking, and financial history, mainly through grants and publication subsidies. Likewise, industrial history has greatly benefited from the Institut d'Histoire de l'Industrie (IDHI), established in 1988 under the aegis of the Ministry of Industry. The Ministry of Finance created its own committee in 1986, the Comité pour l'histoire économique et financière de la France: among other activities, it organized a number of major international colloquia, some highly relevant to business history, and launched, under its own imprint, a now prestigious series as well as a yearly publication, the *Etudes & documents*.

In addition to encouraging and sponsoring historical research, these associations have made considerable archival material available to researchers. They have opened and classified their own archives or those of the companies, ministries, and other institutions with which they are linked, as well as set up oral archives and organized documentation centers. Several other major French companies – including Crédit Lyonnais, Société Générale, Paribas, Crédit Agricole, Assurances Générales de

France, Saint-Gobain, and France Telecom – have established their own in-house historical associations, opened their archives, and put other historical material at historians' disposal. These sources and collections have recently been cataloged in a useful guide edited by Roger Nougaret.[80] Finally, there are the all-important archives of the chambers of commerce and, of course, the collections kept at the National Archives under the classification known as *série AQ*. Apart from a few exceptions, these business history collections have recently been moved from Paris to the Centre des Archives du monde du travail in Roubaix.

THE FRENCH CONTRIBUTION TO BUSINESS HISTORY

In 1986, Jean-Pierre Daviet wrote the following on the state of business history in France, "Quantitatively, France is not up to international standard. Qualitatively, research has moved away from international issues."[81] Have things improved? First, it must be said that this condemnation was too severe, as is often the case when assessing one's own country. Quantitatively, business history was probably more developed in France than in any other European country except Great Britain. Despite undoubted progress, including the publication of a learned journal, the gap has not entirely been filled in this respect, nor has it been by the two other large European economies, Germany and Italy. But convergence appears to be on its way. The matter is, of course, more complex at the qualitative level. Historical research agendas are necessarily defined in a national context, depending on a country's specific questioning at a given time. And although some countries have attracted greater international attention than others, international issues are mostly defined in theoretical and methodological terms. The British and American dominance of the field does not need to be emphasized, and, unlike in other historical fields, French influence has been rather limited in business history. The reasons are to be found not only in the country's position in the world economy and the pattern of its business development, but also in its historiographical traditions and its language.

Business historians in France have on the whole addressed the same issues as their counterparts in other industrialized countries. To what extent have they developed an original approach? As elsewhere, French

---

[80] Roger Nougaret, ed., *Guide des services d'archives d'entreprises et organismes du monde du travail* (Paris, 1998).

[81] Jean-Pierre Daviet, "Bilan et perspectives de l'histoire des entreprises," typescript, Maison des sciences de l'homme, Paris, n.d. [1986].

business historians have primarily been historians and relied on the historian's tools to undertake their research. Although economic theories have
not been ignored, it must be said that French business historians have
not been preoccupied with references to "transaction costs," "bounded
rationality," "path dependency," or "asymmetric information," though, of
course, several of them, for example François Caron, Jean-Pierre Daviet,
Patrick Fridenson, and Michel Lescure, have made ample use of these
concepts. A generation of historians writing on business matters has
been concerned with the social and political dimensions of the subject,
in the tradition of the French *histoire totale*, which predominated in the
1950s and 1960s. This has remained one of the characteristics of business
history in France. Organizational theories have gained in influence in the
past decade.[82] More recently, the move appears to be toward increasing
use of business and management analyses for the study of history. This is
a trend that might narrow the outlook of business historians; this again
is not specific to French business history.

KEY WORKS

Caron, François. *Les deux révolutions industrielles du XXe siècle* (Paris, 1997).
Caron, François, Fabienne Cardot, Maurice Lévy-Leboyer, and Henri Morsel, eds.
     Histoire générale de l'électricité en France (Paris, 1991–6).
Cassis, Youssef. *Big Business. The European Experience in the Twentieth Century*
     (Oxford, 1997).
Cassis, Youssef, François Crouzet, and Terry Gourvish, eds. *Management and Busi-
     ness in Britain and France: The Age of the Corporate Economy* (Oxford,
     1995).
Fridenson, Patrick. "France: The Relatively Slow Development of Big Business in
     the Twentieth Century," in Alfred D. Chandler, Jr., Franco Amatori, and Takashi
     Hikino, eds., *Big Business and the Wealth of Nations* (Cambridge, 1997).
Kuisel, Richard F. *Capitalism and the State in Modern France: Renovation and
     Economic Management in the Twentieth Century* (Cambridge, 1981).
Lévy-Leboyer, Maurice. "La grande entreprise française: Un modèle français?"
     In Maurice Lévy-Leboyer and Jean-Claude Casanova, eds., *Entre l'État et le
     marché. L'économie française des années 1880 à nos jours* (Paris, 1991).
     ed., *Histoire de la France industrielle* (Paris, 1995).
Marseille, Jacques. *Les performances des entreprises françaises au XXe siècle*
     (Paris, 1995).
Woronoff, Denis. *Histoire de l'industrie en France, du XVIe siècle à nos jours*
     (Paris, 1994).

[82] Patrick Fridenson, "Les organisations: Un nouvel objet," *Annales E.S.C.* 44, no. 6 (1989):
     1461–77.

10

Business History in Italy at the Turn of the Century

FRANCO AMATORI AND GIORGIO BIGATTI

STATE OF THE ART AND AN INSTITUTIONAL FRAMEWORK

At the beginning of the new century, Italian business history is in good shape; it represents one of the most lively branches of economic history. At least four important centers for study and research are active; teaching and research in business history is commonplace in universities and their doctoral programs; and corporations as well as financial institutions have opened their archives and sponsored research projects and publications that go well beyond simple commemoration.

Of the four research centers, the Italian Center of Research and Information on the Economy of State-owned Enterprises (CIRIEC) was started in 1956 and since the 1970s has promoted a series of projects and publications on the history of the managers and entrepreneurs of state-owned enterprises.[1] The Center for the Historical and Economic Documentation on Enterprise also focuses primarily on the history of state-owned enterprises. It was started in 1982 on the initiative of the historian Valerio Castronovo and has published a business history series since 1987.

---

[1] See in particular A. Mortara, ed., *I protagonisti dell'intervento pubblico in Italia* (Milan, 1984). CIRIEC has a series dedicated to the history of state-owned enterprises which has been published in Milan since 1987.

Another, the Center for the History of Enterprise and Innovation, which
is promoted by the Chamber of Commerce in Milan, has the ambitious
goal of becoming a large territorial archive.[2]

Probably the most relevant role of business history in Italy has been
played by the Association for the History and Study of Enterprise (ASSI),
which was founded in 1983. ASSI is active in four fields: seminars and colloquia, publications, teaching, and research.[3] Together with the institute
of economic history at the Bocconi University in Milan, ASSI is a leader of
international colloquia on business history. Approximately every twelve
months, ASSI publishes a volume (the *Annali Storia dell'Impresa*), which
has reached eleven issues since starting in 1985. ASSI also produces a journal, initially called *Archivi e impresa* and recently renamed *Imprese e Storia*. Business history articles are also published in Italy by important and
older reviews like the *Rivista di Storia Economica* and *Società e Storia*.

In Italy there exists no academic position dedicated to business history.
However, several full or associate professors of economic or contemporary history practice business history. The nation's best-known school
for business and economics, Bocconi, dedicates a large portion of its
basic course in economic history to business issues. In the academic
year 2000–2001, the University of Milan started a doctoral program in
business history. In addition, various dissertations from the doctoral programs in economic history at important institutions such as Bocconi, the
University of Bari, and the University of Pisa can be considered works of
business history.

The relationship between academics and corporations, at least on the
larger scale, is highly collaborative. Much progress has been made since
Gian Lupo Osti, chief executive officer of Terni, one of the country's
largest major manufacturers of steel, delivered the company's archives
to a first-rate historian, Franco Bonelli. Terni gave its archive with the
intent of constructing the company's history without the motive of a
commemorative publication.[4] Ansaldo, one of the most important Italian

---

[2] See P. Paletta et al., *Guida agli archivi della Camera di commercio di Milano* (Soveria
Mannelli, 1998). For more details on the Center activity see www.csii.it.

[3] In addition to its activities in publishing and seminars, ASSI is a fundamental component
of ICSIM (Instituto per la Cultura e la Storia d'Impresa Franco Momigliano), an institute for
postgraduate studies in economic and business history sponsored by the Region of Umbria
and the provinces (as well as the cities) of Perugia and Terni (where the school is based).
ASSI has also coordinated a major project of the Italian National Research Council (CNR)
on "Small Business in Italy from Unification to the Economic Miracle (1860–1960)."

[4] G. L. Osti, CEO of Terni, delivered the company's archives to a first-rate historian, Franco
Bonelli, saying in an ironic tone that "a pirate as an ancestor does not spoil the best

machinery and engineering corporations,[5] Banca Commerciale Italiana,[6] and Fiat are other examples of large corporations that have opened their archives to researchers. Fiat, the nation's largest industrial group, has not only opened its archives but also sponsored innovative research by some of the nation's most prestigious - as well as independent - scholars.[7]

In 1999 two detailed histories of Italian industries were published. First, the fifteenth volume of Einaudi's prestigious series History of Italy was dedicated to the country's industrial history,[8] with a principal focus on the history of business. Franco Amatori and Andrea Colli's *Impresa e industria in Italia dall'Unità ad Oggi* (Venice, 1999) described the evolution of big business as well as small enterprises that often organized in industrial districts, forming one of the principal characteristics of the Italian industrial system.

THE DIFFICULT BEGINNINGS

Thirty years ago, business history in Italy appeared to be nonexistent. In 1967, Luigi De Rosa, in a wide-ranging review of the orientation of economic history in Italy after the Second World War, noted the scarcity of literature dedicated to industry.[9] De Rosa took note of some volumes that, in his opinion, tried to summarize the subject but inevitably failed. They neglected, in his view, an effective exploration of the stories of the protagonists - companies, entrepreneurs, managers, and workers. Nor did the first sectorial studies on a regional scale fill this gap, even if they were solidly documented. Also notably absent were monographs focusing on single corporations. De Rosa was only able to cite a profile of Fiat founder Giovanni Agnelli, written by Silvio Pozzani (not a historian by

---

genealogical tree"; see "Tavola Rotonda sugli archivi delle imprese industriali," *Rassegna degli Archivi di Stato* 33, no. 1 (1973): 54.

[5] See A. Lombardo, "L'Archivio Storico Ansaldo," *Archivi e imprese*, nos. 11-12 (1995): 110-20.

[6] See F. Pino, "Dieci anni di lavoro d'equipe: Aperti al pubblico tutti i documenti Comit dal 1894 al 1934," *Archivi e imprese*, no. 13 (1996): 133-61.

[7] See Progetto Archivio Storico Fiat, *Fiat, 1915-1930: Verbali dei consigli di amministrazione*, 3 vols. (Milan, 1991); id., *Fiat, 1944-1956: Le relazioni industriali alla Fiat: Saggi critici e note storiche*, 3 vols. (Milan, 1992); C. Annibaldi and G. Berta, eds., *Grande impresa e sviluppo italiano: Studi per i cento anni della Fiat*, 2 vols. (Bologna, 1999).

[8] Franco Amatori et al., eds., *L'industria*, in the series *Storia d'Italia*, vol. 15 (Turin, 1999).

[9] Luigi De Rosa, "Vent'anni di storiografia economica italiana (1945-1965)," in *La storiografia italiana negli ultimi vent'anni*, vol. 2 (Milan, 1970), 857-923, republished in id., *L'avventura della storia economica in Italia* (Rome and Bari, 1990), 115-85.

profession); a collective volume on the railway corporation Società per
le Strade Ferrate Meridionali; and some works on the history of banking,
among which he included his own study on Banco di Napoli.[10]

Strong cultural and ideological obstacles were the cause of this state
of business history. At the time, the orientation of historiography was
characterized by idealistic and Marxist attitudes. These were different
cultures, but both shared a subtle diffidence toward modern industrial
society and its values.[11] In a climate of strong ideological conflicts, corresponding to a renewal of the workers' fight in the factories of the north,
it seemed that there was no room for business history: it was considered
to be apologetic to the capitalistic order.[12] Proof of this attitude can be
found in Giorgio Mori's writing at the Harvard Center for Entrepreneurial
Studies. A typical Marxist, Mori invited those who studied the corporation to focus on the process of production and the relationship between
workers and management. This authoritative scholar effectively pushed
industrial studies in the direction of a history of factories and workers.[13]

There was substantial opposition as well in the business community
itself. As a defensive reaction to what did not seem immediately useful,
many companies tended to destroy their administrative or accounting
documents when these were no longer legally required. Sometimes companies were concerned with the fact that archives could shed light on
episodes that they preferred be forgotten. Increasing this resistance was
the family or oligarchic control of most of the important groups com-
prising Italian capitalism – Fiat, Pirelli, Falck, and Montecatini, to name
but a few. On the other hand, this close relationship between family and
enterprise fostered a great deal of jubilee and commemorative writing.
While these publications tended to celebrate the virtues of the founders
or the results achieved by the corporations, they also were a precious

---

[10] S. Pozzani, *Giovanni Agnelli: Storia di una industria* (Milan, 1962); E. P. d'Entrèves et al.,
eds., *La società italiana per le strade ferrate meridionali nell'opera dei suoi presidenti
(1861-1944)* (Bologna, 1962); L. De Rosa, *Il Banco di Napoli nella vita economica
nazionale (1863-1883)* (Naples, 1964).

[11] See, for instance, the introduction by P. Bairati to E. Conti, *Dal taccuino di un borghese*
(Bologna, 1986), and S. Lanaro, *L'Italia nuova: Identità e sviluppo, 1861-1988* (Turin,
1990), particularly pp. 33-50 on the "holiness of the entrepreneur."

[12] See S. Merli, *Proletariato di fabbrica e capitalismo industriale: Il caso italiano, 1880-
1900* (Florence, 1972).

[13] See G. Mori, "Premesse e implicazioni di una recente specializzazione storiografica
americana: La entrepreneurial history," in *Studi di storia dell'industria* (Rome, 1967),
43-79, as well as the critical considerations of G. Berta in "La storia delle relazioni industriali: Problemi di ricerca," *Archivi e imprese* no. 7 (1993): 63-76.

source of technical and economic information. The limits of these publications are evident, but they provided a way of understanding the image that companies wanted to project to the external world.[14]

THE PIONEERS

During most of the 1960s, little room was available in Italian historiography for business history. Even something as important as Rosario Romeo's work on the history of large Italian industry, *Storia della grande industria in Italia*,[15] warned the reader that a history of industry could not be conceived as a sum of the stories of single industries. He argued that its object was above all the development of the national system in its entirety and within the framework of the nation's economic life. Consistent with these premises, Romeo shed light on the dynamics and the turning points in the development of big business, stressing the ties between industry and government. He did not give much attention to the evolution of technology,[16] or to organizational typologies of large factories, or to commercial policies, or to, in general, all those aspects that only an approach having the enterprise as the unit of analysis could fully clarify.

At the end of the 1960s, things started changing in Italy, even in the stuffy world of economic history. Four years after the conference in Perugia at which De Rosa emphasized the poor state in Italy of business history, a new series of publications strongly modified the situation. Two important works, Castronovo's work on Giovanni Agnelli (the founder of Fiat) and Franco Bonelli's work on Terni (the first big industrial concern in Italy), were published, inaugurating a new season of scholarly efforts. Even if the title suggested a biographical angle, the volume, *Giovanni Agnelli*, was in reality the history of Fiat from its origins to the end of World War II. Castronovo was able to rely on direct corporate sources

---

[14] G. Mori, "La storia dell'industria italiana contemporanea nei saggi, nelle ricerche, e nelle pubblicazioni giubilari di questo dopoguerra," in *Annali dell'Istituto Giangiacomo Feltrinelli*, vol. 2 (Milan, 1959), 264–366.

[15] R. Romeo, *Breve storia della grande industria in Italia* (Bologna, 1961; new edition Milan, 1988). Romeo is one of the most important Italian historians of the twentieth century. He authored a monumental biography about one of the founders of a unified Italy, Camillo Cavour (*Cavour e il suo tempo*, 3 vols. [Bari, 1969–84]) and a famous anti-Marxist essay on the political economy of the rightist ruling class that assumed power immediately after Unification, *Risorgimento e capitalismo* (Bari, 1956; new edition Rome and Bari, 1974): 85–184.

[16] For a first synthesis on this subject, see R. Giannetti, *Tecnologia e sviluppo economico italiano 1870-1990* (Bologna, 1998).

only in a limited way, but by exploiting public archives and creatively using secondary sources, he was able to reconstruct in great detail the evolution of the company. From his work emerged the portrait of a "dual soul" company. On the one hand, it was very dynamic, open to technical innovation, and aggressive on international markets, where about 50 percent of its production was sold. On the other hand, it was a firm that operated in such a way as to enjoy favorable conditions under whichever political power ruled at the time. In fact, the government was decisive to the success of Fiat, from its action in the crisis of 1907 to the prohibition of Ford from producing and selling its vehicles in Italy in 1930.

Just a few years after Castronovo's book was released, Franco Bonelli published a work on Terni, *Lo sviluppo di una grande impresa in Italia: La Terni dal 1884 al 1962*. The book was destined to provide a cornerstone for the field. Bonelli was able to utilize the company's archives to reconstruct the history of the firm, which had been established as a steel producer in 1884 and was progressively transformed into a multisectorial company operating in shipyards, electricity, and electrochemicals. From Bonelli's book emerged the inside story of the strategies adopted by the company's various leaders, of their technological choices, and of their relations with the bank and the government that controlled the company through its financial holding IRI (Institute for Industrial Reconstruction) from 1933 on.

These two volumes stirred so much interest in the scientific community that from the mid-1970s on, it became clear to companies that they needed to open their archives. They found that this openness provided the added advantage of improving their corporate image. When the first census on the assets available in archives began, the damage due to neglect was fully revealed, but at the same time, previously unknown archives were discovered. In working on the documentation found at Banca Commerciale Italiana, the country's most important universal bank, Antonio Confalonieri, a professor of banking, produced the third most significant work in those pioneer years of Italian business history. Confalonieri focused on the relationship between the bank and industrial enterprises from the end of the nineteenth century to the early 1930s, challenging the old thesis of a universal bank as autonomous promoter of industrial initiatives. He emphasized the subordination of industrial credit to normal banking activities at least until the 1920s, when the deep crisis of companies (especially in the steel sector) compelled the banks to become more involved in the firms' management in order to

protect their interests.[17] Confalonieri's positions have been fully confirmed by the research of Peter Hertner, a German scholar who has written on the origins of Banca Commerciale Italiana, on its first management,
and on the relevance in its origins of foreign capital.[18]

In recent years, the works of Confalonieri and Hertner have been
followed by works written by many researchers. From the studies of
Francesca Pino, Roberta Garruccio, and Ferruccio Ricciardi, it is possible to fully evaluate the choices for allocating resources and the banking
know-how of Banca Commerciale's leadership, its financial strategies,
its ties to the international banking community, and its internal organization.[19] Roberto Di Quirico and Giandomenico Piluso have analyzed
Banca Commerciale's expansion abroad, as well as that of the other major universal bank in Italy, Credito Italiano.[20] This is a relevant topic that
puts the experience of Italian mixed banks in the international financial
scene, emphasizing the great openness of some advanced segments of
Italian capitalism. In the past several years, the Italian central bank has
also opened its historical archive and has published an important series of studies on the history of the bank and its financial and monetary
strategies.

FULL AFFIRMATION IN THE 1980S

In 1990 Duccio Bigazzi contributed an important bibliographical essay
that provided an overview of the status of business history in Italy in the

---

[17] A. Confalonieri, *Banca e industria in Italia, 1894-1906*, 3 vols. (Milan, 1974-6); id.,
Banca e industria in Italia dalla crisi del 1907 all'agosto 1914, 2 vols. (Milan, 1982);
id., *Banche miste e grande industria in Italia. 1914-1933*, 2 vols. (Milan, 1994-8).

[18] P. Hertner, *Il capitale tedesco in Italia dall'unità alla prima guerra mondiale* (Bologna,
1984); id., "Banche tedesche e sviluppo economico italiano (1883-1914)," *Ricerche per
la storia della Banca d'Italia*, vol. 1 (Rome and Bari, 1990), 69-101.

[19] See F. Pino, "Note sulla cultura bancaria a Milano nei primi anni '20: Cabiati, Mattioli, e
la Rivista bancaria," *Rivista di storia economica* n.s., 12, no. 1 (1995): 1-55; see also
G. Piluso, "Per una storia della cultura economica dei banchieri milanesi: Formazione,
cultura e istituzioni (1890-1914)," in *Milano e la cultura economica nel XX secolo, I: Gli
anni 1890-1920*, ed. P. L. Porta (Milan, 1998), 425-63; R. Garruccio, "Otto Joel alla Banca
generale: I prerequisiti di una carriera manageriale," in *Storie di imprenditori*, ed. D. Bigazzi
(Bologna, 1996), 159-99; F. Ricciardi, "Gestione e riorganizzazione industriale durante la
crisi: Da Comit a Sofindit (1930-1934)," *Archivi e imprese* 9, no. 18 (1998): 291-343. In
the same issue, see also the articles by Michele D'Alessandro and Carlo Brambilla.

[20] R. Di Quirico, "Il sistema Comit. Le partecipazioni estere della Banca commerciale italiana
tra il 1918 e il 1931," *Rivista di storia economica* n.s., 12, no. 2 (1995): 175-217; Giandomenico Piluso, "Le banche miste in Sud America: Organizzazioni, strategie, mercati
(1905-1921)," *Archivi e Imprese* 7, no. 13 (1996): 7-57.

1980s. Between monographs, essays, and articles, Bigazzi was able to gather almost 1,000 works that had been published between 1980 and 1987. This is a large number even if, as Bigazzi admitted, he considered as belonging to business history studies that were only indirectly related, as their focus was more on factory life or on the analysis of an industrial territory.[21] Even so, it was clear that in less than a decade, hundreds of researchers had become involved in studying topics clearly related to business history – a phenomenon that would have been unthinkable just a few years earlier.

Another important development was the change in methodology. This can be traced in large part to the change in the sociocultural climate of Italy that occurred around 1980. The decline of the hegemony of Marxist ideology and a new and favorable international economic cycle, one in which Italy greatly benefited, brought about a rediscovery of the market and its values. For the first time since the beginning of the twentieth century, investment in stocks was popular – mutual funds were officially recognized in 1983 – and the Milan Stock Exchange became one of the major markets in the developed world. In the end, the terms "entrepreneur" and "enterprise" were – perhaps for the first time in Italy – anything but negative.[22] In this climate, the demand for business history studies exploded, notwithstanding uncertainties in the academic community and a lack of coordination between research programs. Also very important was the fact that around 1980 some interpretations of Italian economic evolution became commonly shared. This constituted a solid framework for young Italians engaged in business history. In particular, we can refer to the works of Luciano Cafagna[23] and, again, Bonelli,[24] who firmly placed Italian economic development within an international framework, emphasizing the special importance for the industrialization of a peculiar Italian actor – the state. These scholars stressed the mix between a heavy component that is bound to the state (e.g., most of the sectors taking part in the Second Industrial Revolution) and a "Manchesterian"

[21] D. Bigazzi, *La storia d'impresa in Italia. Saggio bibliografico: 1980-1987* (Milan, 1990), 22. For an up-to-date bibliographical survey see G. Bigatti, "La storia d'impresa in Italia: Rassegna degli studi," *Annali di storia dell'impresa* no. 10 (1999): 317-75.

[22] See Franco Amatori and Andrea Colli, *Impresa e industria in Italia dall'Unità a oggi* (Venice, 1999), 339-52.

[23] "Profilo della Storia industriale italiana," in *Dualismo e sviluppo nella storia d'Italia*, ed. Cafagna (Venice, 1989), 281-322.

[24] "Il capitalismo italiano: Linee generali di interpretazioni," in *Dal feudalismo al capitalismo*, eds. R. Romano and C. Vivanti, *Storia d'Italia*, vol. 1 (Turin, 1978), 1194-1255.

component deriving from the First Industrial Revolution and caused more by the spontaneous initiatives of entrepreneurial forces. A good example of the latter can be found in the studies of Giovanni Federico on the silk industry, *Il filo d'oro: L'industria mondiale della seta dalla restaurazione alla grande crisi* (Venice, 1994); in Roberto Romano's work on cotton manufacturers, *L'industria cotoniera lombarda dall'Unità al 1914* (Milan, 1992); and in Giorgio Roverato's history of Marzotto, an important Italian wool company, *Una casa industriale: I Marzotto* (Milan, 1986).

Federico traced the fortunes of the Italian silk sector – a decisive one for the "original accumulation" of the nation's economy. With research founded on a broad quantitative basis, he placed the Italian sector in the framework of the development of the world silk market from the beginning of the nineteenth century to the Great Depression. Through this analysis of the sector's evolution, Federico provided a precise portrait of the silk entrepreneur, his constraints, and alternatives.

In his study of cotton firms in Lombardy from Italian unification (1861) until World War I, Roberto Romano emphasized their substantially endogenous origins, even if several of the names of entrepreneurs clearly showed their foreign origins. Among the reasons behind the decision of these businessmen to choose Italy as their field of action was the country's relative proximity to the supply of cotton and the markets offered by the urban network of northern Italy. The cotton manufacturers were also attracted by the region's ample availability of peasant laborers, the expectancy to develop a national market thanks to protective tariffs, and the abundance of water that was easily convertible into energy.

In Roverato's work on the Marzotto family – a dynasty that began at the beginning of the nineteenth century and is still at the top of the textile industry in Italy – one sees clearly the strong will of the founders. They pursued industrialization and technical innovation, forged solidarity with the local community, and practiced a sort of organizational paternalism that would be widely imitated by textile manufacturers in northern Italy.

Historians have been even more attracted to sectors whose existence was made possible by state support, which seems peculiar to the Italian case. The most significant example was the steel industry, which for a long time appeared to be the true industrial problem of the country. An important event in this field of studies was the publication of the research directed by Franco Bonelli under the sponsorship of the Einaudi Foundation. Bonelli's work, which was published as *Acciaio per l'industrializzazione* (Turin, 1982), shed light on the weakness of the

big Italian steel companies from the beginning of the twentieth century
up to the 1930s. The weakness was due to the fact that these companies
were forced to operate in a sort of "cage" created by the cartels. Thriving
private firms that could be considered very competitive in market niches
did not produce sufficient material for a demanding market. So the state
intervened with support for big companies that could sustain a basic
industry for a nation eager to become a world player.

Bonelli's book also described the work of a managerial cohort deeply
involved in national interests. In the 1930s, these managers began a very
innovative restructuring of the sector, based on the creation of a big
new plant with state-of-the-art technology, while undertaking a rigorous
specialization of the other steel works to ensure full and constant work
for all. Bonelli had already shown, in his biographical profile of Alberto
Beneduce, how the state entrepreneur could be a very innovative element in the Italian economy. Beneduce was the technocrat who founded
the state financial holding unit, IRI, in 1933 in order to take over the industrial securities of the banks that had fallen into a deep crisis. Beneduce
designed a structure in which, under state ownership, firms operated not
in a nationalized but rather a market environment.[25]

The greatest expression of this philosophy can be found in the entrepreneurial adventures of Oscar Sinigaglia. Sinigaglia was the man who
in the early 1950s turned into reality the projects of the 1930s for the
steel industry. His case is well documented in the book-length interview by Gian Lupo Osti, edited by Ruggero Ranieri, *L'industria di Stato
dall'ascesa al degrado* (Bologna, 1993). But also within "Beneduce's for-
mula" was the risk of a management expropriated by politicians, which
actually happened after 1960. This tale is described in Osti's book, in
Margherita Balconi's book, *La siderurgia italiana, 1945-1990* (Bologna,
1990), surveying the steel sector, and by Giulio Sapelli and Francesca
Carnevali for ENI in *Uno sviluppo tra politica e strategia: ENI 1953-
1985* (Milan, 1992).[26]

Similar to the steel sector were companies operating in industries
such as heavy machinery, for example, Ansaldo and Breda.[27] Anna Maria

---

[25] F. Bonelli, "Alberto Beneduce," in *Dizionario Biografico degli Italiani*, vol. 3 (Rome,
1966), 455-66. This encyclopedia of biographies is a precious resource for the history of
Italian entrepreneurs and managers.

[26] See also M. Colitti, *Energia e sviluppo in Italia: La vicenda di Enrico Mattei* (Bari, 1979).

[27] *La Breda. Dalla Società Italiana Ernesto Breda alla Finanziaria Ernesto Breda: 1886-
1986* (Milan, 1986); Stefania Licini, "Dall'Elvetica alla Breda: Alle origini di una grande
impresa milanese (1846-1918)," *Società e storia* no. 63 (1994): 79-124.

Falchero's *La Banca Italiana di Sconto 1914-1921: Sette anni di guerra* (Milan, 1990) describes the history of the Banca Italiana di Sconto, Ansaldo's financial arm, during World War I. Marco Doria's *L'Ansaldo: L'impresa e lo Stato* (Milan, 1990) also provides a history of the firm (as more recently does the collective work *Storia dell'Ansaldo*, 7 vols. [Rome and Bari, 1994-2001]).

Ansaldo and Breda ended up in the state shareholdings system. But other companies, even though not formally within the state-owned system, received state support. This is the case with a company like Montecatini, the biggest Italian chemical firm from the 1920s to the 1960s. The volume edited by Franco Amatori and Bruno Bezza, *Montecatini 1888-1966. Capitoli di storia di una grande impresa* (Bologna, 1990), showed that the strong protectionism provided by the state was the cause of the serious problems that struck Montecatini in the 1960s. The state played no role in the chemical sector, neither promoting basic research nor fostering an appropriate antitrust policy.

Even the electric companies, the heart of economic power in Italy in the first half of the twentieth century, owe much of their success to the state, which provided favorable regulations and special financing. However, even though electricity was a critical sector, until the 1970s there was only one work, dating from 1934 by Giorgio Mortara, on the subject.[28] Then, starting in 1985, a new wave of Italian business historians began studying the field. Books appeared by Renato Giannetti[29] and Bruno Bezza (editor),[30] and Pier Angelo Toninelli.[31] More recently, five volumes of a collective history of the Italian electric industry from the 1880s to the 1980s were published under the title *History of the Italian Electric Industry* (Rome and Bari, 1992-4). Within this monumental work is a notable essay by Luciano Segreto on the dynamics of competition between the most important firms.[32]

In the end, the descriptions of the chemical and electric sectors delineate a limited suffrage form of capitalism. Montecatini and Edison,

[28] "Lo sviluppo dell'industria elettrica in Italia," in *Nel cinquantenario della società Edison. 1884-1934*, vol. 2 (Milan, 1934), 83-358.

[29] *La conquista della forza: Risorse, tecnologia ed economia nell'industria elettrica italiana, 1883-1940* (Milan, 1985).

[30] *Energia e sviluppo: L'industria elettrica italiana e la Società Edison* (Turin, 1986); this book is built around a central essay by Claudio Pavese, "Le origini della Società Edison e il suo sviluppo fino alla costituzione del 'gruppo,' 1881-1919," 25-169.

[31] *La Edison: Contabilità e bilanci di una grande impresa elettrica, 1884-1916* (Bologna, 1990).

[32] "Gli assetti proprietari," ibid., vol. 3, *Espansione e oligopolio, 1926-1945* (1993), 89-173.

the most important electric companies, which in the 1950s diversified into chemicals, were epitomes of this form. Each enjoyed a monopoly in its field and suffered difficulties after the Second World War, when a less protected economic environment emerged. Sick giants in the 1960s, they merged in 1966. But the resulting company, Montedison – as described by the journalists Eugenio Scalfari and Giuseppe Turani in *Razza Padrona. Storia della borghesia d'Italia* (Milan, 1974) and by the economists Alves Marchi and Roberto Marchionatti in *Montedison 1966-1989: L'evoluzione di una grande impresa tra pubblico e privato* (Milan, 1992) – was unable to rid itself of its original vices.

The decline of Montecatini and Edison together with the nationalization of the electric industry in 1962 elevated Fiat to the top of the Italian industrial system. Fiat was an enterprise that, as we have seen when considering Castronovo's book on Agnelli, did not disdain the favors of the state, but also wanted to keep the great international industrial companies as its reference points. Fiat's translation of the Fordist experience into the reality of Italy, the so-called hybridization of Fordism, is the dominant theme of other studies appearing after Castronovo's volume. It can be seen in works such as Piero Bairati's biography of Agnelli's sucessor, *Vittorio Valletta* (Turin, 1983), in Duccio Bigazzi's essays on the technical and organizational aspects of Fiat's production,[33] and in Giuseppe Volpato and Franco Amatori's work on the evolution of Fiat's management.[34] Finally, on the occasion of Fiat's centennial anniversary, in a volume consisting of almost 2,000 pages, *Fiat 1899-1999: Un secolo di storia italiana* (Milan, 1999), Castronovo tried to produce a definitive work on the Turinese company. This work is not as successful as his biography of Agnelli. Castronovo seems overwhelmed by the company's archives, and the entire work resembles an extended chronicle.

As the biggest employer in Italy since World War I, Fiat has been the major locus of the class struggle in Italy. Giuseppe Berta traces the most significant phases of social conflicts at Fiat in a series of essays, *Conflitto industriale e struttura d'impresa alla Fiat, 1919-1979* (Bologna, 1998). His broad and deep knowledge of the sources – Berta is responsible for Fiat's historical archives – and the ability to read them in a detached

[33] *La grande fabbrica: Organizzazione industriale e modello americano alla Fiat dal Lingotto a Mirafiori* (Milan, 2000).
[34] G. Volpato, "Produzione e mercato: Verso l'automobilismo di massa," in *Mirafiori, 1936-1962*, ed. C. Olmo (Turin, 1997), 123-60; F. Amatori, "Gli uomini del Professore. Strategie, organizzazioni, management alla Fiat fra anni Venti e anni Sessanta," in *Grande impresa e sviluppo italiano*, eds. C. Annibaldi and G. Berta (Bologna, 1999), 257-34.

as well as learned way, make Berta's work a splendid example of the interaction between industrial relations and business history.

Fiat has not been the only player in the Italian automotive industry over the past century, and the historiography about it reflects this fact. Two niche-oriented but still significant automotive producers were Alfa Romeo and Lancia. Each has been extensively studied. Duccio Bigazzi's volume on the first two decades (1906–26) of Alfa Romeo, *Il Portello: Operai, tecnici e imprenditori all'Alfa Romeo, 1906–1926* (Milan, 1988), is an example of the best case in Italy of a combination of business and social history. In fact, Bigazzi overlapped an analysis of the firm's entrepreneurial strategies with that of the character and behavior of the social actors, entrepreneurs, managers, technicians, designers, and workers. In *Impresa e mercato: Lancia, 1906–1969* (Bologna, 1996), Franco Amatori examined the evolution of Lancia as an independent auto manufacturer (in 1969 it was taken over by Fiat). The focus of his work, which covered the period starting in 1906 with the company's creation, is on the entrepreneurs behind the firm, its moments of fortune and of bad luck, and the company's story as considered within the sector's competitive framework.

On the international scene, the fact that Fiat, a leading European company, is still family-controlled today is certainly an anomaly. But family capitalism is a main feature of the Italian economic system. According to Robert J. Pavan, an American scholar who studied the first 100 Italian companies (by sales) between 1950 and 1970, half of them could be considered family-controlled.[35] In his view, this was a serious obstacle to the full development of an enterprise. Two books that concentrate on the relationship between the owners and managers of a company confirm his observation. Amatori's *Proprietà e direzione: La Rinascente 1917–1969* (Milan, 1989), the story of Italy's most important department store chain, and *Pasta e cioccolato: Una storia imprenditoriale* (Perugia, 1992), G. Gallo's interview of Bruno Buitoni, largely support Pavan's observations. Pavan stressed that up to the 1970s, family control created serious obstacles to the application of the most advanced managerial techniques, even when, as Giulio Sapelli and Duccio Bigazzi clearly demonstrated in their work, those same techniques were known by Italian top and middle managers at the time.[36]

---

[35] *Strutture e strategie delle imprese italiane* (Bologna, 1976).
[36] G. Sapelli, *Organizzazione, lavoro e innovazione industriale nell'Italia fra le due guerre* (Turin, 1978); id., "Gli 'organizzatori della produzione' tra struttura d'impresa e modelli

228 AMATORI AND BIGATTI

IS ITALY A CLASSIC INDUSTRIAL NATION?

With the rise of Italian business history after 1980, we can say that the history of big business in Italy is no longer ignored. The problem is that most of the relevant results of business historiography in the past two decades – works dealing with industries like textiles, steel, heavy machinery, chemicals, and electricity – show Italy to be fairly similar to the classic industrial nations of Europe, like England and Germany.[37] In reality, the consolidated – and well-documented – opinion in the scholarly community is that Italy's competitive advantage is based on labor-intensive industries dedicated to producing goods for household and personal use, which are, in turn, characterized especially by numerous small firms.[38] There are two principal reasons for this historical backwardness – an ideological orientation that sees only large firms as the engines of economic progress and the difficulties of scholarly research due to the scarcity and poor organization of both corporate and public archives.

Nonetheless, some work on small companies has been done, and various volumes as well as essays have been published on the textile and food industries, as well as on steel and machinery. Very important in this respect is a series on the history of various Italian regions published by Einaudi.[39] Compelling historians to work on a local scale has forced them to confront the peculiarities of small firms. But studying small companies in Italy does not mean researching a single firm; instead, an analysis of territorial entities is called for. Within these territories, both a horizontal and vertical division of labor occurred in the production of a single good.[40] The general consensus is that these industrial districts in Italy

culturali," in *Intellettuali e potere, Storia d'Italia*, vol. 4 (Turin, 1981), 591–696; D. Bigazzi, "Modelli e pratiche organizzative nell'industrializzazione italiana," in *L'industria, Storia d'Italia*, vol. 15 (Turin, 1999), 900–94.

[37] See the considerations of L. Segreto in "L'industria calzaturiera in Italia: La lunga rincorsa marchigiana, 1914–1960," in *L'industria calzaturiera marchigiana dalla manifattura alla fabbrica*, ed. S. Anselmi (Ostra Vetere, 1989), 247–53.

[38] See, of course, M. E. Porter, *The Competitive Advantage of Nations* (New York, 1990), 210–25, 421–55.

[39] See, for instance, G. Roverato, "La terza regione industriale," in *Il Veneto*, ed. S. Lanaro (Turin, 1984), 165–230; G. Nigro, "Il caso Prato," in *La Toscana*, ed. G. Mori (Turin, 1986), 823–65; F. Amatori, "Per un dizionario biografico degli imprenditori marchigiani," in *Le Marche*, ed. S. Anselmi (Turin, 1987), 589–627; S. De Majo, "Dalla casa alla fabbrica: La lavorazione delle fibre tessili nell'Ottocento," in *La Campania*, eds. P. Macry and P. Villani (Turin, 1990), 319–70.

[40] On the phenomenon of small business in Italy in historical perspective see A. Alaimo, "Small Manufacturing Firms and Local Production Systems in Modern Italy," in *Small Firms, Large Concerns: The Development of Small Business in Comparative Perspective*, eds. K. Odaka and M. Sawai (Oxford, 1999), 168–93, and his rich bibliography.

number about 100, and most of them are the outcome of a long tradition. A pioneer work in the study of industrial districts is a volume edited by Giovanni Luigi Fontana, *Le vie dell'industrializzazione europea: Sistemi a confronto* (Bologna, 1997). In it the reconstruction of the history of several industrial districts in Italy is compared with similar realities in other areas of Europe. Two more good examples of in-depth studies of Italian industrial districts are a 1998 volume edited by Fontana regarding shoemaking in an area of the Venetian region[41] and another by Andrea Colli examining iron production in the valleys on the eastern side of Lake Como in Lombardy.[42] Both works convincingly illustrate how the history of business and economic issues of industrial districts is clearly intertwined with the social and cultural issues in these areas.

The phenomenon of small businesses in Italy is so pertinent that in 1995 the National Council of Research (CNR) sponsored a study coordinated by ASSI that was articulated in nine units covering a significant part of the country.[43] The goal of the research was not to study individual small firms or industrial districts, but rather to consider small enterprises in different local economic systems. The resulting work examined a variety of areas. Some were metropolitan, such as Milan, Turin, and Naples. Terni, a company town, was studied, as was an area with old craftsmanship traditions in Umbria. A few emerging territories in the central and northeastern parts of the country (a shoemaking district in The Marches region, the food and machinery industries of the mid-sized city of Bologna, and a multisectorial area in the Venetian region) were examined, as was an old industrialized area in the northwest known as the Alto Milanese. What emerged throughout the study was the great vitality and the multiformal aspects of the country's development, the considerable capacity for self-regulation of economic actors, and the failures that occurred when it became necessary to evolve into larger organizations or to form more solid economic institutions.

AN AGENDA FOR THE FUTURE

Business history in Italy appears to be pretty healthy these days, especially in contrast to its state prior to 1980. Nonetheless, there are still many

---

[41] *Cento anni di industria calzaturiera nella Riviera del Brenta* (Fiesso d'Artico and Venice, 1998).
[42] *Legami di ferro: Storia del distretto metallurgico e meccanico lecchese tra Otto e Novecento* (Catanzaro, 1999).
[43] F. Amatori and A. Colli, eds., *Comunità d'imprese. Sistemi locali in Italia tra Ottocento e Novecento* (Bologna, 2001).

empty boxes that need to be filled, either in relation to the peculiarities of Italian history or when comparing the discipline in Italy with that of the most advanced nations. Among these tasks are the completion of basic work, that is, the establishment of precise benchmarks and criteria for the largest 200 Italian businesses in the twentieth century. In part, this work has already been done for the years from 1970 on with the contributions of the economist Enrico Filippi and for the period 1950–70 with the already mentioned work of Robert Pavan. For the years preceding the Second World War, we have R. Giannetti, G. Federico, and P. Toninelli's essay "Size and Strategy of Italian Industrial Enterprises (1907–1940): Empirical Evidence and Some Conjectures" (*Industrial and Corporate Change* 3, no. 2 [1994]: 491–512). This is a pioneering contribution, but by itself it could not overcome a difficulty so typical of the Italian reality. The sources from which the authors drew their findings consider the individual firms rather than the groups to which they refer, which should be the real unit of analysis. Thus, there were serious distortions regarding the true importance of big business. Given these partial contributions, it is still necessary to complete a work toward homogeneity that could lead to a *Scale and Scope*-like book on the Italian case. On the other hand, we need to keep in mind that, if we want to raise a Chandlerian building, we still need the "bricks" (in this case, corporate histories) that have been assembled in large part over the past two decades.

But even when we examine big business, there are still notable holes. For instance, corporations like Olivetti and Pirelli deserve a wide and deep analysis comparable to what has been done for Fiat. In general, we still need to produce important works on subjects such as internationalization, a topic that is important for almost all of industrial Italy over the past decade, and on management and its techniques. In addition, Italian business history is identified almost completely with industrial companies, while other territories – especially those in the service sector – are pretty much unexplored.

In the field of small business, it is evident that there is still much to be done in Italy. In fact, studying small businesses and industrial districts is not sufficient. In the past 30 years, companies constituting a so-called fourth capitalism have emerged in Italy. Positioned between big and small firms, these are usually businesses with annual sales between 200 million and 2 billion U.S. dollars. These enterprises are all focused on globalization and have become significant actors on the national economic scene. It is time for the business historian in Italy to single out their origins and paths.

From its outset, ASSI, which has been described as the principal engine of business history in Italy, expressed a strong desire to do interdisciplinary work and to collaborate in its research with writers in other disciplines like economics and sociology. The result was a series of international weeks in business history[44] from 1985 to 1993 and the creation of a journal, *Industrial and Corporate Change*. But ASSI's relationship with scholars in other disciplines has proved to be more difficult than was foreseen. Above all, historians have felt overwhelmed by economists, and the relationship has been interrupted in recent years. Needless to say, it is hoped that future efforts will be made to encourage dialogue so as to develop the fertile terrain of comparison between history and theory.

Like business history in most other countries, Italian business history has used the economic performance of an enterprise as its reference point. Much less attention has been dedicated to social and environmental issues. This, too, is a serious limitation that needs to be rectified. Finally, it should be pointed out that Italians are still far less prominent in the international arena than their foreign colleagues. Their participation is often small at the annual meeting of the American Business History Conference, and their contributions are too few in important journals like the *Business History Review* and *Business History*. The initiative from which this volume springs is a contribution in this direction.

KEY WORKS

Amatori, Franco, Duccio Bigazzi, Renato Giannetti, and Luciano Segreto, eds. *L'industria*, in the series *Storia d'Italia*, vol. 15. Turin, 1999.

Amatori, Franco and Andrea Colli. *Impresa e industria in Italia dall'Unità a oggi*. Venice, 1999.

Berta, Giuseppe. *Conflitto industriale e struttura d'impresa alla Fiat, 1919-1979*. Bologna, 1998.

Bigazzi, Duccio. *Il Portello: Operai, tecnici e imprenditori all'Alfa Romeo, 1906-1926*. Milan, 1988.

Bonelli, Franco. *Lo sviluppo di una grande impresa in Italia: La Terni dal 1884 al 1962*. Turin, 1975.

Castronovo, Valerio. *Giovanni Agnelli*. Turin, 1971.

---

[44] ASSI's international weeks were organized every other year between 1985 and 1993. The proceedings of 1987 (on Enterprise and Technology) and 1989 (on Enterprise and Finance) were published as volumes authored by G. Dosi, R. Giannetti, and P. Toninelli (*Technology and Enterprise in an Historical Perspective* [Oxford, 1992]) and by V. Zamagni, ed. (*Finance and the Enterprise: Facts and Theories* [London, 1992]).

11

Business History in Spain

ALBERT CARRERAS, XAVIER TAFUNELL, AND EUGENIO TORRES

Business history is an academic field that developed very late in Spain but has nevertheless shown considerable vitality over the last few years. It has its roots in Spanish economic history and has closely followed that discipline's development and lines of research, meanwhile enriching economic history with its microeconomic insights, theories of the firm, and empirical evidence.

The founder of economic history in Spain is the Catalan scholar Jaume Vicens. Vicens argued the need to integrate business and entrepreneurial studies within the framework of his discipline forty years ago. However, no effort was made to forge this link until the 1970s, when the Research Section of the Banco de España (Spanish Central Bank) made seminal contributions to studies on banks and railroads. These papers, together with two other groundbreaking works,[1] invigorated Spanish economic

This essay forms part of research project PB96-0301, funded by *DGES, Ministerio de Educación y Cultura* (Spanish Ministry of Education and Culture).

[1] Gabriel Tortella, *Los orígenes del capitalismo en España: Banca, industria y ferrocarriles en el siglo XIX* (Madrid, 1973), an interpretation of the origins of capitalism in Spain in the mid-nineteenth century, and Santiago Roldán and José Luis García Delgado, in collaboration with Juan Muñoz, *La formación de la sociedad capitalista en España, 1914-1920* (Madrid, 1973). The latter work focused on capital accumulation during the First World War.

history and greatly influenced its subsequent development. As such, they may be considered among the first contributions to the embryonic discipline of business history.

At the risk of oversimplifying, one can say that Jordi Nadal's book, *El fracaso de la Revolución Industrial en España, 1814-1913*, which appeared halfway through the decade, marked the path taken by both disciplines. Nadal (a disciple of Vicens) was the first to put forward a sound general thesis providing the framework for the debate among Spanish economic historians on Spain's failure to industrialize in the nineteenth century. His work is considered the most influential work in Spanish economic historiography.

Spanish economic history in the twenty-five years following publication of Nadal's book has focused on these same issues. The application of quantitative analysis and other New Economic History techniques have produced significant advances in the measurement of economic growth variables. This has allowed assessment of Spain's relative backwardness in comparison with other European countries. Meanwhile, the change in the general focus of analysis toward the *supply side* has yielded a rapid increase in microeconomic studies. These studies focus on firms and entrepreneurs, their role in the Spanish economy, and the extent to which they can be held responsible for the country's backwardness. The emerging discipline of business history – often termed the "economic history of the firm" to emphasize the scientific approach employed – can be traced to the beginning of the 1980s, when academic output in the field began to soar. During this period, three new areas of specialization within economic history began to emerge: agricultural history, industrial history, and demographic history. The first two[2] in particular have contributed to the growth of business history by deepening the knowledge of particular sectors and the firms working in them.

With this proliferation of work in the field, new interpretations of Spanish economic growth during the period of continental industrialization have come about, many challenging the thesis Nadal put forward two decades ago. In his book *De imperio a nación*, Leandro Prados de la Escosura suggested that during the period of continental industrialization, backwardness rather than failure or stagnation characterized the

---

[2] Evidence of their development can be seen in the fact that there are already two specialized journals: *Historia Agraria* (formerly *Noticiario de Historia Agraria*) and *Revista de Historia Industrial*.

Spanish economy.[3] He argued that a weak supply side in the Spanish domestic market rather than a lack of demand was to blame. This situation, in turn, arose from uncompetitive companies operating under a protectionist regime, a failure on their part to penetrate foreign markets, and low industrial productivity. This interpretation has been confirmed by Pedro Fraile's analysis of the opening decades of the twentieth century.[4] Fraile's work adopted an approach closer to that of business history, arguing that the backwardness of the Spanish economy can be explained by its proclivity for monopolistic market structures and a restrictive institutional framework. These limitations put a brake on growth and channeled it into the domestic market but failed to contain either prices or business profits. High prices and profits served special interests but stunted the development of a large national market.

Prados's and Fraile's works both emphasized that the backwardness of the Spanish economy was a problem not simply of demand but also of supply – an analysis that has furthered the cause of business history. However, the current vitality of business history is not solely due to advances in the field of economic history. A reduction of hostility toward firms and entrepreneurs by Spanish society since the restoration of democracy has also contributed to its growth. Previously, both businesses and their owners were associated closely with many of the worst aspects of the Franco regime. External factors played a part in this change, including liberalization, globalization, and the fall of regimes advocating planned economies. The way business organizations adapted to the political and social consensus achieved during the Spanish political transition and the economic crisis between 1975 and 1984, as well as gradual recognition of companies' role in reducing unemployment, have also greatly benefited business history in Spain.

Finally, the belated arrival of the ideas and results of the new business history, particularly through the works of Chandler, has helped the domestic growth of the discipline. Likewise, the new economics of the firm, the theory of transaction costs, neoinstitutionalism, and evolutionary economics have all made contributions. Attracted by the research dynamism in these fields and the acceptance these subjects have gained

[3] Leandro Prados de la Escosura, *De imperio a nación: Crecimiento y atraso económico en España, 1780-1930* (Madrid, 1988).

[4] Pedro Fraile, *Industrialización y grupos de presión: La economía política de la protección en España, 1900-1950* (Madrid, 1991). A critical approach is taken in Jordi Nadal and Carles Sudrià, "La controversia en torno al atraso económico español en la segunda mitad del siglo XIX (1860-1913)," *Revista de Historia Industrial* 3 (1993): 199-227.

in Spanish universities, a growing number of young scholars have decided to make their careers in economic history and business history. In barely ten years, Spanish business history has built up an identity and established itself as an academic discipline in its own right.[5] The literature published to date confirms that scholars drawn from economic history largely make contributions to Spanish business history.[6] However, the output to date is much more wide-ranging than one would expect given the late arrival of the discipline in Spain. Notably the Italian Fondazione ASSI (the Association for the History and Study of Enterprise) has published various papers on the current state of Spanish business history, many of which were subsequently translated into Spanish.[7] These proved controversial, and the subsequent debate revealed wide discrepancies among economic historians regarding thematic and methodological issues. Some historians consider business history to be closer to applied economics. Others show less hesitation when it comes to using available theories. Both groups have tried to systematize economic theories bearing on their own fields, particularly in the light of lessons learned from the development of the discipline in English-speaking countries.[8]

In any event, the increasing historiographic output has found institutional channels that provide a path toward more integrated and systematic development of the discipline. The conferences and meetings on business history are proliferating, and many university departments

---

[5] It is symptomatic that economic historians did not use the term "business history" in a systematic way or apply it to a particular field of study until the end of the 1980s and the beginning of the 1990s. The same occurred with the term "economic history of the firm."

[6] Eugenio Torres, *Catálogo de publicaciones sobre la Historia Empresarial Española de los siglos XIX y XX* (Madrid, 1993); Juan Hernández Andreu and José Luis García Ruiz, eds., *Lecturas de Historia empresarial* (Madrid, 1994).

[7] Luciano Segreto, ed., "La storiografia d'impresa in Spagna: Materiali e temi per una discussione," *Annali di Storia dell'Impresa* 8 (1992): 7-180. For the Spanish version see Gregorio Núñez and Luciano Segreto, eds., *Introducción a la Historia de la empresa en España* (Madrid, 1994).

[8] Pedro Tedde, "La Historia empresarial en España: Una perspectiva general," *Cuadernos de Información Económica* no. 96 (1995): 169-75. See also Sebastián Coll and Gabriel Tortella, "Reflexiones sobre la Historia empresarial: Estado de la cuestión en España," *Información Comercial Española*, nos. 708-9 (1992): 13-24; Jesús M. Valdaliso, "Algunas reflexiones acerca de la Historia empresarial y su desarrollo en España," *Revista de Historia Económica* 11, no. 2 (1993): 417-33; Francisco Comín and Pablo Martín-Aceña, "Rasgos históricos de las empresas en España. Un panorama," *Revista de Economía Aplicada* 4, no. 12 (1996): 75-123; and Jesús M. Valdaliso, "Orígenes y desarrollo de la historia empresarial en España," *Príncipe de Viana. Suplemento de Ciencias Sociales* no. 17 (1999): 91-117.

and public institutions have established lines of research.[9] Changes to curricula in Spanish universities have made it possible to include business history courses in economics and business administration degree studies. However, such courses are almost always optional and vary considerably in scope. The new status of business history has forced economic historians to reflect on the content of academic programs, which reveal a wide range of approaches to both methodology and content. This has made the choice of supporting materials, explanation of their content, and writing the first teaching manuals for the discipline a pressing issue.

Our purpose in the following three sections is to flesh out this skeleton outline of Spanish business history. In doing so, we will address the following fundamental questions: (1) What research has been done on business history and entrepreneurs in Spain? (2) How has this research been carried out? (3) What have been the results of this work? The essay ends with some brief conclusions.

WIDE-RANGING BUT SPARSE OUTPUT

As Ralph W. Hidy wrote in 1975, business history covers a wide range of fields that are influenced by entrepreneurial and business focus, on the one hand, and by researchers' interests and cross-fertilization from kindred disciplines, on the other. Spain is no exception in this respect and reflects these influences despite the short history of the discipline here. We shall select from among the materials available, classifying these under the most common fields of study.

Studies on Entrepreneurs

These studies are still relatively rare and tend to be in the form of biographies of individual entrepreneurs rather than monographs on the characteristics of businessmen in a particular region or industry. In both cases, these works draw heavily on private archives (of both entrepreneurs and companies) or public sources (company records, records of notaries, and

---

[9] Practically all university departments of economic history have faculty members who are interested in carrying out research on business history, provided that public funding is forthcoming. An example of initiatives by other institutions is the Economic History Program run by Francisco Comín and Pablo Martín-Aceña of the Fundación Empresa Pública (Foundation of Public Companies), which is aimed almost exclusively at business history. The foundation has published more than seventy working papers since 1992.

tax records), generally covering the period between the second half of the nineteenth century and the outbreak of the Spanish Civil War in 1936. Notable examples of biographical subjects include Manuel Agustín Heredia and the Larios family, early entrepreneurs from Andalusia; Nicolás María de Urgoiti, the paper tycoon; Ramón de la Sota and Antonio López (the first Marquis of Comillas), ship owners from the Basque country and Cantabria, respectively; Horacio Echevarrieta, the financier; José Fernández, a businessman from Asturias; and Juan Antonio Suanzes, an erstwhile soldier who went on to found the all-powerful National Industry Institute (INI) during Franco's dictatorship.[10] It is surprising that this academic genre is so poorly represented in Catalonia, whose industrialization and work in the field of economic history lit the way for the rest of Spain. There is, however, a work written by Francesc Cabana that is unique, providing a sample of Catalan entrepreneurs' and businessmen's initiatives.[11] It is also remarkable that magnates like the Marquis of Salamanca in the nineteenth century or Juan March in the twentieth century have not been the subject of biographies by economic historians given the attention they received from writers in their own lifetimes. Nevertheless, short biographies of the 100 outstanding Spanish entrepreneurs of the twentieth century have been included in a recent book edited by Eugenio Torres.[12]

Social and political history have also produced studies on entrepreneurs. These fields have analyzed investment behavior and the social and political influence of magnates within the framework of social, political, and economic elites. This analytical perspective developed notably in the 1980s, with one of its principal aims being to discover the role of elites in the transition from liberalism to democracy. A particularly noteworthy work, given the subject of the study, is by Guillermo Gortázar on Alfonso XIII's investments; however, several other works could also be mentioned.[13]

---

[10] Most of them have been published by LID, a publisher specializing in business history: Alfonso Ballestero, *Juan Antonio Suanzes, 1891-1977: La política industrial de la posguerra* (Madrid, 1993); Pablo Díaz Morlán, *Horacio Echevarrieta, 1870-1963: El capitalista republicano* (Madrid, 1999); Martín Rodrigo, *Los Marqueses de Comillas, 1817-1925: Antonio y Claudio López* (Madrid, 2001); Pilar Toboso, *Pepín Fernández, 1891-1982: Galerías Preciados. El pionero de los grandes almacenes* (Madrid, 2001); and Eugenio Torres, *Ramón de la Sota, 1857-1936: Un empresario vasco* (Madrid, 1998).

[11] Francesc Cabana, *Fàbriques i empresaris: Els protagonistes de la revolució industrial a Catalunya*, 4 vols. (Barcelona, 1992-4).

[12] Eugenio Torres, dir., *Los 100 empresarios españoles del siglo XX* (Madrid, 2000).

[13] Guillermo Gortazar, *Alfonso XIII, hombre de negocios: Persistencia del Antiguo Régimen, modernización económica y crisis política, 1902-1931* (Madrid, 1986).

Studies on Business Organizations

There are also social and political historians who have focused on the organizational nature and practices of entrepreneurial collective action, their relationship to workers and trade unions, and their function as political lobbies. Previously, work in these disciplines was biased toward studying social conflict and workers' associations. Research on business organizations has helped a more balanced view to prevail. The most influential works on business organizations are general in scope, while others deal with specific entities. In both cases, the overwhelming majority cover the century up to 1936. The following era has received much less attention. However, economic historians with an interest in neoinstitutional political economy have also made contributions that attempt to explain rent-seeking behavior by private businessmen and business associations in their dealings with the public sector.[14]

Company Monographs

Company monographs are one of the pillars on which Spanish business history is being built. They are similar to company histories, and there are many more of these than of the works mentioned in the preceding two sections. The monographs have often been sponsored by the firms themselves, which in turn have provided both funds and access to archival material. These studies tend to be descriptive, particularly if they have been written to celebrate companies' birthdays. Unfortunately, some of these works are more cosmetic than educational and hence are useless from an academic point of view.

The financial sector has a longer tradition of company monographs, going back to work by the Banco de España's research department on the central bank itself, as well as individual public bank and saving banks initiatives in writing their own histories.[15] However, far fewer private

[14] An overview is found in Mercedes Cabrera and Fernando del Rey, "Los intereses económicos organizados en España. Un siglo en la historia del asociacionismo empresarial," in *La empresa en la historia de España*, eds. Francisco Comín and Pablo Martín-Aceña (Madrid, 1996), 441–56.

[15] Pedro Tedde, *El Banco de San Carlos, 1782–1829* (Madrid, 1988); id., *El Banco de San Fernando, 1829–1856* (Madrid, 1999); Jordi Nadal and Carles Sudrià, *Historia de la Caja de Pensiones: La "Caixa" dentro del sistema financiero catalán* (Barcelona, 1983); Gabriel Tortella and Juan Carlos Jiménez, *Historia del Banco de Crédito Industrial* (Madrid, 1986); and Juan Antonio Lacomba and Gumersindo Ruiz, *Una historia del Banco Hipotecario de España, 1872–1986* (Madrid, 1990).

banks have followed this example, these studies being confined to two medium-sized entities and one large one, the Central Hispanoamericano (currently Spain's biggest bank after its merger with Banco de Santander). More recently, sponsorship by the Fundación Empresa Pública (Foundation of Public Companies) of a set of works on business history has initiated a line of research on the history of public companies. Its most important achievement to date is the publication of a work on INI, a giant public holding company that has had a great impact on Spanish industrialization in the past fifty years.[16] Monographic studies of some of the entities in the holding company are currently underway. Finally, to be added to this list are studies on public companies in the eighteenth and nineteenth centuries (royal factories, state mines, tax monopolies, municipal companies, etc.), which have helped form a preliminary picture of the organizational development of public companies over the past two centuries.[17]

Various utility companies have also commissioned studies, particularly in the electricity, water, and transportation industries. There are monographs in the electrical sector on Hidroeléctrica del Cantábrico, Eléctricas Reunidas de Zaragoza, Sevillana de Electricidad and Fecsa, making the industry one of the best known from the business history standpoint, although there are no existing studies on two large companies, Iberdrola and Endesa. Of the other two utility sectors, there is a history of water supply and urban transport in Madrid. There has also been a spate of works on town infrastructure and services, no doubt reflecting the relative ease with which scholars can now consult municipal archives.

A considerable amount of work has been done on railways. The Banco de España produced an early study on the subject, and a history of the Spanish National Railways (RENFE) was published recently to celebrate the 150th anniversary of the opening of the first railway line in Spain.[18] In the sea transportation field, firms themselves (Trasmediterránea) have sponsored some monographs, while others have had to seek independent funding (Marítima del Nervión). Airlines still await studies. The mining industry was of great importance to the Spanish economy during the nineteenth century; however, there are few studies on Spanish companies in

---

[16] Pablo Martín-Aceña and Francisco Comín, *El INI: Cincuenta años de industrialización en España* (Madrid, 1991).

[17] Francisco Comín and Pablo Martín-Aceña, eds., *Historia de la empresa pública en España* (Madrid, 1991).

[18] Miguel Artola, ed., *Los ferrocarriles en España, 1844–1943*, 2 vols. (Madrid, 1978); and Francisco Comín et al., *150 años de ferrocarriles en España*, 2 vols. (Madrid, 1998).

this sector. There are classic works on foreign companies that did business in Spain, including ones on Tharsis and Rio Tinto.[19] The monograph on Rio Tinto is particularly interesting since it reveals the methods used by the Franco regime to nationalize any vestige of foreign capital during the early period of the dictatorship.[20]

Although the steel industry was at the vanguard of industrialization, there are hardly any studies on some of the most important companies in the sector, such as Altos Hornos de Vizcaya or Ensidesa.[21] What work on the steel industry has been done is very fragmentary. With regard to the shipbuilding industry, there is a monograph on the biggest company, Astilleros Españoles.[22] The companies that participated in setting up Astilleros Españoles, like Euskalduna or la Sociedad Española de Construcción Naval, have also been studied. Other sectors, on which work has gradually appeared, include the chemical industry, foodstuffs, including wines and beverages, and the car industry. The textile industry has largely been based in Catalonia. The pattern has been one of SMEs (small and medium-sized enterprises), and hence studies have dealt less with individual firms than with the industrial fabric of the areas in which mills have been set up.[23]

Sectoral Studies

A fourth field of business history concerns particular regional and national industries. Currently in vogue, these sectoral studies reveal the overall discipline's strong links with economic history. Although the methodological approach employed in these studies is not homogeneous, almost all of the work done analyzes the factors affecting the respective structure of markets and, in particular, the supply side. Sectoral studies are currently attracting most interest in the field of industrial

---

[19] See Sydney Checkland, *The Mines of Tharsis: Roman, French and British Enterprise in Spain* (London, 1967); Charles Harvey, *The Rio Tinto Company: An Economic History of a Leading Mining Concern, 1873-1954* (Penzance, 1981); and Gérard Chastagnaret, *L'Espagne, puissance minière dans l'Europe du XIXe siècle* (Madrid, 2000).

[20] See Antonio Gómez Mendoza, *El "Gibraltar económico": Franco y Riotinto, 1936-1954* (Madrid, 1994).

[21] But there is a recent business history of Duro-Felguera in Germán Ojeda and Ana Viñuela, *Duro-Felguera: Historia de una gran empresa industrial* (Oviedo, 2000).

[22] Stefan Houpt and José M. Ortiz-Villajos, dirs., *Astilleros Españoles, 1872-1998: La construcción naval en España* (Madrid, 1998).

[23] Jordi Nadal and Xavier Tafunell, *Sant Martí de Provensals: Pulmó Industrial de Barcelona, 1847-1992* (Barcelona, 1992).

history. Unsurprisingly, many economic historians have entered business history by this means. This can be clearly appreciated in the pages of *Revista de Historia Industrial,* in a recompilation of works on sectors that played a secondary role in industrialization, and in a recent book paying tribute to Nadal.[24]

Similar growth has come in the field of agricultural history, where one can find various contributions to business history. Almost everything we know of the foodstuffs industry comes from these sectoral studies, and the same is true of much of the literature on mining, particularly for coal and iron. Other important contributions to the field have been made on the Basque and Asturian steel industries and the textile industry both in Catalonia and elsewhere. Likewise, the chemical industry, construction, gas, footwear, insurance sectors, electricity utilities, rail and sea transport, and the financial sector have all benefited from extensive sectoral studies. The field is therefore extremely active. Business history will continue to grow in this direction, judging by the numerous studies currently being undertaken by accomplished scholars and the tried and tested methodology employed.[25]

Other Studies

This section includes a fairly mixed bag of research lines, some of which are now well established. Others have yet to make a name for themselves, although they appear extremely promising in filling the gaps in our present knowledge.

One of the first research lines begun in the 1970s explored the founding of companies. This work drew on official company registers – an invaluable and abundant source of company records. These studies produced a great deal of information on the volume of and fluctuations in company investment, broken down by sectors and industries. The names of entrepreneurs also appear in the records, and attempts have been

[24] Jordi Nadal and Jordi Catalán, eds., *La cara oculta de la industrialización española: La modernización de los sectores no líderes (siglos XIX y XX)* (Madrid, 1994); and Albert Carreras et al., eds., *Doctor Jordi Nadal: La industrialización y el desarrollo económico de España* (Barcelona, 1999).

[25] Among many studies of this kind, see two recently published in English: Núria Puig, "Business and Government in the Rise of the Spanish Synthetic-Dyes Industry: The Case of Fabricación Nacional de Colorantes y Explosivos, 1922-1965," in *Business and Society*, eds. A.-M. Kuijlaars, K. Prudon, and J. Visser (Rotterdam, 2000), 137-58; and Jesús M. Valdaliso, "The Rise of Specialist Firms in Spanish Shipping and Their Strategies of Growth, 1860 to 1930," *Business History Review* 74, no 2 (2000): 267-300.

made to explore the formation of partnerships and organizations. In the past decade, this work has also been enriched by thorough examination of notarial records on firms, thus complementing earlier studies using company records. Yet another source, in this case edited, is company financial yearbooks, available from the early years of the twentieth century on. These have received systematic attention over the past few years from economic historians who are interested in delving into new areas like the history of large companies, profitability trends, and industrial diversification.[26]

Among this second set of studies, work on large companies has been one of the star research areas during the past decade, largely due to the influence of Chandler.[27] We shall return to this theme later. However, we should note in passing that size has not been a determining factor in embarking on similar research on SMEs that might reveal strategies and business behavior differing from those of large companies. The same applies to ownership, for example the distinction between national and foreign companies, although study has recently begun on family companies.[28]

The 1990s began with an awareness of the need in business history to understand a company fully. As such, studies began focusing on all aspects of corporate existence: the ownership structure, the relationship between organization and management, production and sales, labor relations, and accounting systems.[29] It was realized that only thus could one evaluate company strategy and behavior. Publication has also begun of studies on the training of senior managers. While studies of large companies will pay the biggest research dividends, this does not mean SMEs should be excluded, particularly when they involve multiple units.

[26] Albert Carreras and Xavier Tafunell, "La gran empresa en España (1917–1974): Una primera aproximación," *Revista de Historia Industrial* 3 (1993): 127–74; and Xavier Tafunell, "Los beneficios empresariales en España, 1880–1981: Estimación de un índice anual del excedente de la gran empresa," *Revista de Historia Económica* 16, no. 3 (1998): 707–46.

[27] Albert Carreras and Xavier Tafunell, "Spain: Big Manufacturing Firms Between State and Market," in *Big Business and the Wealth of Nations*, eds. Alfred D. Chandler, Jr., Franco Amatori, and Takashi Hikino (Cambridge, 1997), 277–304.

[28] Paloma Fernández-Pérez, "Challenging the Loss of an Empire: González & Byass of Jerez," *Business History* 41, no. 4 (1999): 72–87.

[29] Javier Vidal, "La estructura de propiedad de una gran empresa ferroviaria: Norte," *Revista de Historia Económica* 17, no. 3 (1999): 623–62; Eugenio Torres, "Intervención del Estado, propiedad y control en las empresas gestoras del monopolio de tabacos de España, 1887–1998," *Revista de Historia Económica* 18, no. 1 (2000): 139–73; Carlos Arenas, Antonio F. Puntas, and José I. Martínez, eds., *Mercado y organización del trabajo en España (siglos XIX y XX)* (Seville, 1998); and Carlos Arenas, Antonio F. Puntas, and Jerònia Pons, eds., *Trabajo y relaciones laborales en la España contemporánea* (Seville, 2001).

Lastly, new lines of research have opened up on technological change in firms. This field should make giant strides in the near future, given the influence of evolutionary theory on many researchers. One of the keystones of this theory provides an explanation for technological change.[30] Similarly, the thesis concerning the economic power of banks and the trend toward business concentration, which formerly united many economists and economic historians in the 1970s, is now being reconsidered in light of the analytical tools available for examining industrial economics and mergers. On the other hand, there seems to be little interest in the causes of business failure through an examination of bankruptcy proceedings. Such a study would probably shed light on Spanish entrepreneurs and the soundness (or otherwise) of their business ventures. Unfortunately, such an undertaking would be heroic given the paucity of Spanish legal records and official resistance to making them available – a sorry contrast with other countries.

THE CONTROVERSY OVER METHODOLOGICAL APPROACHES AND THEORIES

How has business history research been carried out in Spain? To date, most work in the field of business history reveals its origins in economic history. This is evident in its empiricism, its use of archive material, the preference for quantitative data series, the use of simple models based on nonexplicit assumptions, and the consideration of the social aspects of economic activity. Studies that use explicit economic analytical models are in a minority. Such works attempt to contrast the corollaries of available theories on businesses and entrepreneurs and make international comparisons with a view to providing new interpretations.

This situation is the result of the development of economic history in Spain since the 1980s – the point in time when the new economic history was making an impact. Thereby was created a school of specialists who considered the discipline to be a social science capable of providing explanations of social phenomena while drawing on an arsenal of economic methods and theory in doing so.[31] The controversy between this conception and what we might call the "traditional view" aimed at

---

[30] See Santiago López and Jesús M. Valdaliso, eds., *¿Que inventen ellos? Tecnología, empresa y cambio económico en la España contemporánea* (Madrid, 1997).

[31] Joseph A. Schumpeter stressed the need to wed theory and history in business history; see "La teoría económica y la historia empresarial" in *Ensayos* (Vilassar de Mar, 1966), 255-72.

explaining past events from an economic perspective, though without losing sight of social aspects, has persisted ever since and now permeates business history. Thus the term "history of companies" suggests a more empirical approach closer to the traditional school, while the term "companies in history" connotes a more analytical approach closer to the New Economic History.

However, not as much divides these two positions as might appear from the foregoing comments. In reality, no scholar in the field would deny the usefulness of explicit economic analytical models in providing explanations or the value of historic and social perspectives in examining economic activity. In fact, the controversy of the past few years seems to be giving way to a general acceptance that any methodology is valid, provided that it yields good explanations of the role of entrepreneurs and firms in Spanish economic growth. A certain eclecticism has been preached and practiced in the use of methodologies and theories for both research and teaching purposes, an attitude that appears more valid than ever. In addition to enriching explanations and stimulating scholarly debate, this broader-minded view reflects developments abroad, where a more worldly approach has now been adopted in the discipline.

As a consequence, business history in Spain has become a discipline in its own right over the past decade. It is worthwhile to look briefly at how the discipline came of age. First and foremost, there was the influence of Chandler, with his works *The Visible Hand* and, above all, *Scale and Scope*. Second, there was the influence of researchers close to the New Economic History school, as well as advocates of transaction cost theory – such as Ronald H. Coase and Oliver E. Williamson – and agency theory – such as Michael C. Jensen and Eugen F. Fama. Third is some of the work on political economy covering the role of the state, such as the theories of economic regulation by George J. Stigler, and public choice – particularly the analysis on rent seeking by Anne O. Krueger and Gordon Tullock. After that came new theories of institutional change (e.g., Douglass C. North), technological change (Giovanni Dosi and Nathan Rosenberg), and the evolutionary theory in general of Richard R. Nelson and Sidney G. Winter. All inspired young scholars who quickly took these ideas aboard. The wide acceptance of these theories is likely to be strongly reflected in future historiographical output. By contrast, other theories, like those on flexible production and industrial districts (e.g., Philip B. Scranton and Giacomo Becattini), or on family companies (Mary Rose), seem to have had much less impact, even though they may provide interesting explanations of the behavior of SMEs and family concerns.

With regard to Chandler's work and the theory of transaction costs, it appears that more attention has been paid to annotations, commentaries, and criticisms than to the practical application of these ideas to specific studies. It is true that these theories have helped orient research and prompt consideration of the form company organization takes in management, production, purchases, and sales, as well as how this develops in terms of size and of horizontal and vertical integration processes (a point all too often ignored by Spanish economic historians). However, few works can be said to draw on the corollaries of these theories. An exception is the line of research begun by Albert Carreras and Xavier Tafunell on large companies. It is based on the methodological approaches in *Scale and Scope* and forms part of the work being done internationally on the role of large companies in the economic growth of industrialized countries.[32]

With regard to evolutionary theory, few studies explore its implications for analyzing institutional and technological change. However, there are two pieces of research that reveal the advantages of this approach. Further, here one can find examples of its application to specific sectors, largely covering SMEs. It is small and medium-sized enterprises for which the explanations offered by the evolutionary theory are most convincing. This development holds good prospects for Spanish business history, as smaller companies have traditionally constituted an important part of the country's economic fabric. The consolidation of this approach within the framework of the methodological pluralism mentioned earlier will also benefit future research. As Pedro Tedde has commented, it seems reasonable to believe that the habitual use of these theories and perspectives of the firm may prove decisive in raising Spanish business history to heights that currently appear unassailable, emulating the breakthrough of its parent discipline, economic history, in the 1980s.[33]

RESULTS: DOMINANT HYPOTHESES

We have come far in our knowledge of Spanish companies in both the recent and more distant past. Works have varied in explanatory scope, but have all served to shed light on one of the main concerns of economic historians, namely, the reasons for Spain's economic backwardness. We

---

[32] See Carreras and Tafunell, "Spain."
[33] Tedde, "La Historia empresarial," 175. See also references in footnote 8.

shall consider the most representative of these works, bearing in mind the arguments that connect them. Accordingly, the order in which they are presented starts with the most general interpretation, the rest addressing specific aspects of the same subject.

Lack of Entrepreneurship

This is the most general hypothesis used to explain Spain's economic backwardness. It bases its argument on the mediocrity of business ventures in the country. According to this hypothesis, few entrepreneurs in Spain merited the name, and most shied away from seeking production efficiency and taking on the competition in a fair fight.[34] The country has failed to succeed for various reasons, among them the preponderance of foreign entrepreneurs, particularly in the nineteenth century; the supine reaction of Spanish businessmen to foreigners' business initiatives; and Spanish entrepreneurs' tendency to seek state protection from their more efficient competitors. Gabriel Tortella has also argued that the cultural values of the old regime played a part. A combination of the Catholic Church's distaste for capitalism, the Spanish Inquisition's stifling of free thought and technological innovation, the low value placed upon education nationally, and, finally, the aristocratic prejudice against anything that smacked of manual work all combined to retard the country's business economy.

This hypothesis has led to a heated debate in which two critical positions can be discerned. The first critique[35] holds that, rather than the lack of entrepreneurship, the reasons for Spain's economic backwardness should be sought in factors such as income distribution, the natural environment, and the role of the state. It is argued that the presence of foreign businessmen per se is poor support for the argument, since such entrepreneurs were also to be found in France and Great Britain, where they did not stifle the formation of a strong class of native entrepreneurs. Likewise, German and Italian businessmen had also sought protection from their foreign rivals. It is argued that this behavior indicates the political clout of native businessmen rather than economic weakness. The notion that poor educational standards explain the shortage of entrepreneurs is also rejected on the grounds that growth in technical and

[34] Gabriel Tortella, *El desarrollo de la España contemporánea: Historia económica de los siglos XIX y XX* (Madrid, 1994), chap. 8.
[35] For a synthesis of these arguments, see Valdaliso, "Orígenes y desarrollo," 95–8.

commercial know-how would have been a consequence of economic development rather than one of its causes.

The second position[36] coincides with the first insofar as it rejects the legacy of the old regime as an obstacle to business activity. However, it stresses that political instability in nineteenth-century Spain, particularly in the period 1790–1840, together with the interventionist and anti-industrial policy applied throughout the period, had a negative impact on business behavior. The idea that educational backwardness hindered the emergence of an entrepreneurial class is also rejected, since tradition and the learning of workshop skills could provide sufficient know-how to carry out business ventures. This theory also holds inadequate resources as an unlikely cause of economic backwardness, though it acknowledges the effects of an endemic shortage of energy and the country's mountainous landscape, which made industrial output and land transport more expensive. Finally, these same authors argue that foreign businessmen as well regularly sought protection from the Spanish government, making them not so different in this sense from native entrepreneurs.

In either event, the hypothesis of a dearth of Spanish entrepreneurship has served to put business in the spotlight of the debate concerning Spanish economic backwardness. It has had the effect of stimulating other hypotheses, the most important of which will now be examined. Some of these new hypotheses have not only helped bring specific difficulties to the fore but have also advocated an analytical framework for explaining entrepreneurial behavior. Exploring this will be Spanish business history's task over the next few years.

The Absence of Large Companies

This hypothesis, formulated by Carreras and Tafunell (1997), has many points in common with the one just mentioned. The authors' work covered large companies in Spain. Although there have been large Spanish companies from the second half of the nineteenth century to the present, this segment shrank considerably after the Spanish Civil War (1936–9) by comparison with what was happening abroad. Before the war, Spain's international ranking of large companies was higher than one would expect from Spain's bantamweight economy.

Measuring the size of companies in terms of their net assets, the biggest Spanish enterprises at the beginning of the twentieth century

---

[36] See Comín and Martín-Aceña, "Rasgos históricos."

were railways, electricity utilities, and mines, which were mainly foreign owned. Around 1990, the companies ranking at the top of the scale were electricity utilities and banks, together with a special case, Telefónica (the national telephone company). However, these were no longer in foreign hands. The Franco regime's obsession with autarchy and its xenophobic nationalist policies, particularly in the early years, were the principal causes of the disappearance of foreign-owned large companies. The early industrial policy of the new regime gave rise to a big expansion of public industrial companies. It was thus during this period that big industries grew to account for their largest-ever share of the national economy. But they were still dwarves when measured on an international scale. Many of these firms later shrank during the industrial crisis of the 1970s and 1980s, except in some notable cases like Repsol, an oil company. The trend over the past few years has been for foreign companies to win back lost ground as the last vestiges of Spain's planned economy disappear.

Carreras and Tafunell presented three main reasons for the absence of large companies in Spain. To begin with, the poverty of the country resulted in thin markets when the first capital-intensive technologies appeared. Such technologies were essential for the development of large companies, and Spain lagged behind. Related to this were limited factors of production, which denied Spain the comparative advantages that tend to breed large companies. Finally, the authors argued, distortions of market mechanisms were caused by state intervention, particularly by policies creating public industrial companies during the Franco dictatorship.

This hypothesis commands fairly wide support. One of the authors' main achievements was to focus much of the debate regarding the scarcity of entrepreneurial initiative on big companies and to open up research into the lack of large enterprises. A more basic but no less useful achievement was the creation of a rank order of the 200 most important companies in the twentieth century and the sectors to which they belonged, thus allowing greater selectivity in future choice of research subjects.

Criticism of Carreras and Tafunell's work covered both the methodology and the content of the study.[37] With regard to content, one critic[38] stressed that the absence of large Spanish companies linked to the Second

---

[37] See Anna M. Aubanell, "La gran empresa en España (1917–1974): Una nota crítica," *Revista de Historia Industrial* no. 5 (1994): 163–70; the authors' response is to be found in Carreras and Tafunell, "La gran empresa en España (1917–1974): Réplica a una nota crítica," *Revista de Historia Industrial* no. 6 (1994): 165–72.

[38] See Valdaliso, "Orígenes y desarrollo," 102.

Industrial Revolution (chemistry, machine tools, electrical goods) was due to technological factors like the shortage of national patents and restrictions on the use of foreign ones. Another criticism[39] held that the state's responsibility for preventing the formation of large private companies lay in the way it facilitated cartels and legal oligopolies rather than in its policy of creating public companies. It was argued that this provided a disincentive to mergers and takeovers and hence deterred the emergence of larger companies. This argument was reinforced by the informal integration of companies that took place when entrepreneurs held stakes in various firms. This phenomenon also bore some relation to the diversification strategies carried out by many enterprises and businessmen. However, the main criticisms of Carreras and Tafunell's hypothesis are reserved for the role they attributed to public companies, a point we shall consider later.

Finally, Carreras and Tafunell argued that some of the harm done to the Spanish economy by the absence of large companies had various causes. Production inefficiencies resulted from an inability to take advantage of economies of scale and scope. Smaller companies had difficulties in improving management and obtaining information on markets and competitors. A lack of large companies created effective barriers to widening markets, particularly international ones. Without large companies' economic clout, there was inadequate investment in technological innovation and marketing. Smaller entities suffered from comparatively lower bargaining power with customers and banks. And, finally, the lack of larger companies limited the ability to take advantage of internal labor markets.

The Predominance of Family-Owned SMEs

The preceding hypothesis indirectly reinforces the notion that SMEs predominated in virtually every Spanish business sector throughout the nineteenth and twentieth centuries. Family ownership of these businesses left its mark on every aspect of their organization, particularly equity holdings and management. However, family groups also exercised strong control in a fair number of large companies. Although there are few monographs on small companies, results tending to support this view[40] have been

---

[39] See Comín and Martín-Aceña, "Rasgos históricos."

[40] See ibid. and Jordi Maluquer de Motes, "La estructura del sector algodonero en Cataluña durante la primera etapa de la industrialización (1832-1861)," *Hacienda Pública Española* no. 38 (1976): 133-48, for a historical interpretation of this hypothesis.

produced by recent research. Among these are studies on the Catalan
textile industry, sea transport, Castillian flour mills, and shoemaking in
the Valencia area. Work on other sectors including agriculture, particularly in the Mediterranean, points in the same direction. Large companies
coexisted with small and medium-sized companies in virtually all sectors of the economy, albeit under different competitive conditions. SMEs
were able to survive by adapting better to short and varied production
runs, unstable business conditions, and boom and bust cycles. SMEs managed despite their difficulties in obtaining external capital and developing
growth strategies. And often they outlived their founders. In addition, in
some areas this coexistence between companies of different sizes led to
the creation of industrial districts and favored the establishment of informal networks inspired by a mixture of personal ties, knowledge, and
mutual trust. This environment helped smaller companies survive and
remain competitive while reducing both the costs and other barriers
to obtaining market information, financing, technology, skilled workers,
and other factors of production.

According to this hypothesis, the structure of Spanish business was
generally similar to that of the rest of Europe, particularly the Mediterranean, where small and medium-sized family businesses have had a long
history. However, the available evidence is still insufficient to identify the
historical traits of SMEs in Spain. Many more comparative studies need to
be done on the business fabric in other Mediterranean countries before
such a conclusion can be drawn.

The Subsidiary Nature of Public Companies

This hypothesis stems from research on public companies carried out
during the past decade. The results of this work have led the two scholars
involved – Francisco Comín and Pablo Martín- Aceña – to talk about the
subsidiary nature of public companies vis-à-vis their private cousins.
These authors[41] believe that public companies already played an important part in the Spanish economy in the nineteenth century. They
point to the number of workers employed in large state-run enterprises
in sectors like mining, weapons production, and tax monopolies, though
management there was later privatized to increase tax revenue. During
the early years of the Franco dictatorship, this state domination of industry was further reinforced. Autarchic policies were adopted, such as the

[41] Comín and Martín-Aceña, "Rasgos históricos."

foundation of INI and the nationalization of the railways, telephones, and public banks. It is also true that state companies grew as well throughout Western Europe after the Second World War. Comparatively, Comín and Martín-Aceña argue, during Franco's long dictatorship, public companies played a subsidiary role to private enterprise to a greater extent in Spain than in other European countries. Proof of this is that public companies were set up in sectors that had been abandoned by private enterprise. Public companies also mounted lifeboat operations, taking over bankrupt private businesses, with nationalized companies confining themselves to providing important public services. Public companies also provided private ones with cheap inputs even when this meant taking a cut in profits. Indeed, public companies sometimes even carried out joint strategies with private enterprises due to the latter's "capture" stratagems. Those defending this hypothesis insist that very few examples can be found that demonstrate autarchy-inspired public companies throttling infant private enterprises or intervening to prevent their conception.

This hypothesis, as indicated earlier, contradicts Carreras and Tafunell's argument that the policy distortions introduced by the Franco dictatorship (i.e., the creation of strategically positioned public companies between 1940 and 1974) were responsible for stifling large private firms and putting foreign capital to flight. In a recent study,[42] these authors, and Torres, note that government policy caused a serious economic setback, since most of the public sector manufacturing companies tanked after 1973 because of their impoverished technology and lack of competitive skills. Nevertheless, some public companies overcame these difficulties and survived, even if most of the lucky few just happened to be operating state monopolies (e.g., oil, telecommunications, and electricity). The results of other recently completed research projects[43] also cast doubts on the subsidiary nature of public companies during the autarchic period, arguing that the creation of state firms clipped the wings of private enterprise. This hypothesis is still provisional in nature, but this research could well yield some of the best results in Spanish business history over the next few years.

---

[42] Albert Carreras, Xavier Tafunell, and Eugenio Torres, "The Rise and Decline of Spanish State-Owned Firms," in *The Rise and Fall of State-Owned Enterprise in the Western World*, ed. Pier Angelo Toninelli (Cambridge, 2000), 208–36.

[43] Antonio Gómez Mendoza, ed., *De mitos y milagros: El Instituto Nacional de Autarquía, 1941-1963* (Barcelona, 2000); and Elena San Román, *Ejército e industria: El nacimiento del INI* (Barcelona, 1999).

The Importance of Foreign Companies in Spanish Industrialization

Economic historians of the 1960s and 1970s viewed in a bad light the role of foreign companies in Spain, as they did in the case of other countries that industrialized late. Fortunately, subsequent work by foreign historians[44] led to a more balanced view that also recognized the benefits of foreign enterprise. These scholars were right when they stated that foreign companies enjoyed certain advantages over native capital, including better organization, better financing, more advanced technology, and greater market knowledge. Foreign companies therefore played an important role in mobilizing natural resources and transferring technology and organizational, commercial, and financial skills, even if Spain was often poorly placed to take advantage of them. Nevertheless, foreign companies did not necessarily put free competition into practice, since many of these firms were set up in sectors with strong monopolistic or oligopolistic tendencies (e.g., railways, explosives, telephones, municipal services, and mining). Foreign firms therefore predominated among large companies in Spain during the second half of the nineteenth century. Spanish experience from the 1960s to the present seems to confirm the notion that foreign firms have had a beneficial effect on Spanish economic growth. This provides a stark contrast to the enforced exile of foreign firms from Spain during the 1940s and 1950s.

The Power of Spanish Banks

Lastly, we should consider a hypothesis that has been deeply rooted in Spanish economic historiography since the 1960s. This hypothesis refers to the mixed commercial and industrial character of private banks and their strong links with companies, particularly large firms. The most important issue is to identify the banks' role in providing financing in poorly developed capital markets. Going beyond the strong ties between banks and big business (largely a result of directors sitting on the boards of both banks and large enterprises),[45] this hypothesis is consistent with

---

[44] See Albert Broder, *Le rôle des interêts étrangers dans la croissance de l'Espagne (1767-1923)* (Paris, 1981); Chastagneret, *L'Espagne*; Checkland, *The Mines;* and Harvey, *Rio Tinto.*

[45] See Juan Muñoz, *El poder de la banca en España* (Madrid, 1970), and a new approach in Maria A. Pons, "Universal Banks and Industrialisation: The Spanish Case, 1939-1975," in *Business History, Theory and Practice*, ed. A. Slaven (Glasgow, 2000), 102-13.

Gerschenkron's contention that banks may play an important role in the development of countries that industrialize late. However, bank financing seemed to benefit bank shareholders more than the recipients of loans. This was especially true of small companies, which not only paid dearly for their borrowings but also were expected to pay them back over very short periods. Both factors discouraged long-term investment in plant and equipment.

Although Spanish banks were of a mixed commercial and industrial character at the beginning of the twentieth century, their industrial vocation left a lot to be desired when compared with, say, German banks or, in another example, when examining their wholesale disposal of holdings during the Spanish industrial crisis of the 1970s. It has occasionally been written that the formation of banking groups revealed the close relationships forged between banks and industry. More likely, this was simply a ruse to gain captive clients rather than an expression of a genuine industrial vocation. In any case, the "old" hypothesis needs to be thoroughly revised – yet another important task that the waxing field of business history in Spain needs to tackle. More empirical data are needed on the relationship between banks and industry. Toward this end, use should be made of some of the tools employed by industrial economics and other fields of economic theory, with which business historians are increasingly familiar.

CONCLUSIONS

During the past ten years, Spanish business history has come of age as a specialist field of study within economic history. It owes a debt to economic history, from which it has received many of its scientific tools and research directions. This is not surprising, since the new specialty sets out to explain the role of entrepreneurs and companies in the development of the Spanish economy over the past few centuries. While it is still far from providing general explanations of Spanish economic development, it has nevertheless made considerable strides in a very short period.

Economic historians have brought a wealth of subjects, methodologies, and research interests to business history, spurred on by their interest in examining theories in a microeconomic context. In the process, they have revealed the complexity of business history issues. These developments by themselves would not suffice to make business history a mature discipline. However, the prospects of achieving this aim will be much brighter if researchers in the field avail themselves fully of the theories and comparative analyses employed abroad. Recent experience gives grounds for optimism, but it would be unwise to forget that the discipline in Spain still has much work to do.

KEY WORKS

Carreras, Albert, Pere Pascual, David Reher, and Carles Sudrià, eds. *Doctor Jordi Nadal: La industrialización y el desarrollo económico de España*. Barcelona, 1999.

Carreras, Albert and Xavier Tafunell. "Spain: Big Manufacturing Firms Between State and Market." In *Big Business and the Wealth of Nations*, edited by Alfred D. Chandler, Jr., Franco Amatori, and Takashi Hikino, 277-304. Cambridge, 1997.

Comín, Francisco and Pablo Martín-Aceña, eds. *La empresa en la historia de España*. Madrid, 1996.

Comín, Francisco and Pablo Martín-Aceña. "Rasgos históricos de las empresas en España. Un panorama." *Revista de Economía Aplicada* 4, no. 12 (1996): 75-123.

López, Santiago and Jesús M. Valdaliso, eds. *¿Que inventen ellos? Tecnología, empresa y cambio económico en la España contemporánea*. Madrid, 1997.

Nadal, Jordi. *El fracaso de la Revolución Industrial en España, 1814-1913*. Barcelona, 1975.

Núñez, Gregorio and Luciano Segreto, eds. *Introducción a la Historia de la empresa en España*. Madrid, 1994.

Torres, Eugenio, dir. *Los 100 empresarios españoles del siglo XX*. Madrid, 2000.

Tortella, Gabriel. *Los orígenes del capitalismo en España: Banca, industria y ferrocarriles en el siglo XIX*. Madrid, 1973.

Valdaliso, Jesús M. "Orígenes y desarrollo de la historia empresarial en España." *Príncipe de Viana. Suplemento de Ciencias Sociales* no. 17 (1999): 91-117.

12

Business History in Greece

The State of the Art and Future Prospects

MARGARITA DRITSAS

Business history is a relatively new area of interest in Greece. The first steps toward its introduction were made only in the late 1980s. Ten years later, it would be fair to say that although the results have not been spectacular, business history has found a place on the agenda of the country's academic researchers. New ground is beginning to be broken in terms of new perspectives and issues.

These developments do not seem to have induced, however, any greater integration within the scientific community. Business history research has remained the pursuit of individual researchers and academics, mainly historians and social scientists. Systematic teaching and team projects in the field remain elusive. The number of monographs and articles produced is small, and there are virtually no full-fledged ongoing case studies of individual big firms. Nor has the publishing of any specialized journal been attempted. Papers tend to appear selectively in the three or four general historical journals published in Greece.[1]

---

[1] *Historica, Histor*, and *EMNE Mnemon*; of these three journals, *Historica* was initiated more as an economic history journal. The other two publish papers on general and social history. Articles on business history have also appeared in *Synchrona Themata (Modern Themes)*, a general social science journal concerned with new perspectives in social science and in history.

The slow development of the subdiscipline is due to several factors. Low institutionalization in the area of economic history itself has been partially responsible for the problem. The long dominance of political history in the curricula of history departments that, moreover, have traditionally included as well the study of archaeology, has hindered the blossoming of economic history and related areas of knowledge. Students of history are usually unprepared to take courses in economic theory or the social sciences. When economic/business history became a novelty in the 1980s, it was never linked to any career path. Motivation to pursue research in business history has therefore been frustrated. Meanwhile, in departments of economics, the few positions in economic history that were established emphasized the study of economic thought rather than the analysis of processes or institutions. Although this situation is changing, the existing positions in economic history are still far from creating any momentum or critical mass.

The principal weakness of business history in Greece is due, however, mainly to the late introduction in the country of economic history. Until the mid-1970s, particular interpretations of Greek development dominated debates among Greek academic historians. Distortions in the system of political and economic power were explained in terms of structural problems of the Greek economy and society, the causes of which were, in turn, sought in past centuries. The introduction of economic history was the result of a renaissance in historical studies in Greece during the mid-1970s, without which the road toward business history would have probably remained closed for a much longer period.[2] For the first time, new sources and new perspectives originating not only in history but also in the social sciences were used for the analysis of the past – more precisely, for understanding Greek social and economic life. Whole areas that had until then been shrouded and relegated to historical "silence" soon became the main objects of historical research. The redirection of Greek history took place under the constellation of Marxist theory, suppressed until then, and now for the first time was

---

[2] Cf. Nicos G. Svoronos, *Histoire de la Grèce Moderne* (Paris, 1953). The author has been an influential figure in Greek historiography. He had long lived in France and adopted the principles of the new history. He had nothing to say about business history, but his writings provided inspiration for younger researchers. For an early reference to the need to incorporate business history perspectives, see Margarita Dritsas, "He Historia ton hellinikon epicheiriseon: Merika prota erethismata" (The History of Greek Business: An Initial Response), in *Afieroma ste Mneme tou N. Svoronou (Homage to the Memory of N. Svoronos)*, ed. Stefanos Papageorgiou (Athens, 1992), 263–71.

able to incorporate modern tools.[3] Questions about economic structure, the agrarian nature of the Greek economy, and its continuity throughout the Byzantine and Ottoman periods became central in the analysis. The study of institutions such as the tax system, the origin and role of social classes, and the rise of the modern bourgeoisie and economic power led to studies about the role of the modern Greek state itself. Studies of the transition to capitalism and capitalist development per se were further steps in the same direction.[4] Documents such as archives, account books and ledgers of merchants, or any kind of information that might lead to measuring and proving or disproving hypotheses began to be systematized. These resources formed the basis for research.

Concurrently, parallel attempts by neo-Marxist economists and other social scientists to explain economic backwardness led to competing programmatic notions of the state, sometimes as an instrument of the dominant capitalist class or as the outcome of changing relations among classes. Meanwhile, any systematic analysis of the business community, state action with regard to business, the study of business institutions themselves, or the study of entrepreneurial practices remained outside the realm of such studies. In contrast, numerous works appeared analyzing the Greek labor movement, state action leading to the regulation of the incipient labor market, and the nature of the working class.[5]

---

[3] In 1975, one year after the collapse of the dictatorship (1967-74) and the return to democratic rule, Svoronos, in his inaugural lecture at Panteion University in Athens on the relationship between political history and history, affirmed his attachment to the "method emanating from Marxist thought" which he considered the best tool for "historical research and for the analysis of reality." N. Svoronos, *Analecta Neohellnikes Historias kai historiographias*, 34, 37-8, 43-52.

[4] Spyros I. Asdrachas, *Oikonomike dome ton Valkanikon choron, XV-XIX eones (Economic Structure of the Balkan Countries, XV-XIX Centuries)* (Athens, 1980); id., *Helliniki Koinonia kai oikonomia XVIII-XIX aiones Hypotheseis kai prosengiseis (Greek Society and Economy, XVIII-XIX Centuries, Hypotheses and Approaches)* (Athens, 1982); id., *Zetemata historias (History Issues)* (Athens, 1983); in chapter 5 of *Zetemata*, he dealt with revenue farming as a form of business in 1790 related to trade, usury, and finance, and drew the theoretical outline of analyzing business in the context of the Ottoman Empire. See also Nicos G. Svoronos, *Le Commerce de Salonique au XVIIIe siècle* (Paris, 1956); id., *Histoire de la Grèce Moderne* (Paris, 1980).

[5] See comprehensive works by George Leontaritis, "To helliniko ergatiko kinema kai to astiko kratos, 1910-1920" (The Greek Labor Movement and the Bourgeois State, 1910-1920), in *Meletemata gyro apo ton Venizelo kai ten epoche tou (Studies on Venizelos and His Era)*, ed. Thanos Veremis (Athens, 1980), 49-84, and Kostis Moskof, *Historia tou Kinimatos tes ergatikis taxis sten Hellada (History of the Labor Movement in Greece)* (Thessaloniki, 1979).

Finally, to the institutional difficulties encountered by economic and business historians, one must add the lack of state action with regard to source material, since there has never been in Greece any coherent statutory policy concerning the preservation of business records. Similar inertia has characterized the actions of organizations and pressure groups such as the Federation of Greek Industrialists and the Chambers of Commerce and Industry, which have been very slow to realize that past experience should be incorporated into present practices.

Any systematic analysis of business activities in Greece, therefore, has rested on the initiative of a limited number of individual researchers, some of whom became interested and got involved without much national or institutional assistance. Despite these constraints, persistent efforts by academics with help from several sponsorships by business firms have made possible the organization of two conferences, the publication of their proceedings, and a number of scientific case studies.[6] Further growth will depend on future developments in academia and on strengthening cooperation and mutual trust between the world of business and the world of business historians. Optimism in this respect is warranted: more and more businesses are gradually realizing the importance of their own histories and the significance of their historical records.[7] Ultimately, further development will also depend on the quality of the work produced. Business histories should be more than

---

[6] See Margarita Dritsas, Håkan Lindgren and Alice Teichova, eds., *L'Entreprise en Grèce et en Europe XIXe-XXe siècles* (Athens, 1991); M. Dritsas, *To Chroma tes Epitychias: He Helliniki viomehania chromaton, 1830-1990 (The Color of Success: The Greek Paint Industry, 1830-1990)* (Athens, 1995); and Margarita Dritsas and Terence R. Gourvish, eds., *European Enterprise: Strategies of Adaptation and Renewal in the Twentieth Century* (Athens, 1997). Other studies refer to archives of both ongoing and defunct firms. See, for example, Christina Agriantoni and Maria-Christina Hadjioannou, eds., *The Athens Silk-Industry Quarter* (Athens, 1995); Vasilis Kremmydas, *Emporikes praktikes sto telos tes Tourkokratias: Mykoniates emporoi kai plioktetes (me vase to archeio tes oikogenias Bate) (Commercial Practices at the End of Turkish Rule: Merchants and Shipowners from Mykonos [Based on the Bates Family Archive])* (Athens, 1993); id., *Emporoi kai Emporika diktya sta chronia tou eikosiena, 1820-1835 (Merchants and Trade Networks, 1820-1835)* (Athens, 1996); Gelina Harlaftis, *A History of Greek-Owned Shipping: The Making of an International Tramp Fleet, 1830 to the Present Day* (London and New York, 1996).

[7] An exhibition on "facets of entrepreneurship in the twentieth century" was organized in November 1999 by the monthly journal *Oikonomike Viomechanike Epitheorise* in Athens. It presented profiles of most of the oldest and largest industrial and banking firms. The accompanying catalog included an introduction on the history of entrepreneurship in Greece; see Margarita Dritsas, ed., *Facets of Greek Entrepreneurship in the Twentieth Century* (Athens, 1999).

chronologies of operations; they should formulate hypotheses and use theory.[8]

EARLY INITIATIVES AND THE ORGANIZATION
OF BUSINESS ARCHIVES

The earliest important initiative combining the organization of archives and historical research was the establishment in the mid-1970s of the Historical Archive of the National Bank of Greece (NBG), containing records going back to the early nineteenth century. This action was instrumental in opening up the field for economic history and subsequently for business history. The opening of the archive was combined with a bank-financed research program, the aim of which was to promote economic history by also assessing the role of the NBG in modern Greek economic development. The project included systematic processing of about 19 million documents. Another 14.7 million await treatment in the depots.[9] The successful running of the program over several years has led to the publication of a series of studies that could well be considered the first modern monographs in Greek economic history.[10]

The NBG project was designed and supervised by Greek historians, many of whom had lived and worked in France at the University of Paris and at the Centre National de Recherche Scientifique (CNRS) or the Ecole des Hautes Etudes en Sciences Sociales. Upon their return to Greece, they were able to put into effect ideas and methodological perspectives emanating largely from the French Ecole des Annales (or new history), which soon achieved a sort of hegemony over Greek history. As a result, alternative perspectives that had developed at the same time or earlier in

---

[8] For example, Nicos Melios and Evangelia Bafouni, *Elais S.A. 1920-1997: Opseis tes oikonomikes tes historias (Elais S.A. 1920-1997: Facets of Its Economic History)* (Neo Falero, 1997); Vasiliki Theodorou, *To ergostasio emaye sten Kea, 1927-1957 (The Emaille Factory in Kea, 1927-1957)* (Kea, 1994); Dimitra Pikramenou-Varfi, *O Spyridon Pavlides kai to glykismatopoieion tou (Spyridon Pavlides and His "Pastry Shop": The Early Years of the First Greek Industry)* (Athens, 1991).

[9] For a progress report of the research program see Gerasimos Notaras, "Fonds d'Archives et Banques Grecques," in Dritsas et al., *L'Entreprise*, 191-202. For details of the electronic handling stage, see George N. Mitrophanis, "Analysis of Historical Information Systems: The Case of the Historical Archive of the National Bank of Greece," in KNE (Centre of Neohellenic Research), *Tetradia Ergasias* (Athens) 21 (1998): 106-25.

[10] The NBG project was headed by the eminent historian S. Asdrachas. It has yielded over fifteen monographs on Greek economic history.

the rest of the world, notably in British or American institutions, did not attract as much interest. The example of the NBG was quickly imitated by other banking institutions, and thus banking history gradually created the base for the subsequent interest in business history.[11] On the other hand, it was soon realized that the archives of the NBG contained the business records of many clients of the bank and of several other firms that came under its control.[12] The former, together with a series of branch studies compiled by the bank, went to form a category entitled Industrial Credit, which featured over 2,000 files from most of the important industrial firms operating in Greece between 1911 and 1960. This was used as the basic source material for a monograph on the relations between industry and banking, more particularly relations between the NBG and industry, during the interwar years.[13]

Another institution, the Centre of Neo-Hellenic Research, has over the years accumulated a number of private business archives.[14] Several

[11] A case in point was that of the Commercial Bank of Greece. Its program was headed by another Greek historian, George Dertilis. The program did not emphasize business or economic history but rather social history and anthropology. Several studies, however, could be considered as entrepreneurial history, for instance Haris Exertzoglou, *Adaptability and Tactics of Greek Overseas Capital* (Athens, 1989), dealing with Greek bankers in Constantinople during the nineteenth century. The program was suspended in the late 1980s. The Agricultural Bank and the Industrial Development Bank (IDB) also imitated the NBG. The IDB's Institute of Technology and Research still sponsors conferences and publishes works generally concerned with the history of know-how and technology in Greek industry.

[12] For instance, the archives of the first sizable modern paint and varnish plant, Iris S.A., were used for writing a business history of the paint and varnish branch, those of a printing firm, Aspiotis Elka S.A., a subsidiary of the bank, and records of the Bank of Athens, an NBG competitor that merged with the NBG in 1952. In addition to these archival entities, other material exists on a number of important early companies, such as the Hellenic Maritime Company, established in 1857, Greek railways, several power plants, and energy supply firms. This material formed the basis of several monographs published in the economic history series of the NBG. See, in particular, Lefteris Papagiannakis, *Oi hellinikoi sidirodromoi, 1882-1910 (The Greek Railways)* (Athens, 1982); Constantinos Papathanassopoulos, *Etaireia Hellinikis Atmoploias (Hellenic Maritime Co.), 1855-1872* (Athens, 1988); Nicos S. Pantelakis, *O Exelectrismos sten Hellada: Apo tin idiotiki protovoulia sto kratiko monopolio, 1889-1956 (The Electrification of Greece: From Private Initiative to State Monopoly, 1889-1956)* (Athens, 1991).

[13] Margarita Dritsas, *Viomichania kai trapezes stin Hellada tou mesopolemou (Industry and Banking in Greece during the Interwar Period)* (Athens, 1990). The study touched upon central issues in business history since it focused on the formation of joint stock companies in Greece, their management patterns and financial strategies, and so on.

[14] For example, records of A. S. Koupas S.A. (1882-1987), a machine repair and manufacturer; Retsinas Brothers S.A. (1872-1981), a cotton spinning company; and the Gerousis family

others belong to the Hellenic Literary and Historical Archive Association (ELIA), a nonprofit organization.[15] Kerkyra Publications, responsible for publishing one of the older economic magazines, the monthly *Industrial Review*, has recently organized and cataloged the archive of one of its founders and owners.[16] The significance of this archive lies in the fact that it was compiled as a basis for the five-volume *Hellenic Business Biographical Dictionary*, published between 1958 and 1960, the first and only one of its kind in Greece. Finally, and not less importantly, in the past few years, several firms have had their records cataloged. One of them, Chrotech S.A., which is the second largest firm in the paint and varnish industry, also commissioned a business history of its paint and varnish branch.[17] Another relatively old firm in the oil business, Elais S.A., now a subsidiary of Unilever, opened a permanent exhibition of documents and memorabilia and published a pamphlet of a brief chronology of its operations.[18] These examples have also shown that a crucial and determining factor in carrying out successful research based on unpublished sources is the rapport between historians and the business world.

Two international conferences, one in 1989 in Athens and one in 1995 in Rethymno, Crete, also contributed to the establishment of business history in Greece. The first one could be considered as marking the official beginning of the interest in the discipline in the country, while the second showed the progress made during the six years that had elapsed. Both conferences – the proceedings of which were later published – included scholars from elsewhere in Europe, and Chandler himself contributed an introduction to the second volume.[19]

archive. These archives are not generally accessible to outside researchers. For details of the Retsinas archive and a brief chronology of the firm history, see C. Agriantoni, " 'Frères Retsinas S.A.': Ascension et déchéance d'une grande entreprise textile de la Grèce," in Dritsas et al., *L'Entreprise*, 213-26; for the Koupas archive, see Andreas Bayas and Eugenia Kremmyda, "Archeiakes ergasies sto archeio A. Kouppa S.A." (Archival Work in the A. Koupas S.A. Archive), in *Tetradia Ergasias* 21 (1998): 59-61; for the Gerousis archive, see Maria-Christina Hadzioannou, "Modes of Adaptation of Greek Diaspora Firms in the Greek Kingdom," in Dritsas et al., *L'Entreprise*, 103-8.

15 Christina Varda, *The Hamburger–Alexopoulos Archive. Catalogue* (Athens, 1997). Information about new acquisitions is published regularly in their monthly bulletin.
16 Margarita Dritsas, ed., *The Archives of Konstantinos Vovolinis, Volume 1* (Athens, 1997); volume 2 is in press.
17 Dritsas, *To Chroma tes Epitychias*.
18 Melios and Bafouni, *Elais S.A.*
19 Dritsas et al., *L'Entreprise*; Dritsas and Gourvish, *European Enterprise*.

APPROACHES AND PARADIGMS

Case studies of ongoing Greek firms are rare. The history of the Greek paint industry[20] is a business history of the whole sector for the period 1830–1990 commissioned by one of the leaders of the industry. The study was based on several companies' archives and on structured and unstructured personal interviews that helped to fill gaps in the documents. The work looked at the development of the industry in relation to other sectors, following its transfer across geographical areas. It identified the types of principal firms that emerged both in the last quarter of the nineteenth century and during most of the twentieth century – dominated still today by what in international terms might be small and medium-sized enterprises (SMEs), although several of them count today as big corporate units. The general evolution of this sector, which is quite representative of Greek development, its modernization process, and its present state, was traced in terms of both external and internal factors. Apart from the variety of business arrangements, several entrepreneurial and corporate strategies and attitudes emerged as particularly important. Changes in the ownership and structure of the leading firms and in the behavioral profiles of their owners followed an intergenerational pattern across the sector. Modest individual enterprises initially, or big firms from their inception, they evolved into family multidivisional units, and some ended up as multinational affiliates. For these modern companies, the mix of family control and managerial sophistication determined their success or failure. Although most of the leaders in the sector would not be considered the Chandlerian type of firm, those that succeeded seem to have effected the "three-pronged investment." Modernization thus embraced planning in regard to the amounts and sorts of capital resources committed, the type of technology used, and control of market conditions.

Concepts used in this study were drawn from economic and social history, rather than from the theory of the firm alone. This choice was imposed by the analysis of business activity in the nineteenth century, in which the role of the entrepreneur appeared to have had greater relevance. Formal qualifications and aspirations, experience and perception of reality, social position, and connections played an important part in affecting not only the style but also the essence of decision making, strategy, and tactics. Accordingly, socioeconomic profiles of businessmen were considered significant for understanding how particular strategies were

---

[20] Dritsas, *To Chroma tes Epitychias*.

designed and what sorts of decisions were made. The approach most often used has been as versatile as possible, combining entrepreneurial and firm analysis, since the dominant pattern of business activity throughout the twentieth century in Greece has been the formation of SMEs. However, big firms have also had an important share in economic development. Modern companies exhibit a great deal of variation in their structure and scope, but generally characteristics of a Schumpeterian type of entrepreneurship are strong, while features of a Chandlerian type, although not dominant, also exist. Resilient SMEs today operate not only in small national or regional markets but also across markets, including the global context. Their survival and prosperity have been a function of their flexibility in dealing successfully with multiple market structures.

The study of the paint industry as a representative branch of the secondary sector has shown that SMEs have functioned and prospered side by side with bigger firms within the same branch and across branches following a variety of ownership patterns – controlled by families, by the state, or by multinationals. The variety of Greek business today will undoubtedly determine to a large extent the terms of the debate in the future, and dilemmas about which theoretical approaches may be more useful are bound to remain unresolved. The study of the paint industry has shown that some degree of eclecticism cannot be avoided. Two questions already invite more systematic attention in the future. One is the problem of size in Greek business and its consequences. If big business has so far remained restricted in Greece, recent evidence shows that in the past decade, important changes have occurred stemming from patterns of succession and from increasing internationalization. Mergers and acquisitions already take place on a substantial scale, although firms do not seem, in general, to eschew their family characteristics. What has emerged as a new feature to be analyzed and assessed is the pattern of national or international business groups run by single families.

The second issue is the need to analyze those big firms – state or privately owned and managed – that often, but not always, combine smaller or larger portions of national and multinational capital and that so far have received little attention. Such an agenda acquires additional importance in Greece, where the role of the state has traditionally been pervasive. The parameters of this problem are also changing in view of the policy of privatization that Greek governments have been pursuing during the past few years. Another topic on which research should focus is the comparison and contrast of the trajectories of firms in equally or more advanced economies, on the one hand, and in countries with similar histories and structures – for instance, other Mediterranean countries – on the other.[21]

The Chandlerian paradigm, so apt for the study of big business in the United States and other parts of the world, can only partially incorporate the specificities of the process of development in latecomers such as Greece. This, however, does not imply that it is irrelevant. On the contrary, it sharpens our insight for comparative analysis. Since embedding the firm in historical development is the basis of Chandler's approach, it helps reveal the diversity of alternative business attitudes and their relation to different structures, thus enhancing our understanding of the variety of business forms operating in national and regional contexts. As the findings of the study about the Greek paint industry suggest, for instance, within the specific Greek market, family ownership and control was not incompatible with bigger size or efficiency, or with rationalization and innovation. At the same time, the pioneer spirit of the founders was supported by the flexibility of family structure in terms of financing and work arrangements. Nor did family ownership preclude managerial hierarchies. Some companies, after the demise of their founders, were able to make the transition to a less "personalized" or even completely nonpersonalized form of organization, while still others managed to combine the personal involvement and initiative of their owners with a managerial hierarchical structure closely approaching a multidivisional pattern.

Another branch of business history covering roughly the same period (1830–1990) concerns the Greek-owned shipping industry.[22] Unlike the history of the paint industry, which was written in Greek, the history of shipping has been written in English and has therefore attracted a wider audience. Shipping has traditionally been considered among the most important forms of Greek economic activity, exhibiting a high degree of continuity and occasional outstanding successes. Several earlier works exist on the economic history of this sector, but the latest one (1996) on maritime history is the most comprehensive, based on the extensive use of a variety of archival materials. Greek shipping was (and still is) based firmly on family structure and has had a strong geographical bond with several Greek islands. The study shows in a very satisfactory

---

[21] A research program is in progress comparing the structure of big business in Mediterranean countries.

[22] Harlaftis, *Greek-Owned Shipping*; this study appeared in translation in Greek (*Historia tes Hellinoktites Naftilias 19os–20os aionas* [Athens, 2001]).

way how the versatility required for successful tramp shipping and bulk cargo carrying was based on the cohesion and ability of the extended family structure and the consequent network formation to meet demand by changing locations swiftly. Using kinship and local human resources (e.g., intermarriage and recruiting crews from their islands of origin), shipping firms had established in the nineteenth century a sophisticated organizational pattern involving important business networks set up around the world. Shipping firms were thus able to gain access to particular markets and eventually to dominate them by efficiently organizing their cargoes and shipping routes. The study also argues that this networking was a specific Greek business strategy, one that, despite the increasing internationalization of the business in the twentieth century and the emergence of new shipowners, allowed for continued dominance of Piraeus as the industry's decision center. The maintenance of the Greek identity as a locus for expertise, communication, financing, shipbuilding, insurance, and so on is shown by the study to be the basis of the Greeks' success.

Apart from these comprehensive business histories of two important branches of economic activity, there are several other studies more limited in scope but still helpful. Among them is the case study of an early silk factory, established in Athens in the mid-nineteenth century, that failed to survive. It outlines the difficulties encountered by both foreign (British) and national (Greek) ownership in adapting to a nonindustrialized environment at a time when exporting cocoons was more profitable than processing them locally for the production of silk. The firm suspended manufacturing in the 1870s and operated as a private merchant company. It then shrank even further, and its facilities were eventually rented out as plots of urban land.[23] The absence of a supportive state policy and a protected home market were identified as the main causes of failure, as well as entrepreneurial behavior that emphasized concern for the security of ownership rather than returns on capital. Other shortcomings were the lack of technical skills and know-how, a permanent liquidity crisis, and managerial deficiencies. The merit of the study is that it shows that timing is important when setting up relatively big firms and that big firms were probably unable to survive unless assimilated into the dominant pattern of family ownership.

[23] Christina Agriantoni, " 'Société Sericicole de la Grèce': Adaptation and Assimilation of a Large Industrial Firm," in *Metaxourgeion: The Athens Silkmill,* eds. Agriantoni and Maria Christina Chatziioannou (Athens, 1997), 83–136.

General works on Greek development from the 1970s and 1980s often include chapters that might be considered fragments of entrepreneurial history since they are concerned with the role of entrepreneurs or with particular business practices. Many obey the logic of dependency theory, while others refer to particular sectors of the Greek economy – for instance, the rural economy – and particular regions. They, too, have been related mostly to banking and are useful because they reveal specific instances of business behavior and strategy.[24]

As already mentioned, in the 1970s and 1980s, within the neo-Marxist discourse of political economy, economic backwardness was seen as due mainly to insufficient or wrong initiatives taken by one class – the Greek "capitalist class," the "bourgeoisie," the "entrepreneurial class," or the "new middle class," depending on the ideological nuances adopted. Regardless of which term was chosen, all of these studies implicitly focused on the role of certain entrepreneurs at a particular time. Practices such as short-term speculative behavior, profit-seeking, and low risk taking were then extrapolated across time and across sectors to be projected as features of a homogeneous class, characteristic of a peripheral or semiperipheral outward-looking economy.[25] Although these were not business history studies and suffer from many methodological weaknesses, they have had an impact on economic and social (entrepreneurial) history. The concept of a monolithic, homogeneous "class" is particularly obvious in one study that focuses on the Greek "capitalists" as creators and creatures of the capitalist system.[26]

---

[24] George Dertilis, ed., *Banquiers, usuries et paysans* (Paris, 1988). For regional history combined with historical geography see Vangelis Prontzas, *Oikonomia kai Geoktesia sti Thessalia, 1881-1912 (Economy and Land Property in Thessaly, 1881-1912)* (Athens, 1992). Extensive use was made of the archives of the Privileged Bank of Epirus-Thessaly and the economic records of the Xenia Monastery. Part of this work focuses on issues of strategy and management of large estates, such as the Xenia Monastery. For the Peloponnesos region and the effects of banking in the area see Thanasis Kalafatis, *Agrotike Piste kai Oikonomikos Metaschematismos ste Peloponneso (Rural Credit and Economic Transformation in North Peloponnesos)*, 3 vols. (Athens, 1990).

[25] For instance, see Nicos Mouzelis, *Modern Greece: Facets of Underdevelopment* (London, 1977); Costas Vergopoulos, *Ethinismos kai Oikonomike Anaptyxe (Nationalism and Economic Development)* (Athens, 1981); id., "The Constitution of the New Bourgeois Class, 1944-1952," in *Greece in the 1940s and 1950s: A Nation in Crisis*, ed. John O. Iatridis (Hanover and London, 1981), 529–59; Constantinos Tsoukalas, *Koinoniki Anaptyxi kai Kratos (Social Development and the State)* (Athens, 1981).

[26] Alice Vaxevanoglou, *Oi Hellines Kefaleouchoi, 1900-1940 (The Greek Capitalists, 1900-1940)* (Athens, 1994). Similar reductionism characterizes another work that includes chapters on the Greek cotton and steel industries: Christos H. Hadjiossif, *He Gerea Selene, He*

Finally, there is a group of monographs based on a variety of archival material that often contain detailed information on early business practices in Greece. Commerce, combined with shipping, has attracted the most attention. The majority of these studies describe the activities of certain groups of entrepreneurs in late-eighteenth- and early-nineteenth-century Greece, which was still under Ottoman rule, such as merchants and shipowners from particular regions (Peloponnesos or Crete or Mykonos) and their commercial relations with other European trade and industrial centers.[27] These monographs include well-documented hypotheses about Greek merchants operating in a precapitalist context who, by dominating trade in the eastern Mediterranean and the Black Sea regions, shaped to a large extent modern capitalism in the area. The works refer mainly to national historiography debates, and none of them was presented as business history at the time. In addition to providing valuable information about early forms of enterprises, they feed into the debate about ethnic entrepreneurial and business cultures operating within larger multiethnic or multinational economic structures.[28] These studies have shown that Greek merchants were efficient entrepreneurs, having established successful firms in the eastern Mediterranean region, but the conditions of their firms' demise still remain rather obscure and need to be researched in more detail.[29]

viomechania sten Helliniki Oikonomia, 1830-1990 (The Waning Moon, Greek Industry and the Greek Economy, 1830-1990) (Athens, 1993).

[27] See Vasilis Kremmydas, *Archeio Hatzipanayotti (The Hatzipanayotis Archive)*, vol. 1 (Athens, 1973); id., *Emporikes praktikes*; idem, *Emporoi kai emporika diktya*; Stefanos Papageorgiou, *O exynchronismos tou Hellena pragmatefti symphone me ta europaika protypa (The Modernization of the Greek Itinerant Merchant in Terms of the European Pattern)* (Athens, 1990).

[28] On Jewish entrepreneurs in Greece before the Second World War see Margarita Dritsas, "Politismiki idiaiteroteta kai epicheiriseis: He periptosi ton evraikon diktion" (Cultural Specificity and Entrepreneurial Practices: The Case of Jewish Networks in Greece in the Early Twentieth Century), in *Hellinikos Hevraismos (Greek Jewry): Conference Proceedings*, ed. Vasilis Kremmydas (Athens, 1999), 303–44.

[29] For new work on Greek merchants using institutional theory to understand their networks and strategies, see Ioanna Pepelassis-Minoglou, "The Greek Merchant House of the Russian Black Sea: A Nineteenth Century Example of a Traders Coalition," *International Journal of Maritime History* 10, no. 1 (1998): 61–104; and Minoglou Louri and Helen Louri, "Diaspora Entrepreneurial Networks in the Black Sea and Greece, 1870-1917," *Journal of European Economic History* 26, no. 1 (1997): 69–104. On banking networks see Margarita Dritsas, "Networks of Bankers and Industrialists in Greece in the Interwar Period" in *Universal Banking in Twentieth Century Europe*, eds. Alice Teichova, Terence R. Gourvish, and Agnes Pogany (London, 1994), 229–45; Margarita Dritsas, Peter Eigner, and Jon Ottoson, "Big Business Networks in Three Interwar Economies: Austria, Greece, Sweden," *Financial History Review* 3 (1996): 175–95.

Areas such as the introduction of new technology and new organizational methods in business have so far been examined mainly by economists and sociologists and cover only recent developments.[30] Emphasis is placed on the role of the state in recent years or on incentives for modernization created by state policy and much less on the initiatives of business firms themselves.[31] Nevertheless, these analyses suggest that closer and more systematic historical research is necessary.

In the 1990s, a number of studies were published about publicly run companies. Most of these are utility firms, founded in the immediate post–Second World War period, with a monopoly over services such as telecommunications, electricity supply, water supply, urban and air transport, and so on.[32] They are the largest firms in the country, constituting, along with a few multinationals, the corporate sector of the economy. As their archives remain inaccessible to researchers, it is no coincidence that none of the studies was written by a historian, the authors usually being former chief executive officers of these firms, appointed by the government in power. The analysis hardly ever traces the history of these companies beyond the span of a decade at most, but it has the advantage of being based on privileged inside information. On the other hand, it tends to be rather biased, and it is often loaded with political rhetoric. Such works, however, were induced by growing political concern about public deficits and managerial deformities of the public sector, and they should be assessed within the changing framework of government policy during the past ten years. Historical analysis of the state sector, and especially of the utilities, will definitely be among the high priorities of Greek business history for the next decade. Consequently, the debate between the Chandlerian and non-Chandlerian paradigms will also be central.

[30] See Antigone Lymberaki, "The Dynamics of Change Under the Surface of Stagnation: Greek Manufacturing in the post-1974 Period," in Dritsas and Gourvish, *European Enterprise,* 247–66; and Maria Petmezidou, "Inter-Firm Collaboration and Innovation: How Do Greek Enterprises Respond?" ibid., 267–84.

[31] See Tassos Giannitsis, ed., *Viomichaniki kai Technologiki Politiki sten Hellada (Industrial and Technological Policy in Greece)* (Athens, 1993).

[32] See Dimitris Papoulias, *O demosios Tomeas se Krise (The State Sector in Crisis)* (Athens, 1991); D. Papoulias and C. Tsoukas, *Katefthynseis gia te metarrythmisi tou kratous (Guidelines for State Reform)* (Athens, 1998); the author was advisor to the secretary of state for industry, subsequently Prime Minister Constantinos Simitis. He was appointed chairman and managing director of the Organisation of Greek Telecommunications (OTE) and later of the Public Electricity Company (DEH). On the latter company see also Stathis Tsotsoros, *Energia kai Anaptyxi ste metapolemiki periodo: H DEH, 1950-1992 (Energy and Development in the Post-War Period: The Public Power Co., 1950-1992)* (Athens, 1995).

CONCLUSIONS AND FUTURE PROSPECTS

If we have to draw some conclusions, a general one should be that business history in Greece, though still not very sophisticated and certainly less developed than in other countries, including Mediterranean ones like Spain and Italy, has definitely gained ground in the past few years. Prospects, moreover, seem to be positive. Many economic historians present their work today as business history, but therein lies a potential danger that all economic history will become business history. There is a need, therefore, to define more rigorously the object of analysis. Apart from this, a future agenda of business history desiderata in Greece will depend on the degree of institutionalization of the new discipline, on the accessibility of sources, and on the state of finances. Above all, it will depend on the interest shown by researchers.

With regard to approaches, it seems that eclecticism cannot be avoided, since it is imposed to a large extent by the empirical reality that we wish to comprehend. More open communication, nevertheless, may eventually lead, through closer cooperation, to particular paths of research. A "Mediterranean connection" would seem to be almost a natural development for countries belonging to the region. Most Mediterranean societies and economies have exhibited important similarities in the process of development during the nineteenth and twentieth centuries. Elements of their business history group them together, as in the dominant presence both of a large state sector and of a multitude of SMEs. The works produced so far by Spanish, Italian, French, and Greek researchers seem to suggest that there is no single, exclusive model that may render intelligible a complex reality. Several models, one stressing the features of large multidivisional enterprises developed in the United States and elsewhere, as well as others that have a more regional relevance, are useful. The same works also point to the need for a synthesis resulting from the development and exploration of alternative perspectives. Any agenda for the future, therefore, should include the analysis of regional and national diversities, and its assessment against that of the Chandlerian and other paradigms. Both big firms, especially those of the state sector, and foreign multinationals operating in Greece should be placed at the center of future analysis and compared with SMEs. Different strategies and structures – formal and informal – regarding processes such as (to mention only a few) the diffusion and appropriation of new technology, the flow of information, investment diversification, labor strategies, and the perception of relations with politics and society at large should be part of such attempts. Entrepreneurial behavior, which has already begun to be researched, seems to have gathered sufficient momentum and will continue to be a central issue. This highlights the need to explore further aspects of social history that might be useful. The construction of a national typology informed by theory would, on the other hand, be put in context, embedding the Greek case in regional and world perspectives. Finally, of equal importance must be the establishment of better channels of communication between historians and social scientists on the one hand, and between historians and the business world on the other.

KEY WORKS

Agriantoni, Christina and Maria-Christina Hadjioannou, eds. *The Athens Silk-Industry Quarter*. Athens, 1995.

Dritsas, Margarita. *To Chroma tes Epitychias: He Helliniki viomehania chromaton, 1830–1990 (The Color of Success: The Greek Paint Industry, 1830–1990)*. Athens, 1995.

———. ed. *Facets of Greek Entrepreneurship in the Twentieth Century*. Athens, 1999.

Dritsas, Margarita and Terence R. Gourvish, eds. *European Enterprise: Strategies of Adaptation and Renewal in the Twentieth Century*. Athens, 1997.

Dritsas, Margarita, Hakan Lindgren, and Alice Teichova, eds. *L'Entreprise en Grèce et en Europe XIX–XXe siècles*. Athens, 1991.

Harlaftis, Gelina. *A History of Greek-Owned Shipping: The Making of an International Tramp Fleet, 1830 to the Present Day*. London and New York, 1996.

Leontaritis, George. "To helliniko ergatiko kinema kai to astiko kratos, 1910–1920" (The Greek Labor Movement and the Bourgeois State, 1910–1920). In *Meletemata gyro apo ton Venizelo kai ten epoche tou (Studies on Venizelos and His Era)*, ed. Thanos Veremis, Athens, 1980, 49–84.

Melios, Nicos and Evangelia Bafouni. *Elais S.A. 1920–1997: Opseis tes oikonomikes tes historias (Elais S.A. 1920–1997: Facets of Its Economic History)*. Neo Falero, 1997.

Moskof, Kostis. *Historia tou Kinimatos tes ergatikis taxis sten Hellada (History of the Labor Movement in Greece)*. Thessaloniki, 1979.

Pikramenou-Varfi, Dimitra. *O Spyridon Pavlides kai to glykismatopoieion tou (Spyridon Pavlides and His "Pastry Shop": The Early Years of the First Greek Industry)*. Athens, 1991.

Svoronos, Nicos G. *Histoire de la Grèce Moderne*. Paris, 1953.

Theodorou, Vasiliki. *To ergostasio emaye sten Kea, 1927–1957 (The Emaille Factory in Kea, 1927–1957)*. Kea, 1994.

13

The State of Business History in Japan

Cross-National Comparisons and International Relations

AKIRA KUDÔ

Japan's economy experienced a bubble, epitomized by stock and real estate speculation, during the second half of the 1980s. It then experienced the collapse of that economic bubble in 1990–1. During the 1990s, the Japanese economy faced an extended period of stagnation evidenced in low growth rates and increased unemployment rates (although there were, of course, alternating phases of good times and bad, i.e., a business cycle). For Japanese firms, too, the 1990s were a difficult decade. The decade caused deterioration in the performance of many firms, and failures affected not only small and medium-sized enterprises but large firms as well. In the retail sector supermarkets and department stores failed, while Hokkaido Takushoku Bank, Yamaichi Securities, and the Long Term Credit Bank of Japan failed one after the other in the financial sector. In the industrial sector or, more specifically, the core automobile sector in which Japanese firms had made world-class achievements, Nissan fell into business difficulties, looked to France's Renault for rescue, and consequently became affiliated with the French automaker.

Mrs. Takeo Kikkawa, Minoru Sawai, and Takao Shiba read the manuscript and gave me their valuable comments. I deeply appreciate their kindness. It goes without saying that any errors and omissions are entirely my own responsibility.

Japanese firms, which had swept over the world with their direct
investment offensive during the 1980s, faced stalemate and failure in their
overseas projects during the 1990s and successively pulled back. The
Japan that had risen so rapidly as an investment and creditor superpower
during the 1980s hit a massive wall in the 1990s. There was a feeling
that Japan might experience in only one generation the rise to and fall
from the status of investment and creditor power that in Great Britain
had taken two centuries to unfold. This drastic change in a relatively brief
period of time seems to have baffled Japanese business historians.

There are three problems concerning the Japanese firm that must be
worked out for the field of business history, a field of historical research
that, like Minerva's owl, always makes its appearance late. These three
problems overlap in layers. The first problem relates to the success of
Japanese firms. This problem is the explication of the causes for the phe-
nomenal achievements of Japanese firms after the Second World War and
especially in the ten years following the first oil crisis in 1973. Hidemasa
Morikawa, who has spearheaded research in business history in Japan,
has written on this point in a review of Alfred Chandler's *Scale and Scope*:

I cannot support the Professor's view that the cause for the stalling of
American capitalism lies in the excessiveness of global oligopolistic competition after the 1960s. Was not oligopolistic competition the condition that
forged organizational capabilities? It was not the intensification of oligopolistic competition that caused American industrial firms to stall but rather their
defeat by Japanese managerial enterprises in that competition. But why were
they beaten? We must ask why Japanese managerial firms won.... We must
study separately how organizational capabilities at large American, German,
British, and Japanese firms, as well as these firms' interrelationships, shifted
and how they were transformed after the 1960s. In so doing, might we
find that the flaws – the vestiges of personal capitalism – which link the
period of American competitive managerial capitalism's greatest prosperity
with its current defeat are immanent in that system? Were Japanese managerial enterprises able to achieve victory exploiting these flaws because they,
painstakingly and over many years, forged and accumulated organizational
capabilities that focused on human skills? It is necessary to shed light on
these kinds of problems.[1]

This was published in 1991. By curious coincidence, the bubble economy burst immediately thereafter. As a precautionary postscript, it should

[1] Hidemasa Morikawa, book review, *Keiei shigaku* (*Japan Business History Review*) 26,
no. 2 (1991): 65–8.

be noted that Morikawa's raising of these questions in no way loses its importance because of this recessionary state of affairs. Both then and now, such questions are important and appropriate.

Second, then, we must ask why the bubble economy occurred. It was a phenomenon that clearly showed the deterioration of Japan's economy, but did Japanese firms have any responsibility for it? Was the bubble economy a necessary consequence of Japanese managerial capitalism or was it rather undesirable deviation? Most centrally, did it demonstrate the failure of the Japanese firm?

Third, we must inquire about the causes for the genuine failures of Japanese firms. Because speculation will necessarily collapse at some point, the collapse of stock and real estate speculation was inevitable, as was the demise of the accompanying bubble economy. But one must ask again about the causes of the subsequent decade-long stagnation.

Japan's economy and enterprises, of course, had experienced crisis conditions numerous times before, even if we limit discussion to the postwar era. One might therefore argue that this period of long-term stagnation really is not worthy of surprise, but is merely a psychological problem or a normal condition for a capitalist economy. With even a bit of investigation into the scale and character of the long-term stagnation, though, it is safe to say that these arguments are based upon either excessive optimism or a thickheadedness unbecoming a crisis.

Where, then, are the causes of long-term stagnation to be found? Should factors external to the firm be named? Even in that case, should we point to international factors – globalization or Americanization – or to Japanese government failures in fiscal, trade, currency, industrial, or competition policies? Or were there problems within the firms themselves? Even within these possible explanations, there is likely room for divergence. For example, was a late response to international changes – such as globalization or Americanization – to blame, or was the cause first and foremost problems inherent in the enterprise system or in Japanese business management?

Taken in this way, all of these arguments – excepting those that trace everything to government failure – may be seen as placing responsibility more or less with the firm. In fact, interfirm relations, the main bank system, and government–business relations (including industrial policy and competition policy) are the main targets of attack in treatments of the Japanese firm by the disciplines of economics and business management. The management system and industrial relations have also come under fire, and even the nature of the production and research and development systems has been called into question.

BUSINESS HISTORY'S UNIQUE CONTRIBUTION

In business history, we must step back and calmly seek the causes rather than casually join the fray. That task requires a new explication of the causes for the generation of the bubble economy, of course, and the causes of the success of Japanese firms. In this sense, the three foregoing questions are piled up in layers. In other words, the history of success and failure of Japanese firms requires a consistent explanation. If industrial relations are emphasized as a factor in success, they may also have to be emphasized as a factor in failure. Taking on this set of three overlapping questions is the task imposed on scholars of Japanese business history.

It is not odd that various explanations should rise and fall with the rapid and dramatic transformation in the facts on the ground. Although uncritical applause under the influence of the success of Japanese-style management was rare in the field of business history, a fair amount of research rapidly grew stale. Business history research in Japan has been unable to respond adequately to this rapid transformation in the Japanese firm and its environment.[2] Hidemasa Morikawa, who has taken the lead in business history research in Japan, has also been a pioneer on this point. He has been quick to propose answers to sets of questions like these, especially on causes for the failure of the Japanese firm.[3] He has pointed out the deterioration of managerial capitalism in Japan and has found the chief cause for that deterioration to be the deterioration in top management. This explanation is not sufficiently persuasive, but the attempt at explanation should itself be highly praised. Japanese business historians have been called upon to continue in Morikawa's footsteps.

This essay takes as its task the description of the current state of business history in Japan as it relates to the Japanese firm. In this case, the current state will be taken to mean the period from the 1970s through the end of the 1990s. Naturally, I will touch on research from

---

[2] See, for example, the Kikkawa piece in Takeshi Yuzawa et al., *Erementaru keiei shi* (*Elemental Business History*) (Tokyo, 2000).

[3] Hidemasa Morikawa, *Toppu manejimento no keiei shi: Keieisha kigyô to kazoku kigyô* (*A Business History of Top Management: Managerial Enterprises and Family Enterprises*) (Tokyo, 1996). Its English version is id., *A History of Top Management in Japan: Managerial Enterprises and Family Enterprises* (New York, 2001).

before this period, research conducted outside Japan and research related to foreign firms as needed. Conversely, and due to my own narrowness of perspective, there will certainly be research that I will fail to touch on, even though it is important. For this I make my apology in advance.

This task is extremely difficult, even if we set aside the multilayered problematization of the three issues previously described. By way of excuse, I note that there is a tremendous volume of business history research in Japan, and this research is extremely varied in its quality. As of the year 2000, the Business History Association (BHA) had more than 850 members. The papers and publications produced by business history scholars (both members and nonmembers) have reached a prodigious volume, as even a glance through the year in review column in the *Keiei shigaku* (the journal of the Business History Association) shows. Moreover, these publications cover various aspects of business history both in Japan and abroad and from the seventeenth century to the present. The yearly review column in the journal has come to be divided among a number of authors each year. That scale of current research is something that I alone could not possibly cover.

So, I will first try to give as objective as possible an overview of the current state of the discipline. Even so, some subjectivity is unavoidable, but at least that part focused on institutionalized aspects will be objective. Next, I will sacrifice objectivity and draw the discussion toward my own interests. That is, I will narrow the focus to the fields of comparative and international relations history, which I think are the most important currents, and then select and introduce several works considered to be representative in those fields (here too I have had no choice but to abandon comprehensiveness). This essay can only hope to introduce in a brief way the current state of business history in Japan.

A SERIES THAT SETS THE RESEARCH STANDARD FOR JAPANESE BUSINESS HISTORY

There is probably no objection to suggesting that the five-volume series *Nihon keiei shi* (Japanese Business History) (Tokyo, 1995) is the publication to pick up first in order to gain an overview of the current state of Japanese business history research in Japan. This series consists of the following volumes with their editors: Volume 1 – *Kinseiteki keiei no hatten (The Development of Early-Modern*

Business) (Shigeaki Yasuoka and Masatoshi Amano, eds.);[4] Volume 2 - *Keiei kakushin to kôgyôka (Business Innovation and Industrialization)* (Matao Miyamoto and Takeshi Abe, eds.);[5] Volume 3 - *Dai kigyô jidai no tôrai (The Arrival of the Age of Large Enterprise)* (Tsunehiko Yui and Eisuke Daitô, eds.);[6] Volume 4 - *"Nihonteki" keiei no renzoku to danzetsu (Continuities and Discontinuities in "Japanese-Style" Management)* (Hiroaki Yamazaki and Takeo Kikkawa, eds.);[7] and Volume 5 - *Kôdo seichô wo koete (Beyond High Growth)* (Hidemasa Morikawa and Seiichirô Yonekura, eds.).[8]

[4] Volume 1 includes the following chapters with authors: Chapter 1 - "Overview: From the Edo Period to the 1880s" (Shigeaki Yasuoka); Chapter 2 - "Merchant Wealth Accumulation and the Form of Enterprise" (Kenjirô Ishikawa and Shigeaki Yasuoka); Chapter 3 - "Business Organization and Business Management" (Masahiro Uemura and Matao Miyamoto); Chapter 4 - "The Employment System and Labor Management" (Shigeaki Yasuoka and Akiko Chimoto); Chapter 5 - "Accounting Organization and Bookkeeping Techniques" (Noboru Nishikawa); Chapter 6 - "Early-Modern Distinctiveness of Business Ideals" (Shigeaki Yasuoka, Makoto Seoka, and Teiichirô Fujita); Chapter 7 - "Business and the Shift of an Early-Modern Paradigm" (Masatoshi Amano).

[5] Volume 2 includes the following chapters with authors: Chapter 1 - "Overview: The 1880s to 1915" (Matao Miyamoto and Takeshi Abe); Chapter 2 - "Building the Base for Business Development" (Kaoru Sugihara); Chapter 3 - "The Sudden Rise of Enterprise, Modern Business, and Traditional Business" (Masayuki Tanimoto and Takeshi Abe); Chapter 4 - "Industrialization, Trading Companies, Shipping, and Finance" (Mariko Tatsuki); Chapter 5 - "The Heavy and Chemical Industries and Engineers" (Minoru Sawai); Chapter 6 - "Meiji-Period Men of Means and the Company System" (Matao Miyamoto and Takeshi Abe); Chapter 7 - "Establishment of the Factory System and Labor Management" (Kônosuke Odaka).

[6] Volume 3 includes the following chapters with authors: Chapter 1 - "Overview: 1915 to 1937" (Tsunehiko Yui); Chapter 2 - "The Structure of Large Enterprise and Zaibatsu" (Haruhito Takeda); Chapter 3 - "From Technology Introduction to Technology Development" (Shin Hasegawa); Chapter 4 - "Modernization of the Factory Management System and Organizational Capacity" (Satoshi Sasaki); Chapter 5 - "Marketing and Distribution Mechanisms in the Interwar Period" (Eisuke Daitô); Chapter 6 - "Funding Procurement in Large Enterprise" (Shôichi Asajima); Chapter 7 - "The Manager's View of Firm and Labor" (Tsunehiko Yui and Masakazu Shimada).

[7] Volume 4 includes the following chapters with authors: Chapter 1 - "Overview: 1937 to 1951" (Hiroaki Yamazaki); Chapter 2 - "Hegemony of the Salaried Managers: The Emergence of the Japanese-Style Managerial Enterprise" (Hideaki Miyajima); Chapter 3 - "The Formation of the Japanese-Style Production System" (Kazuo Wada and Takao Shiba); Chapter 4 - "Japanese Introduction and Transformation of American Business Management Techniques" (Kinsaburô Sunaga and Izumi Nonaka); Chapter 5 - "The Formation of Japanese-Style Employment Relations: Employment Regulations, Wages, and 'Employees' " (Shinji Sugayama); Chapter 6 - "The Transformation of Intermediate Organizations and the Formation of Competitive Oligopoly Structures" (Takeo Kikkawa); Chapter 7 - "The Emergence of Postwar-Style Industrial Policy" (Tsuneo Suzuki).

[8] Volume 5 includes the following chapters with authors: Chapter 1 - "Overview: 1955 to the 1990s" (Hidemasa Morikawa); Chapter 2 - "Long-Term Relational Connections and

A number of compilations of business history research have already been produced in Japan. One representative thereof is the six-volume series supervised by Mataji Miyamoto and Keiichirô Nakagawa, *Nihon keiei shi kôza* (*A Course in Japanese Business History*) (Tokyo, 1976– 7). The five-volume series *Nihon keiei shi* (*Japanese Business History*), published twenty years later, is not only the most current work but also demonstrates the present level of business history in Japan. Comprehensive reviews have naturally pointed out a number of flaws in this series; however, by and large, they praise it highly.[9] The series is not merely an overview but also contains a large number of laboriously crafted pieces with original content.

ACTIVITIES OF THE BUSINESS HISTORY ASSOCIATION

As these organized publishing activities show, research in business history in Japan has been relatively well institutionalized. If one were to trace the development of business history, one would arrive back at the pioneering findings of Yoshitarô Wakimura, Mataji Miyamoto, and others prior to World War II. The institutional foundations of business history as a discipline belong to the postwar period, though. The BHA was established in 1964. This constituted a landmark in the institutionalization of the discipline. The association has published the journal *Keiei shigaku* since 1966. As noted earlier, membership in the BHA as of 2000 exceeded 850, which makes the association among the largest academic organizations in the field of business history in the world. Over 300 business history professors (including associate professors) are affiliated with universities throughout Japan. There are approximately forty chairs of business history (including Japanese business history, Western business history, foreign business history, and general business history) in departments of economics, commerce, and business management at

Enterprise Keiretsu" (Jurô Hashimoto); Chapter 3 - "Postwar Top Management" (Hiroyuki Itami); Chapter 4 - "The Financial System in Postwar Japan: Banks, Enterprises, Government" (Tetsuji Okazaki); Chapter 5 - "Internationalization and Japanese-Style Management" (Hideki Yoshihara); Chapter 6 - "Enterprise and Government: The Third Hand" (Masaru Udagawa and Etsuo Abe); Chapter 7 - "The Appearance and Demise of the Japanese System as Shared Illusion" (Seiichirô Yonekura).

[9] Reviews by Yôtarô Sakudô, Kanji Ishii, Takeshi Ôshio, Satoshi Saitô, and Kiyoshi Nakamura in *Keiei shigaku* (*Japan Business History Review*) 32, no. 1 (1997); and those by Masaharu Uemura, Tetsuji Okazaki, and Satoshi Saitô in *Shakai keizai shigaku* (*Socioeconomic History Review*) 64, no. 5 (1998–9). An English translation of the former is found in the English journal *Japanese Yearbook on Business History* 15 (1998).

universities across Japan. Moreover, courses in business history are as numerous in business management departments and business information
sciences departments as courses in marketing.[10]

Initially, the specialties of BHA members included (and still do) disciplines such as economic history, social history, labor history, history of
technology, business management, and sociology, in addition to business
history. The association came to foster the shared interest in business history among these fields. One factor that contributed to this growth, and
that merits special mention, was the energetic introduction of overseas
research trends. These exercises in comparative business history by
Keiichirô Nakagawa, Yasuo Mishima, Shin'ichi Yonekawa, and others in
the initial period exerted a profound influence on subsequent work.[11] By
dint of efforts such as these, business history established its significance
as an independent discipline. The downside of this process was the lack
of a broad-ranging debate on method in business history, with the result
that the discipline went on without a clear consensus. The overall theme
of the 1999 annual nationwide BHA conference was methodology, and
that was probably the first time that an attempt had been made to deal
with the topic in the history of overall conference themes at the national
meeting.

The activities of the BHA focus on the publication of its journal, *Keiei
shigaku*, but also cover a number of other areas. Aside from sponsoring
an annual national conference, the association has active regional blocs in
Kantô, Kansai, Kyûshû, Chûbu, and Hokkaidô. The activities of the BHA
from its founding through 1984 have been assembled in a volume, *Keiei
shigaku no 20-nen: Kaiko to tenbô* (*Twenty Years of Business History:
Retrospect and Prospect*) (Tokyo, 1985), which was a pioneering attempt
even in international comparative perspective.

The BHA has been engaged in international activities from its establishment. Since 1974 it has sponsored an annual international conference
on business history, known as the Fuji Conference, that has enriched the
comparative business history approach. The results of the research presented at the conference have been published by the University of Tokyo

[10] See the papers and materials for distribution concerning the conference theme "The State
and Issues of Business History Education" at the BHA 2000 annual conference.
[11] Keiichirô Nakagawa, *Hikaku keiei shi kenkyû 1: Hikaku keiei shi josetsu* (*Studies in
Comparative Business History 1: Introduction to Comparative Business History*) (Tokyo,
1981); Yasuo Mishima, *Keiei shigaku no tenkai* (*The Development of Business History*)
(Kyoto, 1961; expanded edition, 1970); Shin'ichi Yonekawa, *Keiei shigaku: Tanjô, hatten,
tenbô* (*Business History: Its Birth, Development and Prospects*) (Tokyo, 1973).

Press (volumes 1–20) and, from the fifth series (1994–8) on, by Oxford University Press. The sixth series, starting in 1999, is currently in process. One of the ripple effects of the Fuji Conference has been the start of bilateral conferences. Starting with a Japanese–German meeting and then adding Japanese–British and Japanese–French meetings, these bilateral conferences have each been held a number of times. The BHA has played a leading role on this front as well, and the bilateral conferences have each yielded a book.[12] Since 1984, the BHA has also published the English-language annual *Japanese Yearbook on Business History*. Its book review columns are probably the most suitable guides for English-speaking readers. In terms of international activities, then, the BHA may be placed in the active category, relative both to learned societies in the humanities and social sciences in Japan and to associations related to business history worldwide. I would like to acknowledge in particular the Taniguchi Foundation's long-standing interest and assistance in this area.

TEXTBOOKS, CASEBOOKS, AND COMPANY HISTORIES

I will now leave the BHA and return to my overview, limiting myself to the institutionalized dimension. A number of textbooks on business history have been published. Those that have an established reputation or have come to be regarded as standards include Tsunehiko Yui and Johannes Hirschmeier's book in English. Yôtarô Sakudô and others and Yoshitaka Suzuki and others have also produced respected textbooks, as has Akio Ôkouchi.[13] A relatively recent work that probably sets the current research standard has been produced by Matao Miyamoto and others.[14] Takeshi Yuzawa and others have produced a work that sets the current academic standard and covers the United States, Britain, and Germany, in addition to Japan.[15] Finally, Masaru Udagawa and Seishi Nakamura

[12] A few examples are: Keiichirô Nakagawa and Tsunehiko Yui, eds., *Organization and Management 1900-1930: Proceedings of the Japan-Germany Conference on Business History* (Tokyo, 1981); and Etsuo Abe and Robert Fitzgerald, eds., *The Origins of Japanese Industrial Power* (London, 1995).

[13] Tsunehiko Yui and Johannes Hirschmeier, *The Development of Japanese Business, 1600-1973* (London, 1975) (also published in Japanese as *Nihon no keiei hatten* [Tokyo, 1977]); Yôtarô Sakudô et al., *Nihon keiei shi (Japanese Business History)* (Kyoto, 1980); Yoshitaka Suzuki, Etsuo Abe, and Seiichirô Yonekura, *Keiei shi (Business History)* (Tokyo, 1987); and Akio Ôkouchi, *Keiei shi kôgi (Lectures on Business History)* (Tokyo, 1991).

[14] Matao Miyamoto et al., *Nihon keiei shi (Japanese Business History)* (Tokyo, 1995).

[15] Takeshi Yuzawa et al., *Erementaru keiei shi (Elemental Business History)* (Tokyo, 2000).

have crafted a textbook designed to attract the interest of beginning students.[16]

Although it is not a textbook, *Kindai Nihon keiei shi no kiso chishiki: Meiji ishin ki kara gendai made* (*Fundamentals of Modern Japanese Business History: From the Meiji Restoration to the Present*) (Tokyo, 1974; expanded edition, 1979), edited by Keiichirô Nakagawa, Hidemasa Morikawa, and Tsunehiko Yui, is a handy, reliable encyclopedia even today. The three-volume series *Sengo Nihon keiei shi* (*Postwar Japanese Business History*) (Tokyo, 1990–1), edited by Shin'ichi Yonekawa, Kôichi Shimokawa, and Hiroaki Yamazaki, is a full-scale treatment of postwar business history. Although research on the postwar period increased by leaps and bounds during the 1990s, especially among younger scholars, this series remains the touchstone of that movement.

In recent years, the publication of casebooks has become prominent. Typical of these works are a four-volume series edited by Hiroyuki Itami, Tadao Kagono, Matao Miyamoto, and Seiichirô Yonekura, *Keesubukku Nihon kigyô no keiei kôdô* (*Casebook on the Business Behavior of Japanese Firms*) (Tokyo, 1998), and a book edited by Masaru Udagawa entitled *Keesubukku Nihon no kigyôka katsudô* (*Casebook on Entrepreneurial Activity in Japan*) (Tokyo, 1999).

The publication of company histories is closely related to business history research, and publication of company histories is flourishing in Japan. The *Kaisha shi sôgô mokuroku* (*General Index of Company Histories*) (Tokyo, 1986; expanded and revised edition, 1996), edited by the Japan Business History Institute, lists more than 8,000 company histories. In some cases, business historians participate in the writing of company histories, which then feed back into business history research. These company histories are especially valuable for the postwar period, for which there are problems of access to internal company materials and thus little case-study research on individual firms. Of course, company histories often have a tendency to turn into hagiographies of the firm or its top management and, as such, have drawn appropriate criticism. Even so, the quality and quantity of company histories in Japan are at a high standard internationally, and Japan can take pride in being one of the several company history superpowers in the world. Some

---

[16] Masaru Udagawa and Kiyoshi Nakamura, eds., *Materiaru Nihon keiei shi: Edo ki kara genzai made* (*Materials on Japanese Business History: From the Edo Period to the Present*) (Tokyo, 1999).

academically important works related to company histories are *Gaikoku kigyô oyobi kigyôsha keieisha sôgô mokuroku* (*General Index to Foreign Company, Entrepreneur, and Manager Histories*) (Tokyo, 1979), edited by the Japan BHA Tenth Anniversary Project Committee; Nobuhisa Fujita, ed., *Shashi no kenkyû* (*Research on Company History*) (Tokyo, 1990); and *Nihon kaisha shi kenkyû sôran* (*Compendium of Japanese Company History Research*) (Tokyo, 1996), edited by the BHA.

THE FLOURISHING OF FOREIGN BUSINESS HISTORY

One of the characteristic features of the study of business history in Japan is vigorous research on foreign business history. The United States, Britain, Germany, and France are the principal subjects of research. In the background of this focus lies Japan's late-developer perspective, wherein the Western firm has traditionally served as the model. Starting from that perspective, comparison with the Japanese firm came to be attempted repeatedly. After 1970 or so, when Japan's economy had finished catching up, changes became apparent in the perspective of foreign business history research and the perspective of comparison with Japanese firms. A more explicit comparison came to be emphasized, and the previous standards, vantage point, and rigors of comparisons were called into question.

Here, limiting myself to monographs, I will introduce only a very small portion of foreign business history research. A number of works on the United States have been published, but here I will limit myself to Haruto Shiomi, Seigo Mizota, Akitake Taniguchi, and Shinji Miyazaki's book on the formation of American big business, *Amerika biggu bijinesu seiritsu shi* (*History of the Formation of Big Business in America*) (Tokyo, 1986). Several books on Britain may be noted – Keiichirô Nakagawa's comprehensive studies, Takeshi Yuzawa's book on railroads, Yoshitaka Suzuki's book on entrepreneurial activities in the age of the Industrial Revolution, Etsuo Abe's book on steel companies, Chikage Hidaka's book on the cotton industry, and Takashi Iida's book on the securities market.[17]

[17] Keiichirô Nakagawa, *Hikaku keiei shi 2: Igirisu keiei shi* (*Comparative Business History 2: British Business History*) (Tokyo, 1986); Takeshi Yuzawa, *Igirisu tetsudô keiei shi* (*Business History of British Railroads*) (Tokyo, 1988); Yoshitaka Suzuki, *Keiei shi: Igirisu sangyô kakumei to kigyôsha katsudô* (*Business History: Industrial Revolution and Entrepreneurial Activities in Britain*) (Tokyo, 1982); Etsuo Abe, *Daiei teikoku no sangyô haken: Igirisu tekkô kigyô kôbô shi* (*The British Empire's Industrial Hegemony:*

Works on Germany include Hisashi Watanabe's book on industrialization, Sachio Kaku's book on the chemical industry, Sachio Imakubo's book on the electric giant Siemens, and Akira Kudô's book on the chemical industry.[18] Works on France include Isao Hirota's work on the economy and society in the interwar period, Jun Sakudô's book on the chemical industry, and Terushi Hara's recent work on the economic history in the interwar period.[19] On Europe in general, there is a collection on contemporary business history, *Gendai Yôroppa keiei shi* (*Contemporary European Business History*) (Tokyo, 1996), which focuses on regional characteristics, edited by Hisashi Watanabe and Jun Sakudô. The foregoing works are just the tip of the iceberg in the thriving field of foreign business history.

Research on developing countries, and especially on Asian business history, has finally come into its own in recent years against a backdrop of economic and business development in that region. Two works that show some of the achievements in this area are Atsushi Mikami's work on family business in India and Fumikatsu Kubo's work on the Japanese sugar industry in colonial Formosa.[20] Asian business history is indispensable for contextualizing Japanese business development in the non-Western European world, providing, for example, comparative materials for generalizing Japanese *zaibatsu* firms as a case of family enterprise.

The Rise and Fall of British Steel Firms) (Tokyo, 1993); Chikage Hidaka, *Eikoku mengyô suitai no kôzu* (*The Decline of the British Cotton Industry*) (Tokyo, 1995); and Takashi Iida, *Igirisu no sangyô hatten to shôken shijô* (*The Development of Industry and the Securities Market in Britain*) (Tokyo, 1997).

[18] Hisashi Watanabe, *Rain no sangyô kakumei: Genkeizaiken no keisei katei* (*The Rhine Industrial Revolution: The Emerging Process of Economic Proto-Sphere*) (Tokyo, 1986); Sachio Kaku, *Doitsu kagaku kôgyô shi josetsu* (*An Introduction to the History of the German Chemical Industry*) (Kyoto, 1986); Sachio Imakubo, *19-seikimatsu Doitsu no kôjô* (*The Late-19th-Century German Factory*) (Tokyo, 1996); and Akira Kudô, *Gendai Doitsu kagaku kigyô shi: IG Farben no seiritsu, tenkai, kaitai* (*A History of the Modern German Chemical Industry: The Establishment, Development and Dissolution of IG Farben*) (Kyoto, 1999).

[19] Isao Hirota, *Gendai Furansu no shiteki keisei: Ryôtaisenkanki no keizai to shakai* (*The Foundation of Modern France: Economy and Society Between the Wars*) (Tokyo, 1994); Jun Sakudô, *Furansu kagaku kôgyô shi kenkyû: Kokka to shakai* (*Studies in the History of the French Chemical Industy: State and Society*) (Tokyo, 1995); and Terushi Hara, *Furansu senkanki keizai shi kenkyû* (*Studies in French Economic History in the Interwar Period*) (Tokyo, 1999).

[20] Atsushi Mikami, *Indo zaibatsu keiei shi kenkyû* (*Business History Research on Indian Family Business Groups*) (Tokyo, 1993); and Fumikatsu Kubo, *Shokuminchi kigyô keiei shi ron: "Jun kokusaku kaisha" no jisshôteki kenkyû* (*The Business History of Colonial Enterprises: Empirical Studies of "Parastatal Companies"*) (Tokyo, 1997).

JAPANESE LARGE-FIRM BUSINESS HISTORY

Business history research on Japanese firms has concentrated on large firms. Thus, *zaibatsu* firms have been the focus of research on the prewar period, and firms belonging to business groups have been the center of research on the postwar era.

One comprehensive survey of prewar *zaibatsu* firms has been produced: *Nihon zaibatsu keiei shi* (*The Business History of Japanese Family Business Groups*), a seven-volume series. It is also worthwhile to mention Yasuo Mishima, Yasuaki Nagasawa, Takao Shiba, Nobuhisa Fujita, and Hidetatsu Satô's book on the Mitsubishi *zaibatsu* during the Second World War, *Dai 2 ji taisen to Mitsubishi zaibatsu* (*The Second World War and the Mitsubishi Zaibatsu*) (Tokyo, 1987). Regarding the research on the prewar *zaibatsu*, I would like to focus especially here on the research of two authors who made great use of a cross-national comparative perspective.

One of these authors is Shigeaki Yasuoka, whose results are collected in several books by him on cross-national comparative history of *zaibatsu*-owned enterprises in Japan and family business in the world. It is his focus on the relationship between ownership and management in the *zaibatsu*-affiliated large enterprises, his attempt at specific cross-national comparisons between the *zaibatsu*-affiliated large enterprises and family-owned enterprises in Asia as well as in the West, and his proposal of the *Gesamteigentum* (whole ownership) concept that have set a new standard.[21] The other author is Hidemasa Morikawa, whose work is collected in a book on the business history of *zaibatsu* in Japanese[22] and an English book: *Zaibatsu: The Rise and Fall of Family Enterprise Groups in Japan* (Tokyo, 1992). While Morikawa accepted Chandler's results from *The Visible Hand* and *Strategy and Structure*, he pushed for a revision of those books' fundamental arguments. Morikawa proposed a perspective that emphasizes individual managers rather than the hierarchical organization of managers. From this perspective,

---

[21] Representative are Shigeaki Yasuoka, *Zaibatsu keisei shi no kenkyū* (*Studies on the Formative History of the Zaibatsu*) (Kyoto, 1970; expanded edition, 1998); id., *Zaibatsu keiei no rekishiteki kenkyū: Shoyū to keiei no kokusai hikaku* (*Historical Research on Zaibatsu Management: A Cross-National Comparison of Ownership and Management*) (Tokyo, 1998).

[22] Representative are Hidemasa Morikawa, *Zaibatsu no keieishiteki kenkyū* (*A Business History Approach to the Zaibatsu*) (Tokyo, 1980); id., *Zaibatsu: The Rise and Fall of Family Enterprise Groups in Japan* (Tokyo, 1992). (The English-language work is not merely a translation of the Japanese.)

Morikawa clarified empirically the dynamism of competition and cooperation between family owners and salaried managers over the right to
manage *zaibatsu* enterprises (*Business History Review* 64, no. 4 [1990]:
716-25).

Research, even on the prewar era alone, naturally extends to various issues, including the differences among *zaibatsu* - such as those between
old and new *zaibatsu* or those due to the industrial sector - and the argument that juxtaposes the idea of the *Konzern* (concern) to the *zaibatsu*
concept. On this score, I offer only one recent work, Shôichi Asajima and
Takeshi Ôshio's book on Shôwa Denkô, *Shôwa Denkô seiritsu shi no
kenkyû* (*Research on the Formative History of Shôwa Denkô*) (Tokyo,
1997).

There is also a great deal of research on postwar business groups and
the large firms affiliated with them. A small sampling of such works
includes a volume on business groups before and after the Second
World War edited by Jurô Hashimoto and Haruhito Takeda; a book written by Masahiro Shimotani on *keiretsu* and business groups; a volume
on some relevant industries' development edited by Haruhito Takeda;
Takeo Kikkawa's work on the continuity–discontinuity debate; a volume on the postwar enterprise system edited by Jurô Hashimoto; a
volume from a Fuji Conference on business groups edited by Takao
Shiba and Masahiro Shimotani; and a volume on interfirm competition edited by Masaru Udagawa, Takeo Kikkawa, and Junjirô Shintaku.[23]
Each of these books works from the premise that there is an issue
in the continuities and discontinuities between the prewar and postwar eras. Further, this problematization is shown quite clearly, especially in Kikkawa's work and in the volume edited by Hashimoto and
Takeda.

---

[23] Jurô Hashimoto and Haruhito Takeda, eds., *Nihon keizai no hatten to kigyô shûdan* (*Business Groups and the Development of the Japanese Economy*) (Tokyo, 1992); Masahiro
Shimotani, *Nihon no keiretsu to kigyô gurûpu: Sono rekishi to riron* (*Japan's Keiretsu
and Business Groups: History and Theory*) (Tokyo, 1993); Haruhito Takeda, ed., *Nihon
sangyô hatten no dainamizumu* (*The Dynamism of Japanese Industrial Development*)
(Tokyo, 1995); Takeo Kikkawa, *Nihon no kigyô shûdan: Zaibatsu tono renzoku to
danzetsu* (*Japan's Business Groups: Continuity and Discontinuity with Family Business Groups*) (Tokyo, 1996); Jurô Hashimoto, ed., *Nihon kigyô shisutemu no sengo shi*
(*Postwar History of the Japanese Enterprise System*) (Tokyo, 1996); Takao Shiba and
Masahiro Shimotani, eds., *Beyond the Firm: Business Groups in International and Historical Perspective* (Oxford, 1997); and Masaru Udagawa, Takeo Kikkawa, and Junjirô
Shintaku, eds., *Nihon no kigyôkan kyôsô* (*Interfirm Competition in Japan*) (Tokyo,
2000).

AN EXAMPLE OF EXPLICIT CROSS-NATIONAL
COMPARISON

As noted previously, the study of business history in Japan has from the outset shown a strong awareness of cross-national comparison. The study of large enterprises has also taken such an awareness as a given. Cross-national comparative business history has been a powerful thread in two recently published collections of essays, a volume edited by Keiichirô Nakagawa and another edited by Hidemasa Morikawa and Tsunehiko Yui.[24] Hiromi Shioji and T. D. Keeley have provided a direct comparison of distribution systems in Japan and the United States in *Jidôsha diiraa no nichibei hikaku* (*A Comparison of Automobile Dealers in Japan and the United States*) (Fukuoka, 1994).

With the partial exception of Yasuoka and some others, however, most of these works (including those coming out of the Fuji Conference and bilateral conferences) stop at implicit comparison. Most important at the present stage are attempts at explicit cross-national comparison. Implicit cross-national comparison tends more or less to assume existing methods and frameworks. If we desire methodological breakthroughs we must actually attempt, with our own hands, explicit cross-national comparison, even if we are hindered by our lack of knowledge. Akio Ôkouchi and Haruhito Takeda's edited volume, *Kigyôsha katsudô to kigyô shisutemu: Dai kigyô taisei no nichiei hikaku shi* (*Entrepreneurial Activity and the Enterprise System: A Historical Comparison of Large Enterprise Systems in Japan and Britain*) (Tokyo, 1993), which approaches this issue head on, is one of a small number of such works. Let us enter this collection of essays and introduce and evaluate them.

[24] Keiichirô Nakagawa, ed., *Kigyô keiei no rekishiteki kenkyû* (*Historical Research on Business Management*) (Tokyo, 1990); and Hidemasa Morikawa and Tsunehiko Yui, eds., *Kokusai hikaku kokusai kankei no keiei shi* (*Business History in Cross-National and International Relations Perspectives*) (Nagoya, 1997). Morikawa and Yui's edited volume contains a number of essays: Keiichirô Nakagawa, "Markets and Business Organization: A Three-way Typology of National Economies"; Yô Ten'itsu, "Cross-National Characteristics of Chinese Family Business"; Yukio Yamashita, "Some Thoughts on 'Motivation': From the Standpoint of Discovering Mankind"; Katsumi Tomizawa, "Specialized Managerial Technicians versus 'Civilian' Managers: The Contest of Two Ethos in Industrial Democracy in Post-World War I America"; Shin Gotô, "Merits and Demerits of Planned Shipbuilding: Its Role in the Postwar Recovery of Japan's Shipping Industry, 1948–1960"; Hidemasa Morikawa, "Government and Business: Suggestions for Cross-National Comparison"; Masaaki Kobayashi, "Cross-National Comparison of Business Modernization: Looking at American Research on Japan."

The book selects Japan and Britain as its objects of comparison and limits itself approximately to the period between the two world wars.[25] Comparison is clearly in mind in almost all of the chapters, which are then paired neatly. The book is a meticulously constructed comparative business history. Two chapters that make particularly worthwhile reading are Ôkouchi's comparison of Nakajima Aircraft and Rolls-Royce and Fujimoto and Tidd's Japanese–British comparison on the introduction of the Ford system. The former chapter relates how Rolls-Royce made pathbreaking achievements in aircraft engine development while Nakajima Aircraft failed to do so, stressing hypothetically the existence or lack of excellent managers as a factor in differentiating performances. The latter chapter traces and compares the history of the transfer and introduction of the Ford system into Britain and Japan in the automobile industry, the sector that is the prototype for American-style mass production and the large-firm system. Both chapters are attempts at extremely desirable forms of comparison that emphasize the importance of comparison in light of international relations.

The book is an attempt to generalize the individual cases at the level of business histories of the respective Japanese and British firms. Even viewed apart from the task of comparison, the book has been put together so that, by reading each chapter, one can obtain an overall picture of Japanese and British firms between the two world wars. The reason for this is that the five themes the book takes up basically cover the whole of business management.

I would like to add some critical evaluations on two points. The first has to do with comparisons with the United States. Ôkouchi notes in his preface, "Viewed globally, the development of American business society was a single, special experience, and while the Chandlerian understanding of the firm and image of history that took the U.S. as a model is one prototype, it is not history's royal road." In the same space Takeda, too, says "The large enterprise system is itself a historical presence. The various features that the system shows must be contextualized and taken up along with the special characteristics of the United States." I would have liked the comparisons with the United States, especially those with

[25] The constituent sections and their authors are as follows: 1 – "Enterprise Form and Holding Company Functions" (Yoshitaka Suzuki and Haruhito Takeda); 2 – "Interfirm Relations and the Business System" (Chikage Hidaka and Haruhito Takeda); 3 – "Distribution Mechanisms and Marketing" (Kazuo Wada and Louisa Rubinfein); 4 – "Production Rationalization and Labor Management" (Tomoji Onozuka and Eisuke Daitô); 5 – "Research and Development and Technological Innovation" (Akio Ôkouchi, Takahiro Fujimoto, and Joseph Tidd).

the American large-enterprise system, to have been executed that clearly throughout the entire book. Above all, whether the subject is production technology or marketing, one cannot talk about business management in any country in the twentieth century, including the interwar period, if one leaves out the transfer of technology and management skill from the United States. It is impossible to proceed without comparison vis-à-vis the United States, not because of Chandler, but because America was America. In this book, too, there is certainly full awareness of this point in the individual chapters. The thought pieces by Suzuki and Wada are particularly aware of this, and such overtones are also strong in other sections. But it seems as though comparison with the United States has been suppressed in the book as a whole.

The other evaluation has to do with the time period this book has covered. The book has been limited to the interwar period and after, when Japan's large-enterprise system might finally be worthy of comparison with that of Britain. In actuality, though, the handling of the time period varies from chapter to chapter. One feels the relative dynamism of the chapters by Suzuki and by Fujimoto and Tidd, in which the interwar period and the period after World War II are given equal treatment. Ironically, the book's strength lies in those places where coverage was not strictly limited to the interwar period. This is probably not a chance outcome. The interwar period was an exceptional one in which the environment of the firm moved from world war to world depression to the formation of blocs in the world economy. It was an exceptional period in the history of the large-enterprise system as well, in which the international cartel was becoming the prototypical organization. The various peculiarities of the period are thus impressed upon the activities of entrepreneurs and upon the enterprise system, and the book pays attention to this important facet. In order to contextualize these peculiarities, the preceding and subsequent periods should be brought into range clearly. By expanding the time period and thus pursuing explicit cross-national comparison more effectively, this book could have been an even more significant work.

RESEARCH THAT PROVIDES METHODOLOGICAL SUGGESTIONS

Explicit cross-national comparison is needed especially due to the keenly felt need for methodological breakthroughs in the field of business history. Conversely, however, it is extremely difficult to do explicit cross-national comparison without a methodologically coherent study. The work of two scholars is suggestive on this point.

One, Shin'ichi Yonekawa, proposed the "contemporary absolute comparison" perspective, from which he actively implemented explicit cross-national comparisons. In the process of pursuing a cross-national comparison of business management in the cotton industry, Yonekawa asserted the importance not of comparison at the same stage, which has traditionally been the method chosen in Japan, but of comparison only in the same era. He gave as his reason for this stance that "Each country's firms participate in the formation of the world market, and what determines their future is nothing other than competition in that market." Yonekawa noted that "They interactively take part and make rules through the world market. This is none other than the realistic base for contemporary cross-national comparison."[26] His long-term study of the management of firms in the cotton industry based on this perspective was recently compiled in a series of volumes.[27] This body of empirical research provides the punch to demolish the methodological discussions that smack of empty theory, and it provides important suggestions for future cross-national comparative research in business history.

The other scholar is Yoshitaka Suzuki. By expanding the Chandler model, Suzuki made cross-national comparisons of the hierarchical structure of large enterprises in the twentieth century and situated the Japanese firm among them. He argued that the firm first internalizes those business resources for which the transaction costs in the market are highest. The firm is then constructed so that it is able to monitor, adjust, and distribute those business resources. Using this perspective, Suzuki attempted to make a typology of business organization. The typology characterized the Japanese enterprise organization as a direct control organization that developed from the internalization of labor markets, as opposed to the American functional organization, in which

[26] Shin'ichi Yonekawa, "The Road to Comparative Business History: Focusing on Industry History," *Hitotsubashi ronsô* 79, no. 4 (1978): 42–59; id., "Comparative Economic History," in *Shakai keizai shigaku no kadai to tenbô* (*Issues and Prospects for Socioeconomic History*), ed. Shakai keizai shi gakkai (Tokyo, 1984), 354–61.

[27] Shin'ichi Yonekawa, *Bôsekigyô no hikaku keiei shi kenkyû: Igirisu, Indo, Amerika, Nihon* (*A Comparative Business History of the Spinning Industry: Britain, India, America, Japan*) (Tokyo, 1994); id., *Tôzai bôseki keiei shi* (*A Business History of Spinning: East and West*) (Tokyo, 1997); id., *Tôzai sen'i keiei shi* (*A Business History of Textiles: East and West*) (Tokyo, 1998); id., *Bôseki kigyô no hasan to fusai* (*Bankruptcy and Debt in Spinning Firms*) (Tokyo, 2000).

goods markets had been internalized, or the British holding company organization, in which primarily capital markets had been internalized.[28] This expansion or universalization of the Chandler model has the potential to bring about the development of a cross-national comparative business history that incorporates national and historical differences in labor and capital markets.

HISTORY OF INTERNATIONAL BUSINESS RELATIONS

As the overseas direct investment of Japanese firms became regularized and business management became more internationalized or globalized during and after the 1970s, attention in the business history field turned to the international expansion of Japanese firms. When inward direct investment finally became regularized in the 1990s, research on the activities of foreign firms in Japan also finally started to become animated. Finally, as some multinational firms transformed themselves into more global firms, there arose a full-scale awareness that research should clarify the activities of Japanese firms in the context of international relations.

The notion that business management should be understood in an international context has a long tradition in Japan. The research of Yoshitarô Wakimura in the prewar period was a pioneering effort in this area.[29] In the postwar era, there were already calls for such awareness at the beginning of the 1960s. By the early 1980s, at least the following three important research agendas, and the empirical research based upon them, had already come into being.

First, Keiichirô Nakagawa proposed a history of international business relations as well as a methodology. In order to clarify international differences in advanced capitalism, Nakagawa held that it was not enough merely to clarify the economic and social conditions within each country. Rather, he wrote, "We compare American and British capitalism not simply for our convenience in understanding American capitalism; we compare them because American capitalism itself is not a historical reality unless it is in the context of international relations with British

---

[28] Yoshitaka Suzuki, *Japanese Management Structure, 1920–80* (London, 1991).

[29] Yoshitarô Wakimura, *Oil, Shipping, Shipbuilding*, vol. 3 of *Wakimura Yoshitarô chosaku shû* (*Collected Works of Yoshitarô Wakimura*) (Tokyo, 1980); and *Cotton, International Trade, Oil Tankers*, vol. 5 of ibid. (Tokyo, 1981).

capitalism."[30] Later, he went so far as to term this sort of research "business history based on international relations theory." At that point, Nakagawa understood international relations as especially meaning relations among organizations. More concretely, Nakagawa tried to explain the genesis and development of the general trading company in Japan in the context of the special international relations embodied in unequal treaties. Nakagawa also carried out a number of projects in the history of international business relations, most notably on the shipping industry.[31]

Shin'ichi Yonekawa then proposed a "contemporary absolute comparison" approach. This has already been introduced as a call for cross-national comparative business history, but it is also clearly a proposal for an international relations perspective. In developing a business history for the cotton industry, Yonekawa started with the recognition that British, American, Indian, and Japanese firms were placed in a competitive relationship in a single world market during and after the last quarter of the nineteenth century. On Yonekawa's research, Nakagawa stated insightfully at an early point, "It opens the way for research based on international relations theory, and I await its findings."[32]

One more methodological suggestion was Sakae Tsunoyama's invocation of world system theory. Tsunoyama wrote, "If dealing structurally with international economic history through the framework of world capitalist system theory is an influential approach, then how international relations theory-based business history ought to respond will be a future topic for discussion."[33] When he took up this issue in his own work, he used Japanese consular reports as source material, and organized research on the information-related interrelationship of firms and governments in the context of international relations.[34]

[30] Keiichirô Nakagawa, "Comparative Economic History and International Relations," in *Hikaku keiei shi kenkyû 1* (*Studies in Comparative Business History 1*) (Tokyo, 1981), 101–16.

[31] Keiichirô Nakagawa, *Ryôtaisenkan no kaiungyô* (*The Shipping Industry between the Wars*) (Tokyo, 1980).

[32] Business History Association, ed., *Keiei shigaku no 20-nen: Kaiko to tenbô* (*Twenty Years of Business History: Retrospect and Prospect*) (Tokyo, 1985), 20.

[33] Sakae Tsunoyama, "Economic History," in *Keiei shigaku no 20-nen: Kaiko to tenbô* (*Twenty Years of Business History: Retrospect and Prospect*), ed. Business History Association (Tokyo, 1985), 47–8.

[34] Sakae Tsunoyama, ed., *Nihon ryôji hôkoku no kenkyû* (*Studies in Japanese Consular Reports*) (Tokyo, 1986). See also id., "Japanese Consular Reports," *Business History* 23, no. 3 (1981): 284–7.

INVIGORATION OF RESEARCH ON THE HISTORY OF INTERNATIONAL BUSINESS RELATIONS

With the exception of the pioneering work of the preceding three authors, there was little research on the history of international business relations through the mid-1980s. After that, however, research activity rapidly grew. The BHA established a project on the history of international business relations at its annual conference, a history of international business relations category was set up in the yearly review column in *Keiei shigaku*, and the *Japanese Yearbook on Business History* put together a special issue on the subject. Individual pieces of empirical research dealing with international relations head on became prominent, even if they were not labeled as history of international business relations.

Research was first concentrated on the business activities of foreign firms in Japan in the first half of the twentieth century. Hisashi Watanabe, making free use of internal company materials, wrote a pioneering series of works that clarified the Siemens Corporation's direct investment in Japan.[35] Masaru Udagawa did pioneering work on foreign companies' direct investment in Japan.[36] Other scholars who made significant contributions in the area of foreign firms in Japan were Tôru Takenaka on Siemens and Meiji Japan; Akira Kudô on the German chemical giant, IG Farben and other German large enterprises in interwar Japan; Takeo Kikkawa on foreign oil companies' prewar enterprises; and Bunji Nagura on Japanese–British relations in the arms and steel industry.[37] Two valuable collections of essays on the subject are the volume on foreign companies in prewar Japan edited by Takeshi Yuzawa and Masaru Udagawa, *Foreign Business in Japan Before World War II* (Tokyo, 1990), and

---

[35] Hisashi Watanabe, "A History of the Process Leading to the Formation of Fuji Electric," in *Japanese Yearbook on Business History*, vol. 1 (1984), 47–71; id., "The Process of Formation for Fuji Electric: Second and Third Phases," in Nakagawa, *Kigyô keiei*, 263–83.

[36] Masaru Udagawa, "Business Management and Foreign-Affiliated Companies in Prewar Japan (Parts 1 and 2)," in *Keiei Shirin* 24, no. 1 (1987): 15–31; no. 2 (1987): 29–40.

[37] Tôru Takenaka, *Siemens to Meiji Nihon* (*Siemens and Meiji Japan*) (Tokyo, 1991); id., *Siemens in Japan: Von der Landesöffnung bis zum Ersten Weltkrieg* (Stuttgart, 1996); Akira Kudô, *Nichidoku kigyô kankei shi* (*A History of Japanese–German Business Relations*) (Tokyo, 1992); id., *I.G. Farben no tainichi senryaku* (*I.G. Farben's Japan Strategy*) (Tokyo, 1992); id., *Japanese–German Business Relations* (London, 1998); Takeo Kikkawa, "Business Activities of the Standard-Vacuum Oil Co. in Japan Prior to World War II," in *Japanese Yearbook on Business History*, vol. 7 (1990), 31–59; Bunji Nagura, *Heiki tekkô kaisha no nichiei kankei shi: Nihon seikôsho to eikoku gawa kabunushi 1907–52* (*History of Japanese–British Relations in an Arms and Steel Company: Japan Steel Works and Its British Stockholders, 1907–52*) (Tokyo, 1998).

Erich Pauer, ed., *Technologietransfer Deutschland - Japan von 1850 bis zur Gegenwart* (Munich, 1992) on Japanese-German transfer of technologies.

On the expansion of foreign firms into Japan as well as Japan's response to it, it is possible to name a number of monographs covering the time period from the end of the Edo shogunate regime and the Meiji Restoration or early Meiji. Chief among these monographs are Kanji Ishii's work on Jardine Matheson and modern Japan; Kazuo Tatewaki's history of foreign banks in Japan; Shin'ya Sugiyama's monograph on a British merchant, Thomas Glover, and Meiji Japan; Toshio Suzuki's English book on Japanese government loan issues and the London capital market; and Naoto Kagotani's book on the Asian international trade network.[38] Tetsuya Kuwahara compiled a useful literature survey on foreign companies' direct investment in prewar Japan.[39] Business activities of foreign firms in Japan in the postwar era remain an item for future study in the business history field.[40]

Works on foreign direct investment and overseas business expansion on the part of Japanese firms include Nobuo Kawabe's monograph on Mitsubishi Trading in the prewar United States; Tadakatsu Inoue's paper on early foreign direct investment; Tetsuya Kuwahara's volume on the business activities of Japanese textile companies in China; Fumio Kaneko's studies of Japanese investment in Manchuria; and Fumikatsu Kubo's study on Japanese business activities in Formosa.[41] Tetsuya Kuwahara's survey in English of the literature on overseas business

[38] Kanji Ishii, *Kindai Nihon to Igirisu shihon: Jardine Matheson shôkai wo chûshin ni* (*Modern Japan and British Capital: With a Focus on the Jardine Matheson Company*) (Tokyo, 1984); Kazuo Tatewaki, *Zainichi gaikoku ginkô shi* (*History of Foreign Banks in Japan*) (Tokyo, 1987); Shin'ya Sugiyama, *Meiji ishin to Igirisu shônin: Thomas Glover no shôgai* (*The Meiji Restoration and a British Trader: The Life of Thomas Glover*) (Tokyo, 1993); Toshio Suzuki, *Japanese Government Loan Issues on the London Capital Market, 1870-1913* (London, 1994); and Naoto Kagotani, *Ajia kokusai tsûshô chitsujo to kindai Nihon* (*Asian International Trade Order and Modern Japan*) (Nagoya, 2000).

[39] Tetsuya Kuwahara, "Foreign Firms' Investment in Japan Before World War II: Based on a Survey of the Secondary Literature," *Keizai Keiei Ronsô* 26, no. 2 (1991): 17-51.

[40] For a pioneering work on foreign firms in Japan, see Hideki Yoshihara, ed., *Gaishi kei kigyô* (*Foreign-Affiliated Companies*) (Tokyo, 1994).

[41] Nobuo Kawabe, *Sôgô shôsha no kenkyû: Senzen Mitsubishi Shôji no zaibei katsudô* (*Research on the General Trading Company: The Activities of Mitsubishi Trading in the Prewar United States*) (Tokyo, 1982); Tetsuya Kuwahara, *Kigyô kokusaika no shiteki bunseki* (*A Historical Analysis of Business Internationalization*) (Tokyo, 1990); Fumio Kaneko, *Kindai Nihon ni okeru taiman tôshi no kenkyû* (*Investment in Manchuria in Modern Japan*) (Tokyo, 1991); and Kubo, *Shokuminchi kigyô keiei shi*.

activities of Japanese firms in the prewar era is also useful.[42] Overseas expansion by Japanese firms in the postwar era remains a topic for future study. Although it does not fall within the framework of business history, one such work that provides suggestions for the direction of future work in business history and that merits mention is Hiroshi Itagaki's edited collection on Japanese direct investment in Eastern Asia, *Nihonteki keiei seisan shisutemu to higashi Ajia: Taiwan, Kankoku, Chûgoku ni okeru haiburiddo kôjô (The Japanese-Style Management and Production System and East Asia: Hybrid Factories in Taiwan, Korea, and China)* (Kyoto, 1997). This volume explains the business activities of Japanese firms, especially in the automotive and electric machinery sectors, in East Asia, with a focus on the international transfer of technology. The book locates research questions in what aspects of the Japanese-style management and production system have or have not been transferred, to what extent transfer has occurred, and the factors that determine the extent to which that transfer has occurred. In other words, this collection looks at the tension between the direct application of the Japanese system and its flexible adaptation to the local environment.

The most recent comprehensive collection of essays is Hidemasa Morikawa and Tsunehiko Yui, eds., *Kokusai hikaku kokusai kankei no keiei shi (Business History in Cross-National Comparative and International Relations Perspectives)* (Nagoya, 1997).[43] Each essay has its own distinct shading of the notion of international relations, and each tests its own approach to the issue in its concerns, methodology, and source materials. The essays also test cross-national comparisons at every turn. The essays by Kikkawa and Takaoka (on the transfer of the supermarket

---

[42] Tetsuya Kuwahara, "Trends in Research on Overseas Expansion by Japanese Enterprises Prior to World War II," in *Japanese Yearbook on Business History*, vol. 7 (1990), 61–81.

[43] The essays that may be considered attempts at a history of international business relations are Tsunehiko Yui, "Technology Transfer Between Japan and Europe in the Interwar Period and Cumulative Innovation: The Case of Tôyô Rayon"; Kazuo Sugiyama, "The Establishment of the Gold Standard and the *Tôyô Keizai Shinpô*"; Takeaki Teratani, "The Establishment of the NBC Kure Shipyard: With a Focus on Hisashi Shintô"; Eisuke Daitô, "The Development of the Spinning Industry in Hong Kong: In the Context of Its Relationship with the Postwar History of the Japanese Cotton Industry"; Masaru Udagawa, "The Industrial Development Activities of Yoshisuke Aikawa: With a Focus on Indigenization of Automobile Manufacture"; Takeo Kikkawa and Mika Takaoka, "The International Transfer of the Supermarket System and Its Japanese Transformation"; Hisashi Watanabe, "The Process of the Establishment of the Duisburg-Ruhrort Harbor Corporation"; Keizô Kawada, "The British Computer Industry and International Relations: From the Late 1950s On"; and Takeshi Yuzawa, "Japanese–British Economic Competition in the Inter-war Period."

system between the United States and Japan) and by Yuzawa (discussing Japanese-British cotton industry talks) are examples of this.

The highest achievement in the history of international business relations at the present stage of the discipline may be Haruto Shiomi and Ichirô Hori, eds., *Nichibei kankei keiei shi: Kôdo seichô kara genzai made* (*Japan–U.S. Relations Business History: From High Growth to the Present*) (Nagoya, 1998). Japanese–U.S. economic relations after World War II have been the most important basic relationship for the Japanese economy and for the world economy, and this volume makes a valuable contribution to its analysis from the perspective of business history. In comparison to research on Japanese–British and Japanese–German relations, which has stalled at the prewar period, this book is quite significant as well.

In the preface, Shiomi observes that Chandler's model, which had broadly influenced the world of business history, met with a "phase shift" in the 1980s, and its utility came under suspicion. While maintaining the "from market to organization" viewpoint that undergirds the Chandler model, Shiomi holds that a new direction, oriented either explicitly or implicitly toward a post-Chandler model approach, has become visible in business history research. Focusing on Yoshitaka Suzuki and Akira Kudô, Shiomi catalogs the history of research in this field in Japan. He then asserts the usefulness of the history of international business relations, because it breaks through the limits of the Chandler model, which has been constructed within the framework of single-country histories.

In addition, the book discusses global firms in twelve key industries and emphasizes the analysis of the global competitive strategies of Japanese and American firms. The authors share three common premises: the establishment of a global, oligopolistic market that entails a "multi-layered global network"; the emergence of global firms of Japanese descent; and the Americanization of Japanese firms and the Japanization of American ones. The book then observes the interrelationships between the Japanese and American firms that are representatives of the global firms in the twelve key industries.[44] The book clearly shows not only the

---

[44] These are as follows: in steel, U.S. Steel and New Japan Steel (Ichirô Hori); in automobiles, General Motors and Toyota (Haruto Shiomi); in electrics, General Electric and Toshiba (Yasuyuki Kazusa); in oil, Exxon/Mobil and Tônen/Idemitsu Kôsan (Takeo Kikkawa); in chemicals, DuPont and Mitsubishi Chemicals (Akira Morikawa); in aerospace, Boeing and

relationships between Japanese and American firms but also the shape of Japanese and American global big business. As such, it is a great step forward in contemporary business history. There are, however, points that warrant criticism. One such point is the considerable difference among the chapters in the shape or denotation of the interfirm relations that are the object of analysis. The shape or denotation of interfirm relations is, of course, multidimensional and includes trade, technology tie-ups, strategic cooperation, and foreign direct investment. If we also add the notion of competitor firms, the application of competitive strategies, and choice qua object of learning, then interfirm relations becomes an even more variegated concept. Also, the nature of the relations between Japanese and American firms differs by sector, and the authors' respective interests, perspectives, and agendas also differ. The availability and accessibility of materials and documents is also a consideration. Thus, it is natural that the aspects that come under study also differ in response to these conditions. But if the book had been given a somewhat more unified perspective, its claims would probably, as a whole, have had more of an impact.

If I were to venture a suggestion, my one additional request would be a characterization of relations between Japanese and American firms in the 1990s. The book tries to narrow its focus to the "phase shift" that took place from the 1970s to the 1980s. One wonders how the authors understand the shift from the 1980s to the 1990s. Based on this book's position – expressed in its afterword – with "the mid-range perspective that ought to be characteristic of business history," how should we characterize the 1990s? Do we move to the "retrading places between Japan and the United States" and "continuing 'almighty America'" perspectives? Or do we emphasize the information technology revolution or the services innovation perspective?

Research on the history of international business relations has finally become regularized. But methodological consideration has been insufficient, and many points have been left in an imprecise state. Even in the

---

Mitsubishi Heavy Industries (Seigo Mizota); in computers, IBM and Fujitsu (Keiji Natsume); in semiconductors, Intel and NEC (Hiroshi Koizuka); in telecommunications, AT&T and NTT (Shinji Miyazaki); in automobile franchise systems, the Big Three and Toyota and others (Hiromi Shioji); in sundries retailing, U.S. and Japan Seven-Eleven (Nobuo Kawabe); and in finance and securities, Merrill Lynch and Nomura Securities (Kazuko Kobayashi). To these chapters are attached a summing-up chapter (Ichirô Hori) and a timeline (Akira Tanaka).

comprehensive collection edited by Morikawa and Yui, the reader finds no essays dealing with method. What scholars are looking for now is clear methodology. Serious thought needs to be given to how arguments that expressly assume Japan's special international context can acquire cross-national universality. The discipline must address a necessary question: is the history of international business relations methodologically independent, or is it rather just a subfield of business history? In the future, scholars must redouble their methodological search in parallel with their empirical work.

TOWARD A GREATER INTERNATIONAL CONTRIBUTION

As I wrote at the outset, Japanese business history scholars have been given the challenge of answering a three-layered set of problems: the success that prevailed until the mid-1980s, the bubble economy of the late 1980s, and the failure of the 1990s. We must coolly observe what actually happened and what sorts of changes actually occurred. In order to do this, it is necessary to locate this single generation within a longer history and to observe from a long-term perspective. It is for precisely this reason that we look forward to business history's unique contribution to knowledge.

What such a turn requires is not a mindset that seeks to explain even as it is fixed within the existing theoretical framework but rather a mindset that seeks, through accumulated observations, to repeat attempts to propose universal frameworks. To assert out of the blue the uniqueness of Japanese business management or, alternatively, to assert a priori its universality ultimately assumes some sort of existing theoretical framework. Terminology, too, should not be a provincial jargon that is bandied about, but should rather express the results of observation using a universal vocabulary. In so doing, new terms should be proposed only when existing ones render expression impossible. This is one of the preconditions for Japanese business history if it is to make more of an international contribution.

The need for an international contribution on the part of Japanese business history is the same as it ever was or even greater. For example, the word *keiretsu* has been used to express a certain type of interfirm relationship – in most cases, a vertical business group. This term, though, may run the risk of misleading readers on the issues surrounding *keiretsu*. It may also run the risk of interfering with the formation of a universal framework through the observation of Japanese cases.

KEY WORKS

Morikawa, Hidemasa. *Zaibatsu: The Rise and Fall of Family Enterprise Groups in Japan*. Tokyo, 1992.

Morikawa, Hidemasa and Tsunehiko Yui, eds. *Kokusai hikaku kokusai kankei no keiei shi* (*Business History in Cross-National and International Relations Perspectives*). Nagoya, 1997.

Nakawaga, Keiichirô, ed. *Kigyô keiei no rekishiteki kenkyû* (*Historical Research on Business Management*). Tokyo, 1990.

Nihon keiei shi (*Japanese Business History*). 5 vols. Volume 1 – *Kinseiteki keiei no hatten* (*The Development of Early Modern Business*); Volume 2 – *Keiei kakushin to kôgyôka* (*Business Innovation and Industrialization*); Volume 3 – *Dai kigyô jidai no tôrai* (*The Arrival of the Age of Large Enterprise*); Volume 4 – *"Nihonteki" keiei no renzoku to danzetsu* (*Continuities and Discontinuities in "Japanese-Style" Management*); and Volume 5 – *Kôdo seichô wo koete* (*Beyond High Growth*). Tokyo, 1995.

Ôkouchi, Akio and Haruhito Takeda, eds. *Kigyôsha katsudô to kigyô shisutemu: Dai kigyô taisei no nichiei hikaku shi* (*Entrepreneurial Activity and the Enterprise System: A Historical Comparison of Large Enterprise Systems in Japan and Britain*). Tokyo, 1993.

Shiomi, Haruto and Ichirô Hori, eds. *Nichibei kankei keiei shi: Kôdo seichô kara genzai made* (*Japan–U.S. Relations Business History: From High Growth to the Present*). Nagoya, 1998.

Suzuki, Yoshitaka. *Japanese Management Structure, 1920–80*. London, 1991.

Yasuoka, Shigeaki. *Zaibatsu keisei shi no kenkyû* (*Studies on the Formative History of the Zaibatsu*). Kyoto, 1970; expanded edition, 1998.

Yonekawa, Shin'ichi. *Bôsekigyô no hikaku keiei shi kenkyû: Igirisu, Indo, Amerika, Nihon* (*A Comparative Business History of the Spinning Industry: Britain, India, America, Japan*). Tokyo, 1994.

14

Chinese Business History

Its Development, Present Situation, and Future Direction

CHI-KONG LAI

Studies of Chinese business have often sought explanations in Chinese business culture and organization, giving particular attention to, among other things, the growth or stagnation of the Chinese economy, state–business relations, and the business practices of *guanxi* (relationship or connections). Several conferences have been organized, and proceedings, journal articles, and books have been published, not to mention a number of M.A. and Ph.D. theses in Chinese, Japanese, German, and English.

The goal of this essay is to review the field and recent trends in Chinese business history. The aims and influence of the sources and Chinese business history publications will be addressed. I will then proceed with an investigation of academic works in Chinese, Taiwanese, Hong Kong, and Western publications, highlighting the differences in the explanation and conceptualization of Chinese business and economic behavior and demonstrating how these are influenced by the regions, disciplines, interests, and personal backgrounds of the scholars. I will also provide some possible research directions in Chinese business history.

A RECENT UPSURGE OF RESEARCH

During the past two decades, there has been growing international interest in Chinese business history research. Institutionally speaking, there
is still no centralized international organization focused on Chinese business history. However, an international Chinese business history newsletter, *Chinese Business History*, is published by the East Asia Program
of Cornell University to encourage scholarly research on Chinese business history. Essays are edited by the Chinese Business History Research
Group: Professor Andrea McElderry of the University of Louisville is the
editor, and Professors Robert Gardella, Chi-Kong Lai, Elisabeth Koll, and
Brett Sheehan are associate editors. This newsletter also offers a variety
of topics on business archives, research directions, and organizational
activities. Recently, a web site has been created for the newsletter.

In China, the Shanghai Academy of Social Sciences (SASS), the Chinese
Academy of Social Sciences, major universities, and government research
institutes are the key Chinese institutions that contribute to the research
in Chinese business history. China has a Chinese Business History Association, which has organized many conferences, with newsletters and
proceedings published by the association. Books and journal articles are
also published by some major research institutes in China, such as the
Shanghai Academy of Social Sciences, the Chinese Academy of Social Sciences, and Xiamen University. Both Nanjing University and Zhongzhan
University are also strong in the field of premodern Chinese business
history. Huazhong Normal University and Fudan University are strong in
modern Chinese business and financial history.

Since 1956, the SASS has been collecting source materials on Chinese
enterprise history.[1] Scholars in the institute have published numerous
monographs on Chinese business history in Shanghai, most of which concerned famous large-scale enterprises. These include machinery firms,

[1] The most important of these are *Liu Hongsheng qiye shiliao* (*Source Materials on Liu
Hongsheng Enterprise Group*), 3 vols. (Shanghai, 1981); *Yongjia qiye shiliao* (*Source Materials on Yong Family's Enterprise Group*), 2 vols. (Shanghai, 1980); *Nanyang Xiongdi
yancao gongsi shiliao* (*Source Materials on the Nanyang Brothers Tobacco Company*)
(Shanghai, 1958); *Yingmei yan kongsi zai Hua qiye ziliao huibian* (*Source Materials on
the BAT Company*), 4 vols. (Beijing, 1983); *Shanghai minzu jiqi gongye* (*Source Materials on the Shanghai Domestic Machinery Industry*), 2 vols. (Beijing, 1966); *Shanghai
minzu xiangjiao gongye* (*Source Materials on the Shanghai National Rubber Industry*)
(Beijing, 1979); *Shanghai shi mianbu shangye* (*Source Materials on the Shanghai Domestic Cotton Cloth Industry*) (Beijing, 1979); Yan Pengfei, Li Mingyang, and Cao Bu, eds.,
Zhongguo Baoxian shizhi (*Source materials on Chinese Insurance Industry*) (Shanghai,
1989).

textile mills, tobacco companies, drug stores, department stores, and other industrial and commercial firms.[2] The institute also publishes a journal entitled *Source Materials on Modern Chinese Economic History*, which was renamed *Jindai Zhongguo* (*Modern China*) in 1991. This journal provides scholars with an important overview of the field of Chinese economic and business history. Under the leadership of Professor Ding Richu, SASS scholars are currently preparing a comprehensive three-volume study entitled *Shanghai jindai jingjishi* (*The Economic History of Modern Shanghai*).[3] The third volume is still not published.

In today's China, even with state-sponsored pluralism, Chinese scholars still face obstacles. The major obstacle is the lack of financial support. Many current works are not being published because China no longer subsidizes their publishers. Another problem is that many academics do not share their materials or archives with others. Since many business

[2] Zhang Zhongli, Chen Zengnian, and Yao Xinrong, *The Swire Group in Old China* (Shanghai, 1991); Zhang Zhongli and Chen Zengnian, *Shasun jituan zai jiu Zhongguo* (*The Sassoon Enterprise Group in Old China*) (Beijing, 1985); Institute of Economics of the Shanghai Academy of Social Sciences, ed., *Jiangnan zaochuanchang changshi, 1865-1949* (*The History of Jiangnan Arsenal*) (Jiangu People's Press [Nanjing], 1983); id., ed., *Shanghai jindai wujin shangye shi* (*The Metal Industry of Modern Shanghai*) (Shanghai, 1990); id., ed., *Zhongguo jindai zaozhi kongye shi* (*The Paper Industry of Modern China*) (Shanghai, 1989); Xu Weiyong and Huang Hanmin, *Yongjia qiye fazhan shi* (*The Development of the Yong Enterprise*) (Beijing, 1985); Institute of Economics of the Shanghai Academy of Social Sciences and the Bureau of Food Supply of Shanghai, eds., *Zhongguo jindai mianfen gong-ye shi* (*The History of Flour Industry in China*) (Beijing, 1987); Institute of Economics of the Shanghai Academy of Social Sciences and Zhongxi Drugstore, eds., *Zhongxi yaochang bainianshi* (*The Hundred Year History of the Zhongxi Drugstore*) (Shanghai, 1990); Fang Xiantang, *Shanghai jindai minzu juanyan kongye* (*The National Cigarette Industry in Modern Shanghai*) (Shanghai, 1989); Institute of Economics of the Shanghai Academy of Social Sciences, ed., *Shanghai Yongan gongsi ti chansheng, fazhan he gaizao* (*The History of the Origins, Development and Reconstruction of the Yongan Company*) (Shanghai, 1981); id., ed., *Shanghai jindai baihuo shangyeshi* (*The History of Modern Department Stores in Shanghai*) (Shanghai, 1988); id., ed., *Longteng huyue bashinian Shanghai Zhonghua Zhiyue chang chang shi* (*The History of the Zhonghua Drugstore in Shanghai*) (Shanghai, 1991); Zheng Yukui, Cheng Linsun, and Zhang Chuanhong, *Jiu Zhongguo di ziyuan weiyuanhui: Shishi yu ping-jia* (*The National Resource Council in Old China: Historical Fact and Evaluation*) (Shanghai, 1991); Xu Xinwu, *Jiangnan tubu shi* (*The History of Domestic Cloth in Jiangnan Area*) (Shanghai, 1992); Xu Dingxin, *Zhongguo jindai qiye di keji liliang yu keji xiaoying* (*Chinese Modern Enterprise and Its Technological Power and Efficiency*) (Shanghai, 1995); Pang Junxiang, *Zhongguo jindai guohuo yundong* (*The National Product Movement in Modern China*) (Beijing, 1996).

[3] Ding Richu, ed., *Shanghai jindai jingjishi* (*The Economic History of Modern Shanghai*), vols. 1 and 2 (Shanghai, 1994-7). Professors Huang Hanmin and Sheng Zuwei will be responsible for editing volume 3.

historians cannot access others' materials, there are obstacles to contesting others' research.

In Taiwan, there is a research group on Chinese economic history at the Academia Sinica directed by Professors Wang Yeh-chien and Liu Ts'ui-jung. Business historians work at various institutes at the Academia Sinica and at some major universities. The Sun Yat-sen Institute for Social Sciences and Philosophy at the Academia Sinica organized and sponsored eight international conferences on Chinese maritime history. The institute also published eight conference proceedings on Chinese maritime history entitled *Essays in Chinese Maritime History*.[4] Altogether, the proceedings include almost 100 essays on various aspects of maritime history, such as maritime trade, the tributary system, silver and world economy, overseas Chinese communities, and maritime Taiwan in historical perspective. Most of the participants were from Taiwan, but some were from the United States, Japan, China, Korea, Hong Kong, and Australia.

In Taiwan, case studies exist on the hong merchants,[5] the Tainan business group,[6] the silk industry of modern China,[7] and a study of the operational and managerial structure of the Chinese railway industry.[8] The Institute of Modern History has also published some collections of business materials[9] and the oral histories of many businesses. These materials will shed light on the actors' own perspectives regarding the operation of their businesses. In Hong Kong, Professor Chuan Han-sheng (Quan Hansheng) and David Faure supervised several M.A. and Ph.D. theses

---

[4] See Editorial Committee on the Chinese Maritime History, ed., *Chung-kuo Hai-yang fa-chan shih lun-wen chi (Essays in Chinese Maritime History)*, vols. 1 and 2 (Taipei, 1984-6); vol. 3, ed. Chang Yen-hsien (Taipei, 1989); vol. 4, ed. Wu Chien-hsiung (Taipei, 1991); vol. 5, eds. Ping-Tsun Chang and Shih-Chi Liu (Taipei, 1993); vol. 6, ed. Chang Yen-hsien (Taipei, 1997); vol. 7, ed. Tang Shi-yeoung (Taipei, 1999); vol. 8, ed. Te-lan Chu (Taipei, 2002).

[5] Kuo-tung Ch'en, *The Insolvency of the Chinese Hong Merchants, 1760-1843*, Monograph Series, no. 45 (Taipei, 1990).

[6] See Heieh Kuo-hsing (Xie Guoxing), *Corporation Development and the Taiwan Experience* (Taipei, 1994).

[7] See Chen Tsu-yu (Chen Ciyu), *The Silk Industry of Modern China, 1860-1945* (Taipei, 1989).

[8] See Chang Jui-te (Zhang Ruide), *The Peking-Hankou Railroad and Economic Development in North China, 1905-1937* (Taipei, 1987).

[9] *Haifangdang (Archives on Maritime Defense)* (Photo-offset reproduction of Zongli Yamen papers) (Taipei, 1957); *Kuangwudang (Archives on Mining)* (Taipei, 1960); Dai Zhili (Tai Chih-li), comp., *Sichuan baolu yundong dialiao huizuan (Collection of Historical Materials on Sichuan Railway Protection Movement)* (Taipei, 1994); *Qingji Huagone chuguo shiliao (Source Materials on Chinese Coolies in Qing China)* (Taipei, 1995).

on Chinese economic and business history, some of which have been published in monographs and articles.[10] In its efforts to build a field critical to the understanding of business and social change in modern China and other East Asian regions, Hong Kong University Press supports a new book series, Business, Innovation and Society in Modern East Asia. Chi-Kong Lai, Tim Wright, and David Faure are the coeditors, and Han-wai Ho is an associate editor.

Institutions in the United States, Hong Kong, and Australia also organized conferences on Chinese business history. In February 1991, about twenty scholars attended a symposium on the Qing state's relationship to the private economy organized by the University of Akron. In October 1995, the University of Akron sponsored another workshop on "Scholarly Research on Chinese Business History: Interpretive Trends and Priorities for the Future." The conference attracted about thirty academics. The Division of Humanities of the Hong Kong University of Science and Technology organized two special conferences on "Merchant and Local Cultures" in August 1994 and September 1995. The South China Research Group offers both workshops and field trips to villages and cities in South China every year. The Center of Asian Studies of Hong Kong University organized three workshops on Chinese business history in July 1996, July 1998, and July 2000. The most recent one was on the history of the Chinese Chamber of Commerce. Other business history meetings on topics such as the history of the Chinese business networks and the International Conference on Shanghai business have been organized recently by the Asian Business History Center at the University of Queensland, Australia. There were also many conferences on overseas Chinese business activities, Chinese business networks, hometown ties of Chinese merchants, and the history of Chinese banking taking place in Leiden (1997), Brisbane (1997), Oxford (1998), and Singapore (1997 and 1999). The increasing number of conferences and publications indicates that the field is growing.[11]

[10] For example, Ho Hon-wai (He Hanwei), *The Early History of the Beijing Hankou Railroad* (Hong Kong, 1979); Lee Muk-miu (Li Mumiao), *The Development of Yongs' Enterprise, 1912-1921* (Hong Kong, 1989).

[11] There have been several international conferences on Asian business history: the International Symposium on the Chinese Chamber of Commerce and Modern China, Tianjin, July 1998; the International Conference on "Creating Hometown: Chinese Migrants and Native-Place Community," Hong Kong University of Science and Technology, July 11-15, 2001; the International Conference on Asian Trading Networks, Zhongshan University, China, December 2001. There were also two workshops on Chinese business history: the

THE LITERATURE ON LATE IMPERIAL
CHINESE BUSINESS

There is a general consensus that late imperial China possessed a highly commercialized and commodity-oriented economy. It also had a private market. Although economic expansion was present, it did not exhibit signs of developing into an industrial capitalism.

Why did China not develop an industrial revolution? The explanation for this rests on the classical Smithian approach, which focuses on the dynamic role of the market in China facing the population pressure on land and resources. By the 1800s, the population had doubled since the 1700s; while this was happening, there was no corresponding increase in the level of productivity and technology.[12] China in the 1700s may have seen economic expansion; however, there was no mechanism to sustain this growth.[13] The detailed explanations of the internal mechanics of the Chinese economy have been the seminal contribution of Mark Elvin in what he terms the "high-level equilibrium trap."[14] Elvin's work was highly influential among other scholars, some of whom have advanced theories along these same lines.

One of the most important approaches to Sino–Western trade was made by Han-sheng Chuan, who indicates that considerable maritime trade was conducted during the Ming and Qing dynasties. He argues that the expanding monetary economy of China was due to the inflow of silver bullion. Four major articles on the silk and silver trade are collected together in Chuan's *Zhongkuo jianjishi luncong* (*Collected Works on Chinese Economic History*) (Hong Kong, 1972). During the past two decades, Chuan has published numerous articles on silk and the Maritime Silk Road.[15] In January 1987, Chuan gave six lectures on Chinese economic history at the National Ching-hua (Qinghua) University in Taiwan. Later, the lectures were published as *Ming Qing jianjishi*

International Workshop on Labor Relations in Asia, sponsored by the Asian Business History Center, The University of Queensland, July 21–2, 2000; and Diaspora Entrepreneurial Networks, C. 1000–2000, Sept. 21–2, 2001, Corfu, Greece.

[12] Bin Wong, *China Transformed: Historical Change and the Limits of European Experience* (Ithaca, NY, 1997), 48–54.

[13] Phillip Richardson, *Economic Change in China, c. 1800–1950* (Cambridge, 1999), 56.

[14] Mark Elvin, *The Pattern of the Chinese Past* (Stanford, 1973).

[15] See the *Journal of the Institute of Chinese Studies* 8, no. 1 (1976): 71–86; *Collected Essays in Memory of Former Director Mr. Qian Siliang*, vol. 4 (Taipei, 1984), 635–49; *Collected Essays from the Second International Sinological Conference of the Academia Sinica* (Taipei, 1989), 93–4; and the *Journal of the New Asia Institute* 16, no. 1 (1991): 1–22.

yanjiu (*Research on Ming-Qing Economic History*) (Taipei, 1987). The first three lectures were on Chinese maritime trade. During the late sixteenth and eighteenth centuries there was a large infusion of silver into the Chinese economy, which was very important to the facilitation of trade. It was also crucial to the development of China itself, possibly being the most important factor in the development of the silk and porcelain industries. The silver imports, however, contributed to a strong inflationary tendency and increased monetization of the economy. China therefore depended on a large and steady influx of silver to maintain economic stability and growth. This trade network had extensive dealings with the areas of Amoy, Canton, and Southeast Asia. Recently, Ng Chin-keong, Wang Gungwu, Anthony Reid, and Takeshi Hamashita have discussed Chinese trading networks during this period.[16]

China's inflow of silver derived from the tea trade of the eighteenth century. Recently, there have been numerous studies in this field. Robert Gardella's discussion of the Fukien tea trade and the world economy is a case in point.[17] The British paid huge amounts of silver for tea imports. Tea had become Britain's national drink, and by the early nineteenth century the British were consuming 30 million pounds of Chinese tea each year. However, the British managed to find a product that the Chinese were interested in – opium. Even though the Chinese government banned the imports, opium was smuggled into China. Again, China suffered an imbalance of trade with the outflow of huge amounts of silver used in buying opium. This drain of silver contributed to a severe economic crisis – prices fell and land taxes doubled. The drain of silver and the depreciation of copper cash were the causes of the economic crisis. Government mints and forgers had been debasing the cash by reducing the content and the weight of their coins. Widespread hoarding of the more valuable silver also exacerbated the shortage. The drain of

[16] See Ng Chin-keong, *Trade and Society: The Amoy Network on the China Coast, 1683-1735* (Singapore, 1983); Wang Gungwu, "Merchants without Empire: The Hokkien Sojourning Communities," in *The Rise of Merchant Empires: Long-Distance Trade in the Early Modern World, 1350-1750*, ed. James D. Tracy (New York, 1990), 400-21; Anthony Reid, "The Unthreatening Alternative: Chinese Shipping in Southeast Asia, 1567-1842," *Review of Indonesian and Malaysian Affairs* 27, nos. 1 and 2 (1993): 13-32; Takeshi Hamashita, "The Tribute Trade System and Modern Asia," *Japanese Industrialization and the Asian Economy*, eds. A. J. H. Lathan and Heita Kawakatsu (London, 1994), 91-107. Also see Hsi-Yü Chen, *Chung-kuo fan-ch'uan yü hai-wai mou-i* (*Chinese Junks and Foreign Trade*) (Amoy, 1991).

[17] Robert Gardella, *Harvesting Mountains: Fujian and the China Tea Trade, 1757-1937* (Berkeley, 1984).

silver from China contributed to the outbreak of the Opium War with the Europeans.

The United States also played an important role in the China trade. There are numerous studies on this subject. Most of them focus on the performance of American firms[18] and the American opium trade.[19]

THE LITERATURE ON MODERN CHINESE BUSINESS HISTORY

With the coming of the West, Chinese hegemony in East Asian trade was lost. Many scholars state that the treaty port system in place between 1842 and 1943 led to a hybridization of Chinese and Western practices. Others argue that China was able to experience a boost in trade and hence economic growth.[20] In the face of the foreign competition, China tried to adopt Western technology. There have been numerous recent studies on shipbuilding and shipping companies in the field, such as the Shanghai S.N. Company (Russell and Company), Jardine Matheson and Company, Swires Company, the China Merchants' Company, and the Minsheng Shipping Company.[21]

On the issue of foreign trade and investment, Dwight H. Perkins, Thomas G. Rawski, and L. Brandt adopted a quantitative analysis approach to China's economy characterized by a focus on output gains and increases in per capita income. Using this approach, they found that there was substantial growth in the agricultural sector and in the rural economy.[22] At the same time, exaggeration of the role of the West in the economic change of China is not supported. Rather, the outcome of China's economy is seen as the result of a natural market-oriented advantage, moved along by supply and demand and not merely dictated by the West. However, the drawbacks of this calculation are that there is a

---

[18] See Ernest R. May and John K. Fairbank, eds., *America's China Trade in Historical Perspective: The Chinese and American Performance* (Cambridge, 1986).

[19] Jonathan Goldstein, *Philadelphia and the China Trade, 1682-1846: Commercial, Cultural and Attitudinal Effects* (University Park and London, 1978).

[20] See Yen-p'ing Hao, *The Commercial Revolution in Nineteenth-Century China* (Berkeley, 1986).

[21] W. E. Cheong, *Mandarins and Merchants: Jardine Matheson & Co., a China Agency of the Early Nineteenth Century* (London, 1979); Colin N. Crisswell, *The Taipans: Hong Kong's Merchant Princes* (Hong Kong, 1981); Maggie Keswick, ed., *The Thistle and the Jade: A Celebration of 150 Years of Jardine, Matheson & Co.* (London, 1982).

[22] Richardson, *Economic Change*, 32, 76-8; L. Brandt, *Commercialization and Agricultural Development: Central and Eastern China: 1870-1937* (Cambridge, 1987); T. Rawski, *Economic Growth in Prewar China* (Berkeley, 1989).

problem with the method of calculation, and the data are also question-able.[23] In addition, some of the calculations are circumstantial.

The previously accepted themes about China's business during the early twentieth century have been seriously reconsidered since the 1980s. The emerging interpretations have challenged traditional views taken by Chinese and Western historians. The study of Chinese business history has gone from an "emphasis on failure" to "an emphasis on success." Western histories in the field from the 1950s to the 1970s were dominated by modernization theory. Meanwhile, Chinese scholars' studies were dominated by Marxist and Maoist orthodoxies. Both emphasized the failures and backward nature of Chinese capitalist busi-ness.[24] Chinese business historians developed histories that condemned imperialist policies and justified the need for communism in China, while Western economic historians developed theories that emphasized why the modernization of China failed. This essay looks only at those theories that have influenced the historiography of late-nineteenth- and early-twentieth-century China and at the emerging historical research, which is presenting a different view of Chinese business practices and the development of the Chinese economy.

Chinese historians encountered many constraints during the post-1949 era. In his edited book *The Chinese in the Early Twentieth Century*, Tim Wright recognizes the restrictions that Maoist policy placed on Chinese business and economic historians. When Mao reigned in China, the writings of business historians were controlled by the state. Vari-ous opinions were unacceptable. Criticism or praise in the pre-Mao era was viewed as an attack on the government. These circumstances re-stricted the institution of the historians and caused them to write party history rather than accurate business history. To legitimize the Commu-nist regime, histories about the development of capitalism during the early twentieth century focused on the negatives and on the class strug-gle. Chinese interpretations adhered to Marxist concepts and focused on the relations of the means of production and the class struggle.

Contemporary Chinese historians no longer face the restrictions en-countered during Mao's reign. Wright stresses that recent reinterpreta-tions are occurring as a result of state-sponsored pluralism. New studies

---

[23] Mark Elvin, "Skills and Resources in Late Traditional China," in *China's Modern Economy in Historical Perspective*, ed. Dwight H. Perkins (Stanford, 1975), 96.

[24] Tim Wright, ed., *The Chinese Economy in the Early Twentieth Century: Recent Chinese Studies* (New York, 1992), 1–2.

do not blame Chinese culture for the lack of development. Instead, they blame the exploitive imperialist relationships as providing an obstacle to China's development. Chinese capitalism was not as underdeveloped as was previously claimed. Concurrently, Western historians are also reevaluating their previous judgments of the early-twentieth-century Chinese economy. With the criticism of modernization theory, Western historians are reinterpreting the failures and, more important, the successes of the Chinese economy.[25] Western historians are also reevaluating the cultural biases that inundated modernization theories.[26]

Traditionally, historical accounts deliberated over the many negative aspects of foreign investment in China. These negatives included upsetting "the economy by ruining the handicraft industries and disrupting agriculture."[27] These arguments were emulated by Mao, who claimed that foreign capital was developing a "commodity economy," and through its creation it was bringing about an end to China's self-sufficient natural economy and destroying its handicraft industries. He argued that foreign influence put pressure on China's industry, hampered development, and basically made China a "semicolony."[28] The foreign powers' autonomy with regard to navigation of waterways, developing their own currencies, and so on crippled the national economy and caused the people to degenerate into an abnormal condition. A prominent thesis that sought to explain the role of foreign powers was the "absorption thesis." It went against international trade theory by suggesting that trade between rich and poor countries could actually damage the poor countries. Many Chinese business historians today also consider the exploitive imperialist relationships an obstacle to China's development, but most would not go so far as to support such a thesis. Conversely, many contemporary historians are looking at the positive effects of foreigners on China.

---

[25] See Jane Kate Leonard and John R. Watt, eds., *To Achieve Security and Wealth: The Qing Imperial State and the Economy, 1644-1911* (Ithaca, NY, 1992); Tim Wright, "Overcoming Risk: A Chinese Mining Company During the Nanjing Decade," Occasional Paper Series of Asian Business History, no. 1 (Brisbane, 1998), 4.

[26] See Paul A. Cohen, *Discovering History in China: American Historical Writing on the Recent Chinese Past* (New York, 1984); and David Shambaugh, ed., *American Studies of Contemporary China* (Washington, DC, 1993).

[27] Chi-Ming Hou, *Foreign Investment and Economic Development in China, 1840-1937* (Cambridge, Mass., 1965), 1.

[28] Mao Zedong (Mao Tse-tung), *Selected Works of Mao Tse-tung* (Beijing, 1965), 314. Also see Wu Chengming, "Introduction: On Embryonic Capitalism," in *Chinese Capitalism, 1522-1840*, ed. Xu Dixin and Wu Chengming (London, 2000), 1.

In 1965, Chi-ming Hou argued in his book *Foreign Investment and Economic Development in China* that foreign investment was not an intrusion in China, but was beneficial to both foreigners and China. According to Hou, the foreign presence contributed to the economy by bringing significant trade, investment, and technology.[29] Hou also acknowledged the tremendous amounts of infrastructure that foreign investment created. Foreign countries owned the majority of China's transport, iron, and coal industries. One would argue that Hou's interpretation failed to recognize the imperial nature of such ownership. He did recognize the advantages that foreign business provided, but he also claimed that Chinese businessmen themselves enjoyed advantages derived from their intimate knowledge of their own markets. Chinese markets in places like Manchuria were negatively affected by foreign influence. Foreign industries in Manchuria did not encourage or use the domestic market's goods and therefore did not encourage development. Although there were elements of imperialism overall, economic historians such as Tom Rawski still insist that "China's pre-war industrial history demonstrates the positive impact of foreign trade on industrial progress."[30]

Economic historians like Hou, Rawski, and Richardson deny the absorption thesis. Instead of looking at the negatives, they look at how foreign influence contributed to China. Many argue that foreign imports dominated China and therefore destroyed many of China's domestic production opportunities. Rawski insists that foreign imports were a valuable indicator for domestic manufacturers, who would begin producing the imported goods when the demand warranted it. Rawski argues as well that the absence of a strong Chinese government actually benefited the Chinese economy by allowing for this type of market development. Strong barriers could have left Chinese industry with either expensive reproductions of imports or no such goods. Richardson argues that, with the exception of wartime, China's terms of trade were continuously improving throughout the early twentieth century. He also claims that the moderate trade deficit that existed could hardly be considered to have drained China of its wealth.[31]

While many business historians are looking at the positives of foreign investment in China, they do not go so far as to say that foreign investment created Chinese capitalism. Richardson insists that development in

[29] Hou, Foreign Investment, 127.
[30] G. Thomas Rawski, *China's Transition to Industrialism* (Ann Arbor, 1980), 27.
[31] Richardson, *Economic Change*, 47.

China was not an "impact-response phenomenon" brought on by foreign involvement. As he puts it, "foreign trade and investment flowed through, and became part of, an existing and evolving commercial system." Some Chinese business historians state that the "equipment, markets and techniques for the new enterprises were all fundamentally dependent on the West or on changes induced by the West."[32] Some Chinese business historians present the case that China was developing independently of Western influence. For example, Bin Wong, Gary Hamilton, and Chi-Kong Lai hypothesize that China was developing commercialism without capitalism before the European disruption.[33]

In *China's Transition to Industrialism* (Ann Arbor, 1980), Rawski discusses the many industrial advances made in China from 1911 to 1937. During this period, China's industries experienced significant growth in production. China focused on the development of certain industries through "output expansion and import substitution." Rawski concludes that by 1937, these developments created the foundation of a modern "producer sector." Contrary to some accounts, foreign companies did not dominate the developing industries. Richardson concluded that during the 1930s, 70 percent of Chinese workers were employed by Chinese producers and were manufacturing two-thirds of the country's goods.

One of the problems business historians confront when interpreting the early-twentieth-century economy is the lack of reliable government or private statistics for the period prior to the 1950s. As a result, the realities of the economy have been constantly debated. Past historians like Hou looked for reasons why modernization was limited. Newer scholars are taking a more positive approach.

The successes of modernization in China have in the past been ignored. In his book, Hou states that China was an undeveloped nation showing only a significant tendency toward modernization. On the other hand, in his *Economic Growth in Prewar China* (Berkeley, 1989), Rawski suggests that there was strong growth throughout the economy and that the sustained increases indicated the onset of modern economic growth. He states that the growth experienced by China's industry is comparable with the growth that was occurring at the same time in Japan. Rawski's findings are not accepted by all, but most agree that his more optimistic

---

[32] Wright, ed., *The Chinese Economy in the Early Twentieth Century: Recent Chinese Studies*, 12.

[33] Gary Hamilton and Chi-Kong Lai, "Consumerism without Capitalism," in *The Social Economy of Consumption*, eds. Benjamin Orlove and Henry Rutz (Lanham, 1989), 253–79, reissued in Rajeswary Brown, ed., *Chinese Enterprise History* (London, 1996), 315–38.

interpretations are at least improvements on past historical accounts of the period.

Research institutions in China are now also revising their views of the 1920s and 1930s. Recent works by the SASS and the Nankai Institute of Economics are denying the former view that modernization attempts were failures. Wu Chengming of the Chinese Academy of Social Sciences has also abandoned the theory that China was experiencing a serious economic crisis during this period, though there were limited rural crises during this time. Bin Wong is not so confident about the predictions of Rawski. He believes that the capitalist factories in port cities were products of the West. He claims that early-twentieth-century industrialization was basically a market phenomenon in Chinese cities, often with foreign capital and foreign management.[34]

Bin Wong points out that the steady growth figures that Rawski accounts for pertain to only a small proportion of the Chinese population. According to Rawski, China would have experienced continuous growth if it hadn't been for the Japanese invasion. Wong questions Rawski's thesis, saying that it doesn't take into account the challenges of incorporating the large mass of China. David Faure also notes the size of China as an obstacle that limited the influence of urban industrialization on rural areas.[35] Wong asserts that such growth would have required the existence of a strong state. He compares China's circumstances before the Japanese invasion with the European experience. Europe experienced over a century of obstacles when trying to industrialize its rural areas. Throughout the process, European governments had to play a large role by protecting and creating the capital to eventually develop these areas. According to Wong, this type of government involvement did not occur in China during the first half of the twentieth century.

The status of China's agricultural sector during the early twentieth century is also under debate. Mao theorized that foreign currency was destroying China's traditional self-sufficient agricultural economy. More popular historical accounts also argue that agricultural production was stagnant. David Faure suggests that the sheer size of China limited the influence that the modernizing cities could have on the rural areas. New theories are suggesting that foreign investment was actually influencing an increase in output in certain rural areas. The work of Rawski and

---

[34] Bin Wong, *China Transformed*, 53–67.

[35] David Faure, "The Chinese Bourgeoisie Reconsidered: Business Structure, Political Status and the Emergence of Social Class," Occasional Paper Series in Asian Business History, no. 3 (Brisbane, 1998), 1.

Brandt argues that there was evident growth in Chinese agriculture. Statistics demonstrate that there was a demand for cash crops like soya beans in Manchuria and that there was a strong demand for silk through the late 1920s. There was also an increased demand for raw materials, particularly cotton, which were used by the modern industries. It is important to realize that these figures represent only moderate change in output. Commercial crops still accounted for only 10 percent of the land and, as pointed out by Faure, rarely did this production threaten the self-sufficiency of the rural areas. Rawski's works predict that if the spread of industry China experienced during the 1930s had continued, it would have extended modern technology to agricultural production.

There is also debate over whether foreign imports were damaging the rural areas' important handicrafts. Hou argues that the handicraft industry adapted to changing demands and produced other goods, suggesting that this industry retained its important role in rural areas. Unfortunately, as Hou points out, there are no data for rural unemployment, so this hypothesis can never be proven.

STATE – BUSINESS RELATIONS

The role of government intervention in Chinese economic growth is one of the major topics of controversy in Chinese business history. Scholars like Kenneth Pomeranz, David Pong, Kwang-Ching Liu, Chi-Kong Lai, and William Kirby placed great emphasis on the role of the government as the initiator and promoter of industrialism. Other historians, such as Rawski, Parks Coble, and Marie-Claire Bergere, question the significance of the government's role in Chinese industrialization and suggest that where the government did take initiatives, they were usually unsuccessful. In this literature, scholars have considered the changing role of the government in Chinese industrialization as a whole.

Marion Levy and Shih Kuo-heng argued in *The Rise of the Modern Chinese Business Class* (New York, 1949) that the traditional and archaic practices of Chinese businessmen inevitably led to failures. They noted the prevalence of nepotism as a major example of outdated business practices. Likewise, Confucian values and the absence of aggressive competition figured in other Western interpretations as sources of failure. These types of judgments were also made by Albert Feuerwerker in *China's Early Industrialization: Sheng Hsuan-huai (1844–1916) and Mandarin Enterprise* (Cambridge, 1958), his study of the failure of the China Merchants' Steam Navigation Company. Feuerwerker sees in this failure of the late nineteenth century the telltale signs of nepotism and overwhelming bureaucracy. Chi-Kong Lai, however, has challenged this view in his own work on the China Merchants' Company.

More recently, Bin Wong and Marie-Claire Bergere have also contradicted such assumptions. Wong points to the "economic miracle" of Japan as evidence that Confucian beliefs are not a barrier to modernization. Bergere counters these theories by looking at the successes of the overseas Chinese and the histories of the early European bourgeoisie.[36]

New works are also looking at how many Chinese businessmen benefited from traditional practices. In *China's New Business Elite* (Berkeley, 1997), Margaret M. Pearson states that the continued prominence of clientism during the golden age was evidence that Chinese businesses were still in a sense archaic. On the other hand, Bergere compares the Chinese methods with those of the French bourgeoisie, claiming that they were not backward and cannot be blamed for the lack of economic development in China. Bergere also identifies the many benefits of family businesses. She claims that the family arrangement gave Chinese businesses "flexibility, dynamism and buoyancy when faced with crises."[37] The diversified expansion of family businesses enabled families to transfer funds to failing segments so that they could survive in the tumultuous environment.

Studies are also looking at how Chinese businessmen combined traditional practices with those from the West. The businessmen during the golden age began stressing the importance of the individual over family structures. According to Wright, Chinese businesses were eager to assimilate new management methods; Rawski sees the successful industries being orchestrated by Chinese who were familiar with Western markets and methods. Many successful Chinese enterprises incorporated Western business styles and reworked them into Chinese practices. In Wellington K. K. Chan's "Personal Styles, Cultural Values, and Management: The Sincere and Wing On Companies in Shanghai and Hong Kong, 1900–1941," he demonstrates how the Wing On company was able to fuse the business practices of both cultures to be successful.[38]

Bergere claims that a Chinese bourgeois class existed in the early twentieth century but that it was too weak to come to power. Her findings

---

[36] Marie-Claire Bergere, *The Golden Age of the Chinese Bourgeoisie, 1911–1937* (Cambridge, 1989), 140.

[37] Ibid., 141.

[38] In Kerrie L. MacPherson, ed., *Asian Department Stores* (Honolulu, 1998), 66–89.

demonstrate that during the 1920s, the bourgeoisie was increasingly recognized as a coherent social class that had been freed of many of the past constraints inflicted on merchants. However, with this new freedom the merchant class grew wealthier, but it failed to emerge as a source of civil society.

In an attempt to demonstrate class divisions in pre-Mao China, Chinese historians portrayed the bourgeoisie as a powerful element in Chiang Kai-shek's government. Bergere claims instead that the bourgeoisie was stripped of its political power and found its resources being excessively absorbed by the troubled Nationalist government. Likewise, Margaret M. Pearson asserts that Chiang Kai-shek's government established a coercive state–business dualist relationship. The government ended the autonomous nature of merchant organizations while demanding large sums of money from them. Faure states that the changes of the early twentieth century "brought about vast and rapid changes in rituals and manners that spread far and wide in Chinese society. Such changes had spread from the cities and their consequence was to produce a city–rural divide rather than a class divide."[39]

CHINESE BUSINESS IN COMPARATIVE PERSPECTIVES

Bin Wong has also worked along the lines of the Smithian dynamics in attempting to describe the similarities and differences between China and Europe. He compares the similarity of the dynamics of economic change in China and Europe and then demonstrates the important qualitative leap that Europe took, which differentiated it from China. He also argues that Europe was able to do this by getting resources from outside its normal perimeters. While being very careful not to use the yardstick of Western comparison, he tries to reconstruct the trajectory for China independently of the Western one. Within his comparison, he highlights the fact that the state's Confucian political system worked along different lines from those of governments in the West. In *The Great Divergence* (Princeton, 2000), Kenneth Pomeranz also compares China and Europe in the making of the modern economy. The ideal Chinese political system was centered on the agrarian economy with a rural industrial base, complemented with cash crops to balance supply and demand. This was the typical and most widely accepted lifestyle, which was considered a noble one and in accordance with Confucian morals. The state

[39] Faure, "Chinese Bourgeoisie Reconsidered," 18.

traditionally did not view commercialism as appropriate and considered it an unimportant source of revenue. The traditional view was that the true gentleman was one who was morally sound and frugal as opposed to one who pursued wealth and glory by commercialization. Hence, scholars have acknowledged that China's economy had its strengths and weaknesses, though its weaknesses became exacerbated when China began to interact on the international scene in the nineteenth century. It has also been agreed that the Qing government had accepted general responsibility for the people, encouraged agricultural expansion, promoted the development of commercial handicraft production, regularized land taxes, reorganized the granary system, and controlled the money supply.[40]

Along different lines, G. William Skinner has contributed a seminal work dividing China into nine different macroregions.[41] This micro and regional approach respects the fact that China is not homogeneous and that each province is unique. It also demonstrates that the earlier Western-centered approach involved a very simplistic perception of change and reaction to change in China. As a country with a richly diverse culture and vastly different people and backgrounds, China's different regions would naturally react in very diverse ways to change. Every region in China had different degrees of economic progress, and their economic structures differed greatly. The experiences of the treaty ports cannot be directly compared with those of inner states in the hinterland. There were vastly different degrees of exposure and reaction. Bin Wong's recent work overlooks this and takes the entire Europe and China as one entity, not highlighting the heterogeneity of Europe.

FUTURE DIRECTIONS

Recent historical accounts have demonstrated how biases have shaped and structured past histories of China. As Western and Chinese historians' work begins to evolve, a more coherent understanding of China's business practices will emerge. The compilation of the source materials on Chinese maritime history by historians will provide more access to research on Chinese business history. New archaeological findings provide more material to reconstruct the business world in China. The primary sources, archaeological reports, and other research aids that are becoming available will allow a more comprehensive and accurate view of the business past to emerge.

[40] Richardson, *Economic Change in China, c.1800–1950,* 27.
[41] G. William Skinner, *The City in Late Imperial China* (Stanford, 1977), 212–15.

Overall, newly available sources – such as the extant archives of the China Merchants' Steam Navigation Company and the Minsheng Company – will enable scholars to frame more serious questions. Sherman Cochran has provided some valuable suggestions on the direction of the field.[42]

Future research topics should consider the relationships between the central offices and branches of enterprises. In the past, historians had to look at the operation of the business as a whole unit. But newly available sources will enable scholars to look at how branches deal with the central office or the monitoring procedures and methods used by the central office to control branches. Recent studies on stock markets and other newly available materials from company archives will enable scholars to look at company law and corporate structures. Companies' records, including their own magazines, catalogs, and posters, may help researchers better understand marketing strategies and management styles. Some newspapers, such as *Shenbao* and *North China Herald*, also have marketing intelligence sections. Business historians could draw on autobiographies, company promotional materials, pamphlets, calendar posters, and paintings to reconstruct the untold story of changing consumer styles in modern China. There are many contracts and much documentation of legal disputes available in company archives. Business historians could study the legal aspects of Chinese business, such as whether law or custom matters more in business dealings in China. There are a number of studies on Chinese business networks, but there is still no clear understanding of what a network is or what is especially Chinese about business networks. New material can help us better understand the relationship among emigration patterns and how forms of trading affected the network structure. In the past, scholars focused only on the positive aspects of networks, but interview materials could provide insights into their negative and dysfunctional aspects as well. Some company archives contain information on industrial design, engineering, and industrial technology. The University of California's Berkeley Library houses translations of Western science texts into Chinese. These kinds of materials could help us understand one of the more neglected topics in this field.

In sum, we need to have more case studies of individual enterprises in order to frame higher-level analyses; thus, access to archives and new

[42] Sherman Cochran, "An Assessment of Chinese Business History Five Years After Our Inaugural Issue," *Chinese Business History* 6, no. 1 (1996): 1–2.

316   LAI

materials is of the greatest importance. After we have studied sufficient numbers of cases, we can piece them together to form a more conclusive account of how Chinese business functioned in both the distant and the more immediate past, and hence how that past may continue to shape the rapidly evolving present.

KEY WORKS

Brown, Raj, ed. *Chinese Business Enterprise*. 4 vols. London, 1996. This is the best collection of essays on Chinese business history.

Cochran, Sherman. *Encountering Chinese Networks*. Berkeley, 2000. Chan, Wellington K. K. *Merchants, Mandarins, and Modern Enterprise in Late Ch'ing China*. Cambridge, 1977. These books are the best studies on Chinese enterprise.

Faure, David. *China and Capitalism: Business Enterprise in Modern China*. Hong Kong, 1994; Eastman, Lloyd E. *Family, Fields and Ancestors: Constancy and Change in China's Social and Economic History, 1550-1949*. New York, 1988. These two books are the best short histories of business and economic change in the long run.

Goodman, Bryna. *Native Place, City, and Nation: Regional Networks and Identities in Shanghai, 1853-1937*. Berkeley, 1995. This is the classic work on Chinese native place associations.

Hamilton, Gary, ed. *Business Networks and Economic Development in East and Southeast Asia*. Hong Kong, 1991. This is the best book on Chinese business networks.

Hao, Yen-p'ing. *The Commercial Revolution in Nineteenth Century China*. Berkeley, 1986. This book is especially helpful for understanding issues of Sino-Western business relations, foreign investment, and international trade.

MacPherson, Kerrie L., ed. *Asian Department Stores*. Honolulu, 1998; Watson, James L., ed. *Golden Arches East: McDonald's in East Asia*. Stanford, 1997. These two books are the best works on Chinese consumer culture.

McElderry, Andrea and Bob Gardella, eds. *Scholarly Research on Chinese Business History: Interpretive Trends and Priorities for the Future*. Armonk, NY, 1998. This is the best introduction to the field of Chinese business history.

Rowe, William T. *Hankow: Commerce and Society in a Chinese City, 1796-1889*. Stanford, 1984; Kwan, Man Bun. *The Salt Merchants of Tianjin*. Honolulu, 2001. These are the best case studies on regional business development.

Wright, Tim. *Coal Mining in China's Economy and Society, 1895-1937*. Cambridge, 1984. This is a very informative book on Chinese enterprise management.

——— ed. *The Chinese Economy in the Early Twentieth Century*. New York, 1992. This book is a good overview of Chinese perspectives on Chinese business history.

15

Business History in Latin America

Issues and Debates

MARÍA INÉS BARBERO

To present an outlook of business history in Latin America is by no means a simple job. It is a territory consisting of twenty countries that have many features in common but also significant differences among them. These differences show up not only at the economic, social, or political levels but also in their cultural traditions, as well as in the development of social sciences and business history. As James Baughman pointed out, the "chronic disease" of Latin American historiography has been to survey and hence overgeneralize about twenty diverse nations.[1]

Despite such conditions, this essay aims to present some of the major lines in the evolution of this discipline in Latin American countries, from the sixties to the present, and to provide a brief description of the field's current trends and the major issues under debate. It does not intend to provide an exhaustive tour through Latin American business history, but rather to offer, through an overall view, a synthesis that will enable comparison with the experience of other countries and regions, and to reflect on its strengths, weaknesses, and future prospects.

To date, the course of business history has been studied in depth only in the most developed countries. An overview of the Latin American

[1] Baughman, "Recent Trends in the Business History of Latin America," *Business History Review* 39 (Winter 1965): 425-39.

scenario is a first step toward studying the business history of the later-developed nations and toward thinking of a more general typology that will include the countries of other continents. Before considering these subjects it is worth noting, as has been pointed out by other authors, that a definition of business history in Latin America has some conceptual difficulties.[2] The terms *historia de empresas* and *historia empresarial*, with which it is designated, encompass the following three different areas, which at times overlap with each other: business history in a comparative sense, company histories in terms of empirical case studies, and entrepreneurial history as the study of individual pioneers. Latin American historians emphasize the distinction between *historia de empresas* and *historia empresarial*. The former focuses on the evolution of companies and their relationship with the economic and social changes in the environment. The latter, using a more Schumpeterian approach, privileges the historic analysis of the actions of entrepreneurs, the development of entrepreneurial groups, and their contribution (or failure therein) to innovation and development.

LATIN AMERICAN BUSINESS HISTORY UNTIL 1990

Any historiographical review of business history in Latin America requires a distinction between the production of foreign Latin Americanists, mainly North American and European historians, and that of Latin American historians. Such a distinction is made above all for analytical purposes, as until the late eighties there was a notorious disproportion between the studies made in the more developed countries and the domestic production of Latin American countries. Such a gap was not limited to the field of business history, but rather reflected – with only a few exceptions – the insularity of Latin American historiography, mainly in social and economic history.

The existing reviews of business history in Latin America usually include in their introductory statements references to two special issues on this subject that were published by *Business History Review* in 1965 and 1985.[3] The comparison between these volumes, with an interval of twenty years between them, is an appropriate starting point for a first

---

[2] Rory Miller, "Business History in Latin America: An Introduction," in *Business History in Latin America: The Experience of Seven Countries*, eds. Carlos Dávila and Rory Miller (Liverpool, 1999), 1–16.

[3] *Business History Review* 39 (Winter 1965); 59 (Winter 1985).

evaluation of the transformations that took place in this subject from its origins to its ascendancy as a specific field within Latin American economic history.

In the 1965 edition, its compiler, James Baughman, emphasized the insignificant attention that both business history and economic history in general had received among Latin Americanists up to that date, where research had concentrated on political, military, religious, and diplomatic history. Business history did not constitute a well-defined area, and many general papers, such as studies on growth or development, were the only work in the field.

Another characteristic was that most of the historic research on companies in Latin America was addressed to foreign investments, while publication on local enterprises was much less, particularly regarding industrial firms.[4] A third element worth noting was the small proportion of Latin Americans among the researchers.

The 1985 special issue highlighted the transformations that had occurred during the two decades in which business history established itself as an autonomous subject both in the United States and in a number of European countries. Its editor, H. V. Nelles, remarked on the way in which the changes in historiographical fashions had affected Latin American studies, promoting research on the economic and social milieus of business enterprises from the colonial period.[5] The noticeable changes could be seen in different areas. To begin with, the avalanche of scholarship in Latin American studies was accompanied by an increasing interest in new issues and new methods. Secondly, the multiplication of studies had gradually modified some preconceptions regarding Latin American history and had allowed for a rediscovery of the essentially commercial character of colonial societies, encouraging the studies of merchant communities and the social context of entrepreneurship.

The studies on economic and social history had also been enriched by the debates sparked on imperialism, the historical roots of underdevelopment, and dependence. The discussions on free-trade imperialism, and in particular the research promoted from Great Britain by D. C. M. Platt, boosted the studies on commercial relationships and foreign investments in the nineteenth and twentieth centuries. Developmentalism

---

[4] The book by Thomas Cochran and Ruben Reina about an Argentine industrial firm, Siam Di Tella, was an exception, but it was a commemorative book; see Cochran and Reina, *Entrepreneurship in Argentine Culture* (Philadelphia, 1962).

[5] H. V. Nelles, "Latin American Business History since 1965: A View from North of the Border," *Business History Review* 59 (Winter 1985): 543–62.

and dependency theory, in turn, helped invigorate the field of economic history by offering new conceptual frameworks for research and by shifting explanations of development away from religion and culture toward factor endowments, public policies, and international economic relationships.

Progress was also reflected in the contents of the articles included in the 1985 special issue, which showed a growing interest in nineteenth- and twentieth-century history and the increasing use of archival materials. However, 50 percent of the papers still dealt with the study of foreign business in Latin America, affected to a large degree by the debates on imperialism and dependence.

Both compilations fundamentally summarize the work of North American and European Latin Americanists, who approached business history issues from the standpoint of economic and social history. The references to "domestic" productions of Latin American countries are very few, mainly because of the scarcity of work on firms or businessmen made by Latin American historians. Notwithstanding the progress achieved in the two decades that elapsed between the publications, it is apparent that by the mid-eighties business history did not constitute a well-defined subject, even among the foreign scholars who did research on Latin American history. It was rather a by-product of economic and social history, inasmuch as it began to involve itself in enterprise and entrepreneurial issues. For this reason, despite the significant contributions of many of the works and with some exceptions, it isolated Latin American business history from the discipline in developed countries, and kept it apart from the theoretical frameworks and debates that had been enriching the development of the discipline since the sixties.

In Latin American historiography, the development of business history as a specific subdiscipline did not occur until the eighties. However, in both the sixties and the seventies, subjects inherent in entrepreneurial history began to be discussed in the context of larger debates dealing with Latin American development and underdevelopment held by historians, economists, and sociologists.

The sixties and the seventies were more important for the development of economic and social history than for the specific growth of business history, which was only starting. In Latin America, the historiographical renovation that extended the field of historical studies to the economy and the society was just beginning by the late fifties.

Regarding business history, during these years there was a strong predominance of deductive views based on the theory of modernization,

Latin American structuralism, dependency theory, and Marxism. Most scholars devoted to economic or social history were concerned with investigating the basic causes of Latin American backwardness. Discussion of the entrepreneurship or of firms, if any, was peripheral to the principal focus of their attention. Interest in companies and entrepreneurs appeared subordinate to the study of development, underdevelopment, and industrialization. The subjects dealt with most fully in the research carried out in those years concerned the existence – or lack thereof – of an industrial bourgeoisie in Latin American countries, that class's specific characteristics in comparison to those of more industrialized countries, and its capacity to lead economic, social, and political transformation processes.

In the theory of modernization and structuralism, the core of the analysis concerned the study of the innovative capacity of industrial entrepreneurs and their ability to lead economic development. An example of this approach was research carried out by the Economic Commission for Latin America (ECLA) in different Latin American countries, addressing the characteristics of businessmen and their innovative capacity, but without involving the historical dimensions of the question.[6] Among dependentists and Marxists, in a more or less explicit fashion, the study of entrepreneurship was connected with the debates on the transition from feudalism to capitalism and with discussions on the viability of capitalism and of social class alliances. The most radical perspectives, such as André Gunder Frank's, asserted that local business elites had been incapable of developing an autonomous growth process.[7]

Nevertheless many of the works, whose original purpose was to discuss problems of the present, started to look to the past. The debates concerning entrepreneurship led to the study of the origin and construction of the entrepreneurial sector and opened the field for business history. In the case of Argentina, this tendency involved the study of the past, looking for an explanation for the "structural weakness of the industrial businessmen."[8] In the Brazilian case, Warren Dean's pioneer work started

[6] Fernando H. Cardoso, *Ideologías de la burguesía industrial en sociedades dependientes (Argentina y Brasil)* (Mexico, 1971); E. Zalduendo, *El empresario industrial en América Latina: Argentina*, mimeo, 1963.

[7] Frank, *Capitalism and Underdevelopment in Latin America: Historical Studies of Chile and Brazil* (New York, 1967).

[8] O. Cornblit, "Inmigrantes y empresarios en la política argentina," in *Los fragmentos del poder*, eds. T. Halperín Donghi and T. Di Tella (Buenos Aires, 1969), 389–437; D. Cuneo, *Comportamiento y crisis de la clase empresaria* (Buenos Aires, 1967).

a debate focused on the relationship between agrarian and industrial businessmen and the role of immigration in building the entrepreneurial sector.[9] In Chile, an ECLA scholar stressed that Chilean entrepreneurs tended, from the mid-nineteenth century on, to consumption rather than to investment, and held this sector responsible for "frustrated development."[10]

Starting early in the seventies, the theoretical frameworks of the sixties were increasingly questioned. At the same time, the historical research on topics concerning companies and entrepreneurs started to grow. While in the preceding decade general views prevailed about development (or underdevelopment) processes, the seventies brought an expansion of sector and regional studies. On the basis of the empirical evidence obtained, a revision of the generalizing interpretations of the sixties began. One of the most appealing topics for historians was the rise and composition of the business class, and this subject produced different kinds of research. To begin with, works concentrated on the national origin of entrepreneurs, encompassing research on both European immigrants and local entrepreneurs. A feature common to all Latin American countries, European immigrants played an outstanding part in the building of entrepreneurship. In addition to Argentina, Chile, Uruguay, and Brazil, immigrants had an important role in entrepreneurial activity in Mexico, Colombia, Venezuela, and Peru.

Also beginning in the seventies was an important research line on the origins and building of the Latin American bourgeoisie. Special attention was given to the development of entrepreneurial groups, to the accumulation mechanisms, and to the diversified investments derived from an originally mercantile activity. Though this research was mainly interested in the process of bourgeoisie-building in Latin American societies in their transition to capitalism, it was based on case studies that offered interesting empirical material for the study of the birth of entrepreneurial groups and their different social origins. Examples of this kind of work are the articles edited by Enrique Florescano on the origins and development of the bourgeoisie that were discussed in an international conference in Lima in 1978.[11]

Regional and sectoral studies in connection with this topic also expanded in the seventies and covered a wide range of themes, providing

[9] Dean, *The industrialization of São Paulo, 1880-1945* (Austin, 1969).
[10] A. Pinto, *Chile, un caso de desarrollo frustrado* (Santiago de Chile, 1965).
[11] Florescano, ed., *Orígenes y desarrollo de la burguesía en América Latina* (Mexico, 1985).

an important contribution to business history. Works on agriculture, railways, manufacture, trade, and banking multiplied in all countries, Mexican and Colombian historiography being pioneers in this field. In both countries, where regional differences are deep, the argument privileged by business history has been the study of the origins and activities of regional entrepreneurial groups.

BUSINESS HISTORY IN LATIN AMERICA
IN THE PAST DECADE

With the eighties began the greatest expansion of business history in Latin America. In spite of limitations that will be pointed out, during this period interest in the field grew significantly and research multiplied. Although research continued along the lines drawn in the preceding decades – the building and characteristics of the entrepreneurial sector, along with sector and regional studies – the number of case studies and research on firm archives increased, offering a larger empirical base. The opening and restructuring of economies and the challenge of competition contributed to a reassessment of firms and entrepreneurs as economic agents, thus reinvigorating business history.

Starting in the mid-eighties, business history began to emerge as a specific research area within economic history, a trend that strengthened in the nineties. There were multiple reasons for this, but no doubt the new macroeconomic conditions helped to increase the interest in commercial firms and entrepreneurs and in their historical performance. The debt crisis, the liberalization of economies, the gradual pullback of the entrepreneurial state, and in general the adoption of neoliberal policies by governments conferred on private enterprise a role ever more relevant in economic activity. Within that context, historic studies on companies and businessmen began to offer new keys to the reading and interpretation of the present and the past. The changes in the general historiographic context also helped encourage the study of the history of firms inasmuch as it invigorated the interest in new subjects, new individuals, and new interdisciplinary alliances. At the same time, the process of political democratization offered new possibilities of institutional meetings among Latin American researchers and their colleagues in the North Atlantic world, which contributed to the encouragement of research and to extension of the conceptual frameworks available.

The bottom line is that business history is increasingly a space occupied by historians, as opposed to the preceding stage, in which studies

of firms and entrepreneurs were led by economists and sociologists. It
may be asserted that the firm has become a historic subject. It should
be noted that the growth of business history has not been consistent. Its
major development has been achieved by Mexico and Brazil, followed
by Argentina, Colombia, and Chile, while in the rest of Latin America
it is still emerging.[12] This expansion may be measured by various indi-
cators. In the first place, the bibliography on business history in Latin
America that was published after 1960 reveals a considerable increase
in production since the eighties. Early in the nineties the first historiographic results of the progress of this discipline began to appear,[13] and
in 1996 a volume edited by Carlos Dávila was published that offered a
review of the evolution of business history in seven countries (Argentina,
Brazil, Chile, Colombia, Mexico, Peru, and Venezuela). In 1996 this work
was translated into English.[14] The publications have prefaces by Carlos
Dávila and Rory Miller, respectively, that include remarks on the trends,
achievements, and issues pending.

The publication of the results of research has significantly increased
and now encompasses a very broad terrain, including case studies of domestic and foreign companies, biographical studies of entrepreneurs and
entrepreneurial families, works on entrepreneurial alliances, and sector
and regional studies. At the same time, the presence of Latin American
business history has become increasingly apparent at international conferences of Americanists[15] and more recently at international economic
history congresses.[16] The conferences on the economic history of several Latin American countries have included symposia on business history
from early in the nineties. In this respect, the action of the Associação
Brasileira de Pesquisadores em História Econômica should be stressed.

---

[12] As Rory Miller points out, research has advanced much faster in some countries than in
      others for "institutional, economic and academic reasons," such as the degree of polit-
      ical freedom, the availability of funds, or the role played by the state. Miller, "Business
      History," 2.

[13] Mario Cerutti, "Estudios regionales e historia empresarial en México (1840-1920)," *Revista
      Interamericana de Bibliografía* 43, no. 3 (1993): 413-28; María Inés Barbero, "Treinta
      años de estudios sobre la historia de empresas en la Argentina," *Ciclos* 8 (1995): 179-200;
      a new version of this article has been published in Italian in *Imprese e Storia* 19 (1999):
      107-30.

[14] Carlos Dávila L. de Guevara, ed., *Empresa e historia en América Latina* (Bogotá, 1996).
      An English version was published in 1999; see footnote 2.

[15] In Amsterdam (1988), New Orleans (1991), and Stockholm (1994).

[16] At the Twelfth International Economic History Congress in Madrid (1998), María Inés
      Barbero and Mario Cerutti organized a C Session on "Business History in Late Industrialized
      Countries."

Since 1991, this association has promoted international conferences on entrepreneurial history that take place during Brazilian congresses on economic history. The proceeds of such conferences, which have been published, offer a global outlook of the status of that discipline in the country discussed, and include as well works on theoretical issues and papers relative to other Latin American nations.[17]

In contrast to the progress of research and the presence of entrepreneurial history at conferences, the institutionalization of the discipline at universities has been very slow. Except for Colombia,[18] there are very few courses on business history, which no doubt is slowing the growth of that discipline. Nor, with few exceptions, are there specialized research centers. In the past few years, the collaboration of scholars has increased, thanks to their attendance at congresses, the organization of symposia, the publication of collective works, and the creation in 1999 of the Iberian-American Network of Entrepreneurial Studies, organized by historians at the Universidad Autónoma de Nuevo León, Mexico. As a result of this network, and the initiative of a number of colleagues, research has multiplied and there has been noticeable progress in comparative history.[19]

Based on the production of the last two decades, we may outline a list of subjects and issues that emerge as the central elements of recent research. In general, Latin American business history is relatively backward in comparison with other historiographies. The gap is apparent not only in comparison with countries that have an important tradition in business history, like the United States and the United Kingdom, but also in comparison with countries that have made important progress in the past few decades, like Italy and Spain. Nevertheless, this backwardness is shared with many less developed countries, where interest in business history has been relatively marginal until recently.[20] A review of the production

---

[17] T. Szmrecsányi and R. Maranhao, eds., *História de Empresas e Desenvolvimento Economico* (São Paulo, 1996); II Congreso Brasileiro de História Economica – 3ª Conferência Internacional de História de Empresas, *Anais* (Niteroi, 1997). The more recent conferences have published their results in CD-ROM, such as the 1999 Economic History Congress in Curitiba, Brazil, the 1999 Economic History Conference in Montevideo, or the 1998 and 2000 Economic History Conferences in Argentina (Quilmes and Tucumán).

[18] In Colombia, business history is taught in schools of business administration.

[19] In recent years, Latin American historians from Mexico, Colombia, Brazil, Argentina, and Uruguay have organized conferences, seminars, and publications that have included comparative studies.

[20] D. Thripati, "Interpreting Indian Business History," mimeo, Twelfth International Economic History Congress, Madrid, 1998.

of the eighties and the nineties reveals the extent to which the gap has gradually been reduced in the last two decades and allows a diagnosis of the strengths and weaknesses of business history in Latin America.

The first thing to be noted is the multiplication of research and, with that, the increase in the empirical evidence available. There has been a gradual advance from the predominance of global interpretations of a deductive nature to case studies, as a stage in the construction of a new synthesis and concepts reflecting the specific conditions of Latin American countries. Such studies encompass a vast spectrum, which includes not only industrial firms but also agricultural, mining, and transportation companies, banks, trading companies, and so on. There has also been a parallel growth of interest in the nineteenth and twentieth centuries.[21]

As Rory Miller notes, progress in research has been based on "the discovery and use of a much wider range of source material than might have been expected when research in this area commenced."[22] The principal sources of information used by business historians were notarial registers, taxation and company records available in national and regional archives, business archives, daily and weekly newspapers, specialized business publications, and, for the modern period, oral history.[23]

This trend constitutes a decisive contribution, since it permits historians to review the validity of interpretations based on either theoretical models or generalizations of the evidence obtained from local studies. As Carlos Dávila pointed out in reference to the constraints of the psychologistic-culturalistic theories on the origin of the Colombian bourgeoisie, historic research permits discussion of the vast generalizations that simplify reality and are based on the abstractionism and rigid embrace of theoretical schemes.[24]

Among the subjects that have been revised thanks to progress in historical research are the birth and development of entrepreneurial groups, the role of immigrants and domestic elites in the origins of industrialization, the industrial development before the 1929 worldwide

---

[21] Dávila, *Empresa e historia*, includes complete lists of publications in the seven countries considered. See also María Inés Barbero's surveys of Argentina (1995, 1999; see footnote 13).

[22] Miller, "Business History," 11.

[23] In Brazil, a collection of five volumes containing interviews with businessmen was published at the beginning of the 1990s. C. Aquino, ed., *História Empresarial Vivida: Depoimentos de Empresarios Brasileiros Bem sucedidos* (Rio de Janeiro and São Paulo, 1991).

[24] Carlos Dávila L. de Guevara, "El Empresariado Antioqueño (1760-1920): De las interpretaciones psicológicas a los estudios históricos," *Siglo XIX* 5, no. 9 (1990): 12-74.

depression, and the relationships between entrepreneurs and governments. For example, consider the works published in Mexico and Colombia on the regional bourgeoisie, which emphasize the role of the region as
a framework of analysis for the development of entrepreneurial groups
and the importance of commerce as a starting point for accumulation
and diversification.[25] On the role of immigrants, there have been very
important debates in Brazilian historiography regarding regional diversities in the origins of industrial businessmen. Warren Dean's thesis on
the prevalence of foreigners, based on the case of São Paulo, has been
contested by researchers on Minas Gerais and other regions, where the
role of local families was more important.[26]

Case studies, both of companies and of businessmen, have reevaluated
the entrepreneurial abilities and the extent of industrial development
prior to 1930, and have reconsidered the image predominating until the
seventies, which stressed the weaknesses of the entrepreneurial sector
in primary export economies. These studies have also begun to look
at firms from within and to analyze aspects such as strategy, structure,
performance, technology, innovation, forms of financing, and forms of
ownership. Research on company records has developed, and articles
and books have been published in different Latin American countries on
single firms' trajectories.[27] In 1986, financed by ECLA and other organizations, an edited work was published on the technological capacity
of Latin American industry. As it was conducted within the conceptual
framework of the evolutionary theory of the firm, many case studies
included analysis of the companies' histories.[28]

---

[25] Mario Cerutti, *Propietarios, empresarios y empresa en el Norte de México* (Mexico,
2000); Carlos Dávila L. de Guevara, "Estado de los estudios sobre la historia empresarial
de Colombia," in Dávila, ed., *Empresa e historia,* 137-70.

[26] See the discussions on Dean's thesis in C. Lewis, "Historia empresarial brasileña, c.1850-
1945: Tendencias recientes en la literatura," in Dávila, *Empresa e historia,* 35-58. See also
S. de O. Birchal, "Empresarios Brasileiros: Um estudo comparativo," *VII Seminario sobre
Economia Mineira* (Belo Horizonte, 1995), 393-427.

[27] Examples of this kind of publication are, for Argentina: J. Forteza, B. Kosacoff, M. I. Barbero,
F. Porta, and A. Stengel, *Going Global from Latin America. The Arcor Case* (Buenos Aires,
2002); L. Gutiérrez and J. C. Korol, "Historia de Empresas y crecimiento industrial en la
Argentina. El caso de la Fábrica Argentina de Alpargatas," *Desarrollo Económico* 111
(1988): 401-24; for Brazil: E. von der Weid and A. Rodrigues Bastos, *O fio da meada:
Estrategía de expansão de uma indústria textil - Companhia América Fabril* (Rio de
Janeiro, 1986); for Mexico: Mario Cerutti, *Burguesía y capitalismo en Monterrey (1850-
1910)* (Mexico, 1983).

[28] J. Katz et al., *Desarrollo y crisis de la capacidad tecnológica latinoamericana: El caso
de la industria metalmecánica* (Buenos Aires, 1986).

Although it is not possible to summarize briefly the richness of the studies of the past two decades, there are some issues that stand out as specific to the history of Latin American firms and provide it with distinct characteristics. The first observation arising from an overall view is that entrepreneurial history has developed much more than business history. In other words, the main subject of study has been entrepreneurs (men, families, groups) rather than firms. This may be ascribed to various factors. This is the direction followed by business history in Latin America from its inception. The predominance, to the present day, of family firms – even among large enterprises – is another factor that has fostered the study of entrepreneurs rather than firms. One example is the recent research by Mario Cerutti on entrepreneurship in Monterrey, where he analyzes the history of family groups that from the second half of the nineteenth century have retained control of some of the largest companies in the north of Mexico.[29] Moreover, the characteristics of Latin American markets, in which social networks explain as much as contractual relationships, naturally led business history to be strongly inclined toward social history.

Such an inclination does not necessarily imply a constraint, but rather the possibility of analyzing the social and cultural dimensions of companies, the strategies of the actors, and their social networks. Latin American business historiography can, in this respect, help strengthen this perspective, which is usually confined to a marginal position by economic or organizational approaches. Due partly to its inclination to social history and partly to the absence of interest in business theory, Latin American business history is closer to non-Chandlerian or post-Chandlerian perspectives than to what has been the predominant paradigm ever since the seventies. To a certain extent, it may be asserted that it is postmodern without having passed through modernism. Until the nineties, the influence of Alfred Chandler was almost nonexistent – evidence of the insularity of business history in Latin America. This was a result of the poor training of local historians, as well as of their scarce interest in taking part in the theoretical debates of the discipline. It also demonstrates the contrast between Latin American realities and the context in which the Chandlerian paradigm was constructed. One of the main deficits of Latin American business history has been what Colin Lewis designated, in reference to the Brazilian case, as "scarcity of business theory," and which Mario Cerutti has ascribed to the lack of the

[29] Cerutti, *Propietarios*.

necessary technical and theoretical background for most scholars, mostly historians and sociologists.[30]

This situation has gradually improved over the past decade and, although most of the production remains very descriptive, there appears to be – above all in Argentina, Brazil, and Mexico – an increasing interest in theory. This has resulted from the increased interaction among Latin American, North American, and European scholars. A considerable boost was provided by the development of business history in Spain since the eighties, increasing the number of publications in Spanish.

Regarding the Chandlerian paradigm, there are at least three stances worth noting in Latin American business history. The most critical one is the one that questions to what extent the "organizational synthesis" (as defined by Louis Galambos) is the most adequate conceptual framework. From this point of view, Chandler's critics are closer to alternative proposals arising from both North American and European historiography.[31] These critical visions maintain that the Chandlerian model is not the one best suited for the study of Latin America, where big firms are distinctly different from those in the United States, where the state has played a decisive role in the economy, and where the study of small and medium-sized companies is a key issue in the analysis of the historic development of domestic economies.[32]

A second line of investigation applies Chandlerian concepts within an eclectic paradigm, admitting the specificity of local realities while rescuing the value and functionality of concepts such as "strategy," "structure," "three-pronged investments," and so on. This trend also adopts the inductive path proposed by Chandler for the construction of concepts, as well as the comparative method.[33] A third line, which partly

---

[30] Lewis, "Historia empresarial brasileña"; Cerutti, "Estudios regionales."

[31] The edition of the proceedings of the "2ª Conferência Internacional de História de Empresas" in Brazil starts with a conceptual section including articles by Steven Tolliday and Pier Angelo Toninelli, who offer a critical vision of the Chandlerian paradigm and a defense of alternative approaches. See Szmrecsányi and Maranhao, *História de Empresas*.

[32] In his paper "Historia de Empresas e Historia Economica do Brasil," Flavio De Saes says that "a modelo de Chandler tem pouca relaçao com a realidade da empresa nos paises desemvolvidos e que sua tentativa de aplicaçao estrita certamente irá a ignorar os aspectos mais relevantes da história da empresa" ("The Chandlerian model has little relation with the reality of the firm in underdeveloped countries and its use in a strict manner does not take into account the more relevant aspects of business history"). *Anais da 4ª Conferencia Internacional de História de Empresas* (Curitiba, 1999), CD-ROM.

[33] Examples of this approach are María Inés Barbero's and Armando Dalla Costa's research in Argentina and Brazil. See, for example, Barbero, *El Grupo del Banco de Italia y Rio*

intersects the second one, uses the Chandlerian paradigm to compare the development of large firms in Latin America to the model of the American managerial company. A collective work on the history of the big firms in Mexico, edited by Mario Cerutti and Carlos Marichal, includes some works that use Chandlerian concepts and compare Mexican and American experiences.[34]

In the study of large firms, a particularly important subject is the evolution and characteristics of the various types of firms that have operated in Latin America. Among these are the large private companies owned by local investors, the affiliates of multinational companies, and the state-owned companies that played a prominent role until the end of the eighties. Regarding the large domestic companies, a research subject that has advanced in the past few years has been the development of economic groups with diversified investments, the most frequent type of organization from the final decades of the nineteenth century. As many authors point out, economic groups constitute a key issue, because they reveal organizational patterns of the large enterprise, which are different from those prevailing in more industrialized countries and which are specific to late joiners.[35] The study of Latin American groups in an historical context has shown to what extent this pattern of industrial organization was a response to the strategies of family firms and the conditions of markets. Regarding the first case, it has been proven that groups tended to diversify in order to reduce risk and to profit from new opportunities offered by the modernization process.[36] Firms integrated and diversified in markets with high transaction costs, scarce and expensive inputs, and relatively small size.[37] Research on this topic has been very important in Mexico, with the study of regional economies and of the birth and development of family groups, but it started only at the end of the eighties in other countries, such as Argentina, Uruguay, Chile, and Colombia.

---

de la Plata, and Dalla Costa, Perdigáo e a estrategia de uma empresa familiar, both in Segundas Jornadas de Historia Económica (Montevideo, 1999), CD-ROM.

[34] Marichal and Cerutti, eds., Historia de la Gran Empresa en México (Mexico, 1999); see the articles by Carlos Marichal, Sandra Kuntz, and Arturo Grunstein.

[35] N. H. Leff, "Industrial Organization and Entrepreneurship in the Developing Countries: The Economic Groups," in Economic Development and Cultural Change (Chicago, 1978), 661-75; A. Amsden and T. Hikino, "La industrialización tardia en perspectiva histórica," Desarrollo Económico 137 (1995): 3-34.

[36] Cerutti, Propietarios.

[37] M. I. Barbero, De la Compañía General de Fósforos al Grupo Fabril: Origen y desarrollo de un grupo económico en la Argentina (1889-1965), in AAVV, Problemas de investigación, ciencia y desarrollo (San Miguel, 2001).

For obvious reasons, the question of foreign investment has had a privileged place in Latin American historiography. Research on the history of enterprises and entrepreneurs has matured in the past fifteen years. It has focused on the study of transport companies, public utilities companies, banks, mining companies, and companies investing in the primary sector, concentrating on the period previous to 1930.[38] With a few exceptions, research on the manufacturing sector and the contemporary period is still pending.[39] The works published in this field provide significant empirical and theoretical evidence that is relevant to comparative historical studies. These works concern, among other things, the significance of direct investment in the last decades of the nineteenth century, the complexities of the relationships between foreign firms and governments, the diverse origin of capital, and the various forms of external investment. The last issue is particularly relevant, since case studies have helped confirm the limitations of concepts such as "multinational enterprise" or "transnational enterprise," which are not adequate to understand the complexity of the various types of firms developing from the end of the nineteenth century. Such confirmation has boosted the use and construction of alternative concepts such as "free-standing companies," "holding companies," "mixed companies," "investment groups," "entrepreneurial networks," and so on. In the words of Carlos Marichal, "it would appear insufficient for historians to use only the Chandlerian model of evolution of big corporations to analyze all the structures of companies and financial and entrepreneurial groups which already operated in Latin American economies long before 1930."[40]

Another issue, relative to foreign companies, is that of their relationship with the local environment and the dynamics of their establishment in various countries, including questions such as the alternative forms of

[38] A complete list of the publications on these topics is available in Dávila, *Empresa e historia*. See also Carlos Marichal, *Las inversiones extranjeras en América Latina, 1850-1930* (Mexico, 1995).

[39] Recent contributions in this area are the studies by María Inés Barbero on Pirelli in Argentina, by Delia Espina on IBM in Brazil, and by Rory Miller on British companies. See Barbero, "Grupos empresarios, intercambio comercial e inversiones italianas en la Argentina. El caso de Pirelli," *Estudios Migratorios Latinoamericanos* 15-16 (1990): 311-41; Espina, "The History of IBM in Brazil," mimeo, Twelfth International Economic History Congress, Madrid, 1998; id., "O papel das Empresas Multinacionais na Industrializaçao Periferica: Um Estudo da Trajetória da IBM no Brasil," in Szmrecsányi and Maranhao, *História de Empresas*, 335-45.

[40] Marichal, "Introducción," in *Las inversiones extranjeras en América Latina, 1850-1930*, 11-25.

establishment or the role played by government regulations in attracting foreign investment. These issues are crucial in analyzing the strategies of multinational enterprises and the specific characteristics developed by affiliates in the various countries of destination. Research reveals to what extent big firms have been forced to change their strategies and adjust to local conditions in the countries in which they operate, where institutional instability and strong regulations were until recently the rule.[41] A very rich emerging issue is the study of Latin American multinational firms, on which an edited publication has recently appeared.[42]

Another field with significant development from the seventies on has been the history of banking, thanks to the greater access to archives and to the increasing interest shown by historians in financial and monetary issues. The works published so far have helped historians studying the correlation between financial development and economic growth, the role of banking in industrial development, and the different kinds of banks operating in Latin America from the end of the nineteenth century.[43]

Typical of the past few years have been efforts aimed at elaborating syntheses that will gather the evidence provided by the increased research. Examples are collective works with reviews of the status of the discipline in various countries, as well as essays on the historical characteristics of entrepreneurship.[44] Also worth noting is the progress in the field of comparative history both at the domestic and continental levels.[45] A key aspect of Latin American business history is the study of the relationship between the processes of economic modernization and the characteristics and performance of companies. The main contribution in this field has been work combining analysis of economic evolution in general with information originating in case studies, offering a

[41] For example, Delia Espina's research on IBM in Brazil shows how this branch company had to develop a strategy quite different from that of the mother company in order to function in a state-regulated market by introducing product lines already discontinued in other countries. Espina, "The History of IBM in Brazil."

[42] D. Chudnosky and B. Kosacoff, eds., *Las multinacionales latinoamericanas: Sus estrategias en un mundo globalizado* (Buenos Aires, 1999).

[43] Carlos Marichal, "Historiografía de la Banca Latinoamericana. Su despegue," in Szmrecsányi and Maranhao, *História de Empresas*, 47–67.

[44] E. Lahmeyer Lobo, "Características dos Empresários do Setor Privado no Brasil"; Sergio de Oliveira Birchal, "O Empresario Brasileiro: Um Estudo Comparativo," both in II Congreso Brasileiro, *Anais*, 275–86 and 114–28, respectively.

[45] Cerutti and Marichal, *Historia de la gran empresa*; Mario Cerutti, ed., *Empresarios, capitales e industria en el siglo XIX*, special issue of *Siglo XIX* 5, no. 9 (1990).

renewed perspective thanks to the linkage between the macro, secto-rial, and micro levels.[46] The strengthening of institutionalist approaches within economic history has helped boost interest in companies, as well as in the relationship between institutional contexts and the performance of economies.

ACHIEVEMENTS AND RESEARCH AGENDA

The development of business history in Latin America over the past two decades has been largely positive. It has defined itself as a specific area of study in which research and publications have flourished. There has also been progress in catching up to business history in the United States and Europe, although there is a long way to go. This process involves both challenges and opportunities. Among the challenges, the largest one is no doubt that of adjusting the conceptual frameworks prepared for other contexts to specific Latin American realities. Regarding the op-portunities, Latin American business history may provide new evidence for comparative history and help enrich the theoretical and methodolog-ical debates.

One of the main achievements has been the development of empirical research, overcoming the deductive trends that predominated until the end of the seventies. Thanks to the empirical evidence obtained, some myths prevailing until the end of the seventies, such as the presumed absence of entrepreneurship or the unlimited power of foreign com-panies in Latin American countries, have been destroyed. The greatest strides have been achieved in the characterization of the specific na-ture of firms and business institutions, which differ strongly from their counterparts in the North Atlantic world. Among the differences worth mentioning are the slow development of capital markets and managerial capitalism, the significant role of diversified economic groups, the per-sistence of family firms, the role of social networks, the importance of immigration as a source of entrepreneurship, and the role of commerce and banks in financing other activities.

Regarding entrepreneurial behaviors, the results are less satisfactory and the interpretations are still strongly biased ideologically. In this field,

---

[46] S. Haber, *Industry and Underdevelopment* (Stanford, 1989); F. Rocchi, "Building a Nation, Building a Market: Industrial Growth and the Domestic Market in Turn-of-the-Century Argentina" (Ph.D. thesis, University of California at Santa Barbara, 1998); W. Suzigan, *Industria Brasileira: Origem e desenvolvimento* (São Paulo, 1986).

there are two big issues under debate. The first one is to what extent
short-term strategies, the aversion to risk, or the preference for liquidity,
rather than for long-term investment, may have been generated by strong
uncertainty.[47] The second is to what extent the high level of protection
and regulation of the economies from the early thirties to the late eighties
is correlated with the lack of competitiveness and innovation on the part
of entrepreneurs.[48]

Despite its progress, Latin American business history is still confronted
with constraints of various kinds. Although many taboos that prevented
the scholars from studying entrepreneurship have disappeared, mutual
distrust persists. It is still difficult to gain access to companies' archives,
and in general, entrepreneurs avoid commissioning academic historians
to write commemorative histories. In turn, some scholars still are prej-
udiced against entrepreneurship, either by taking a hypercritical stance
or by assigning it an heroic role a priori.

A second problem is that the institutional insertion in business history is comparatively limited, and interdisciplinary research is just beginning. The experience of other countries shows that under different
circumstances, the development of this discipline could undoubtedly be
greater. One of the major deficits concerns the study of firms. As pointed
out earlier, entrepreneurial history is more fully developed than company
history. The stories of individual companies and the analysis of forms of
organization and ownership, management, technology, competitiveness,
and financing are very few. Studies of the legal environment and the industrial relationships at the factory level are almost nonexistent.

A topic scarcely analyzed, despite its significance, is state-owned companies, partly attributable to the difficulty of gaining access to their files.
Nor are there enough studies on the domestic affiliates of foreign companies. The study of small and medium-sized firms is still pending. Research
on this field has been done mostly by economists and sociologists, rather
than by historians, mainly due to the lack of sources. Largely because
of the weakness of company histories, to date there are very few comparative studies or synthetic works with enough empirical evidence on
the specific traits of Latin American companies compared with those in
other countries.

[47] See, for example, J. Sabato, *La clase dominante en la Argentina moderna* (Buenos Aires,
1988); and J. Schvarzer, *La industria que supimos conseguir* (Buenos Aires, 1996).
[48] R. Cortés Conde, *Progreso y declinación de la economía argentina* (Buenos Aires, 1999);
P. Lewis, *La crisis del capitalismo argentino* (Buenos Aires, 1993).

The future growth of business history in Latin America depends mainly on the ability of scholars to overcome the present constraints. The biggest challenge lies in incorporating theoretical frameworks and strengthening the connections with other historiographies, developing in turn the ability to understand local conditions at both the empirical and conceptual levels. Progress has been made in that direction in the past fifteen years, and it should continue.

KEY WORKS

Cerutti, Mario. *Propietarios, empresarios y empresa en el Norte de México.* Mexico, 2000.

Cerutti, Mario, ed. *Empresarios, capitales e industria en el siglo XIX. (Colombia, Argentina, Brasil, México, Uruguay y España)*; special issue of *Siglo XIX* 5, no. 9 (January–June 1990).

Chudnosky, Daniel and Bernardo Kosacoff, eds. *Las multinacionales latinoamericanas: Sus estrategias en un mundo globalizado.* Buenos Aires, 1999.

II Congresso Brasileiro de História Econômica/3ª Conferência Internacional de História de Empresas. *Anais,* vol. 4. Niteroi, 1996.

Dávila, Carlos and Rory Miller, eds. *Business History in Latin America: The Experience of Seven Countries.* Liverpool, 1999.

Dean, Warren. *The Industrialization of São Paulo, 1880–1954.* Austin, 1969.

Fortezza, Jorge, Bernardo Kosacoff, María Inés Barbero, Fernando Porta, and Alejandro Stengel. *Going Global from Latin America. The Arcor Case.* Buenos Aires, 2002.

Heras, Raúl García. *Transportes, negocios y política. La Compañía Anglo Argentina de Tranvías, 1876–1981.* Buenos Aires, 1994.

Marichal, Carlos and Mario Cerutti, comps. *Historia de las grandes empresas en México, 1850–1930.* Mexico, 1997.

Palacios, Marco. *Coffee in Colombia (1850–1970).* Cambridge, 1980.

Peres, Wilson, ed. *Grandes empresas y grupos industriales latinoamericanos.* Mexico, 1998.

Szmrecsányi, Tamás and Ricardo Maranhao, orgs. *História de empresas e desenvolvimiento economico.* São Paulo, 1996.

PART III

Comparative Business History

16

Family Firms in Comparative Perspective

ANDREA COLLI AND MARY B. ROSE

At the end of the twentieth century, family firms remained numerically important in virtually all economies and continued to make valuable contributions in terms of both employment and wealth generation. In Europe in the mid-1990s, the overwhelming majority of registered companies were family-owned, ranging from 70 percent in Portugal to over 95 percent in Italy. In the United States, 12.2 million family firms generated almost one-third of the gross domestic product and employed 37 percent of the workforce.[1] While most family firms are small or medium-sized, and while many are destined to be short-lived, a significant number in the mid-1990s were large, long-established international businesses. A third of the companies in the Fortune 500 listing of the largest American firms were family-controlled and include Ford, Bechtel, Mars, Estée Lauder, and Levi Strauss. There is a similar array of prominent names in Europe such as Michelin, Bic, and L'Oréal (France); Tetrapak, the Wallenberg group, and IKEA (Sweden); Lego (Denmark); Fiat, Benetton, Armani, Ferrero, and Barilla (Italy); and C&A and Heineken (the Netherlands). In South and East Asia, family and business remain culturally inseparable, and networks of small family firms have often been characterized as alternatives

---

[1] See F. Neubauer and A. G. Lank, *The Family Business: Its Governance for Sustainability* (Basingstoke, 1998), 10.

to Western hierarchical organizations. Examples of large family firms include Tata (India) and Kikkoman (Japan), while the giant Korean *chaebol*
is as well a family business. Thus, while family-dominated groups such as
the *zaibatsu* in Japan were swept away during the American occupation,
elsewhere family business groups remain an important characteristic in
many economies.[2]

Scholars of personal capitalism vary widely in their perceptions of
what constitutes a family firm, and notions are often molded by nationally distinctive economic, cultural, and institutional conditions, which
themselves may shift over time. Definitions vary. In some models, the
family firm is an owner-controlled enterprise. Others require that the
family hold the majority of company shares and control management.
Another model calls for at least two generations of family control, in
which a minimum of 5 percent of the voting stock is family-held.[3]

There is a general consensus, however, that family firms represent
an appropriate response to market failure and high transaction costs
during early industrialization. Equally, in mature economies, small and
medium-sized family firms operating in dynamic and flexible networks
are believed to be highly efficient and likely to enjoy an international competitive advantage in rapidly changing niche markets. Most controversy
has centered on the damaging effects of large family-controlled firms in
mature economies. These may reflect concentrations of political as well
as economic power that nonetheless lack the organizational capabilities
needed for the pursuit of dynamic strategies.[4]

The aim of this essay is to explore this debate, highlighting the dangers
of considering "family business" as a generic term rather than as one that

---

[2] Neubauer and Lank, *Family Business*, 10; M. Kets de Vries, *Family Business: Human
Dilemmas in the Family Firm: Text and Cases* (London, 1996), 4; A. Amsden, *Asia's
Next Giant* (Oxford, 1986); G. G. Hamilton and R. C. Feenstra, "Varieties of Hierarchies
and Markets: An Introduction," *Industrial and Corporate Change* 4, no. 1 (1995): 51-92;
H. Morikawa, *Zaibatsu: The Rise and Fall of Family Enterprise Groups in Japan* (Tokyo,
1992).

[3] For these definitions see, for instance, P. Poutziouris and F. Chittenden, *Family Businesses
or Business Families?* (Leeds, 1996), 6-7; Derek F. Channon, *The Strategy and Structure
of British Enterprise* (London, 1973), 161.

[4] Such a perspective is stressed by Alfred D. Chandler in his well-known *Scale and Scope*,
(Cambridge, Mass., 1990), 296, and also – in a country-specific perspective – for instance
by F. Amatori, "Growth via Politics: Business Groups Italian Style," in *Beyond the Firm*, eds.
Masahito Shimotani and Takao Shiba (Oxford, 1997) 109-34, and Andrea Colli and Mary B.
Rose, "Families and Firms: The Culture and Evolution of Family Firms in Britain and Italy
in the Nineteenth and Twentieth Centuries," *Scandinavian Economic History Review* 47
(1999): 24-47.

may be both culturally and politically loaded and hence variable internationally. In this context, while models of business behavior emphasize predominantly economic variables, such as those of the so-called new institutionalists, they become unworkable if firms are not placed in their correct social context. As Granovetter and Swedberg argued, "Economic action is socially situated. It cannot be explained by reference to individual motives alone. It is embedded in ongoing networks of personal relationships rather than being carried out by atomized actors."[5]

Only in this way can national differences in the capabilities and behavior of family firms be understood. Inevitably, networks are often made up of family or familylike connections and have been associated with the distinctive characteristics of personal capitalism. Within such networks, informal "rules of the game" are a reflection of the shared values and attitudes that underpin trust. Casson has extended this methodology to look at the extent to which a dynastic motive may strengthen trust among family members and discourage recruitment of outsiders. What his analysis does not do, however, is explore the distrust and conflict that can destroy family firms, especially in Western societies, during intergenerational succession.[6]

This essay will therefore link an internationally comparative analysis of family firm behavior to what management specialists, in both the United States and Europe, have described as the crucial issue of family business – leadership succession and the governance issues associated with it.

FAMILY BUSINESS: THE STATE OF THE DEBATE

The publication of Alfred Chandler's *Strategy and Structure* in 1962, *Visible Hand* in 1977, and *Managerial Hierarchies*, edited by Chandler and Daems, in 1980 revolutionized the way business historians viewed the shifting nature of international competitive advantage and the rise of the modern business corporation. Chandler's work also had a profound influence on the way in which the capabilities of family businesses were assessed, especially during the Second Industrial Revolution. The American-style managerial corporation, in mainly capital-intensive industries, where ownership was divorced from control, became the template

---

[5] Mark Granovetter and Richard Swedberg, *The Sociology of Economic Life* (Boulder, 1992), 9.

[6] M. Casson, "The Economics of the Family Firm," *Scandinavian Economic History Review* 47, no. 1 (1999): 10–23.

against which all other models were measured. There was an assumed convergence toward it during the twentieth century. While Chandler himself does not draw a neat division between family and managerial companies, it is clear that the distinction between family and managerial capitalism has been overemphasized, providing a deterministic interpretation of the emergence of the modern corporation. In this framework there is little space for the family enterprise, which has instead been identified with inefficient forms of industrial development.[7]

This "stages" approach to business change has proved as controversial as it has been influential. It has sparked a debate, especially with respect to family business, that has continued into the twenty-first century. Chandler, while attracting many disciples, also provoked skeptics to question how far his model captured the experience of business change inside and outside the United States. In this context, much work has centered on the characteristics and capabilities of the family firm.

The first, admittedly tentative, findings in this debate were presented at a session of the 1982 Budapest International Economic History Congress entitled "From Family Firm to Professional Management: Structure and Performance of Business Enterprise," coordinated by Leslie Hannah. The aim of the workshop was to reassess the relevance of the contribution of families in capital-intensive industries of the Second Industrial Revolution. Rather than assuming that their influence was limited to the traditional and labor-intensive sectors, papers moved away from the common Anglo-American comparisons to show that, in Europe generally, the transition to managerial capitalism was – and to a certain extent remains today – slow and incomplete. A clear-cut division of ownership from control is historically misleading.[8] In addition, the papers questioned how far the shortcomings of the management of family firms had been demonstrated in all circumstances. In particular, the so-called Buddenbrook effect of third-generation decline was questioned and thought to be wanting.

Subsequent debate has focused on the extent to which family control has helped or hindered business performance, both within Britain and among such European latecomers as France, Italy, and other

---

[7] This is the perspective adopted, for instance, by William Lazonick, *Business Organisation and the Myth of the Market Economy* (Cambridge, 1991).

[8] Leslie Hannah, *From Family Firm to Professional Management: Structure and Performance of Business Enterprise* (Budapest, 1982), 2.

Mediterranean economies, where family firms have dominated both traditional and advanced sectors.[9] While interpretations emphasizing the sclerotic tendencies of family firms undoubtedly oversimplify the Chandler thesis, others have emphasized the flexibility of small family firms operating in industrial districts in Europe and also in the United States. A perspective investigated by P. Scranton in *Proprietary Capitalism: The Textile Manufacture at Philadelphia, 1800–1885* (Cambridge, 1983), for example, highlighted the competitive capabilities of Philadelphia's proprietary capitalists in textile production in high-income markets in the nineteenth-century United States. More recently, the industrial districts of northern Italy, with their clusters of family firms, have become the basis of renewed competitive advantage.[10] Alongside the discussion of the dynamism of family firms in skill-intensive niches, there has also been an increasing discussion of the persistence of long-lived family firms in capital-intensive industries. However, analysis has shown that actual family involvement in both ownership and control may vary widely from case to case and from country to country.[11]

The movement toward a better understanding of the role of family firms in Western countries' modern industrial development has therefore been considerable. Discussion has emphasized the extent to which the kind of organizational structure adopted by an enterprise is the result of a complex array of forces rather than simply being related to technological issues. The relationship between the evolution of production technologies, capital intensity, and organizational structure is not therefore perceived mechanistically; considerable emphasis is given to the impact of institutional variety. In this context, efficiency becomes the result of a compromise in which culture and history play a significant

---

[9] For a recent overview see Youssef Cassis, *Big Business: The European Experience in the Twentieth Century* (Oxford, 1997).

[10] There is an enormous amount of research focusing on this issue; see, for instance, V. Capecchi, "In Search of Flexibility: The Bologna Metalworking Industry, 1900–1992," in *World of Possibilities: Flexibility and Mass Production in Western Industrialisation*, eds. Charles F. Sabel and Jonathan Zeitlin (Cambridge, 1997), 381–418; and Andrea Colli, "Networking the Market: Evidence and Conjectures from the History of the Italian Industrial Districts," *European Business History Yearbook* 1 (1998): 75–92.

[11] See, for instance, Andrea Colli and Mary B. Rose, "Families and Firms: The Culture and Evolution of Family Firms in Britain and Italy in the Nineteenth and Twentieth Centuries," *Scandinavian Economic History Review* 47 (1999): 41–6; for a general overview see Roy Church, "The Family Firm in Industrial Capitalism: International Perspectives on Hypotheses and History," *Business History* 35, no. 4 (1993): 26ff.

role. With their emphasis upon important historical forces, the legal environment, and the implications of the social embeddedness of family business, these approaches cast doubt on the widespread applicability of American managerial capitalism. As Thomas McCraw observed in *Creating Modern Capitalism*, "The history of American capitalism is extraordinarily significant, but it offers only one among many models of successful development."[12]

Over the past twenty years, there has been intensive work on European family firms, on their history, and especially on the relationship established between organization, performance, national culture, and traditions. Following the Budapest Conference, family business was immediately proposed for the tenth Fuji Conference in 1985. At the beginning of the nineties, on the other hand, the debate surrounding *Scale and Scope* focused on personal capitalism.[13] Equally, there was a special issue in 1993 of *Business History*,[14] and several meetings and conferences have resulted in a number of articles and books. Notable among them is Margarita Dritsas and Terry Gourvish's volume of articles, *European Enterprise: Strategies of Adaptation and Renewal in the Twentieth Century* (Athens, 1997). In addition, in 1996 the theme of family business was included in the Elgar series *Critical Writings in Business History*, with a book edited by Mary B. Rose. The editorial introductions to these volumes highlight the growing complexity of the debate and the need to reevaluate the role and capabilities of family firms.

Outside Europe, family firms had an important part to play in the twentieth century and have been extensively studied, especially by those favoring sociological, as opposed to purely economic, interpretations of business behavior. The big, diversified, and family-owned business on the *zaibatsu* model has been analyzed as a distinctive type of family grouping that survived in Japan until it was abolished during the American occupation following the Second World War. In this context, it is clear that the shift toward a separation between ownership and control was more closely connected to political and strategic factors than to natural forces. In Asia more generally, although there are networks of small and medium-sized family firms, what is especially striking is the well-known and pervasive economic and political power of family groups, such as

---

[12] Thomas McCraw, ed., *Creating Modern Capitalism* (Cambridge, Mass., 1998), 302.

[13] "Scale and Scope: A Review Colloquium," *Business History Review* 64, no. 4 (1990): 690–735.

[14] Geoffrey Jones and Mary B. Rose, *Family Capitalism*, special issue of *Business History* 35, no. 4 (1993).

the Korean *chaebol* or the Indonesian giant Chinese conglomerates.[15] The same trends are found in Latin America, where large, diversified, family-controlled industrial conglomerates (*grupos*) dominate national markets.[16]

The Asian case is an important example of the key role of cultural and institutional frameworks in shaping the form of big business in newly industrialized economies. It provides an empirical test of assumptions that also hold true for European countries,[17] and it enabled Church to conclude that "international comparisons expose the weaknesses of historical explanation based on structural rather than behavioral factors."[18] In so doing, it becomes possible to stress the positive influence of institutional and social conditions on the way in which families run large, diversified businesses. Equally, this research highlights the difficulties in solving agency problems linked to managerial structures when suitable monitoring instruments are absent or inefficient.

What has emerged in recent years is a growing awareness of the need to move beyond the classic dichotomy between family and managerial firms and, in doing so, abandon the determinism of convergence. Current research on family firms has become multidisciplinary, drawing upon sociology, politics, and management as much as economics and history. There has been a growing tendency to analyze the role of family firms in the different stages of growth of a defined national economic system. Significant case study evidence in various Western countries now shows that family firms may have a positive influence in some sectors, especially in services, compared with publicly owned and managerial companies in other spheres. The issue of performance has also been a crucial element when related to corporate governance patterns in both family and managerial enterprises. In other words, it is necessary to clarify the relationship between property structure and performance (in whichever way measured) across space and time. Chandler, of course, has much to say of relevance here, having introduced these dimensions

---

[15] For the Indonesian case, see R. Robinson, *Indonesia: The Rise of Capital* (Sydney, 1986); S. G. Redding, *The Spirit of Chinese Capitalism* (New York, 1993); Y. Sato, "The Salim Group in Indonesia: The Development and Behaviour of the Largest Conglomerate in Southeast Asia," *The Developing Economies* 10, no. 2 (1993): 100-15. For a general overview and a basic bibliography, see Jones and Rose, *Family Capitalism*, 14ff.

[16] I. Lansberg and E. Perrow, "Understanding and Working with Leading Family Businesses in Latin America," *Family Business Review* 4, no. 2 (1991): 2.

[17] Jones and Rose, *Family Capitalism*, 4, 10.

[18] Church, "The Family Firm," 35.

to explain national differences in *Scale and Scope*. The persistence of family firms in the capital-intensive industries of the Second and Third Industrial Revolutions should not be viewed as a reflection of the inability of European and Asian entrepreneurs to understand and adopt the managerial models of the American corporation. Instead, the enduring presence of a particular form of business organization can be seen as evidence of its efficiency against a particular institutional framework rather than as a failure.

LEADERSHIP SUCCESSION AND GOVERNANCE

The notion that family firms are embedded in social networks of trust implies that shared values and attitudes influence both family and business behavior. This approach has lain at the heart of recent work on family business, where informal rules underpin external networks with other firms and with other types of organization, particularly the state. Moreover, international comparisons reveal significant differences in behavior between firms in nations with diverging cultures and varying types of family relationships. The impact of these forces also applies to the internal arrangement of firms, where social norms – relating to family behavior and the aspirations of individual business leaders – may shape such strategies as leadership succession. Increasing attention to this aspect of family firm behavior marks a shift from interest in the external impact of the family firm to its internal management.

In uncertain environments, the family has provided and continues to provide protection against the economic consequences of adverse events, especially in the sphere of management and the choice of future leaders. Where the objectives of family and firm are united, close networks of trust have the advantage of ensuring a combination of incentives, effective monitoring, and loyalty to protect against the danger of managerial impropriety.[19]

There is ample historical evidence to support the idea that families, religious groupings, and local business communities became internal markets for managerial labor in this way. In Britain, examples abound of this kind of personal capitalism in the nineteenth century. Though in the interwar period there were cases of outside recruitment of executives and some movement toward the professionalization of

---

[19] R. A. Pollak, "A Transaction Cost Approach to Families and Households," *Journal of Economic Literature* 23, no. 2 (1985): 581–608.

management – in, for example, the brewing industry – inside promotion was the norm at all levels of British management until the 1950s.[20] In the early-nineteenth-century United States, the managers employed by the Boston Associates, both in their early mill towns and in commercial management, were drawn from within an extended circle of trusted contacts. While the shift from personal to managerial capitalism was one of the distinguishing features of the Second Industrial Revolution in the United States, firms such as Ford remained family-dominated into the twentieth century. Equally, a legacy of Philadelphia's proprietary capitalism was a capacity to secure continued family control of businesses through the creation of spinoff firms to accommodate subsequent generations well into the twentieth century.[21]

Similarly, in continental Europe, family succession was the norm in the nineteenth and early twentieth centuries. In southern Europe today, the family business is synonymous with insider succession. In Italy, therefore, "the idea that a company is a personal or family domain seems to materialise as a persistent culture."[22] In the Far East, Japanese *zaibatsu* were held together by the financial ties of collective family ownership, but in the interwar period they were managed professionally. However, if these giant groupings drew their managers from outside the family, the likening of these men to "adopted sons" implies an allegiance to business and family objectives.[23] After the Second World War, the American

---

[20] Peter L. Payne, "Family Business in Britain: An Historical and Analytical Study," in *Family Business in the Era of Industrial Growth: Its Ownership and Management*, eds. A. Okochi and S. Yasuoka (Tokyo, 1984), 60–85; M. B. Rose, "The Family Firm in British Business, 1780–1914," in *Business Enterprise in Modern Britain*, eds. Maurice W. Kirby and Mary B. Rose (London, 1994), 61–87; Terry R. Gourvish and Richard G. Wilson, eds., *The British Brewing Industry, 1830–1980* (Cambridge, 1994), 381–92.

[21] Peter D. Hall, "Family Structure and Economic Organisation: Massachusetts Merchant, 1700–1850," in *Family and Kin in Urban Communities, 1700–1930*, ed. Tamara Hareven (New York, 1977), 87–100; H. V. Wortzel, "Changing Patterns of Management in Lowell Mills," in Okochi and Yasuoka, *Family Business in the Era of Industrial Growth*, 83–99; Philip Scranton, "Build a Firm, Start Another: The Bromleys and Family Firm Entrepreneurship in the Philadelphia Region," *Business History* 35, no. 4 (1993): 115–41.

[22] Keetie E. Sluyterman and Hélène J. M. Winkelman, "The Dutch Family Firm Confronted with Chandler's Dynamics of Industrial Capitalism, 1890–1940," *Business History* 35, no. 4 (1993): 152–83; Jurgen Kocka, "The Entrepreneur, the Family and Capitalism," *German Business History Yearbook* (1981): 53–82; the quotation is taken from Franco Amatori, "Italy: The Tormented Rise of Organisational Capabilities between Governments and Families," in *Big Business and the Wealth of Nations*, eds. Alfred D. Chandler, Jr., Franco Amatori, and Takashi Hikino (Cambridge, 1997), 270.

[23] H. W. Strachan, *Family and Other Business Groups in Economic Development: The Case of Nicaragua* (New York, 1976), 41–2; Mark Fruin, "The Family as a Firm and the Firm as

occupation of Japan marked the demise of the family-owned groupings in Japan; but elsewhere, such as in India and Latin America, family succession remained the norm in the firmly entrenched business groupings.[24]

If the external behavior of family firms is influenced by the cultural norms of their host society, the culture of individual family firms is inextricably linked to the hopes and aspirations of the founders or their successors. Since the outlook of any business is intimately tied to its leaders, changes at its head can influence business culture, a firm's internal and external relationships, and the way these change through time. Thus: "For the entrepreneur, the business is essentially an extension of himself. . . . And if he is concerned about what happens to his business after he passes on, that concern usually takes the form of thinking of the kind of monument he will leave behind."[25]

A desire for internal stability is entirely understandable; however, dynamism and innovation in a rapidly changing environment are more likely when firms recruit from outside. Conversely, a preference for insider succession in mature family firms can create inward- rather than outward-looking business cultures in firms, which can then become almost impervious to change.

If family succession tends to reduce the risk and potential transaction costs of changes in business leadership, the process can be problematic and conflict-ridden. Any institution, and particularly a family firm, can be likened to the "lengthening shadow of one man." However, since "a shadow is a fleeting thing and if the firm is to persist beyond the lifetime of its founder, [its] leadership must pass from one generation to the next."[26] In Western family businesses, leadership succession represents one of the most traumatic internal shocks an organization will face.[27] Though succession is by no means the only factor determining the survival or prosperity of family businesses, the conflict-ridden nature of generational transition has been identified as one of the principal reasons why family

a Family in Japan: The Case of Kikkoman Shoya Company Ltd.," *Journal of Family History* 5, no. 4 (1980): 432–49; M. Chen, *Asian Management Systems: Chinese, Japanese and Korean Styles of Business* (London, 1995), 166–7.

24 Strachan, *Family*, 38–42.

25 The quotation is in Neubauer and Lank, *Family Business*, 145.

26 Steven M. Davis, "Entrepreneurial Succession," *Administrative Science Quarterly* 13, no. 2 (1968): 402–3.

27 Mary B. Rose, "Beyond Buddenbrooks: The Family Firm and the Management of Succession in Nineteenth-Century Britain," in *Entrepreneurship, Networks and Modern Business*, eds. Jonathan Brown and Mary B. Rose (Manchester, 1993), 127–43.

firms, especially in Anglo-Saxon societies, are often short-lived.[28] Even a casual reading of the specialist family firm management literature, much of it relating to American and British firms, confirms the view that the passage of a business from a founder to his or her successor is likely to be fraught with difficulty.[29]

Historical evidence supports this idea. In nineteenth-century Britain, although numerous forces, including inheritance laws and strong parental authority, led to a dynastic approach to business, there were often serious problems associated with creating continuity in family firms. The principal reason why smooth generational transition was and is so rare in family firms is that it involves personalities and interpersonal relationships of the most delicate nature. Moreover, so intertwined are the public and private dimensions of the family business that disputes can have repercussions for both family and firm. In sharp contrast with the situation in Asia, where the elderly are revered as part of an extended family, in the West many family firm conflicts have stemmed from the frustration and perceived damage to firms when aging business leaders have been reluctant to retire.[30]

Precisely how family business owners have prepared for their own demise has varied through time, but ultimately the "mature firm and its aging operators had to face the issue of succession."[31] Formal planning for family firm succession, especially the involvement of outsiders, was a comparative rarity in both Britain and the United States in the nineteenth century. In both of the countries, for example, although considerable evidence of familial meritocracies and shop-floor training in many firms gives a lie to unthinking nepotism, the existence of a formal succession strategy was a comparative rarity.[32] In the twentieth century, on the other

---

[28] S. Dutta, *Family Business in India* (New Delhi, 1997), 32.

[29] On these issues see, for instance, R. G. Donnelly, "The Family Business," *Harvard Business Review* 42, no. 2 (1964): 96; H. Levinson, "Conflicts That Plague the Family Business," *Harvard Business Review* 49, no. 3 (1971): 90–5; L. B. Barnes and A. Hershon, "Transferring Power in the Family Business," *Harvard Business Review* 54, no. 5 (1976): 105; P. B. Alcorn, *Success and Survival in the Family Owned Business* (New York, 1982), 2; W. Beckhard and W. G. Dyer, "Managing Change in the Family Firm: Issues and Strategies," *Sloan Management Review* 24 (1982–3): 59–61; W. G. Dyer, *Cultural Change in Family Firms: Anticipating and Managing Business and Family Transitions* (San Francisco, 1986), 3–13; and G. R. Ayres, "Rough Justice: Equity in Family Business Succession Planning," *Family Business Review* 3, no. 2 (1990): 3–22.

[30] Rose, "Beyond Buddenbrooks," 136; Dutta, *Family Business in India*, 77.

[31] P. Scranton, "Learning Manufacture: Shop Floor Schooling and the Family Firm," *Technology* 27, no. 3 (1986): 44.

[32] Rose, "Beyond Buddenbrooks," 136–40; Scranton, "Learning Manufacture," 44.

hand, failures in succession planning could lead to the involvement of management consultants whose reports, by challenging the prevailing culture of a family business, were often so controversial that they were rejected, leaving no alternative but to "go public."[33]

In Italy, experience and the solution of the succession problem have varied between large and small family firms. In industrial districts, the high turnover of firms often means that succession never becomes an issue. Where it is faced, sons or heirs often do not enter their parents' firm. Rather, the establishment of stem firms, sometimes in related areas, solves the internal problem of the family while contributing to the dynamism of the district in ways identified in other regions of the world with similar industrial characteristics. In medium-sized firms, such as Italy's "pocket multinationals" (i.e., small and medium-sized family-owned enterprises active in niche markets worldwide),[34] the issue of succession is far more significant and is currently a key issue, as many of these firms were founded in the early 1950s. Succession in these firms is rarely planned and is almost always familial. Only rarely are consultants used other than to manage the financial implications of transition. Second- and third-generation succession is problematic in Italy because of the usually large numbers of heirs. It is here that the consultant has the most prominent role in drawing up agreements restricting the entry of family members.[35] The position is different again in the large, old family enterprises, where family ownership is limited to relatively few shares thanks to syndicate agreements. Managerial hierarchies are found in these firms, though they rarely function without family interference.

In the latter part of the twentieth century, the threat of extreme family conflict in Western family firms encouraged the substitution of formal

[33] M. B. Rose, "Entrepreneurial Legacies and Leadership Succession in British Business in the 1950s," in *The Entrepreneur and Organization: Comparative Perspectives*, eds. Michael J. Lynskey and Seiichiro Yonekura (Oxford, 2002), 252–70.

[34] See Carlo Mario Guerci, *Alle origini del successo: I campioni della media impresa industriale italiana*, Il Sole 24 ore (Milan, 1998); Franco Amatori and Andrea Colli, *Impresa e industria in Italia: Dall'Unità ad oggi* (Venice, 1999), 325ff; Guido Corbetta, *Le medie imprese* (Milan, 2001).

[35] A situation stressed by the contemporary literature on leadership succession in family firms, especially that produced by consultants. See, among the most recent research, C. E. Schillaci, *I processi di transizione del potere imprenditoriale nelle imprese familiari* (Turin, 1990); G. Piantoni, *La successione familiare in azienda: Continuità dell'impresa e ricambio generazionale* (Milan, 1990); C. Demattè and G. Corbetta, *I processi di transizione delle imprese familiari* (Milan, 1993); V. Bertella, *La pianificazione del ricambio generazionale nell' impresa familiare* (Padua, 1995).

for informal rules and structures to ease the transition within firms. A formal code of corporate governance creates, as outlined in the Cadbury Report, a "system by which companies are directed and controlled."[36] This has been likened to a political constitution that describes "the organs of the business, their tasks, the extent and limits of their power, their internal structure, the composition of their membership and their mode of operating" and reduces the prime areas of conflict within the family firm. Although such constitutions and the use of formal family meetings have increased in popularity in Europe, Latin America, and Australia, in recent years only 15 percent of family firms in the Western world have effective family meetings.[37]

The problem of intergenerational conflict, which accounts for the frequent demise of Western family firms after a single generation, is not replicated in all cultures. The durability in India of family businesses over several generations has been explained in terms of a combination of distinctive attitudes to the family and to family members that minimize the degree of conflict. Close ties between business families and the major political parties since Independence have also contributed. As in many countries where family firms thrived in the twentieth century, the family is a crucial dimension of Indian culture. "The center of the Indian social identity is the family. Family businesses are not merely an economic structure, for most ... individuals, they are a source of social identity. There is a strong social obligation to continue one's father's work."[38]

Certainly there is competition and rivalry within any Indian business family, but a number of forces reduce the level of outright hostility. In the first place, most Indian business families are extended rather than nuclear; as many as five generations may live under one roof. This in itself can encourage greater conformity to the norms of other generations than might be found in the West. Secondly, a formality whereby a person is referred to by hierarchical position stifles much intergenerational conflict. Finally, whereas in the West father–son tensions represent the prime source of conflict, in India the certainty of succession of fathers by sons has tended to encourage compromise. Delayed retirement is comparatively rare.[39]

---

[36] Neubauer and Lank, *Family Business*, 60.
[37] Ibid., ix, 72–4.
[38] Dutta, *Family Business in India*, 91.
[39] Ibid.

CONCLUSIONS

We have traced the shifting controversy surrounding the impact of family firms in modern and mature economies, which reaffirms the need to place business in its social, historical, and institutional as well as its economic context. The role of personal networks has emerged as critical to family firm behavior, while the aims of family and firm remain intertwined. This has had implications for the study of both the external relations of business and their internal strategies.

During the last two decades of the twentieth century, family business was often at center stage in the debates surrounding organizational change in business. Analysis matured from a defense of personal capitalism to the discussion of international variations in business capabilities generally and family firms in particular. It remains to be seen how far multidisciplinary approaches to the study of family firms will move analysis forward. However, the numerical significance of family business alone, and its prominence as a field of managerial study, means that business historians will continue to take family firms seriously.

KEY WORKS

Church, Roy. "The Family Firm and Industrial Capitalism: International Perspectives on Hypotheses and History," *Business History* 35, no. 4 (1993): 17-43.

Dritsas, Margarita and Terry Gourvish. *European Enterprise: Strategies of Adaptation and Renewal in the Twentieth Century.* Athens, 1997.

Dutta, S. *Family Business in India.* New Delhi, 1997.

Hannah, Leslie. *From Family Firm to Professional Management: Structure and Performance of Business Enterprise.* Budapest, 1982.

Jones, Geoffrey and Mary B. Rose. *Family Capitalism.* Special issue of *Business History* 35, no. 4 (1993).

Neubauer, F. and A. G. Lank. *The Family Business: Its Governance for Sustainability.* Basingstoke, 1998.

Okochi, A. and S. Yasuoko, eds. *Family Business in the Era of Industrial Growth: Its Ownership and Management.* Tokyo, 1984.

Rose, Mary B. "Beyond Buddenbrooks: The Family Firm and the Management of Succession in Nineteenth-Century Britain." In *Entrepreneurship, Networks and Modern Business*, edited by Jonathan Brown and Mary B. Rose, 127-43. Manchester, 1993.

"The Family Firm in British Business, 1780-1914." In *Business Enterprise in Modern Britain,* edited by M. W. Kirby and Mary B. Rose, 61-87. London, 1994.

Family Business. Cheltenham, 1996.

17

Multinationals

GEOFFREY JONES

The study of the business history of multinationals has generated an extensive literature that, although drawn on and inspired by Chandlerian concepts, has also developed a strong identity of its own. The literature has at least three distinctive features. First, there has been an attempt to develop comparative frameworks and to explore issues using cross-national comparisons. Second, there has been considerable interaction between business historians and economic theorists of the multinational. Third, business history research has made an impact on, and is cited in, the wider literature on contemporary multinationals written by economists and international business theorists.[1]

PIONEERS

In one sense, the literature on the history of multinationals has a long ancestry. Foreign direct investment (FDI) – along with portfolio investment – forms one component of foreign investment as a whole, and the extensive historical literature on nineteenth-century capital flows contains valuable insights on international business. However these

---

[1] John H. Dunning, *Multinational Enterprises and the Global Economy* (Wokingham, 1992); R. E. Caves, *Multinational Enterprise and Economic Analysis*, 2nd ed. (Cambridge, 1996).

studies, and later ones by economic historians, focused on capital flows
and did not make the distinction between portfolio flows of capital and
FDI, which involves ownership as well as control. It was in the United
States that the earliest studies of FDI and multinationals began. These
studies predated the invention of the term "multinational" around 1960.
During the interwar years, a number of U.S. academics published FDI
estimates and analyses of the growth and impact of multinational enterprises. These included discussions of the management and technological
as well as financial aspects of these firms. However, studies of multinationals and direct investment were constrained by the general neglect of
firms and entrepreneurs in mainstream economics. The work of Edith
Penrose on the theory of the firm, which included explicit discussions
of the international operations of firms, was an outstanding exception.[2]

The United States accounted for up to 85 percent of new FDI out-
flows in the two decades after the end of the Second World War, and
during the 1960s the rapid expansion of U.S. multinationals abroad stimulated new interest in the historical origins of U.S. international business.
The Multinational Enterprise Project, directed by Raymond Vernon at the
Harvard Business School, created a vast database that traced the historical
growth of the largest U.S. multinationals of the period. This remains the
largest database on the historical growth of multinationals. For example,
Chandler used it in *Scale and Scope*. However, Vernon's methodology of
tracing back historically the growth of contemporary large firms considerably distorted the growth pattern of multinationals.[3]

The growth of business history in the United States after the Second
World War saw the publication of a series of case studies of large U.S. firms
that operated internationally. An outstanding example was the commissioned history of Standard Oil of New Jersey (later EXXON).[4] However, it
was the study of Ford's international growth by Mira Wilkins and F. E. Hill
in 1964, *American Business Abroad: Ford on Six Continents* (Detroit,
1964), that had the most profound consequences for scholarship in the

---

[2] F. A. Southard, *American Industry in Europe* (Boston, 1983); C. F. Remer, *Foreign In-
vestment in China* (New York, 1933); Cleona Lewis, *America's Stake in International
Investments* (Washington, D.C., 1938); Edith Penrose, *The Theory of the Growth of the
Firm* (London, 1959).

[3] James W. Vaupel and Jean P. Curhan, *The Making of Multinational Enterprise* (Cambridge,
Mass., 1969); id., *The World's Multinational Enterprises* (Cambridge, Mass., 1974).

[4] Ralph W. Hidy and Muriel E. Hidy, *Pioneering in Big Business* (New York, 1955); George
Sweet and Evelyn H. Knowlton, *The Resurgent Years, 1911-1927* (New York, 1956);
Henrietta M. Larson, *New Horizons* (New York, 1971).

history of multinationals. Subsequently Wilkins embarked on an historical study of all U.S. multinationals. The publication of her *The Emergence of the Multinational Enterprise* (Cambridge, Mass., 1970), followed by its companion volume, *The Making of Multinational Enterprise* (Cambridge, Mass., 1974), were landmark events. Wilkins's volumes produced the first – and still the only – business history of all U.S. firms engaged in FDI from the nineteenth century to the 1970s. The books – based on company and government archives, published sources, and interviews – are among the major achievements of twentieth-century business history, both in their scope and in their methodology. In contrast to most contemporary researchers, Wilkins did not confine her attention to leading manufacturing enterprises, but also included the service and national resource sectors, small firms, and many firms that had disappeared over time. Wilkins set the standard for the next thirty years of research on the history of international business.

Another major pioneer, John H. Dunning, a British scholar, was also concerned with U.S. multinationals. Dunning's study of U.S. manufacturing and multinational investment, *American Investment in British Manufacturing Industry* (London, 1958), traced their historical origins back to the nineteenth century and identified the key managerial, technological, and other variables affecting their investment decisions. The origins of Dunning's subsequent "eclectic paradigm" are already apparent in this study.

Although Dunning's work focused subsequently on developing the theory of the multinational enterprise, he also made a second major impact on the business history of multinationals through his historical estimates of the size of FDI. Researchers in the 1960s assumed that the historical origins of FDI and the multinational were to be found in the United States. Europe's large capital exports in the late nineteenth century were assumed to be overwhelmingly portfolio in composition. For example, the first study of the historical growth of British multinationals, published by John M. Stopford (*Business History Review*, 1974), was as an outgrowth of Vernon's multinational enterprise project. Stopford took the view that only 10 percent of British foreign investment before 1914 was FDI and sought to explain why British manufacturers were so slow to emulate their American counterparts in establishing affiliates abroad.

In the mid-1970s Dunning and his collaborator, Tom Houston, proposed in *UK Industry Abroad* (London, 1976) a radical revision of this interpretation, arguing that about one-third of total British foreign investment before 1914 involved some managerial "control" even though its

institutional forms were rather different from the U.S. model. This became the basis of Dunning's estimates of the size of world FDI at the
benchmark dates of 1914 and 1938. These estimates, first published in
an article included in *The Growth of International Business* (London,
1983), greatly raised the level of FDI in the world economy before 1914
and identified Western Europe, especially the United Kingdom, as the
main home region for FDI. This reinterpretation was echoed in the work
of other economists as well as that of Mira Wilkins.[5] Despite the frailty of
such quantitative estimates, the reinterpretation by Dunning and others
set the stage for a major research effort on the history of multinationals.

NATIONAL PATTERNS

It is a measure of Wilkins's achievement that comparatively little new
research has been conducted on the history of U.S. multinationals over
the past twenty years. Over the same period, research on European and
Japanese firms has demonstrated that the pattern of multinational growth
seen in the case of American firms was by no means replicated elsewhere.
The United Kingdom, as the home of the greatest proportion of world
FDI before 1950, attracted much attention. During the 1980s, business
historians were especially concerned with establishing the scale and determinants of British manufacturing multinational investment. A variety
of methodologies were employed. In the absence of any reliable FDI
statistics before the 1960s, in his research S. J. Nicholas counted the
number of manufacturing affiliates established by British companies. He
explicitly applied transaction cost theories to explain their growth and
showed that this growth could be explained as a response to transac-
tional market failure. British firms grew across borders by internalizing
markets for proprietary assets, such as technology and brands, because
such markets were subject to high transaction costs.[6]

Geoffrey Jones employed a more Chandlerian approach, undertaking
a number of in-depth archivally based case studies of British multinational

---

[5] Irving Stone, "British Direct and Portfolio Investment in Latin America before 1914," *Journal of Economic History* 37, no. 3 (1977): 690–722; Peter Svedberg, "The Portfolio – Direct Composition of Private Foreign Investment in 1914 Revisited," *Economic Journal* 88 (1978): 763–77.

[6] Stephen J. Nicholas, "British Multinational Investment before 1939," *Journal of European Economic History* 11, no. 3 (1982): 605–30; id., "Agency Contracts, Institutional Modes, and the Transition to Foreign Direct Investment by British Manufacturing Multinationals before 1939," *Journal of Economic History* 43, no. 3 (1983): 675–86.

manufacturing companies. The role of protectionism in stimulating such investment emerged clearly from these studies. Jones also discussed the performance of the British firms abroad, which appeared to suffer from precisely the managerial weaknesses of the kind that could be predicted from the Chandlerian critique of "personal capitalism." The complexities of measuring performance and the difficulties of generalization about the subject led to an inconclusive debate on the subject. More recent research in the area of performance and competence has switched attention to the resources and services sectors.

In 1986 Mira Wilkins returned to the different types of firms engaged in British FDI before 1945 and thus opened another area of debate. She noted that the predominant corporate form of British FDI had a distinctly non-American shape. It consisted of thousands of firms registered in Britain to conduct business exclusively abroad that did not grow out of existing domestic enterprises. They usually specialized in a single country, where they might own a plantation or a utility. Dunning included such firms in his revised FDI estimates, and Wilkins now gave them a name: "free-standing firms."[7]

The existence of these free-standing firms has stimulated a large debate, not least among transaction costs theorists anxious to explain them. Among business historians, a number of issues have been explored. Wilkins emphasized the lean managerial structures of the British free-standing firms. Tiny head offices usually consisted of little more than a board of part-time directors, with most financial, legal, and technical functions contracted out. There were no U.S.-style managerial hierarchies. As a result, Wilkins argued, they had no sustainable advantage in countries such as the United States and disappeared during the early twentieth century, although they persisted longer in countries that lacked strong local management. British business historians have responded by arguing that although the absence of U.S.-style managerial hierarchies made the free-standing form unsuitable for high-technology manufacturing industries, these governance structures were much more effective in Britain's large overseas service and resource investments.

For example, Jones, in *British Multinational Banking 1830–1990*, argued that British banks in the nineteenth century managed their large

---

[7] Mira Wilkins, "Defining a Firm: History and Theory," in *Multinationals: Theory and History*, eds. Peter Hertner and Geoffrey Jones (Aldershot, 1988), 80–95; id., "The Free-Standing Company, 1870–1914: An Important Type of British Foreign Direct Investment," *Economic History Review* 61, no. 2 (1988): 259–82.

overseas branch networks by using socialization strategies of control. They were effective in minimizing potential agent–principal conflicts and reducing the need for large head offices to monitor staff. These overseas banks also continued in existence long after 1914, deriving substantial advantages from incumbency but also capable of renewing their strategies in the face of changed circumstances. Further research has established that free-standing firms were by no means an exclusively British phenomenon. Wilkins and Harm G. Schröter edited a major volume, *The Free-Standing Firm in the World Economy* (Oxford, 1999), that explored both their comparative and theoretical dimensions.

A further ongoing debate has concerned the place of free-standing firms within wider business networks. Although European free-standing companies were nominally independent of one another, they were often linked in various ways. Wilkins identified ten different types of "clusters" of British free-standing companies, which form around various interest groups and producers of services. In *Merchant Enterprise in Britain* (Cambridge, 1992), Stanley Chapman explored a similar theme in his identification of thirty British "investment groups," consisting of networks of British companies associated through cross-shareholdings or interlocking directorships. At the heart of these networks were often merchants or trading companies. Chapman documented that these investment groups sometimes reached a formidable size. This ran counter to the Chandlerian view that the problem with British business from the late nineteenth century was its inability to create larger units. However, in other respects, Chapman supported the Chandlerian critique of personal capitalism. Chapman viewed the investment groups as "primarily a device to maintain the wealth and power of the family (or families) that constituted the particular business." They had inadequate management and by 1914 seemed fated for extinction.

The view that these investment groups suffered from weak management – as opposed to a distinctly non-American type of management – has been criticized by various business historians. Geoffrey Jones suggested in *Merchants to Multinationals* (Oxford, 2000) a more dynamic picture. Rather than being regarded as primarily financial in function, this research implied that the British trading companies should be seen as entrepreneurial enterprises that used their knowledge of countries and products to search out new opportunities for trade. They set up organizational systems and flexible organizations to exploit the opportunities. These characteristics were most evident in the expanding world economy before 1914 but were still evident in the interwar years. Compared to the United States, Jones argued, the managerial competencies of the British firms looked fragile. However, they were real, resting in areas of knowledge and information, and worked well for complex business groups based on trade and resource exploitation in developing countries. Meanwhile the post-1945 history of British multinationals is still being explored. In this period the British maintained their position as the world's second largest multinational investor after the United States, despite the alleged managerial shortcomings of their firms. From the 1960s, the bulk of British FDI was shifted from the Commonwealth to elsewhere in Europe and especially to the United States. Jones has examined the post-1945 strategies and performance of British service sector companies in particular, but research remains to be done on British multinational enterprise in this period.[8] The rewards of this work will be great, not least if a correlation can be established between the strong propensity to invest abroad and the underperforming British domestic economy.

Research on the history of multinational enterprises in other European countries was initially less vigorous than in Britain, although more recently a stream of publications has emerged. Lawrence G. Franko published a study, *The European Multinationals* (London, 1976), that suggested a "Continental model" of multinational enterprise. This work utilized Vernon's Harvard database, but its conclusions were limited by the same methodological problems.

Peter Hertner pioneered archivally based case study research on multinationals based in Germany. German firms were very active in the first stages of multinational growth before 1914, though they preferred international cartels in the interwar years and, after the Second World War, opted more for exporting than for FDI. In a series of articles, Hertner examined the growth of German multinational investment in chemicals and electricals, as well as branded consumer goods, and made important studies of German FDI in banking and the electro-technical industry, especially in Italy. This research was extended and developed by Harm Schröter, whose work included detailed studies of the growth of German multinational investment in the chemical industry, as well as surveys of the history of German multinational investment as a whole. There have

[8] Geoffrey Jones, "British Multinationals and British Business since 1850," in *Business Enterprise in Modern Britain from the Eighteenth to the Twentieth Centuries*, eds. Maurice W. Kirby and Mary B. Rose (London, 1994), 172–206. British firms were particularly strong in branded foods and beverages, including alcohol. For their role in a comparative perspective, see Teresa da Silva Lopes, "Brands and the Evolution of Multinationals in Alcoholic Beverages," *Business History* 44, no. 3 (2002): 1–30.

also been important studies of the history of German FDI in the United States by T. R. Kabisch, and more recently on German multinationals in the United Kingdom before 1914 by Antje Hagen, which involved the construction of a large-scale database of firms.[9]

A number of features of German international business have attracted particular attention. In the wake of the loss of most German FDI as a result of the First World War, German firms opted for strategies that lessened risks in their overseas business, notably cartels. Schröter has written extensively as well on the causes and consequences of this phenomenon. New research on the history of Germany's multinational metal trading companies has also been important. Susan Becker has compared the international strategies of Metallgesellschaft and the Belgian firm Vieille Montagne. In her study on German metal traders before 1914, Becker examines closely the use made of cartels and long-term relationships as alternatives to FDI.[10]

Throughout the other European countries, a striking difference has been shown in the propensity of firms of different countries to engage in FDI. In the twentieth century, Dutch, Swedish, and Swiss firms undertook substantial FDI. These firms benefited from their countries' neutrality – although the Netherlands was occupied in the Second World War – which meant that their foreign investments were spared the disruption of the German case. In contrast to the American experience, small and family-owned enterprises were often active foreign investors, and firms went abroad early in their corporate careers. In its colonial orientation and its use of free-standing companies, Dutch FDI had some similarities to British FDI. However, Dutch manufacturing firms also made large investments in neighboring European countries. Generally, Dutch firms were inclined to invest abroad due to the "small economy" effect – that is, their

---

[9] Peter Hertner, "German Multinational Enterprise before 1914: Some Case Studies," in Hertner and Jones, *Multinationals*, 113–34; Harm Schröter, "Die Auslandsinvestitionen der deutschen chemischen industrie 1870 bis 1930," *Zeitschrift für Unternehmensgeschichte* 35, no. 1 (1990): 1–22; id., "Continuity and Change: German Multinationals since 1850," in *The Rise of Multinationals in Continental Europe*, eds. Geoffrey Jones and Harm G. Schröter (Aldershot, 1993), 28–48; T. R. Kabisch, *Deutsches kapital in den USA von der Reichsgründung bis zur Sequestrierung (1917) in Freigabe* (Stuttgart, 1982); Antje Hagen, *Deutsche Direkinvestitionen in Grossbritannien, 1871–1981* (Stuttgart, 1997).

[10] Harm G. Schröter, "Risk and Control in Multinational Enterprise: German Businesses in Scandinavia, 1918–1939," *Business History Review* 62, no. 3 (1988): 420–43; Susan Becker, *Multinationalität hat verschiedene Gesichter: Formen internationaler Unternehmenstätigkeit der Société Anonyme des Mines et Fonderies de Zinc de la Vieille Montagne und der Metallgesellschaft vor 1914* (Bonn, 1999).

domestic market was so small that they had to look elsewhere for growth opportunities.[11] However there were also idiosyncratic factors in their growth. For example, as W. Ruigrok and R. van Tulder demonstrated in *The Logic of International Restructuring* (London, 1995), the Dutch refusal before 1910 to comply with international patenting law facilitated the growth of Dutch margarine and electrical firms by enabling them to freely copy innovations from elsewhere, although they could utilize such technology only within the Netherlands.

The literature on the history of Swiss multinationals is scarcer, largely because of data access problems, but there has been a major survey by Harm Schröter, as well as studies of particular sectors, such as trading companies. Though part of a small economy, Swiss firms were active abroad in a wide range of manufacturing and other sectors, though Swiss banks, for example, were notably slow to invest abroad. Swiss multinationals were clear beneficiaries of neutrality. Nestlé's position as one of the most successful foreign multinationals in Japan, for example, rested on its unbroken presence in that country since 1933, as well as its highly successful instant coffee product.[12]

There is a more extensive literature on the historical development of Swedish multinationals, which was extensive before 1914, even though Sweden was a capital-importing economy. The strong interest in business history in Sweden has resulted in the publication of a series of case studies of major Swedish multinationals such as Ericsson and Swedish Match. Kurt Lundgren has attempted a general explanation of the propensity of Swedish firms to engage in multinational investment, identifying the Swedish ability to learn from and improve on foreign technologies as a key factor generating ownership advantages. Per Boje's recent study has now provided an account of the history of Danish multinationals, as well as foreign multinationals in Denmark, before 1950.[13]

[11] Ben Gales and Keetie E. Sluyterman, "Outward Bound: The Rise of Dutch Multinationals," in Jones and Schröter, *Rise of Multinationals*, 65–98; Keetie E. Sluyterman, "Dutch Multinational Trading Companies in the Twentieth Century," in *The Multinational Traders*, ed. Geoffrey Jones (London and New York, 1998), 86–101.
[12] Harm G. Schröter, "Swiss Multinational Enterprise in Historical Perspective," in Jones and Schröter, *Rise of Multinationals*, 49–64; Youssef Cassis, "Swiss International Banking, 1890–1950," in *Banks as Multinationals*, ed. Geoffrey Jones (London, 1990), 160–72.
[13] Ragnhild Lundström, "Swedish Multinational Growth before 1930," in Hertner and Jones, *Multinationals*, 135–56; Ulf Olsson, "Securing the Markets: Swedish Multinationals in a Historical Perspective," in Jones and Schröter, *Rise of Multinationals*, 99–127; Kurt Lundgren, "Why in Sweden?" *Scandinavian Economic History Review* 43, no. 2 (1995): 204–25; Per Boje, *Danmark Og multinationale Virsomheder før 1950* (Odense, 2000).

The literature on the multinationals of other European countries is more scattered. The history of French multinationals remains largely at a firm or regional level. Ludovic Cailluet has recently examined the role of the French government in French multinational strategies after the Second World War, while Mira Wilkins has written a survey of the history of French multinationals in the United States.[14] Christian Bellak has examined the case of Austria, a small European economy with relatively little FDI over the long term.[15]

A number of business historians have explored general patterns in the history of European multinationals as a whole. In a series of studies, Wilkins compared the experience of individual European countries, both individually and collectively, with that of the United States. Jones and Schröter found evidence of a distinctive Continental model of multinationals, notably a tendency for more collaborative forms of international business than is seen in their U.S. counterparts, with a greater focus on growth rather than acquisition strategies. Schröter himself made a major contribution to comparative business history in his 1993 study of the multinationals from small European countries before 1914.[16]

The history of Japanese multinationals has also produced a considerable literature. T. Kuwahara has shown that although quantitatively small, Japanese multinational investment had grown to a relatively large size compared to the Japanese economy as a whole by the interwar years.

---

[14] There are major studies of the internationalization of French manufacturing firms such as St. Gobain. Jean-Pierre Daviet, *Un destin international: La Compagnie de Saint-Gobain de 1830 à 1939* (Paris, 1988), is a classic work. The best available survey of the multinational growth of French firms is found in Patrick Fridenson, "France: The Relatively Slow Development of Big Business in the Twentieth Century," in *Big Business and the Wealth of Nations*, eds. Alfred D. Chandler, Jr., Franco Amatori, and Takashi Hikino (Cambridge, 1997), 207–45; Ludovic Cailluet, "Nation States as Providers of Organisational Capability: French Industry Overseas, 1950-1965," *European Yearbook of Business History*, vol. 2 (1999), 71–90; Mira Wilkins, "French Multinationals in the United States: An Historical Perspective," *Enterprises et Histoire* 3 (1993): 14–29. There is an interesting regional study by Samir Saul, *La France et l'Egypte de 1882 à 1914* (Paris, 1997).

[15] Christian Bellak, "Austrian Manufacturing MNEs: Long-Term Perspectives," *Business History* 39, no. 1 (1997): 47–71.

[16] Mira Wilkins, "The History of European Multinationals: A New Look," *Journal of European Economic History* 15, no. 3 (1986): 483–510; id., "European and North American Multinationals, 1870-1914: Comparisons and Contrasts," *Business History* 30, no. 1 (1988): 8–45; Geoffrey Jones and Harm G. Schröter, "Continental European Multinationals, 1850–1992," in Jones and Schröter, *Rise of Multinationals*, 3–27; Harm G. Schröter, *Aufstieg der Kleinen: Multinationale Unternehmen aus fünf Kleinen Staaten vor 1914* (Berlin,1993). The latest European research can be sampled in Hubert Bonin, ed., *Transnational Companies (19th-20th Centuries)* (Paris, 2002).

Japanese manufacturing FDI was heavily concentrated in cotton textiles, especially in China, and the international growth of this industry has been the object of several studies. The history of the overall success of Japanese multinationals, and their distinctive characteristics, is the subject of a series of articles by Mira Wilkins.[17]

Multinational enterprise has originated overwhelmingly from a small group of economies in North America, Western Europe, and Japan. Even in the year 2000, less than 10 percent of world FDI originated from elsewhere. Yet since the 1960s, FDI from Asia and Latin America has been of significance in its regional context, and economists and others have debated the extent to which Third World multinationals differed from those in developed countries. Multinational companies from developing countries are generally not located in high-technology sectors, and in the case of many firms, family ownership is usually important. In their preference for making their initial investments in geographically or culturally proximate countries they resemble their Western and Japanese counterparts, and it is hard to discern a truly distinctive Third World type of multinational.[18]

HOST ECONOMIES

Less has been written about the historical impact of multinationals than about the causes and determinants of multinational growth. There are serious problems faced by researchers on this topic, including great uncertainties about the distribution of FDI before the 1960s, the large number of host economies, and the methodological problems in assessing impact. A full consideration of the impact of foreign firms on a host economy requires business historians to move beyond the archives of those firms into a greater engagement with the economic and other features of that country. It is a step that few have taken. The result is a rather patchy literature, with a dearth of comparative studies on the impact on different host economies.

[17] Tetsuya Kuwahara, "Trends in Research on Overseas Expansion by Japanese Enterprises Prior to World War 2," in *Japanese Yearbook on Business History*, vol. 7 (1990), 61–81; Mira Wilkins, "Japanese Multinational Enterprise before 1914," *Business History Review* 60, no. 2 (1986): 199–231; id., "Japanese Multinationals in the United States: Continuity and Change, 1879–1990," *Business History Review* 64, no. 4 (1990): 585–629.

[18] Louis T. Wells, *Third World Multinationals* (Cambridge, Mass., 1983); Roger van Hoesel, *Beyond Export-Led Growth: The Emergence of New Multinational Enterprises from Korea and Taiwan* (Rotterdam, 1997).

In his historical estimates of the size of FDI, Dunning estimated that about two-thirds of world FDI in 1914 and 1938 went to developing countries, mostly in Latin America and Asia. This was mostly engaged in natural resource exploitation and related services. After the Second World War, there was a rapid rise in the relative importance of the developed world as a host for multinationals, with the result that by 1970 only one-third of world FDI was in the developing world, mostly Latin America. This geographical shift reflected both the rapid postwar growth of U.S. manufacturing investment in Western Europe and the nationalization of many multinational resource and service investments in developing countries beginning in the 1950s. Wilkins has been the only business historian to venture into this area. She ranked host economies in 1914 and 1929 by the size of inward FDI, though she was unable to give actual figures for 1914. This exercise produced a subtly different view from that proposed by Dunning, as Wilkins considered the United States and Canada as among the world's largest host economies at both benchmark dates. She also considered a number of Western European countries, led by the United Kingdom, as major hosts.[19]

The long-term role of the United States as a major host as well as home economy were the subjects of Wilkins's major book, *The History of Foreign Investment in the United States to 1914* (Cambridge, Mass., 1989). Wilkins's pathbreaking survey of foreign investment in the United States from the colonial era to 1914 reveals the long-term importance of FDI in that country. By 1914 the United States was the world's largest debtor nation, and Wilkins demonstrated the impact of foreign firms in many sectors, from chemicals and breweries to oil and mining and cattle ranching. Foreign investors, Wilkins argued, opened up U.S. resources, introduced new technology, and greatly assisted U.S. industrialization. Controversially, Wilkins declined to make a sharp distinction between FDI and portfolio flows, and consequently she undertook the heroic task of surveying all foreign investment in the United States. Wilkins is now researching the post-1914 history of foreign investment in the United States. Geoffrey Jones and Lina Gálvez-Muñoz recently edited *Foreign Multinationals in the United States* (London, 2001), which examined the management and performance of foreign multinationals in the United States since 1945. These issues were subsequently explored by Jones in a case study of the performance of Unilever, the Anglo-Dutch

[19] Mira Wilkins, "Comparative Hosts," *Business History* 36, no. 1 (1994): 18–50.

consumer goods multinational in the United States between 1945 and 1980 (*Business History Review* 76, no. 3 [2002]: 435-78).

Historically the United Kingdom has been Europe's largest host economy and, appropriately, it has also attracted most attention from researchers. Dunning's early study of the impact of U.S. multinationals on Britain was followed, after an interval of three decades, by a new wave of interest in the subject by business historians. In 1988 Jones published a study of the impact of foreign multinationals on British industry before 1945. Although inward FDI remained quantitatively small in terms of the economy as a whole in this period, foreign firms were important in introducing new technologies, products, and marketing methods into British industry, creating employment and improving labor management practices. Foreign firms also sometimes provoked a vigorous competitive response from British-owned firms, which stimulated them to innovate. Subsequently Frances Bostock and Jones developed a large database on inward FDI into Britain between the 1850s and the 1960s that has been used to analyze the industrial and geographical distribution of foreign firms investing in the United Kingdom. This research explored the reasons for the choice of entry mode, the evolutionary pattern of growth, and exit patterns. The study demonstrated that a significant proportion of foreign investment in the United Kingdom was short-lived. Subsequently Hagen and Jones have examined the history of German and Swiss multinationals in Britain, while Godley has described in detail a leading inward investor in the nineteenth century - Singer Sewing Machines.[20]

The impact of foreign multinationals on other European host economies has not received as much attention. There is a detailed study of U.S. firms in Germany by Fritz Blaich and a collection of articles on the impact of foreign firms in Germany edited by Hans Pohl, while Charles Cheape has examined the strategies of U.S. multinationals in Nazi Germany.[21] There is a lack of overall surveys for other Western European

[20] Geoffrey Jones, "Foreign Multinationals and British Industry before 1945," *Economic History Review* 41, no. 3 (1988): 429-53; Geoffrey Jones and Frances Bostock, "U.S. Multinationals in British Manufacturing before 1962," *Business History Review* 70, no. 2 (1996): 207-56; Andrew C. Godley, "Pioneering Foreign Direct Investment in British Manufacturing," *Business History Review* 73, no. 3 (1999): 394-429.

[21] Fritz Blaich, *Amerikanische Firmen in Deutschland, 1890-1918* (Wiesbaden, 1984); Hans Pohl, ed., *Der Einfluss ausländischer Unternehmen auf die deutsche Wirtschaft vom Spätmittel alter bis zur Gegenwart* (Stuttgart, 1992); Charles Cheape, "Not Politicians But Sound Businessmen: Norton and Company and the Third Reich," *Business History Review* 62, no. 3 (1988): 444-66.

countries, but detailed studies of particular themes, such as German investment in Italy before 1914, multinational investment in Spain, and British investment in Switzerland are available.[22] Tsarist Russia, a major host economy before 1914, is a special case. The role of foreign companies in Russia's pre-1917 growth has long been a subject for research, and there is a large literature in existence. In the Soviet era, the impact of foreign firms on prerevolutionary Russia was hotly debated by Russian scholars. More recently, research on foreign business in Russia has applied the concept of the free-standing company to explore the institutional forms employed.[23]

The history of foreign multinationals in Japan is heavily influenced by the discussion of why the level of inward FDI has always been very low and remains so at the beginning of the twenty-first century. Restrictions by the Japanese government have traditionally been seen as the reason for this situation. The major study by Mark Mason of U.S. multinationals in Japan, *American Multinationals and Japan* (Cambridge, Mass., 1992), deepened the debate by suggesting that domestic Japanese business was highly influential in shaping foreign investment policies to block or impede unwanted foreign investors.

Business historians have shown that although the amount of foreign multinational investment in Japan was never great, it was nonetheless significant. Before the 1930s in particular, Japan's investment regime was quite liberal. Some of the most prominent U.S. multinationals, including Ford, General Motors, ITT, General Electric, and Otis Elevator, invested in Japan and were highly significant in terms of organizational and technology transfer, if sometimes involuntarily. Akira Kudô has examined the impact of I.G. Farben, the giant German chemicals company, on Japan. I.G. Farben's involvement in Japan included a variety of modes – exporting,

---

[22] Peter Hertner, *Il capitale tedesco in Italia dall Unità alla Prima Guerra Mondiale* (Bologna, 1984); id., "The German Electrotechnical Industry in the Italian Market before the Second World War," in Jones and Schröter, *Rise of Multinationals*, 155–72; Charles Harvey and P. Taylor, "Mineral Wealth and Economic Development: Foreign Direct Investment in Spain, 1851–1913," *Economic History Review* 60, no. 2 (1987): 185–208; Antonio Gómez Mendoza, *El "Gilbraltar Economic": Franco y Rio Tinto, 1936–1954* (Madrid, 1994); Geoffrey Jones, "Multinational Cross-Investment between Switzerland and Britain, 1914–1945," in *Switzerland and the Great Powers, 1914–1945*, ed. Sébastien Guex (Geneva, 1999), 427–59.

[23] Fred V. Carstensen, *American Enterprise in Foreign Markets: Singer and International Harvester in Imperial Russia* (Chapel Hill, 1984); Natalia Gurushina, "Free-Standing Companies in Tsarist Russia," in *The Free-Standing Company in the World Economy, 1830–1996*, eds. Mira Wilkins and Harm G. Schröter (Oxford, 1998), 160–201.

licensing, and FDI - and collectively, the technology and management transfer had a major impact on the Japanese chemical industry, including its distribution system.[24] The most extensive collection of essays on the historical impact of foreign firms in Japan is the volume edited by Yuzawa and Udagawa, *Foreign Business in Japan before World War II* (Tokyo, 1990).

The historical impact of multinationals on developing countries has an extensive but very diffuse literature, often drawing more inspiration from debates on imperialism than on international business. A number of general studies have examined foreign firms in Asia and Latin America as a whole, and these studies or collections remain essential starting points.[25] India and China were major host economies before the middle of the twentieth century, and there are studies of the role and impact of foreign firms on their economies.[26] On China, a number of the large foreign multinationals active in the country, such as BAT, the Hongkong Bank, Swires, Jardine Matheson, and a group of large Dutch firms, have been the subject of extensive case studies. Meanwhile, Cochran has recently shown how Japanese, Western, and Chinese firms responded in a variety of organizational forms to the challenges of doing business in China between 1880 and 1937.[27]

---

[24] Akira Kudô, "IG Farben in Japan: The Transfer of Technology and Managerial Skills," *Business History* 36, no. 1 (1994): 159-83.

[25] On Asia, the classic studies remain George C. Allen and Audrey G. Donnithorne, *Western Enterprise in Far Eastern Economic Development* (London, 1954) and *Western Enterprise in Indonesia and Malaya* (London, 1957). There are essays on British multinationals in Asia in Richard P. T. Davenport-Hines and Geoffrey Jones, eds., *British Business in Asia since 1860* (Cambridge, 1989). On Latin America there is Desmond C. M. Platt, *Latin America and British Trade, 1806-1914* (London, 1972); id., ed., *Business Imperialism, 1840-1930* (Oxford, 1977); and Rory Miller, *Britain and Latin America in the 19th and 20th Centuries* (London, 1993).

[26] On India, see B. R. Tomlinson, "Colonial Firms and the Decline of Colonialism in Eastern India, 1914-1947," *Modern Asian Studies* 15, no. 3 (1981): 455-86; id., "British Business in India, 1860-1970," in Davenport-Hines and Jones, *British Business in Asia*, 92-116; Maria Misra, "Entrepreneurial Decline and the End of Empire" (Ph.D. diss., Oxford University, 1994). On China there is a survey of the literature in Jürgen Osterhammel, "British Business in China, 1860s-1950s," in Davenport-Hines and Jones, *British Business in Asia*, 189-216.

[27] On BAT, see Sherman G. Cochran, *Big Business in China: Sino-Foreign Rivalry in the Cigarette Industry, 1890-1930* (Cambridge, Mass., 1980), and Howard Cox, *The Global Cigarette* (Oxford, 2000). On Hongkong Bank, see Frank H. H. King, *The History of the Hongkong and Shanghai Banking Corporation*, 4 vols. (Cambridge, 1984-91). On the two British trading companies, see Robert Blake, *Jardine Matheson: Traders of the Far East* (London, 2000); E. LeFevour, *Western Enterprise in Late Ch'ing China* (Cambridge, Mass., 1971); Sheila Marriner and Francis E. Hyde, *The Senior: John Samuel Swire, 1825-1898* (Liverpool, 1967); Z. Zhongli, C. Zengrian, and Y. Xinrong, *The Swire Group in Old*

In the case of Latin America, recent major business history studies have included the role of Canadian utilities in Mexico and Brazil.[28] There is as well M. C. Eakin's detailed case study, *British Enterprise in Brazil*, which considers in depth the social, economic, and cultural impact of a British mining company active in Brazil between 1830 and 1960. In the more recent past, Helen Shapiro in *Engines of Growth: The State and Transnational Auto Companies in Brazil* (Cambridge, 1994) has explored the creation of the Brazilian automobile industry by multinationals since the 1950s. She shows both the positive impact that multinationals can have on the manufacturing sector of a developing economy and the ways that host government policy shapes that impact.

NEW DIRECTIONS

Over the past decade, the focus of the business history literature on multinationals has shifted. The growth of multinational investment in services - which now comprise over 50 percent of the world stock of FDI - has prompted new interest in the history of internationalization in services. Previously, and despite Wilkins's inclusion of services in her studies of multinationals, business historians were inclined to go with the trend in international business research and to concentrate on manufacturing. During the 1990s this imbalance was corrected.

Among the services, perhaps the most research has concerned the history of multinational banking. This was a distinctive and important form of early multinational business that European-owned banks pioneered in the nineteenth century and continued to dominate until the 1960s. This first stage of multinational banking typically took the form of "overseas banks," and the past decade has seen major studies of such banks published. Multinational trade and shipping have also been the focus of new interest. Trading companies, long studied by Japanese business historians, have begun to receive the attention of European business historians. Jones has recently published a study of British trading companies from the nineteenth century to the present day, *Merchants to Multinationals*

China (Shanghai, 1995); Frans-Paul van der Putten, *Corporate Behaviour and Political Risk. Dutch Companies in China 1903-1941* (Leiden, 2001); and Sherman Cochran, *Encountering Chinese Networks* (Berkeley, 2000).
[28] Christopher Armstrong and H. V. Nelles, *Southern Exposure: Canadian Promoters in Latin America and the Caribbean, 1896-1930* (Toronto, 1988); D. McDowell, *The Light: Brazilian Traction, Light and Power Company Limited, 1899-1945* (Toronto, 1988).

(Oxford, 2000).[29] One of the interesting features of this research is the identification of competitive advantages and management systems that were often quite different from those of manufacturing firms. There are strong parallels between trade and shipping, and shipping – itself a subject that has long interested business historians – is also receiving new attention. In particular, Gelina Harfaltis's long-term study of the Greek shipping industry, *A History of Greek-Owned Shipping* (London, 1996), has made a pathbreaking contribution to the understanding of the dynamics of multinational shipping.

Among professional services, the history of multinational advertising agencies and accountancy firms[30] and multinational management consultancies has been explored. Management consulting, as a knowledge rather than capital-intensive activity, formed only a tiny part of world FDI after the Second World War, yet it was very significant in transferring U.S. (and later Japanese) management techniques across borders, with firms serving in some countries as quasi-business schools for the training of managers.[31] However, there remains no business history literature on multinational strategies in other professional services, such as law, and other types of service have also been neglected. The only general study of the history of multinational retailing is Stanley Hollander's book, *Multinational Retailing* (East Lansing, 1970). The

[29] Earlier major studies of British international merchants in the nineteenth century are Stanley Chapman, *Merchant Enterprise in Britain* (Cambridge, 1992), and Charles Jones, *International Business in the Nineteenth Century* (Brighton, 1987). For other European trading companies, see Jones, *Multinational Traders*; Hans de Geer, *A. Johnson & Co. Inc., 1920-1995* (Stockholm, 1995); Joost Jonker and Keetie Sluyterman, *At Home on the World Markets. Dutch International Trading Companies from the 16th Century until the Present* (The Hague, 2000); Hubert Bonin, *CFAO Cent Ans de Compétition* (Paris,1987); Hubert Bonin and Michael Cahen, eds., *Négoce blanc en Afrique noire. Histoire du commerce à longue distance en Afrique noire du 18e au 20e siècles* (Paris, 2001).

[30] Douglas C. West, "From T-Square to T-Plan: The London Office of the J. Walter Thompson Advertising Agency, 1919-70," *Business History* 29, no. 2 (1987): 199-217; id., "Multinational Competition in the British Advertising Agency Business, 1936-1987," *Business History Review* 62, no. 3 (1988): 467-501; Keetie E. Sluyterman, "The Internationalisation of Dutch Accounting Firms," *Business History* 40, no. 2 (1998): 1-21.

[31] Christopher McKenna, "The Origins of Modern Management Consulting," *Business and Economic History* 24, no. 1 (1995): 51-58; Matthias Kipping, "The U.S. Influence on the Evolution of Management Consultancies in Britain, France and Germany since 1945," *Business and Economic History* 25, no. 1 (1996): 112-23; id., "American Management Consultancies Company in Western Europe, 1920s to 1990s: Products, Reputation and Relationships," *Business History Review* 72, no. 2 (1999): 190-220; Celeste Amorim, "Catching-Up? The Evolution of Management Consultancies in Portugal and Spain," *European Yearbook of Business History*, vol. 2 (1999): 179-209.

history of international construction management, though identified by Wilkins and Jones as of major interest, has no historical study.

Service firms often employed "network" forms of organization when they operated abroad. In parallel with other areas of business history and in line with developments in contemporary business, there has been new interest in such networks and in collaborative arrangements generally. The literature on "business groups" and "clusters" of free-standing companies forms part of this trend. The role of networks in the international operations of Greek merchants has been explored by Ioanna Minoglou, and the international cartels of the interwar years have also been reexamined, often showing them in a more dynamic and even positive light than was previously believed.[32] International cartels were not limited to the interwar years, and Debora Spar has presented in *The Co-operative Edge* (Ithaca, 1994) a particularly insightful account of the long-running international cartels in gold and diamonds.

Business history research on multinationals has proved a dynamic and stimulating area over the past three decades. It has continued to engage the attention of a wide range of scholars, and the topics covered continue to grow, as indicated by the recent publication of a study that took the origins of the multinational back to 2000 B.C.[33] In its frequent interaction with theory and in its internationally comparative focus, the history of multinationals has established itself as a distinctive subarea of the discipline.

KEY WORKS

Hertner, Peter and Geoffrey Jones, eds. *Multinationals: Theory and History*. Aldershot, 1986. A first attempt to bring together research on multinationals by business historians and economists.
Jones, Geoffrey. *The Evolution of International Business*. London, 1996. The first survey of the history of multinationals worldwide since the nineteenth century.

[32] Ioanna Pepelassis-Minoglou, "The Greek Merchant House of the Russian Black Sea: A Nineteenth Century Example of a Traders' Coalition," *International Journal of Maritime History* 10 (1998): 61–104. The most valuable collections of essays on international cartels are Akira Kudo and Terushi Hara, eds., *International Cartels in Business History* (Tokyo, 1992) and Dominique Barjot, ed., *International Cartels Revisited* (Caen, 1994). Clemens Wurm, *Business, Politics and International Relations* (Cambridge, 1993), discusses the policies of European governments toward cartels. Geoffrey Jones, ed., *Coalitions and Collaboration in International Business* (Aldershot, 1993) contains a collection of essays on the subject.
[33] Karl Moore and David Lewis, *Birth of the Multinational. 2000 Years of Ancient Business History-From Ashur to Augustus* (Copenhagen, 1999).

Jones, Geoffrey and Harm G. Schröter, eds. *The Rise of Multinationals in Continental Europe*. Aldershot, 1993. This contains essays on the major European countries, which makes research available to English speakers.

Wilkins, Mira. *The Emergence of Multinational Enterprise*. Cambridge, Mass., 1970. The pioneering study on the history of U.S. multinationals before 1914.

The Maturing of Multinational Enterprise. Cambridge, Mass., 1974. The second volume of Wilkins's classic study, which surveys the history of U.S. multinationals between 1914 and 1974.

The History of Foreign Investment in the United States to 1914. Cambridge, Mass., 1989. The most recent study by Wilkins, which examines foreign multinationals in the United States before 1914.

Wilkins, Mira and Harm Schröter, eds. *The Free-Standing Company in the World Economy, 1830–1996*. Oxford, 1998. Contains many new perspectives on the institutional forms used in foreign direct investment.

18

Business–Government Relations

Beyond Performance Issues

MATTHIAS KIPPING

Governments have played an important role in business matters ever since the Industrial Revolution. As numerous studies have shown, there has been a very close relationship between the formation of the modern nation state and industrialization.[1] In Germany and Italy, for example, the Second Industrial Revolution, that is, the development of the large-scale production of oil, chemicals, pharmaceuticals, steel, and automobiles toward the end of the nineteenth century, took place at about the same time as political unification. In most industrialized countries, the influence of the state in business matters increased considerably during the twentieth century – even outside exceptional times of war and national crisis. Especially after World War II, many governments in developed as well as less developed countries actively intervened at the industry and firm level.

The author would like to express his gratitude to the staff at the Institute of Innovation Research of Hitotsubashi University near Tokyo, where the first draft of this essay was completed, for providing large numbers of books and photocopies from the library; to Patrick Fridenson, Neil Rollings, Franco Amatori, and Geoffrey Jones, as well as three anonymous referees for many helpful comments and suggestions; and again to the editors for their patience during the revision process. The usual disclaimer applies.

[1] For a general overview, see Sidney Pollard, *Typology of Industrialization Processes in the Nineteenth Century* (London, 1990), and David S. Landes, *The Wealth and Poverty of Nations* (New York, 1999).

A reversal of this trend took place only during the last two decades of the twentieth century, when most governments started privatizing previously state-owned companies and public services and deregulating a vast array of business activities.[2] In addition to bringing much needed resources into public budgets, these efforts were based on economic arguments. Thus, according to the so-called agency theory, publicly owned enterprises are likely to perform less well because they are not subject to the discipline of financial markets.[3] In addition, the state as an owner usually pursues other objectives in addition to or instead of profit maximization.[4] Regarding regulation, economists argued that the relevant public agencies had been "captured" by the companies they were supposed to regulate, leading to inefficient outcomes.[5] During the same period, national governments increasingly ceded some of their powers to both supranational and regional entities.[6]

Business historians have made a significant contribution to the understanding of the changing relationship between the public and private spheres and the complex interaction between government institutions and business organizations. There are several edited volumes and comprehensive summaries on the topic.[7] Most of the country-based essays

---

[2] See, among many others, Herbert Giersch, ed., *Privatisation at the End of the Century* (Berlin, 1997); Daniel Yergin and Joseph Stanislaw, *The Commanding Heights: The Battle between Government and the Marketplace That Is Remaking the Modern World* (New York, 1998); Christopher McCrudden, ed., *Regulation and Deregulation: Policy and Practice in the Utilities and Financial Services Industries* (Oxford, 1999); and Nicola Bellini, "The Decline of State-Owned Enterprise and the New Foundations of the State–Industry Relationship," in *The Rise and Fall of State-Owned Enterprise in the Western World*, ed. Pier Angelo Toninelli (New York, 2000), 25–48.

[3] At least in theory, these markets sanction inferior performance through takeover and replacement of top management; for a detailed development and critique of these arguments, see Colin Mayer and Tim Jenkinson, "The Assessment: Corporate Governance and Corporate Control," *Oxford Review of Economic Policy* 8, no. 3 (1992): 1–10.

[4] For example, Raymond Vernon speaks of "a confusion of goals" in the "Introduction" to *State-Owned Enterprise in the Western Economies*, eds. Vernon and Yair Aharoni (London, 1981), 7–22.

[5] This is due not only to a failure of government, but also to the rent-seeking behavior of these companies, i.e., their efforts to obtain favorable treatment from the regulators rather than to improve their competitiveness; cf., in general, Jean-Jacques Laffont and Jean Tirole, *A Theory of Incentives in Procurement and Regulation* (Cambridge, Mass., 1993).

[6] For example, Kenichi Ohmae, *The End of the Nation State: The Rise of Regional Economies* (London, 1995); and Susan Strange, *The Retreat of the State: The Diffusion of Power in the World Economy* (Cambridge, 1996).

[7] Such collections include Martin Chick, ed., *Governments, Industries and Markets* (Aldershot, 1990); Steven W. Tolliday, ed., *Government and Business* (Aldershot, 1991); Hideaki Miyajima, Takeo Kikkawa, and Takashi Hikino, eds., *Policies for Competitiveness:*

in this volume also contain a review of the relevant literature for the particular country. Instead of providing another summary, this essay will analyze the current state and the future directions of historical research on business–government relations. I argue that most economic but also many business historians appear to have been overly preoccupied with issues regarding the performance and effectiveness of government intervention in business matters. This is due to the influence of mainstream economic theories, which focus on markets (and firms) and see government intervention as an exception, justifiable only in very specific circumstances, if at all. In order to identify available alternatives to this limiting perspective, the essay will present other (nonperformance-related) issues, addressed in the historical literature on business–government relations.

The essay consists of three main sections. The first section offers an overview of the dominant discourse in historical research on the role of government in business matters, which focuses largely on questions of "economic efficiency." It highlights the foundation of this approach in mainstream economics. The remaining sections focus on two issues in which business historians have looked beyond the economic effects of business–government relations. One of them concerns the forms of government intervention in industrialized countries, where historical research has helped elucidate the origins of different regimes and their subsequent development. The other deals with the interaction between the public and private spheres, where historians have examined in detail many of the actors involved in the process, including representatives from government, public administration, and business, as well as various intermediaries such as trade associations. Both issues have also been of interest to scholars from other academic disciplines. The concluding section of this essay therefore suggests closer cooperation between business historians and other social scientists.

A LIMITING PERSPECTIVE: THE "FIXATION" ON ECONOMIC EFFICIENCY

In his book *Socializing Capital* (Princeton, 1997), the historical sociologist William Roy has offered an explanation "for the rise of the large

Comparing Business-Government Relationships in the "Golden Age of Capitalism" (Oxford, 1999). One of the most recent summaries is by Thomas K. McCraw, "Government, Big Business, and the Wealth of Nations," in *Big Business and the Wealth of Nations*, eds. Alfred Chandler, Jr., Franco Amatori, and Takashi Hikino (New York, 1997), 522–45.

industrial corporation in America" (the subtitle of his book) around the turn of the twentieth century, which differs significantly from what he termed the predominant "efficiency theory." The latter view is epitomized by the work of Alfred D. Chandler, Jr., who, according to Roy, shares with classical, neoclassical, and institutional economists "the assumption that there is a selection process that ensures that more efficient economic forms will prevail over less efficient forms" (p. 7). Whereas Chandler insists on the economic superiority of the large-scale managerial enterprise (under changed technological and market conditions) and thus the inevitability of its rise, Roy highlights the openness of the process that determined "how the modern boundaries between the political and the economic were constituted" (p. xiv). In his view, the actual outcome can be explained only by analyzing this process and the individuals and groups involved – including government, which he identifies as a central actor.

Efficiency theory has not only shaped the way in which a whole generation of business historians has charted the rise of big business around the world, it has also influenced the way in which they interpreted the influence of government: once again in close similarity with the views of classical and neoclassical economics. These give absolute priority to market mechanisms and see public intervention as justifiable only when the working of market forces alone would not lead to the optimal allocation of resources. Such cases of "market failure" are clearly defined and rather exceptional. They concern the so-called natural monopoly, when economies of scale allow only one efficient producer to be present in a given market.[8] More recently, so-called institutional economics has put more emphasis on the firm as an alternative coordinating mechanism to the market, thus making an important contribution to the understanding of the emergence and development of managerial enterprise (see the essay by Lazonick in this volume). However, regarding the role of the state, institutional economics also limits it to a few, possibly even fewer cases of antitrust violations.

Similarly, Chandler, and business historians working in his tradition, usually pay little attention to the role of the state in comparison to the

---

[8] For a more extensive and rigorous development of these arguments, see William J. Baumol, *Welfare Economics and the Theory of the State* (London, 1965), and Joseph E. Stiglitz et al., *The Economic Role of the State* (Oxford, 1989). Some economists, such as Friedrich Hayek, consider state intervention not only as generally inefficient but also as somewhat morally reproachable; see especially his book *The Road to Serfdom*, first published in 1944 in London and frequently reprinted thereafter.

market and the managerial enterprise. Government is, at most, seen to
provide the legal and regulatory framework in which companies operate. When it comes to an evaluation of public policy toward business, the
overall assessment is fairly negative. This is, for example, the general tenor
of the majority of contributions to the volume *The Rise and Fall of State-
Owned Enterprise in the Western World*, edited by Pier Angelo Toninelli
(New York, 2000). Thus, for the Italian case, Franco Amatori concluded
that "the marriage of the state with the market in an environment such
as Italy's, where a bureaucratic state did not (and still does not) exist and
where public institutions are dominated by political forces, merits only a
negative judgment after sixty years of experience."[9] Nevertheless, he and
other authors have highlighted the positive role of state-owned companies in the modernization of the country during the 1950s and 1960s.[10]

   In his contribution to the volume *Big Business and the Wealth of
Nations*, edited by Alfred Chandler, Jr., Franco Amatori, and Takashi
Hikino (New York, 1997), Thomas McCraw highlighted – and lamented –
the fact that "numerous first-rate economists" and "scholars of business administration, such as Alfred Chandler, Michael Porter and Bruce
Scott . . . provide only partial answers and leave much unexplained" regarding the role of government in economic development.[11] He also
pointed out that some of the countries with considerable government
involvement, notably Japan and South Korea, had some of the highest
growth rates in the post–World War II period, the same being true,
incidentally, for Italy – a story poorly understood by the "orthodox
economists."[12] In order to find "more satisfactory explanations" for this

---

[9] Amatori, "Beyond State and Market: Italy's Futile Search for a Third Way," in Toninelli, *Rise
   and Fall*, 128–56, quote on 154.

[10] Ibid.; Gianlupo Osti, *L'industria di Stato dall'ascesa al degrado*, interview with Ruggero
   Ranieri (Bologna, 1993), and Ruggero Ranieri, "Learning from America: The Remodelling
   of Italy's Public Sector Steel Industry in the 1950s and 1960s," in *The Americanisation of
   European Business*, eds. Matthias Kipping and Ove Bjarnar (London, 1998), 208–28; for
   a comparison of the government's role in the development of the Italian and Dutch steel
   industries, see also Matthias Kipping, Ruggero Ranieri, and Joost Dankers, "The Emergence
   of New Competitor Nations in the European Steel Industry: Italy and the Netherlands,
   1945–1965," *Business History* 43, no. 1 (2001): 69–96.

[11] McCraw, "Government, Big Business," 544.

[12] Ibid., 543; see also the volume *America versus Japan*, which he edited earlier (Boston,
   1986), where he took a more critical stance and advocated a tougher U.S. response in order
   to force the Japanese government to assume an arm's-length relationship with business.
   For the active (and positive) role of government in South Korean economic development,
   see the many publications by Alice H. Amsden, e.g., "South Korea: Enterprising Groups
   and Entrepreneurial Government," in Chandler et al., eds., *Big Business*, 336–67.

apparent paradox, McCraw suggested "greater communication between academic disciplines," namely, economists, business historians, and political scientists.

His suggestion seems to have fallen on deaf ears. Most of the historical studies of public policy toward business continue to be driven by neoclassical economic theories and attempts to measure the effect of government involvement.[13] Thus, in their summary chapter for the edited volume *European Industrial Policy: The Twentieth-Century Experience* (Oxford, 1999), James Foreman-Peck and Giovanni Federico conclude that "industrial performance since the Second World War has been unprecedentedly successful" in most Western European countries "despite, rather than because of interventionist national industrial policies."[14] But neither they nor the contributors provide much evidence to justify such an obviously paradoxical conclusion. The latter actually show that government intervention was not an exception – as mainstream economists would suggest – but rather the rule in most European countries during the twentieth century. Foreman-Peck and Federico base their own negative assessment partially on a comparison of the concentration of industrial activities in the United States and Western Europe – a measure that they themselves describe as "imperfect" – and mainly on the claims of economic theory: "[U]nless there were market failures that warranted such policy interventions, then the political goals at which they were normally targeted must have imposed economic costs."[15]

To be fair, Foreman-Peck and Federico would probably not consider themselves business historians, but rather economic historians or historical economists. And neither do all economists or, for that matter, most business historians share such views. Among the economic historians and economists with a more favorable assessment of an active government role, one might mention Alexander Gershenkron and John Kenneth Galbraith. In his contribution to the volume *The Rise and Fall*

[13] Earlier collections on industrial policy and state-owned enterprises have a similar focus on performance and, on the whole, also reach rather negative conclusions: for example, *Big Business and the State. Changing Relations in Western Europe*, ed. Raymond Vernon (London, 1974); Vernon and Aharoni, eds., *State-Owned Enterprise*. Since this essay wishes to engage with current debates, it focuses on the most recent examples of this approach.

[14] James Foreman-Peck and Giovanni Federico, "European Industrial Policy: An Overview," in *European Industrial Policy*, 426–60, quote on 428.

[15] Ibid., 427–8. The argument regarding industrial concentration is taken from Paul Krugman, *Geography and Trade* (Cambridge, Mass., 1991). The latter is one of the most vociferous critics of proactive government policies; cf. id., "Competitiveness: A Dangerous Obsession," *Foreign Affairs* 73, no. 2 (1994): 28–44.

of State-Owned Enterprise, Yair Aharoni also tried to show that public enterprise was not always inferior to private enterprise in terms of
performance. For example, the state-owned railways in Canada appear
to have been at least as efficient as, and possibly even more efficient
than, their private counterparts both in Canada and in the United States.
Aharoni states at the same time that these findings have to be taken with
considerable caution, given the limited availability of data in general and
comparable data in particular.[16] A comparative study of seven different industries to identify the *Sources of Industrial Leadership*, edited by David
C. Mowery and Richard R. Nelson (New York, 1999), also comes to a more
positive conclusion regarding the effect of (and actual need for) a limited, sector-specific industrial policy. It concludes, "the conditions that
establish comparative advantage, or industrial leadership, are not givens,
but are actively constructed." Governments should nevertheless refrain
from picking winners, because this has proved largely ineffective.[17]

Geoffrey Jones and Maurice Kirby summarized the view of many
business historians in their introduction to the volume *Competitiveness and the State: Government and Business in Twentieth-Century
Britain* (Manchester, 1991) when they suggested that "governments can
enhance the competitiveness of market economies, with policies that involve more than clearing away the obstacles preventing the operation of
perfectly competitive markets."[18] Further, business history literature in
the United Kingdom has largely concluded that the government should
have intervened more.[19] Regardless of their positive rather than negative
assessment of the government's role, all of the previously mentioned

---

[16] Yair Aharoni, "The Performance of State-Owned Enterprises," in Toninelli, ed., *The Rise
and Fall*, 49–72.

[17] See Richard R. Nelson, "The Sources of Industrial Leadership," in *Finance, Governance,
and Competitiveness in Japan*, eds. Masahiko Aoki and Gary R. Saxonhouse (New York,
2000), 239–56, quote on 253.

[18] Geoffrey Jones and Maurice Kirby, "Competitiveness and the State in International Perspective," in *Competitiveness and the State*, 1–19, quote on 4.

[19] This point has been made strongly for the interwar period by Steven Tolliday, *Business,
Banking, and Politics: The Case of British Steel, 1918-1939* (Cambridge, Mass., 1987),
and for the war and postwar periods by Nick Tiratsoo and Jim Tomlinson, *Industrial Efficiency and State Intervention: Labour 1939-51* (London, 1993); id., *The Conservatives
and Industrial Efficiency, 1951-64. Thirteen wasted years?* (London, 1998), as well as
the work of many of those writing on the role of the state-owned firms; cf. Terence R.
Gourvish, "British Business and the Transition to a Corporate Economy: Entrepreneurship
and Management Structures," *Business History* 29, no. 4 (1987): 18–45, esp. 39. See also
the influential volume *The Decline of the British Economy*, eds. Bernard Elbaum and
William Lazonick (Oxford, 1986).

scholars nevertheless remain focused on questions of effectiveness, performance, competitiveness, and so on. However, such a focus, while possibly of interest to certain economists, seems to impose unnecessary limits on business historical research. A good example on this point is the question of cartels. They were present in most industrialized countries from the end of the nineteenth century and for much of the twentieth – clearly a paradox from the point of view of neoclassical economic theories, which see them as an aberration from the competitive market mechanism and therefore as inefficient.[20] Under the influence of these economic theories, there have been endless debates among economic and business historians about the impact of cartels on the economy. For example, two neoclassical economic historians have blamed restrictive business and labor practices and the failure of the British government to introduce a more efficient competition policy for lower growth rates in the United Kingdom after 1945 compared to other industrialized nations.[21] Two other historians have contested this view. They suggest that the level of competition was actually sufficient, and highlight instead the failure of companies to adopt a number of simple productivity-enhancing techniques.[22] Yet other scholars take a positive view of the effect of cartels, claiming that continued cartelization might have contributed to the favorable economic developments in Western Europe after World War II by providing a more stable and predictable operating environment for companies.[23]

It seems highly unlikely that these debates will ever be resolved. There is simply not enough evidence, regarding either the degree to which an economy was actually cartelized or the economic costs or benefits of cartels – which is where the economic theories came in. The point here

---

[20] See, for an overview, Harm G. Schröter, "Cartelization and Decartelization in Europe, 1870–1995: Rise and Decline of an Economic Institution," *Journal of European Economic History* 25, no. 1 (1996): 129–53; for detailed case studies see the articles in *Coalitions and Collaboration in International Business*, ed. Geoffrey Jones (Aldershot, 1993) and in *Competition and Collaboration of Enterprises on National and International Markets (19th–20th Century)*, ed. Hans Pohl (Stuttgart, 1997).

[21] Steve N. Broadberry and N. F. R. Crafts, "British Economic Policy and Industrial Performance in the Early Post-War Period," *Business History* 38, no. 4 (1996): 65–91.

[22] Jim Tomlinson and Nick Tiratsoo, " 'An Old Story, Freshly Told?' A Comment on Broadberry and Crafts' Approach to Britain's Early Post-War Economic Performance," *Business History* 40, no. 2 (1998): 62–72; id., "Americanisation Beyond the Mass Production Paradigm: The Case of British Industry," in Kipping and Bjarnar, *Americanisation*, 115–32.

[23] Wendy Asbeek Brusse and Richard Griffiths, "The Incidence of Manufacturing Cartels in Post-War Europe," in *Cartels and Market Management in the Post-War World*, ed. Carlo Morelli, Business History Unit Occasional Papers (London, 1997), no. 1, 78–117.

is that it might be equally or even more interesting (and relevant) to look at other questions with respect to cartel agreements rather than their economic effect. One might ask, for example, why governments in certain countries made them illegal earlier than in others or why such an attitude became more commonplace after World War II. It is questions like these that business historians are well equipped to address, as we will see in the remainder of this essay.

The subsequent sections give some examples of areas where business historical research has made a contribution beyond questions of the economic consequences of government intervention. The first concerns the national differences in business–government relations and their development over time, and the second deals with the interaction between the various public and private actors involved in the policy-making process.

NATIONAL SYSTEMS: EXTENT AND FORMS OF GOVERNMENT INTERVENTION

As noted earlier, much of the historical research has shown that the idea of an economy driven exclusively or even mainly by firms and market mechanisms is a fiction. As a matter of fact, a mixed economy has dominated in most of the industrialized world at least since the Second Industrial Revolution. Business historians appear well placed to examine the different forms of public intervention in business matters and their development over time. Their research can help avoid possible oversimplifications by introducing nuances to the more systematic approach of scholars in other disciplines.

Thus, it has become commonplace to distinguish Anglo-American-style capitalism, with its limited government influence and the domination of financial objectives and markets, from a different form of capitalism exemplified by Germany and Japan. In the second type, governments have been involved much more extensively in economic development, and companies pursue other objectives in addition to or instead of maximizing profits and shareholder value.[24] Business historical research shows that such a contrast might be somewhat exaggerated. Thus, regarding the United States, Bill Becker and Lou Galambos have challenged the predominant view of very limited government

[24] Michel Albert's *Capitalism vs. Capitalism* (New York, 1993, French original: Paris, 1991) seems to have been particularly influential in this respect. For the many others, consult "corporate governance" in any decent library catalog.

involvement.[25] Focusing on public ownership, the latter suggests that, at least until the middle of the twentieth century, the American experience was rather similar to developments in other industrialized countries. Major examples of public ownership in the United States include utilities built and operated by the states or municipalities, and federal government control over public land and its use, as well as the post office. Developments between the United States and other industrialized nations therefore started to diverge only in the post–World War II period, when direct government influence in the latter increased significantly.

In the Japanese case, by contrast, business historians have contributed to a demystification of the role of the Ministry of International Trade and Industry (MITI), which had been seen as a major engine of industrial development and international expansion in the earlier literature.[26] As detailed industry and company studies have shown, Japanese firms and managers more often than not rejected the suggestions and pressures of the ministry. This was the case, for example, regarding the project of a people's car in the 1950s, the concentration of the automobile and chemical industries in the 1960s, and the joint development of computer equipment in the 1970s.[27] While not completely discounting the role of public policy, business historians have also highlighted the role of entrepreneurial initiative and of intense competition among the different companies and enterprise groups as a major driver for the expansion of Japanese industry during the 1950s and 1960s and as the basis for its subsequent success in export markets.[28]

[25] William H. Becker, "Managerial Capitalism and Public Policy," *Business and Economic History* 21 (1992): 247–56; Louis Galambos, "State-Owned Enterprises in a Hostile Environment: The U.S. Experience," in Toninelli, *Rise and Fall*, 273–302.

[26] Chalmers Johnson, *MITI and the Japanese Miracle: The Growth of Industrial Policy, 1925–1975* (Stanford, 1982); James E. Vestal, *Planning for Change: Industrial Policy and Japanese Economic Development, 1945–1990* (Oxford, 1993).

[27] For the first two examples, see Hidemasa Morikawa, "Japan: Increasing Organizational Capabilities of Large Industrial Enterprises, 1880–1980s," in Chandler et al., eds., *Big Business*, 307–35; for the latter, see Marie Anchordoguy, "Mastering the Market: Japanese Government Targeting of the Computer Industry," *International Organization* 42 (1988): 509–43, and id., *Computers Inc.: Japan's Challenge to IBM* (Cambridge, Mass., 1989).

[28] For a summary, see Takeo Kikkawa and Takashi Hikino, "Industrial Policy and Japan's International Competitiveness: Historical Overview and Assessment," in Miyajima, Kikkawa, and Hikino, *Policies for Competitiveness*, 19–39; see also Hiroyuki Odagiri and Akira Goto, *Technology and Industrial Development in Japan: Building Capabilities by Learning, Innovation, and Public Policy* (Oxford, 1996); for the very instructive example of the steel industry see Seiichiro Yonekura, *The Japanese Iron and Steel Industry, 1850–1990: Continuity and Discontinuity* (Basingstoke, 1994).

Many authors have seen France as another case where government intervened extensively in business matters. Especially after World War II, the French state exercised considerable influence through a system of indicative planning, price controls, and public ownership of many key industries and companies.[29] However, detailed historical research shows that the government's role and its actual impact should not be overestimated. In many cases, even in the nationalized industries, managers had considerable room to maneuver. Most government policies affecting business were negotiated directly with representatives of the companies or industries concerned. It was not uncommon for the civil servants in the responsible ministries to side with the industrialists rather than the politicians.[30] This more complex interaction between public and private is confined neither to the post–World War II period nor to the country's national industrial policy. Thus, in his examination of *Mercantile States and the World Oil Cartel, 1900-1939* (Ithaca, 1994), Gregory P. Nowell shows that the thesis "that the French state had the power to overcome the resistance of the private sector and implement a national program of oil independence" was a far cry from a reality marked by "complicated backstairs influence, subtlety, and intrigue."[31]

It is these complex interactions that business historians seem well placed to examine. Regulation is one area where this has already been

---

[29] The apparent success of this model had attracted the interest of many Anglo-American scholars before the "Japanese miracle" became more fashionable; see, e.g., Andrew Shonfield, *Modern Capitalism. The Changing Balance of Public and Private Power* (Oxford, 1965); Stephen S. Cohen, *Modern Capitalist Planning: The French Model*, 2nd ed. (Berkeley, 1977); John Zysman, *Political Strategies for Industrial Order. State, Market, and Industry in France* (Berkeley, 1977). For a more recent examination, see Elie Cohen, *Le Colbertisme "High Tech": Economie des Telecom et du Grand Projet* (Paris, 1992).

[30] See, for an overview, Matthias Kipping, "Les relations gouvernement–monde des affaires dans la France de l'après-guerre: Adaptations et adaptabilité d'un système original," *Histoire, économie et société* 20, no. 4 (2001): 577-96; for the nationalized companies, and especially the highly instructive example of the car producer Renault, see Patrick Fridenson, "Les entreprises publiques en France de 1944 à 1986," *Annali di storia dell'impresa* 3 (1987): 144-55; id., "Atouts et limites de la modernisation par en haut: Les entreprises publiques face à leurs critiques (1944-1986)," in *Le capitalisme français XIXe-XXe siècle: Blocages et dynamismes d'une croissance*, eds. Patrick Fridenson and André Straus (Paris, 1987), 175-94.

[31] Quotes on 288 and 290. Similarly, in her Ph.D. thesis, "Multinational Investment in East Central Europe between 1918 and 1948: Entrepreneurship, Institutional Forms and Government–Business Interplay" (University of Reading, 2000), Laura Stanciu shows how the French banks exploited the rivalry between the Ministry of Finance and the Ministry of Foreign Affairs to extract concessions and gain significant degrees of freedom for their business activities in East Central Europe during the interwar period.

done very successfully and has helped to highlight the differences in national regimes and their origins.[32] Not surprisingly, much of the pioneering work in this respect has been done in the United States, where regulation was the predominant form of government intervention during the twentieth century.[33] Thomas McCraw and Richard Vietor have been especially important in tracing the origins and evolution of these regulatory efforts.[34] A good example for international comparisons in this area has been the development of financial regulations – even if many authors continue to be preoccupied with economic efficiency and performance aspects.

Thus, for many of the industrialized economies, financial and banking historians have traced the role of banks in the development of industrial activities and the efforts of governments to regulate the financial system.[35] Their work shows how the regulatory framework evolved over time in an ad hoc rather than a planned manner, often in response to financial crises. It also highlights the fact that governments usually did not get directly involved in financial regulation, but delegated the regulatory tasks to independent central banks. Most of them were founded during the nineteenth century and were publicly owned – the major exception being the Bank of England, established in 1694 and nationalized only in 1946.[36] As detailed historical research has shown, almost all of them continued to compete with commercial banks in providing finance to industry during most of the nineteenth and the early twentieth centuries. This obviously interfered with their responsibility for the stability of the banking system as a whole – and with what economic theory would consider efficient. Most of them only gradually reduced their commercial

---

[32] For instance, a considerable part of the evidence for the interplay between the different public and private actors in the recent overview volume *Global Business Regulation* (Cambridge, 2000), by John Braithwaite and Peter Drahos, is based on (business) historical research.

[33] See especially the various editions of Clair Wilcox, *Public Policies Toward Business* (Homewood, 1955). Cf. also Tony Freyer, *Regulating Big Business: Antitrust in Great Britain and America, 1880-1990* (Cambridge, 1992).

[34] Thomas K. McCraw, "Regulation in America: A Review Article," *Business History Review* 49, no. 2 (1975): 159-83; id., *Prophets of Regulation* (Cambridge, Mass., 1984); Richard H. K. Vietor, *Contrived Competition: Regulation and Deregulation in America* (Cambridge, Mass., 1993).

[35] See Rondo Cameron, ed., *Financing Industrialisation* (Aldershot, 1992); Richard Sylla, Richard Tilly, and Gabriel Tortella, eds., *The State, the Financial System and Economic Modernization* (Cambridge, 1999).

[36] See, among others, Carl-Ludwig Holtfrerich, Jaime Reis, and Gianni Toniolo, eds., *The Emergence of Modern Central Banking from 1918 to the Present* (Aldershot, 1999).

activities to assume the role of "lender of last resort." The Bank of England probably became the first to do so in the 1870s.[37]

In terms of regulation, the Bank of England as well as the British government took a rather hands-off approach during most of the twentieth century, leaving it largely to the banking industry to regulate itself. Even where formal rules and legislation existed, the governor of the Bank of England preferred to use persuasion rather than legal action to make industry members conform. However, few dared to refuse his suggestions, given the bank's power to impose a number of sanctions.[38] The United States, by contrast, developed a much tighter regulatory framework during the twentieth century, following a period of laissez-faire that produced a major crisis of the financial system in 1907, when only the intervention of leading private bankers, such as J. P. Morgan, averted its collapse.[39] Subsequently, the U.S. government created its version of a central bank in 1913, a federation of twelve Federal Reserve Banks presided over by a Federal Reserve Board.[40] The regulatory system was tightened considerably during the 1930s to deal with a large number of banking failures. The Glass–Stegall Act of 1933 not only separated commercial and investment banking, it also established rules for capital requirements and deposit insurance, supervised by several powerful regulators.

When comparing these two systems, there is no clear evidence that tighter, more formal regulation produces a better outcome from the point of view of society. During the twentieth century, the banking industry in Britain was remarkably stable. In the United States, by contrast, the rate of banking failures at the state and local levels remained fairly high even after the regulatory reforms of the 1930s. The last and possibly most extreme example was the savings and loan crisis of the late 1980s. In order to avoid a major disaster, the U.S. federal government had to intervene and bail out the failed financial institutions. But once again, the possible performance differences are not necessarily the most interesting issues resulting from this research. What financial and business historians have shown was the interrelation between the industry structure, the banking failures,

---

[37] Forrest Capie, "Banking in Europe in the Nineteenth Century: The Role of the Central Bank," in Sylla et al., eds., *The State*, 118–33.

[38] Forrest Capie, "The Evolving Regulatory Framework in British Banking," in Chick, *Governments*, 127–41.

[39] Cf. Braithwaite and Drahos, *Global Business Regulation*, 92–93.

[40] See Richard Sylla, "Shaping the U.S. Financial System, 1690–1913," in Sylla et al., *The State*, 249–70. He has argued that the Fed was not an "innovation," but a return to the system of public finance of the late eighteenth century.

and the regulatory efforts. Thus, from the end of the nineteenth century, a few large banks with an extensive branch network dominated British banking. This made supervision much easier than in the United States, where a large number of institutions continued to operate at the local and state levels.

The need to examine the different public and private actors involved in the financial services sector also becomes clear from an historical study of financial regulation and crises in Norway during the twentieth century.[41] It demonstrates that a lack of public supervision of commercial banks, nonlife insurance companies, and brokerage firms was a main reason for their massive expansion and speculation during World War I, leading to the crises of the 1920s. Savings banks and life insurance companies experienced neither a similar war-related boom nor such substantial crises, because public inspectors worked actively and successfully to prevent them from speculating in the stock market, shipping, and so on during the war. As regards the banking and insurance crisis of the 1980s, the study argues that a long-term decrease in the supply of resources during the 1960s and 1970s – combined with the implementation of a major organizational reform of public supervision in the mid-1980s – made it impossible for the supervisory institutions to prevent or counteract the crisis.

This overview of financial regulation demonstrates again that the main contribution of historical research has not necessarily been an assessment of the performance of the different regulatory regimes. Instead, financial and business historians have helped to elucidate the origins and evolution of financial regulation, as well as the complex interaction between governments and business, in this case made even more complicated by the involvement of independent central banks. The following section will look in more detail at the contribution of business historians to the study of the policy-making and implementation process in modern industrialized countries.

OPERATING ON THE BORDERLINE: BUSINESS–GOVERNMENT INTERACTION

One of the particular ways in which historians have made an important contribution to the study of business–government relations is their

---

[41] Gunhild J. Ecklund and Sverre Knutsen, *Vern mot kriser? Norsk finanstilsyn gjennom 100 ar* (Bergen, 2000). The author would like to thank Gunhild Ecklund for providing him with an English summary of the major arguments in this book.

in-depth analysis of the decision-making process involving actors from both the public and private spheres. This is, for example, very apparent in historical studies of the oil industry. Based on the use of business and government archives, business historians have explored the interaction between the oil companies and both home and host governments, rejecting notions of all-powerful states and all-powerful companies and instead showing the complex interaction between them.[42]

The same is true for the development of cartel policy, which, as has been noted, is one of the most developed areas in the historical research on business–government relations. Most scholars interested in this issue would probably agree that after 1945 there was a gradual but perceptible shift in government policy toward horizontal collaboration, both in Europe and in Japan. Historical research has revealed the extent of the changes in government and business policy toward cartels and the drivers behind these changes. During the interwar period, many governments, especially in Europe, considered international agreements between producers as a form of economic cooperation and integration.[43] By contrast, the international trade regime and economic integration in the post–World War II period were founded on principles of unrestricted access and market competition.[44]

Some authors have seen these developments as the result of the dominant military, political, economic, and ideological position of the United States in the international economy. Thus, a recent publication has asserted that the antitrust legislation was "exported" from the United States and more or less imposed on reluctant industrialists in Germany and France with the help of a small group of modernizers within the national governments.[45] Not surprisingly, it is based on a highly selective

[42] Nowell's work has already been mentioned. This is also the principal theme of Geoffrey Jones, *The State and the Emergence of the British Oil Industry* (London, 1981), and is explored in James Bamberg's two volumes on *The History of the British Petroleum Company* (Cambridge, 1994 and 2001).

[43] See, for example, Clemens Wurm, ed., *Internationale Kartelle und Aussenpolitik: Beiträge zur Zwischenkriegszeit* (Stuttgart, 1989).

[44] For the emergence of these new regimes in Western Europe, see, among many others, Christoph Buchheim, *Die Wiedereingliederung Westdeutschlands in die Weltwirtschaft 1945-1958* (Munich, 1990); Alan S. Milward, *The Reconstruction of Western Europe 1945-51*, 2nd ed. (Berkeley, 1987); id., *The European Rescue of the Nation-State* (London, 1992).

[45] Marie-Laure Djelic, *Exporting the American Model: The Postwar Transformation of European Business* (Oxford, 1998). For the German case, similar views had been asserted earlier by Thomas A. Schwartz, *America's Germany: John J. McCloy and the Federal Republic of Germany* (Cambridge, Mass., 1991).

use of government archives and the American occupation authorities in Germany. In-depth historical research, which draws on government and business sources, reveals a more complex picture. In both countries, opinions about merger and cartel control, as well as the creation of larger European markets, were divided within government and business. Among those most actively lobbying for open and competitive European markets were representatives of the downstream industries. Their concern was the effect of restrictive practices in raw material production on the prices and quality of their inputs.[46]

This research also shows that those in favor of and those opposed to cartels both used the U.S. example as an argument. The former referred to the compulsory cartelization under the New Deal, whereas the latter highlighted the apparent superiority of the American model of oligopolistic competition.[47] The changes in European competition policy and market integration thus resulted from the combined efforts of politicians, civil servants, industry, and some labor representatives in Europe, who believed that only more competitive markets would lead to an improvement in productivity, output, and living standards. Whether this is actually true in terms of efficiency and welfare is almost impossible to determine empirically.[48] In any case, it should be clear that business historians have made their major contribution not in terms of a spurious evaluation of the economic effects of cartels, but regarding the process leading to the adoption of stricter legislation – and its subsequent enforcement, which appears to have been less strict than its original proponents might have hoped.[49]

Apart from the detailed examination of changes in competition policy, historical research has also highlighted the active role of business and its representatives in policy making in general and their participation in European integration efforts in particular. There are extensive

---

[46] For the German case, see Volker R. Berghahn, *The Americanization of West German Industry, 1945-1973* (Cambridge, 1986); for the debates and changes in France, see Matthias Kipping, "Concurrence et compétitivité: Les origines de la législation anti-trust française après 1945," *Etudes et Documents* 6 (1994): 429-55.

[47] Cf. Matthias Kipping, *Zwischen Kartellen und Konkurrenz. Der Schuman-Plan und die Ursprünge der europäischen Einigung 1944-1952* (Berlin, 1996), esp. 224-57 and 350-2.

[48] Because the changes destroyed any base case against which comparisons could be made, such an assessment has to be based on a number of assumptions, which automatically reduces its scientific value.

[49] See, for this aspect, Dirk Spierenburg and Raymond Poidevin, *Histoire de la Haute Autorité de la Communauté Européenne du Charbon et de l'Acier. Une expérience supranationale* (Brussels, 1993).

historical studies of the political activities and influence of trade associations in France and Germany.[50] Much of this work has focused on the role of these associations in the process of European integration.[51] The role of the Federation of British Industries in economic policy making and its attitude toward European integration have been the subject of a recent research project. Work on the origins and role of tripartite bodies such as the National Economic Development Council is ongoing.[52] All of these studies provide important insights into the business efforts to shape government policy in a wide variety of areas, including not only competition and trade, but also tax, financial, and research policy. They also show how these business associations generally tried to use their role as intermediaries with government to obtain or reinforce their own legitimacy toward their members.

There are a number of related areas where historical research has only just started. These concern the wide variety of business interest groups that emerged at the European level during the postwar period. Some of them appear to have had an important impact on the integration process. Thus, from 1949 on, the Council of European Industrial Federations (CEIF) made considerable – but not always successful – efforts to influence national and European policies.[53] A more recent example is the European Round Table (ERT), which brings together the chief executives of some of the largest companies in Europe. It has played an important role in initiating and shaping the Economic Union's single

---

[50] For example, Philippe Mioche, *La sidérurgie et l'Etat en France des années quarante aux années soixante* (Thèse d'Etat, University of Paris IV, 1992); Werner Bührer, *Der Bundesverband der Deutschen Industrie, 1949-1999* (Paderborn, 2002). Both authors have also published numerous articles on these subjects.

[51] For example, Werner Bührer, *Ruhrstahl und Europa: Die Wirtschaftsvereinigung Eisen- und Stahlindustrie und die Anfänge der europäischen Integration, 1945-1952* (Munich, 1986); Thomas Rhenisch, "Die deutsche Industrie und die Gründung der Europäischen Wirtschaftsgemeinschaft" (Ph.D. diss., European University Institute, 1994); Marine Moguen, "Les organisations patronales françaises et allemandes face à l'intégration européenne (1949-1961)" (Ph.D. diss., University of Paris X-Nanterre, 1999).

[52] See Alan McKinlay, Helen Mercer, and Neil Rollings, "Reluctant Europeans? The Federation of British Industries and European Integration, 1945-63," *Business History* 42, no. 4 (2000): 91-116; Astrid Ringe and Neil Rollings, "Responding to Relative Decline: The Creation of the National Economic Development Council," *Economic History Review* 53, no. 2 (2000): 331-53.

[53] Cf. Matthias Kipping, " 'Operation Impact': Converting European Business Leaders to the American Creed," in Kipping and Bjarnar, *The Americanisation*, 55-73; a large number of relevant papers were presented at an international conference on "Les réseaux économiques dans le processus de construction européenne," Brussels, October 16-18, 2002.

market program.[54] In this context, the growing role of private lobbyists and large firms of regulatory experts needs to be investigated further. They seem to have taken on some of the intermediary functions previously carried out by the business associations.

Such intermediary institutions, founded by business, sometimes with the support of government, are not only relevant for policy making. As historical research has shown, they have also played an important role in knowledge diffusion. In Germany, for example, they were crucial in the widespread diffusion of scientific management methods – a task left to private consultancy firms in Britain.[55] Apparently, in countries such as Japan and Norway, semipublic associations also disseminated new management ideas, both before and after World War II.[56] In Britain by contrast, businesses remained rather skeptical of these efforts, especially if these institutions were seen as too strongly government-driven.[57] More directly comparative research seems necessary in order to shed more light on the conditions under which these kinds of institutions, operating on the borderline between the public and private spheres, emerged and were able – or not – to ensure knowledge and information flows between the two.

Historical research has also made significant progress on the emergence and development of another institution operating on the borderline between governments and businesses: management education. Following the pioneering work of Robert Locke,[58] there have been several edited volumes on the development of business education, focusing

[54] Maria Green Cowles, "Setting the Agenda for a New Europe: The ERT and EC 1992," *Journal of Common Market Studies* 33, no. 4 (1995): 501-26. For another example, see Wyn Grant and D. Coen, "Corporate Political Strategy and Global Policy: A Case Study of the Transatlantic Business Dialogue," *European Business Journal* 13, no. 1 (2001): 37-44.

[55] Matthias Kipping, "Consultancies, Institutions and the Diffusion of Taylorism in Britain, Germany and France, 1920s to 1950s," *Business History* 39, no. 4 (1997): 67-83.

[56] See Rolv Petter Amdam and Ove Bjarnar, "The Regional Dissemination of American Productivity Models in Norway in the 1950s and 1960s," in Kipping and Bjarnar, *Americanisation*, 91-111; Seiichiro Yonekura, "The Functions of Industrial Associations," in *The Japanese Economic System and Its Historical Origins*, eds. Tetsuji Okazaki and Masahiro Okuno-Fujiwara (Oxford, 1999), 180-207.

[57] Cf. Nick Tiratsoo, "High Hopes Frustrated: The British Institute of Management as an Agent of Change, 1947-1963," in *Deindustrialization and Reindustrialization in 20th-Century Europe*, eds. Franco Amatori, Andrea Colli, and Nicola Crepas (Milan, 1999), 143-54.

[58] *The End of the Practical Man: Entrepreneurship and Higher Education in Germany, France and Great Britain, 1880-1940* (Greenwich, Conn., 1984) and *Management and Higher Education since 1940: The Influence of America and Japan on West Germany, Great Britain and France* (Cambridge, 1989).

especially on developments in the United States, Western Europe, and Japan.[59] Most of their contributions have highlighted the influence of businesses and business representatives on the form and content of management education provided by the state.[60] In many instances, businesspeople did not shy away from setting up private educational institutions if they were not satisfied with the existing public ones. The chambers of commerce seem to have played a particularly active role in this respect, for example in the foundation of the French *Ecoles de commerce* or the German *Handelshochschulen* at the end of the nineteenth and the beginning of the twentieth centuries. Incidentally, the latter were later integrated into the existing public universities, mainly due to the academic ambitions of their professors.

All of these studies once again highlight the complexity of the interaction process, in this case involving not only governments and businesses, but also the academic community itself. The situation becomes even more complex when the developments involve international exchanges of people and ideas. Thus, for example, in the Americanization of European management education after World War II, a major role was played not only by the governments, businesses, and educational institutions, including the Harvard Business School, but also private foundations, namely, the Ford Foundation, and religious orders, such as Opus Dei and the Jesuits in the case of Spain.[61]

Another related dimension of the relationship between business and government can only be mentioned here rather than developed in detail. It concerns the individuals moving during their careers between the public and private spheres – a phenomenon known as *pantouflage* in France and *amakudari* in Japan but also widespread in other countries such as the United States. Historical studies on these kinds of individuals are very promising, especially regarding their contribution to the transfer

---

[59] *Management Studies in an Academic Context*, eds. Lars Engwall and Elving Gunnarsson (Uppsala, 1994); *Management, Education, and Competitiveness: Europe, Japan and the United States*, ed. Rolv Petter Amdam (London, 1996); *Management Education in Historical Perspective*, eds. Lars Engwall and Vera Zamagni (Manchester, 1998).

[60] On the last aspect in particular, see *Inside the Business School: The Content of European Business Education*, eds. Rolv Petter Amdam, Ragnhild Kvålshaugen, and Eirinn Larsen (Oslo, forthcoming).

[61] Cf. *Missionaries and Managers: American Influences on European Management Education, 1945–60*, eds. Terry Gourvish and Nick Tiratsoo (Manchester, 1998); *The Ford Foundation and Europe (1950s–1970s)*, ed. Giuliana Gemelli (Brussels, 1998); Núria Puig, "Educating Spanish Managers: The United States, Entrepreneurial Networks, and Business Schools in Spain, 1953–1975," in Amdam et al., eds., *Inside the Business School*.

of ideas between the two spheres, but have only just started from a business historical point of view.[62]

Overall, these examples drawn from the work of business historians show that the borderline between the public and private spheres is largely imaginary and artificial. It was crossed by individuals and institutions when it came to making specific policy decisions, but also on a more permanent basis by intermediary and educational institutions. In all these cases, historical research has revealed a high degree of interaction between representatives of government, public administration, businesses, and their representatives, as well as a wide range of semipublic, semiprivate institutions. It also has demonstrated that in many instances alliances and coalitions, in favor of or against particular policies, were formed not within but across the divide.

CONCLUSION AND OUTLOOK

This essay has highlighted that business historians have made an important contribution to our understanding of the relationship between business and government. They have shown, for example, that government influence in industrialized countries should neither be overestimated nor underestimated, thus avoiding simplifying generalizations regarding, for example, the extent of government intervention in the United States and Japan. At the same time, business historians have examined the origins and subsequent development of the different forms of government intervention – ranging from regulation to public ownership. Another important aspect of business–government relations examined by business historians concerns the complexity of the interaction process. This research has demonstrated that neither governments nor businesses can be seen as unitary and/or all-powerful actors. Policy making usually occurs across the divide between the public and private spheres and often involves intermediary institutions.

This essay has also argued, somewhat provocatively, that these important contributions were obscured by a preoccupation or fixation of many business historians on the performance or economic effects of

---

[62] See, for example, Volker R. Berghahn, *America and the Intellectual Cold Wars in Europe: Shepard Stone between Philanthropy, Academy, and Diplomacy* (Princeton, N.J., 2001), and the chapters on management education in *Managerial Enterprise and Organisational Adaptability in France and Japan*, eds. Patrick Fridenson and Tsunehiko Yui (London, 2003). Cf. for the French case Christophe Charle, "Le pantouflage en France (vers 1880–vers 1980)," *Annales ESC*, 42, no. 5 (1987): 1115-37.

government involvement in business matters. This, it seems, is due either
to business historians sharing some of the assumptions of neoclassical
economics regarding the limited role of the state or to the fact that they
engage in debates with economic historians/historical economists who
base their work on these kinds of theories. The ultimate objective of
this essay is to show that many of these discussions are futile, because
there is insufficient evidence to resolve these questions – for example,
regarding the effect of cartels. Instead, it is suggested, business historians
should turn their attention to other issues, such as the ones mentioned
previously, where they appear better placed to make a significant contribution. These issues might not be of interest to neoclassical economists,
but they are equally relevant and are the subject of debates in other
academic disciplines.

As McCraw has already noted in his previously mentioned survey,
one of the keys in making progress in the examination of business-
government relations is closer collaboration between different academic
disciplines. Following the preceding argument, his list (economists, business historians, political scientists) needs to be amended, though. Among
the economists, it might be most useful to establish closer relationships
with those working outside a strictly neoclassical framework, that is,
those more willing to accept the reality of a mixed economy. More importantly, organizational sociologists should certainly be added to the
list. To give but one example regarding national differences in business-
government relations, it would appear particularly useful to engage with
scholars examining the institutional context or "business system" in
which economic activities take place.[63] Rather than interpreting national
differences as a deviation from one theoretically derived, economically
efficient "model," this literature sees diversity as normal and is interested
in the interrelation between organizations and their environment – with
the state forming an important and active part of this environment. The
temporal dimension plays an important role in this approach, because
the institutional context changes over time, imposing new constraints
on the organizations within it. At the same time, these organizations are
also seen to play an important part in the change process. This admittedly

---

[63] It is impossible to give even a brief overview of this literature, which so far has received
very limited attention among business historians; see the numerous books written or
coedited by Richard Whitley at the Manchester Business School. Much of this tradition goes
back to an influential article by Mark Granovetter, "Economic Action and Social Structure:
The Problem of Embeddedness," *American Journal of Sociology* 91, no. 3 (1985): 481–
510.

simplified view of a rich literature should sound familiar to most business historians – certainly more so than neoclassical claims of government intervention confined to exceptional cases and condemned to inefficiency.

KEY WORKS

Bourdieu, Pierre. *The State Nobility: Elite Schools in the Field of Power.* Cambridge, 1998.

Braithwaite, John and Peter Drahos. *Global Business Regulation.* Cambridge, 2000.

Chandler, Alfred, Jr., Franco Amatori, and Takashi Hikino, eds. *Big Business and the Wealth of Nations.* New York, 1997.

Foreman-Peck, James and Giovanni Federico, eds. *European Industrial Policy: The Twentieth Century Experience.* Oxford, 1999.

Holtfrerich, Carl-Ludwig, Jaime Reis, and Gianni Toniolo, eds. *The Emergence of Modern Central Banking from 1918 to the Present.* Aldershot, 1999.

Jones, Geoffrey, ed. *Coalitions and Collaboration in International Business.* Aldershot, 1993.

Porter, Michael. *The Competitive Advantage of Nations.* London, 1990.

Schumpeter, Joseph A. *Capitalism, Socialism and Democracy.* New York, 1942.

Toninelli, Pier Angelo, ed. *The Rise and Fall of State-Owned Enterprise in the Western World.* New York, 2000.

Vietor, Richard H. K. *Contrived Competition: Regulation and Deregulation in America.* Cambridge, Mass., 1993.

19

The Opportunities for Business History at the Beginning of the Twenty-First Century

ALFRED D. CHANDLER, JR.

Some of the greatest opportunities for business history at the beginning of the twenty-first century are those offered by recording the creation and evolution of the electronic-based industries. These industries evolved primarily after World War II. No other set of industries had a more far-reaching impact in transforming life and work during the second half of the twentieth century. Nor was any major industrial evolution shaped by so small a number of enterprises. Finally, and most important of all, their dramatic and epic stories are still largely unknown. Very few historians have turned to recording their progress. Of these, almost none would call themselves business historians. I say this because I've just completed a preliminary sketch of the evolution of the consumer electronics industry, the closely related computer industry, and the larger information technology industry.

By contrast to the paucity of the history of electronic-based industries, there is a plethora of studies on individual enterprises and industries of the Second Industrial Revolution, which created the foundations of the industrial economy of the twentieth century. An explanation for this discrepancy calls for an understanding of the institutionalizing of the subdiscipline of economic history, a process that occurred immediately after World War II with the coming of the Economic History Association and the publication of its *Journal of Economic History.* For the next two decades economic history was taught and written primarily as history. In the 1970s, however, economic history changed dramatically and increasingly began to be taught and written as economics.

ECONOMIC HISTORY AS HISTORY

During the discipline's initial years, the primary unit of analysis was the business enterprise and the industries in which it operated. The presidents of the Economic History Association were historians, and numerous published articles in its journal focused on enterprises and their industries. The leading economic historians, in turn, produced broader studies of the American economy. These leaders included Thomas Cochran, Harold Williamson, Edward Kirkland, and Frederick Lane, among many others. Broader studies on the larger economy followed, including those by Cochran and William Miller, *Age of Enterprise*; Kirkland, *A History of American Economic Life*; Williamson, *Growth of the American Economy*; and Lane's economic history of Venice during its golden years. These scholars were historians. At that time, economists also focused on enterprises and industries. Joseph Schumpeter, one of the world's leading economists, stressed that the historical perspective was essential to the discipline of economics. Indeed, Schumpeter's *Business Cycles*, by focusing on the business enterprise and its industries, provided an outstanding example of the potential of economic history as history.

These were the mentors of my generation of economic historians. For in 1948 Schumpeter and another Harvard economist, Arthur C. Cole, formed the Center for Entrepreneurial History at Harvard. At the Center, Cochran and a German scholar, Fritz Redlich, were the intellectual leaders (Schumpeter died in January 1950). Talcott Parsons, the translator of Max Weber and recently appointed chairman of Harvard's Department of Sociology, also provided a major intellectual influence. In this setting, the focus remained on business enterprises and industries and the larger implications of their histories.

By bringing graduate students to the Center, Cole and Cochran turned it into the training ground of young economic historians, including among others such young scholars as David Landes, Bernard Baylyn, myself, Peter Mathias from Britain, and Maurice Lévy-Leboyer from France. The economists included Douglass North, Hugh Aitken, and Henry Rosovsky. At the Center, both groups of students focused on single business enterprises and their industries. Then at dinner discussions they related their research to broader industrial and economic developments.

In their initial writings they followed the Center's approach. As one of this group, I was particularly fortunate, for my dissertation was on Henry Varnum Poor, who was a pioneer business journalist from 1849 to the 1860s, editor of the *American Railroad Journal*, and later publisher of *Poor's Manual of Railroads*. By reading Poor's weekly journal, I could see the creation of the nation's first big businesses and, with them, the beginnings of modern finance, management, and competition. At the same time, I learned from Thomas Cochran, who was writing his *Railroad Leaders, 1845–1890*, based on the letters of sixty-one chief management executives. His book – which covers all aspects of their activities – remains a classic of economic history as business history. At the Center too, I had a chance to communicate regularly with Edward C. Kirkland, whose *Men, Cities, and Transportation* is a model study of how the railroad companies and their industry transformed the New England economy.

After I published the book on Henry Poor and the railroads, I began to focus on the evolution of the large industrial enterprise that initially appeared in response to the national and international markets opened up by the railroad and steamship. The resulting book, *Strategy and Structure*, published in 1962, reflected the teachings of Parsons, Weber, and Cochran. It emphasized that a successful strategy, that is, the determination of long-term goals and objectives, required a structure that integrated the firm's functional capabilities with its functional activities of product development, production, and marketing. This volume further stated that if changes in strategy were not accompanied by changes in structure, inefficiencies resulted. Based on the corporate records of DuPont, General Motors, Standard Oil of New Jersey (EXXON), and Sears Roebuck, that study gained a large audience, aroused new interest in corporate strategy, and is still in print. My point here is that comparable opportunities exist today for economic history as history in recording and analyzing the evolution of the products of the new electronics technologies and a third industrial revolution.

A multitude of books appeared in the 1950s and 1960s on individual business enterprises, industries, and economies. Thomas Cochran and William Miller's *Age of Enterprise*, for example, considered the broad social and political implications of industrial change. In these years, major issues were being debated. For example, the creators of these enterprises were often portrayed either as robber barons or as industrial statesmen, a discussion that is still being carried on today in the media. In the early years of the American Economic History Association, scholars focused largely on questions of who, where, when, and how; they asked why institutional and economic change occurred and sought their answers in historical sources – internal company records, interviews, trade journals, articles, and monographs.

ECONOMIC HISTORY AS ECONOMICS

The shift from economic history as history to economic history as economics took place largely in the 1970s with Robert Fogel and the coming of cliometrics. The major salvo of the new approach was explicit. In 1971 Fogel, with Stanley Engerman, edited a collection of essays, *The Redefinition of American Economic History*. Their stated goal was to "introduce students to the quantitative revolution in historiography and the far-reaching substantive revisions produced by the new methodology." The essays in their book, they pointed out, were "to show the power of simple economic theory and mathematics in illuminating the problems of American life." With the coming of the quantitative revolution, the focus of American economic history was no longer to be the business enterprise and the industries in which it operated, except possibly as a source for quantitative economic data.

As Fogel and Engerman indicated, the quantitative revolution was beginning to transform the discipline of economics. In the late 1970s, graduate students in economics at Harvard were required to take Alexander Gershenkron's course in economic history. In the early 1980s, that requirement was replaced by a required course in mathematics. Some time later, two such courses were required. I recently attended a conference at Harvard of economists who were reviewing the status of their discipline. One major concern was that economics was becoming a refuge for second-class mathematicians.

Let me stress that I make these points in no way to downplay the value of economic history as economics. I do so to indicate why so little history has been written about individual electronic-based companies and the industries in which they operated. For example, Peter Temin, Naomi Lamoreaux, and Daniel Raff have proposed a new synthesis based on coordination to replace the older organizational synthesis, one stressing markets and hierarchies, that was developed to explain the Second Industrial Revolution. Their synthesis is exceptionally well suited to the understanding of the new electronic-based industries. I was surprised, therefore, that the one reference to those electronic technologies was an example of one IBM clone, Dell Computer.

More useful is the work of the economists who established the ten-year-old journal *Institutional and Corporate Change*; they include David Teece, David Mowery, Giovanni Dosi, and the evolutionary economist Richard Nelson, all of whom have provided valuable data on and analyses of electronic-based industries. Such books as David Mowery and Richard Nelson, *Sources of Industrial Leadership: Studies of Seven Industries*, and Richard Nelson, *National Innovation Systems: A Comparative Analysis*, provide essential data on the evolution of the computer industry. These volumes are outstanding examples of what practitioners of economic history as economics can achieve. They focus on the enterprises and the national industries in which they operate. Indeed, the chapters in the Mowery and Nelson book should be required reading for all business historians. But because they do not ask the historian's questions of when, where, how, by whom, and therefore why, or describe and evaluate the competitive interaction that occurred in the commercialization of the products of the new technology, their analyses actually enhance the opportunities for business historians, opportunities that I am about to describe.

THE OPPORTUNITIES IN THE HISTORY OF CONSUMER ELECTRONICS

I have just completed an initial sketch of the evolution of two industries – *Inventing the Electronic Century: The Epic Story of the Consumer Electronics and Computer Industries* – so let me begin with consumer electronics. That industry began with radio. Two enterprises commercialized, that is, brought the technology into public use: Radio Corporation of America (RCA), a joint venture of the three leading U.S. electrical and telecommunication manufacturers (General Electric, Westinghouse, and AT&T), and Telefunken (a joint venture of the two European leaders, Siemens and AEG). After World War II knocked out Telefunken, RCA took the lead in commercializing television worldwide. It was then solely responsible for color television, a major managerial and technological achievement. In the 1960s, however, it began to self-destruct by diversifying, first in attempting to compete with IBM in the production of mainframes and then by becoming a conglomerate, purchasing, among others, Hertz Rent A Car, frozen-food companies, savings and loan enterprises, and others. RCA died in the late 1970s, taking with it a number of smaller U.S. enterprises. The latter were acquired by Japanese companies and Europe's Philips.

In the same brief historical period, from the late 1960s to the late 1970s, the Japanese industry led by Sony and Matsushita conquered world markets. Sony became the world's foremost commercializer of products of new technologies in consumer electronics including the Walkman, Triton Color TV, the VCR, the CD (and CD-ROM), and the DVD. Matsushita became the industry's most successful firm in product development, production, and marketing worldwide. By the late 1980s, these two, with Sanyo and Sharp, had driven both the U.S. and European consumer electronics companies out of their own home markets. Japan's achievements are unparalleled in the annals of industrial history, a particularly spectacular performance in a mass-producing, mass-marketing, high-tech industry.

Almost nothing has been written about the process that led to this achievement. The books written in English are Robert Sobel's brief review of RCA's history, Margaret Graham's *RCA and the Radio Disc*, a biography of David Sarnoff by an RCA executive, and a journalistic account of Sony's expansion.

Precisely because of the tiny number of players involved, their story provides a real-life documentation of the paths to competitive success and failure worldwide in high-tech industries. The technological and institutional infrastructure of the new consumer electronics industry was determined in the crucible of international competition between four companies in the 1970s and 1980s – RCA, Sony, Matsushita, and Philips.

Sony provides a model for the successful strategy of commercializing new technologies by using the learning and income from the previous set of successful innovations. Matsushita's story is different and unique. In 1952, Matsushita arranged to acquire the technical capabilities of the Dutch company Philips in return for 35 percent of the Japanese company's equity. It then concentrated on enhancing its functional capabilities in product development, production, and marketing. These learned capabilities permitted it to enter related electronic commercial, industrial, and even information technology markets. As a result, by 1962 only 28 percent of its sales revenues of $64 billion came from consumer electronics.

The story of Europe's Philips provides still another fascinating chapter for business, industrial, and technological historians. Philips played a critical role in providing the technical capabilities that Matsushita and Sony used to commercialize their new products. Then it was driven out of business by these same two Japanese firms and Sharp. Philips had on its own attempted to produce a CD for television, comparable to the earlier

CD-ROM for computers, losing half a billion dollars in the effort. As a result, it lacked the funds necessary to build a DVD factory and exited the consumer electronic industry almost entirely at the end of the 1990s. Again, this relatively unknown story provides an intriguing opportunity for description and analysis by business historians.

THE OPPORTUNITIES IN THE EVOLUTION
OF THE COMPUTER INDUSTRY

The evolution of the computer industry also has an exciting, largely untold story. In no major industry has a single enterprise so shaped its evolution as did IBM in computers. During the half century since the electronic computer industry began, IBM has dominated in terms of revenues and product lines developed. Moreover, in no other industry have the leader's most successful competitors been those that produced products that the leader had commercialized. In the late 1970s, the Japanese industry became competitive by making and marketing IBM plug-compatible mainframes. By the late 1980s, the most successful producers of computers were those that produced and marketed IBM personal computer clones.

In 1963 IBM's revenues were three times those of its major U.S. competitors combined. In 1984 they were six times those of its nearest competitors, Digital Equipment and Japan's Fujitsu; in 1996 they were two and a half times those of its largest competitors, Japan's Fujitsu and Hewlett-Packard.

IBM had, of course, been the dominant enterprise in the data-processing industry well before the coming of the electronic computer. Its evolution provides a classic illustration of first-mover advantages. From its beginning in 1914, it created an integrated learning base to commercialize a new data-processing punched-card technology. By the 1920s, its initial factory in New York and a new one in Europe were supplying its worldwide marketing organization with electrically driven data-processing equipment. In 1927 Remington Rand, the first mover in typewriters, entered the industry by acquiring a small maker of punched-card tabulators. But during the 1930s, Remington Rand never gained more than 15 percent of the market. After World War II, Remington Rand acquired two of the four projects developing high-speed analytical devices for military purposes. In 1951 it introduced the UNIVAC, the first giant commercial computer, but IBM immediately followed with its own 700 computer.

IBM's continued dominance did not, however, come from its 700 computer. It rested on the replacement of electric power by electronic technology for its punched-card tabulators. In 1954 came its 650 computer, powered by vacuum tubes (an invention at the end of World War I), followed by its 1400, powered by a transistor that was first licensed by AT&T in 1952. The 1400 was leased at $2,500 a month, the cost of a middle-sized punched-card tabulator. Its revenues of $2 billion helped to finance the commercializing of the world's most successful data processor, the System 360, a family of compatible computers.

In 1963, before the announcement of the System 360, IBM's computer revenues were $1.24 billion; Rand's were $145.5 million. Thomas Watson, Jr., the executive most responsible for the change from data processing through electricity to electronics, noted: "While our great million dollar 700 got the publicity, the 650 became computing's Model T" (*Inventing the Electronic Century*, 87–8).

In the 1970s the System 360 all but ruled the world. The attempts of the two major U.S. companies, RCA and GE, to build a comparable family of mainframes failed, with large losses in funds and research time. The Japanese and European computer makers were even less successful. The most successful competitors were those that commercialized products on either side of IBM's 360's price and performance standards; these included the much smaller Digital Equipment, with its stripped-down minicomputer, and Control Data's supercomputer.

Then in 1970 Gene Amdahl, the designer of the System 360 and its successor, the System 370, left IBM to start his own enterprise, producing a plug-compatible System 370. Unable to raise the $40 million required to produce his system, he turned to Japan's Fujitsu, which received him with elation and, in turn, made his plug-compatible equipment available to other Japanese computer makers. With the acquisition of Amdahl's technology, Japan's industry quickly captured its own rapidly growing domestic market for computers. Then in the early 1980s, the four European computer producers turned to Fujitsu, Hitachi, and NEC to acquire plug-compatibles on an original equipment manufacturer (OEM) basis, that is, to be sold as products of the European companies.

With this sudden expansion of their market, the same three companies (with Toshiba and Mitsubishi Electric) concentrated on the mass production of a memory chip, which had been invented by Intel. In the briefest period of time during the early 1980s, the Japanese five knocked out the U.S. memory industry, forcing Intel and the four other major U.S. producers to shut down their memory chip plants.

The U.S. computer industry nevertheless recovered through the introduction at that moment of the microprocessor, and with it the personal
computer. Here again IBM played the critical role. The personal computer had been initially commercialized by young hobbyists in the late
1970s. In 1980 IBM's managers set up a unit in Boca Raton, Florida, to
mass-produce and mass-market a personal computer and to do so within
a single year. The unit's revenues were $500 million at the close of the
first year, close to Apple's $600 million. By 1983 and 1984 they had soared
to $5.5 billion. Moreover, IBM's personal computer was an open system
to be licensed by any applicant. Within a brief time 200 clones poured
into the market. While few of the clones survived, the U.S.-produced
and U.S.-mass-marketed personal computer transformed the computer
industry.

IBM itself gained little from its mass-produced personal computer.
Indeed, it suffered heavy losses in its mainframe business. But IBM clones
conquered world markets. And every clone had to use an Intel chip and a
Microsoft operating system. The resulting advantages of scale and scope,
plus Microsoft's control over applications, made these two the world's
most powerful computer companies. By the early 1990s, Apple was the
only major survivor of the pre-IBM producers that had its own proprietary
operating systems.

Although the Japanese missed out on the personal computer revolution, the rapidly growing demand for computing power created by
the swift expansion of local and wide area corporate computer networks (LANS and WANs) and the privatized Internet brought a second
Japanese challenge in the early 1990s. Critical here was the development
of the workstation using another microprocessor, the reduced instruction set computing (RISC) chip, which, with a UNIX operating system,
became the primary competitor to the IBM personal computer clones.
This technology – developed by Sun Microsystems and the U.S. makers of minicomputers – was quickly acquired by the Japanese computer
companies.

By 1996, as recorded by *Datamation*, a leading trade journal, the
four Japanese companies shared with IBM the revived market for large
systems. In servers, the heirs of the workstation – IBM, Hewlett-Packard,
and Compaq – led in revenues received, with NEC, Toshiba, Fujitsu, and
Hitachi following. More surprising, in desktops, where IBM and Compaq
were at the top, with close to the same revenues, three of these four
Japanese companies followed. In software, IBM remained the world's
leading revenue producer; then came Microsoft, followed by Hitachi,

Fujitsu, and NEC. By 1996 the European industry had all but died. It had become a major outlet for the Japanese manufacturers.

Although the briefest facts of the computer and the broader information technology industry are no better known than those of consumer electronics, more has been written on the producers of computers than on those of audio and video. Kenneth Flamm of the Brookings Institution has published two excellent books, *Targeting the Computer* and *Creating the Computer*, which provide excellent brief reviews of the industry's story into the 1970s. He has done so by focusing on the computer-making enterprises and their national industries. Martin Campbell-Kelly and William Aspray, in *Computer,* focus on the early years of the industry, with only three short chapters on the microprocessor era. They do not mention the Japanese challenge, nor do two detailed books on Microsoft, nor does Paul Cerruzzi's excellent study on the evolution of computing technology. Martin Fransman, *Japan's Computer and Communication Industry*, which focuses on NEC, and Marie Anchordoguy, *Computers, Inc.*, set the stage for Japan's challenge but say little about capturing the European market in mainframes and the industry's swift domination in memory chips. Very little has been written about the move of the core companies into the client server (RISC chips and UNIX operating systems) technology that permitted them to mount a major challenge to the United States in the early 1990s, when the marriage of the corporate WANs and the Internet completed the basic infrastructure of the new electronic-based century.

I hope that this review of the opportunities for writing the history of electronic-based businesses and industries – the industries that created the infrastructure for the new electronic century – will encourage economic historians trained as historians to return to the history of business enterprises and their industries. If they do, they will be able to open a new field of historical investigation. Moreover, because so few enterprises were involved in commercializing the products of the new electronic devices, historians will be able to analyze the competitive successes and failures not only of companies but of major industries – successes and failures that led to worldwide domination or the near death of crucial national industries. As was the case with the writing of economic history as history a half a century earlier when the industries of the Second Industrial Revolution were center stage, scholars can then develop new concepts of growth and adjust existing theories of institutional change based on the commercialization of new science-based technologies. For example, the unparalleled success of Japan's consumer electronics industries confirms William Lazonick's theoretical approach to global competition. Lazonick stresses that an innovative enterprise (as differentiated from an optimizing one) becomes successful not just by using its productive capabilities, but also by creating and enhancing organizational capabilities through continued learning. Clearly, the history of the consumer electronics industry verifies his theory. Compare the performance of Sony and Matsushita to that of RCA. Sony's unsurpassed record of commercializing new products was based on learning acquired by commercializing a previous new technology. Its product innovative record is unsurpassed in the annals of modern industry. Matsushita's success was based on entering new product lines on the basis of continued learning in product development, production, and marketing; by contrast, RCA self-destructed by entering markets in which it had no learned capabilities. IBM's story is roughly the same. Once the Japanese industry acquired the necessary new technology they continued to learn by commercializing new products from it, whereas the Europeans were unable to do so.

The electronics story also provides an opportunity to describe and further understand the symbiotic relationship between large and small companies (a subject that concerns such business historians as Philip Scranton and Jonathan Zeitlin). That relationship is strikingly clear in electronics. In the high-tech industries, neither the large nor the small can live without the other. In Europe the output of Siemens and Nixdorf in computers and that of Philips in consumer electronics were able to attract small suppliers and niche firms. In the United States, where IBM dominated the product line in hardware and software, a supporting nexus appeared along Boston's Route 128 to supply a multitude of products that could be incorporated into Digital Equipment's stripped-down minicomputer. Silicon Valley came into its own in the late 1960s, when the demand for components for mainframes and minicomputers exploded. Compare that growth to the swifter growth of the Tokyo/Osaka industrial district created to support four Japanese consumer electronic firms. Beginning in the 1970s, they started their successful invasion of the United States and then the European markets. When the large-scale production of plug-compatible mainframes began in the late 1970s, the number of suppliers and niche firms increased dramatically. This combination became particularly significant as audio, video, and information technologies became integrated into the new electronically based infrastructure. Having lost its consumer electronics component, the U.S. Silicon Valley nexus will be handicapped as the electronic technology of the twenty-first century evolves. In Europe a supporting nexus of small enterprises no longer exists.

I close by urging professionally trained business historians to respond to the opportunities described here. If they do not, who will? The economists writing economic history still focus primarily on quantitative data and mathematically based models and ask economists' questions. Their work is essential for understanding the broad evolving story of the information age. Business historians will benefit from their studies. Those who write business history as cultural history will probably not make the business enterprise and its industries the focus of analysis. But those who do can now open up new areas of historical investigation and advance broader concepts and theories about institutional change by asking the historian's questions of when, where, how, by whom, and, therefore, why the new technologies that were commercialized appeared. This new generation of business historians can do so by using the traditional historical sources – a wide variety of articles, monographs, trade journals, corporate and government records – analyzed in the well-established ways outlined in this book.

Index

uncertainty: and historical
alternatives approach, 65–6; and
innovative enterprise, 35
United States: business history of
compared to France, 194;
business history and studies of
multinationals, 354–5; economic
relations with Japan, 294–5; and
family firms, 339, 343, 347; as
host economy, 364; and
multinational investment in
Britain and Netherlands, 143;
and present status of business
history, 83–110
Universidad Autónoma de Nuevo
León, 325
universities: business administration
in Scandinavian, 147; and
business history courses in
Spain, 235–6; and French
business history, 210; and
German business history, 180–1,
187. *See also* education
University of Akron, 302
University of Bochum, 179
University of California, 315
University of Copenhagen, 150
University of Milan, 216
University of Queensland, 302
University of Zurich, 176
utilization, of productive resources,
48–9
utopian romanticism, and
alternatives approach, 77–9

Vancoppenolle, Chantal, 132
Van Iterson, Ad, 133
Van Schelven, Arnout L., 121–2
Veenendaal, August, 137
Verein für Social politik, 171
Verein der Wirtschaftsarchivare,
178, 180
Verein für wirtschaftshistorische
Studien, 176

Vernon, Raymond, 354, 373n4
Vernus, Pierre, 209
Vicens, Jaume, 232
Vietor, Richard H. K., 96, 383
Viñuela, Ana, 240n21
Visible Hand, The (Chandler, 1977),
51–4, 91–2, 94, 95
Volpato, Giuseppe, 226
Vries, Johan de, 113

Waarden, Frans van, 140
Wadsworth, John E., 134
Wakimura, Yoshitarô, 289
Wardley, Peter, 117
Watanabe, Hisashi, 282, 291
Watson, Katherine, 135
Weiner, M., 131
Wengenroth, Ulrich, 179
Werkgroep Bedrijifsgeschiedenis,
113
Whisler, Timothy R., 119
Whitley, Richard, 392n63
Whittington, Richard, 118
Wilcox, Clair, 383n33
Wilkins, Mira, 100–101, 354–5, 356,
357, 358, 362, 363, 364
Williamson, Oliver E., 17, 18–19
Wilson, Charles H., 3, 44n20, 115
Wilson, John F., 160, 161
Wilson, R. G., 118
Winkelman, Hélène, 121
Winter, Sidney G., 21
Witt-Hansen, J., 163n26
women's studies, and
postmodernism in business
history, 27
Wong, Bin, 309, 310, 312, 313
Woodbridge, George, 86
works history, and German business
history, 176–7
world system theory, and Japanese
business history, 290
Woronoff, Denis, 203
Wright, Tim, 302, 306